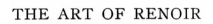

THE ART OF RENOIR

BOOKS WRITTEN BY STAFF MEMBERS OF THE BARNES FOUNDATION

THE ART IN PAINTING
Albert C. Barnes

THE AESTHETIC EXPERIENCE
Laurence Buermeyer

AN APPROACH TO ART
Mary Mullen

ART AND EDUCATION
Dewey, Barnes, Buermeyer, Mullen, de Mazia

ART AS EXPERIENCE
John Dewey

PRIMITIVE NEGRO SCULPTURE
Paul Guillaume and Thomas Munro

THE FRENCH PRIMITIVES AND THEIR FORMS
Albert C. Barnes and Violette de Mazia

THE ART OF RENOIR
Albert C. Barnes and Violette de Mazia

THE ART OF HENRI-MATISSE
Albert C. Barnes and Violette de Mazia

THE ART OF CÉZANNE
Albert C. Barnes and Violette de Mazia

AUGUSTE RENOIR

Self-Portrait (253), circa 1910

THE ART OF
RENOIR

BY

ALBERT C. BARNES
AND
VIOLETTE DE MAZIA

WITH A FOREWORD BY
JOHN DEWEY

ONE HUNDRED AND
FIFTY-EIGHT ILLUSTRATIONS

Published by
THE BARNES FOUNDATION PRESS
MERION, PENNA.

Printed in the United States of America
By William J. Dornan
Collingdale, Pennsylvania

TO

NELLE E. MULLEN

IN GRATITUDE FOR SERVICES OF UNIQUE VALUE
IN THE CREATION OF THE BARNES FOUNDATION
AND IN CARRYING OUT ITS WORK

FOREWORD

THE authors have covered in this volume the artistic work of Renoir and the method that must be used in any intelligent approach to the understanding and appreciation of art in all its forms. Their treatment of these topics leaves nothing for me to add, and contains nothing that I should wish to change.

The Barnes Foundation, however, is an educational institution, and this volume, like those which preceded it, is a fruit of educational activities. The method and material of the present work have a definite bearing not only upon education in the plastic arts, but upon education in general. Although this implication will be evident to the book's intelligent readers, there is perhaps some reason for underscoring it. At all events, in responding to the honor of an invitation to write some introductory words, it is of the educational phase of this work and of the Barnes Foundation that I shall speak.

For many years, I have thought and taught that experience is an interaction between the self and some aspect of its environment. Purposeful, intelligent action is the means by which this interaction is rendered significant. In the course of such action, objects acquire meaning and the self becomes aware of its own powers, since, by intelligent control of the environment, it directs and consolidates its own capacities. Purposeful action is thus the goal of all that is truly educative, and it is the means by which the goal is reached and its content remade. Such activity is of necessity a growth and a growing. It begins when an infant makes his first purposeful adaptions to his surroundings; as he makes them, he acquires attitudes and habits which enable him to widen his purposes and to discover and use the means and methods of achieving larger purposes. In this process of intelligent living there is no inherent limit. It should go on from infancy to death. Arrest of continuous growth is a form of premature decay and death.

In intelligent living, in directed interaction of the self and its world, action (in the limited sense of the word), emotion, and understanding are all involved. Intelligent adaption of self to surrounding objects and events brings these functions into balance. Thought then becomes knowledge and insight; emotion becomes interest; motor responses become mastery of things and qualities about us and of the human potentialities relevant to them. Arrest of the process of growth is really the arrest of intelligent living, of education. Growth, intelligent living, education have many enemies. These enemies are powerful. They are, unfortunately, re-enforced by the practices which dominate the professed agencies of education, the schools and the institutions called educational.

Every one-sided emphasis upon routine and mechanical habit is such an enemy. At the outset, impulses which have not yet been ordered into effective modes of action predominate because of the absence of any purpose or meaning. The problem is to secure the intelligent direction of such impulses. But the schools—in the name of efficiency and under the pressure of those mechanical forces that are so strong in the present social environment—substitute for intelligent direction the formation of rigid and thoughtless habits. Through such inadequacies, the acquisition of knowledge is transformed into the amassing of mere information; memory, instead of being the ally of judgment, is converted into a substitute for it. Facts and principles are "learned" in isolation, whereas *in intelligent living* they are so intimately connected with each other that they are active agencies for grasping meaning and enhancing values. A conformity that restricts then takes the place of what otherwise could have been a never ending voyage of discovery. Emotions which, when connected with the meaning of objects and with purposeful action, are *interests* attaching the self to the changing world, are left free-floating. Instead of giving secure anchorage, they dissolve into reveries that come between the self and the world. All of these breaks and arrests in growth, in intelligent living, in education, characterize traditional learning as practiced in the educational institutions of today.

The method employed in the volume to which these words are prefixed avoids the disorder just noted, a disorder which has permeated current ways of appreciating and understanding art. For, quite apart from set courses in the production and understanding of painting and other art forms (where the disorder is not unknown), the effects of the institution of traditional learning have deeply influenced attitudes in all modes of experience. I know of no statement of the relation of scientific method to intelligent living—the real meaning of science—equal to that found in the early pages of the first chapter of the present volume. Yet, since the material of science is itself often taught in our institutions of learning with little regard to science *as the method of observation and of interpretation of what is observed,* there is small cause for wonder that the scientific method has as yet found little recognition in other phases of human experience, and especially in art. We need not be surprised that, in the teaching of the arts, there has grown up the idea that the fine arts and the method of intelligence—for that is what scientific method is— are polar opposites in any study and understanding that is objectively grounded. In the artistic range of experience, more than in any other, the habit of separating mind (active in observation and reflection), and emotion, is deep-seated. In this range the evils of this habit are most conspicuous. Education, essentially a training of perception, is abandoned. Private emotion, and judgment that is also private, because they are not based on an awakened perception of objects and their relations to one another, come between the self and the perceptible world.

It makes little difference whether the teacher engages chiefly in giving instructions about "facts" or endeavors to stir what is usually called "appreciation." The former concerns biographies of artists, the history of schools, the technique of handling materials —whether the subject be painting or literature. But facts are something *about* objects; they are used instead of the direct perception of objects. Appreciation becomes an effort to stir the emotions. Emotions *are* involved in all genuine perception. But they are a factor in appreciation only when they are responses to objectively perceived elements and relationships progressively discovered in the object itself—whether a painting, a poem, a symphony or a so-called scientific object.

The teacher, if gifted with imagination, can engage in poetic utterance about the work of art and charm the pupil. This process has elements of value lacking in the accumulation of dry facts about the work. But while the teacher's flight of fancy may have a basis in the background of his own experience, the pupil, who lacks this basis, will let his imagination work along the lines of his own private desires and feeling, and, in the end, will be still further removed from the ability to direct his emotions to the object as an object. The result is that his possible interest in increasing his perception of works of art is diverted into interest in pursuing his own lines of reverie. When the method of the teacher leads the pupil to *see* in the object features and relations he had not seen before, both teacher and pupil come into intellectual and emotional control of the situation. Then the habit of objective seeing is formed, and the habit operates in subsequent seeing. The information acquired, instead of being put into dead storage, becomes an active resource. Experience is immediately enriched, and the capacity for growth, for continuing experience, is expanded and directed.

To learn to see anything well is a difficult undertaking. It requires the activity of the whole personality. Learning to perceive demands the interaction of the whole personality with things about it. This is true whether one is seeing a picture or painting it, mastering golf, building a new type of bridge, or reading the poetry of Keats.

Since my educational ideas have been criticized for undue emphasis upon intelligence and the use of the method of thinking that has its best exemplification in science, I take profound, if somewhat melancholy, ironic, satisfaction in the fact that the most thoroughgoing embodiment of what I have tried to say about education, is, as far as I am aware, found in an educational institution that is concerned with art. I do not know whether it is matter for surprise that education in the esthetic field should be the first to do the obvious and simple thing. But I do know that hardly a week—certainly not a month—passes that I do not receive a letter, sometimes from a teacher, sometimes from a student, which asks why there is such a gap between educational theory and educational practice; that does not ask, in effect, why teachers and students who wish to do productive work—work productive in experience, intelligence and interest—should be so hampered and harassed. I have ventured, therefore, into this brief summary of educational theory because this volume of the Barnes Foundation is so adequate an exemplification of what that theory means in practice. It is a reward, as well as an honor, to be associated with an educational institution that is engaged in vital education.

JOHN DEWEY

PREFACE

THE principal problem encountered in recording this study of Renoir has been to glean from the vast amount of accumulated material the indispensable essentials that could be included in a single volume of a size suitable for practical use as a guide for objective study. The problem was set by the fact that Renoir painted probably more pictures than any other important artist, and the difficulty of its solution was that only by a detailed study of his work of all periods could there be obtained the objective evidence of a growth in experience and of a fulness of its expression which are scarcely to be equaled in the entire history of painting.

The study began more than twenty years ago in the collection of a dozen important Renoirs, and it has been continued uninterruptedly as the collection grew to the present number of one hundred and seventy-five pictures by the same artist, each new acquisition bearing within itself recognizable marks of a continuous growth in the painter's experience and of his progressively increasing ability to record new and richer experience in his pictures. At an early stage the study yielded a thrill of adventure which led to a survey of practically all the significant work of Renoir to be found in the museums and important private collections in America and Europe.

A second vital problem was how to make the accumulated material helpful to students in the terms of their own experience, a problem which necessitated devising methods that would establish meaningful connection between the objective matter and the relevant attributes common to all normal human beings. The needed guidance was found in the general concepts of method, experience and education as originated by John Dewey, and as these were developed by ourselves during the nineteen years which have elapsed since we first proved by experimentation the practical value of Professor Dewey's ideas when applied to an objective study of pictures as an insight to esthetic experience.

Inasmuch as the objective and subjective phases are inseparable parts of any fruitful study of paintings, the first four chapters of this volume are devoted to a brief discussion of the rationale of the method employed and to a summarized statement of the underlying principles of psychology upon which is based our objective study of the paintings.

Our research necessitated an extensive inquiry into the Venetian and the eighteenth century French traditions in order to learn what Renoir took from those sources and what creative use he made of his derivations. The products of the investigation were a very considerable number of new and significant facts relating to the traditions themselves and to Renoir's enormous additions to the plastic and human values in the work of his predecessors. The results of this phase of our research appear for the first time in this volume.

Our principal indebtedness is to N. E. Mullen, L. V. Geiger and Mary Mullen whose extensive experience and rare skill in research work in this particular field made the study possible. We are indebted also to Laurence Buermeyer for reading the greater part of the manuscript and making many important suggestions. A service of enormous value was rendered by Georges Keller in obtaining photographs and catalogue data about a large number of particular paintings. Durand-Ruel and Grete Ring also very kindly provided a number of photographs not otherwise available.

ALBERT C. BARNES
VIOLETTE DE MAZIA

Merion, Pa., March, 1935.

CONTENTS

BOOK III

RENOIR AND THE TRADITIONS

CONTENTS

LIST OF ILLUSTRATIONS *

* Numbers in brackets after titles refer to numbers in "Catalogue Data,"
Appendix, p. 441.

BOOK I
INTRODUCTION

CHAPTER I

METHOD

It is a familiar fact that the appreciation of art is vitiated by every sort of whim, fancy, and superstition. The average person, lacking any understanding of what the painter aimed to do, looks at a painting with the expectation of being given information, told a story, moved to the same sort of emotion that the thing in actual life would incite, or perhaps of being inspired to elevated and edifying sentiments. Even if he disavows any knowledge of art, he is probably under the impression that what he does *not* know is a set of arbitrary rules, comparable to those of tennis or chess. If he turns for enlightenment to what usually passes for education in art, he is only too likely to be confirmed in his error or to be led to the additional error of supposing that the biography of the artist, and the technical means of putting paint on canvas, are the key to the understanding he seeks. The result is that he comes away with no impression specifically relevant to what he has looked at, and that there are as many opinions about a work of art as there are persons who have observed it. He presumes that the only alternative to chaos, under these circumstances, is authority, and consequently it is frequently supposed that good art is that which qualified critics pronounce to be such, though of course what qualifies the critics remains a mystery.

A parallel state of affairs formerly prevailed in the understanding of Nature. Many natural scenes and processes, storms and sunsets, deserts and fields with blooming flowers have an obvious appeal to feelings either unpleasant or pleasant, and all primitive peoples consequently conceived Nature as controlled by powers friendly or hostile to human beings, and to be controlled by direct personal appeals. This was the period of animism and magic, which humanity outgrew only as it learned to disregard its own immediate emotions about Nature, and seek verifiable information about objective physical processes. No such information, however, is possible to any one who relies upon his untutored senses, upon habits of interpretation which remain chaotic

3

and infected by subjectivity; hence animism was at first superseded merely by alchemy and astrology.

The change merely continued the conception of natural processes
as intrinsically characterized by their effect upon our own welfare
—metals are in themselves base or precious, for example, and the
positions of the stars are directly related to human welfare. No
real science was possible until a method of investigation was
discovered, a method which wholly eliminated the idiosyncrasies
of the particular observer from the object to be understood, and
hence something which made the observations and interpretations
of one individual verifiable by another. The scientific ideal, in
other words, is that of complete objectivity, and its justification
is found in the fact that by science, and by science alone, has
the course of natural processes been brought under control. Science, in short, by excluding the individual's whims and fancies
from the determination of what objectively exists, has made the
physical world infinitely more amenable to the individual's en-
lightened purposes. The satisfactions denied him have been
imaginary, those provided have been real.

A similar passage from dreams to reality in the world of art
can be made only by the same means—the use of method based
upon objective fact. The possibilities inherent in a painting reveal
themselves to the untutored eye as little as do those of a piece
of coal. Art, like science, involves a departure from the ways of
activity and seeing things which the experiences of practical life
impose; and the appreciation of art, like the understanding of
science, requires a grasp of the artist's specific purpose. No activity, no perception of anything, is possible except by virtue of a
set of meanings and habits, qualities to be identified in the objects
about us, and dispositions to perform specific acts when the
identification has been made. The habits common to eating, dressing and undressing, getting about safely and expeditiously, using
the necessary minimum of language, are so familiar, the process
of their acquisition is usually so completely forgotten, that they
are likely to seem as natural as breathing, and to require no
method. This means only that the method has been wholly absorbed
by the mind and needs no conscious attention; it exists, however,
in our readiness to notice the objective facts in a situation which
sets off the familiar response.

Every perception, as we shall see in detail in Chapter II, involves selection from among the many qualities of an object,

of those relevant to our interests, and the amplifications of such qualities by appropriate meanings stored up in our minds by past experience. This selection and supplementation, which are automatic in our most familiar activities, emerge into consciousness whenever a new form of action has to be acquired. Learning to sail a boat, drive an automobile, play tennis, speak a foreign language, involves, in addition to new muscular coördinations, sensitivity to a new set of stimuli and a grasp of the meanings that attach to them. The sensitivity and set of meanings are correlative: we notice only the characteristic things that point to consequences to be sought or avoided, and the only sort of meanings which we need or can consider are those which have objective indications in an existing situation.

Our interests, our general purposes, determine what we shall notice, how we shall interpret it, and what we shall do about it; and conversely, our ways of seeing, interpreting and doing, constitute our general interests, which are real and efficacious only in so far as they have taken form in definitely organized habits. Such organized habits, though rarely formulated in words, constitute methods without which we cannot perceive, think or act.

Just as the chauffeur, the tennis-player, the physician and the engineer have their individual sensitivity and corresponding store of meanings, so also has the artist. The dramatist or novelist is interested in human experiences, individual and collective; he seeks to portray character, depict situation or incident, and to accomplish this he requires a sensitive responsiveness to every aspect of personal and social relationships, the complication of human motives and the molding of individuality by convention and environment. His medium is that of language, and his command of his medium is shown in his sensitiveness to the use of words, his ability to characterize his subject-matter precisely, vividly, and effectively by the meanings, images and feelings which speech embodies. The painter is likewise interested in objective things and situations, but not in their causes or consequences, and not in the stream of consciousness of the persons who may appear in his pictures. What his eye is trained to see and his mind to organize and enrich, is the visible appearance of things, their shape and color, their texture and the manner in which they are composed in groups. These discoveries he embodies in colored pigments applied to canvas, and his command of his medium appears in his ability to make his paintings a true record of what his senses and imagination have grasped in the objective world. The driving force of his activity is the emotion which the world, in its visible aspect, arouses in him; but unlike the ordinary man, whose feelings spur him to produce practical changes in the things he sees, the artist expends his energy in sharpening his vision, refining and deepening his perceptions, discovering a richer plastic and human significance in the object of his interest.

In Chapter III the way in which this process of expression goes on and its outcome in the creation of form, will be described in detail; what is important for the present is the objective reference of any work of art, the fact that it records a discovery and that the discovery can be verified, the artist's experience shared, only by one who has himself learned to see.

From the fact that meanings are indispensable to seeing, it follows that art and intelligence are inseparably connected. Intelligence, as we shall see in Chapter IV, is nothing but the use of meanings to illuminate existing situations, to bring to bear upon present problems the results of past experience. The scientist sees largely by means of instruments, microscope, spectroscope, thermometer, and the like, which reveal qualities which his unaided senses are not acute enough to discover; these instruments embody the results of past reflection, and make present reflection possible. The artist needs no mechanical aids to perception, but he too requires instruments and these are found in the traditions of painting. The traditions of art constitute the working capital of every artist; they are the records of what painters have in the past discovered and revealed as significant; and the ultimate test of any painter's importance is his ability to add contributions of his own, by means of which his successors may carry further the work of discovery. The intelligence of the painter manifests itself in his use of the traditions to illuminate for him the world which he seeks to depict; of the Venetian, for example, to open his eyes to the rich colorfulness of things, and to the function of color in building up forms, composing masses and welding together the picture as a whole.

Every tradition may be regarded as a way of seeing and a manner of organizing; by extracting from the whole body of traditions the elements which serve best the purpose of his individual vision, the painter displays his intelligence in creating his individual form. This intelligent use of traditions constitutes his method; without it he could do nothing, he would have no esthetic personality to express.

The parallel between art and science in their common objective reference, and their reliance upon method freed from personal idiosyncrasy, involves no derogation to the personality of the artist. We have already noted that objective science yields human values wholly inaccessible to hit-or-miss observation and guesswork colored by desire or prejudice; it does so because it is not a mechanical registration of brute force, but an intelligent search for significant fact. Similarly, the artist does not put down indiscriminately on canvas whatever is before him: he selects and rejects in accordance with the requirements of his design.

Design in the artist corresponds to the specific purpose which makes each science select from concrete things only the qualities or aspects which are relevant to its problems. There is no single formula which describes physical things truly for the purposes of all sciences, and no one way of envisaging the color, mass, line and illumination of an object which is prescriptive for all painters. No two men ever view anything from precisely the same point of view: every true individual, because of his natural endowment, his experience, the influences which have shaped him, the force of his individual personality, sees his world in his own unique way. The objectivity of the artist does not consist in an attempt to be like everybody else, to submit himself to a standard set by the average. What it does consist in is giving a definite form, recognizable by others, to his own vision; in reshaping what he makes, eliminating what is adventitious and supplying what his raw material may not itself display at all, until the form finally achieved is a fully objective expression of his individual reaction to the world.

In defining the conditions of success in art, we have also by implication defined those of failure. An artist who has not mastered tradition can see nothing significant or important; if he attempts to paint he can only tell a story, produce a document, or enter into a losing competition with the camera. Mere acquiescence in tradition, however, is equally futile; it qualifies a painter only as an academician. Since he exercises no initiative or individuality, he remains a copyist; he is a parasite upon tradition, his esthetic status is the same as the scientific status of some one who has read in a text-book that water is H_2O but has no idea how the fact is known or what implications it carries with it. To the academician tradition is a means not to reflection and vision but to the avoidance of either: it takes him not toward but away from the real world. Far from contributing to the advance of artistic insight, he hinders it by adding the weight of his example to the inertia against which all progress has to struggle.

This sketch of the distinctive purpose of art and the conditions of success in it, in defining the method of the artist, has indicated also the only possible method for the understanding of the work of art. The artist is interested in seeing an object in its full significance, not merely in noting in it the indications of its practical bearing in our welfare. To acquire this more comprehensive interest of the artist is thus the first step to be taken in grasping the record of his experience. What he sees is not only more finely differentiated in its detail, it is more comprehensively ordered, more organically unified, than what we are ordinarily capable of perceiving. The principle of its unification is that of **plastic form,** the balanced union of color, line, light and space, by which an object is created which has an imaginative reality denied to the world of literal fact, and also incomparably greater human significance. Any method for the proper study of plastic art must therefore be based upon the conception of plastic form, which defines the only relevant aim of all painting.

Since the artist's ability to see and organize, to create form, depends upon the meanings supplied by the traditions, understanding of his accomplishment depends equally upon possession of these meanings; in their absence no differentiation between the artist and the academician is possible. Since the individual design, the specific purpose which governed the painting of a particular picture, determines the extent and manner in which each of the plastic means is used, their organization also must be grasped and entered into. To suppose that all painters have identical purposes is merely academicism carried to its final conclusion. Since the achievement of a profound esthetic vision, a distinctive personal form, is gradual and involves accumulative growth and enrichment of experience, the artist's work can be fully grasped only if the progress of his development is traced, together with the progressive incorporation in his form of more and more material both from the traditions and from the actual world.

A study of art based upon such a method promises results of the same verifiable objectivity as those of science. Since it does not appeal at any point to mere emotion, it eliminates an otherwise ineradicable source of confusion and blindness; since it can be applied only by the constant exercise of personal observation and intelligent applications of meanings, it eliminates also the appeal to dogmatic authority which is no less fatal than mere emotionalism to real understanding. It obviously provides no rule of thumb, applicable by every one; but no more does science: none of the significant results of science can be tested and judged except by the highly trained and specially qualified.

Since personality remains essential in art, and a measure of personal incompatibility seems to be inherent in experience, the enjoyment of a particular artist's work as distinguished from a judgment of its value, will probably always vary with the individual observer. The variations which actually exist at present, however, are the outcome chiefly of confusion or distraction, such as irrelevant preferences in subject-matter; with the shift of interest to plastic essentials, these may be more and more uprooted. From the intelligent use of objective method, in a word, may be expected a personal response as completely relevant to the work of art as are the judgments of a chemist or biologist to the processes of the physical world.

CHAPTER II

LEARNING TO SEE

The fundamental error in all unenlightened intercourse with works of art is that no account is taken of the axiom that to see means to perceive what in any object or situation makes it significant for experience. Most of the looking at pictures, by those untrained to see, is a search for something to be recognized as already familiar from past experience: it is totally unrelated to the experience which prompted the artist to make of the painting a record of what he saw and felt in his intercourse with a particular objective situation. A beholder who does not see and feel the particular meaning of the painting as an expression of the artist's reaction to the world, is merely looking, not seeing; and such looking is productive of no more benefit than such other essentially similar diversions as looking at a photograph album or the colored illustrations in a magazine. To have a landscape stir up the pleasant memory of a familiar scene, or a portrait that of a friend, is merely to recognize, not to perceive; that is, to refresh one's memory, not to grow in experience by increasing the value of what one already knows through perception of new relationships and values. Recognition, in other words, is seeking a resting place in the past instead of being alive in the present. How widespread is this confusion of values on the part of the layman, and even in what passes for education in art, can be grasped only by a first-hand study of the situation.*

Seeing a picture, that is, perceiving its meaning as an embodiment of an artist's experience in his contact with the world, differs in no essentials from the perceiving of any other object in life, whether the object be a chair, a spark-plug, a map, or what not. In each case, perception, in the true sense of the word, must include two ever-present and determining factors: the qualities of the object itself as they appear to the senses, and the contribution of the individual's mind and body to what the senses communi-

* See "Art and Education," a collection of essays by Dewey, Barnes, etc., pp. 191-202, Barnes Foundation Press, Merion, Pa., 1929.

cate. It is only when these two elements interact, mutually affect each other in a single, continuously unfolding, uninterrupted process, that perception furnishes the material of experience.

The impact upon the senses of each of the qualities of the object is a stimulus to a set of reactions in the percipient, and each successive impact and reaction modifies the significance of those preceding, and establishes new sets of relationships. Unless this uninterrupted flow of new and mutually-affecting relationships takes place the object is not grasped as a composite entity, an individual thing with its own identity, a form conveying a particular meaning for us as an experienced object. Perception, in short, is an organic blending of data furnished by the alert senses of a live animal with the accumulated store of the meanings of past experience, through which the data are digested and assimilated as a new and integral part of the total fund of experience. The process entails a continuous reorganization of the motor-energies of the perceiver and an ever-changing series of readjustments between the new material and the background of accumulated meanings which constitute mind.

It is obvious from the nature of the perceptive process that a defect in any of its aspects results in faulty perception, and, perforce, stunted experience: if the senses are not constantly alert, only isolated parts of the object are taken in; a break in the continuity of interaction between what the senses furnish as nutriment and the perceiver's store of knowledge, prevents new accretions to that store; a limited range of accumulated past experience means an inferior and impoverished store of fuel to be kindled by the sense stimuli into the warmth of new experience.

The foregoing account of the essentials of the psychology of perception makes clear how dependent the value of any artist's work, and indeed of any scientist's, is upon the *quality* of the author's perceptions. The work is never an inventory of objective facts but an embodiment of the interaction of these facts with the background of experience of the worker. Correspondingly, in any study of the work of artist or scientist the subjective element qualifies the objective, and this entails judgment, a judgment of values; in this again the conditions of success are alert senses, a rich background of experience, and a continuous interaction of what is furnished by these two factors. It follows, therefore, that the work of artist or scientist, as well as the study of that work by an outsider, may be gauged intelligently only by fixing the attention upon the control of the material of perception in both its subjective and objective aspects.

This attitude is expressed in all intelligent intercourse with our world: to be relieved of a throat affection, one consults an experienced laryngologist in preference to a general practitioner of medicine; if the specialist is not available, the family doctor, instead of a layman friend, is requisitioned. The reason is that first-hand observation of objective facts is meaningful in proportion to the quality of the background of the stored values of experience brought to bear upon interpreting the significance of what is observed. A painting, like the throat affection, has its own objective marks of identity determinable by perception; in both cases, each attribute stands not alone but as an element in a composite of other and mutually-affecting elements. In the perception of paintings, as of other things, the eyes are but as the sentinels at the outposts whose duty it is to report to headquarters—the mind of the army—every sign that may indicate a situation calling for the conjoined action of all the organization's forces. If the sentinel fails to see the sign of possible danger or advantage, or if headquarters fail to grasp its significance when it is reported, there is no chain of interactions, and either loss of opportunity or disaster may result. To scrutinize a painting for the objective qualities which make it a work of art, is a process of discrimination and this practice finds its counterpart in all intelligent effort to appraise values, in any realm of experience whatsoever. Even a dog practices it before he growls at a stranger or shows the signs of pleasure in greeting his master.

Discrimination in any situation in life entails a picking to pieces of the situation in order to effect a reunification of the pieces in a form representing an appraisal of values. To stigmatize as mere dissection this indispensable first step toward discrimination, is to deny the basic rôle of analysis in the only kind of appraisal of values entitled to respect: judgment based upon objective facts. Only as each constituent part is isolated and examined for what it is in itself, can its fitness to the whole be determined. Thus analysis itself is inseparably connected with the unification, the resynthesis of the elements picked apart, which embodies the sought-for values. The creative artist exercises such analysis not only in what he selects from Nature for his own interpretation but every time he transforms a significant trait characteristic of a preceding tradition—and no artist ever fails to make such selections from

Nature or such drafts upon the past. The trait has to be abstracted, picked out, from its original setting before it can be utilized as working material in a new creation. The abstraction is a mark of the insight which enables the artist to grasp what is significant in a traditional form and recast it in his own expression. The failure either to make the abstraction or to use the abstracted material creatively is the abiding characteristic of academic art.

This looking back at the past by the artist and his incorporation of selected meanings in the expression of new experiences, are paralleled by the dual process of perception and expression in every normal human being, and by every social movement as civilization progresses. What was most significant to human beings of past generations is retained by each subsequent advance in civilization, and the inherited values are enriched by other and equally basic human experiences born of the interaction of creative beings with an ever-changing environment. Such accretions constitute the most vital strand in the thread of life because they are the medium through which contemporary events are expanded in range and deepened in significance by what was most important in the preceding ages. The accretions also verify and deepen the significance of worthwhile experience of the past.

Each expression of significant experience is so deeply rooted in human nature that it survives the attacks of the contemporary critics who, insensitive to fresh experiences in a new and different world, stagnate in the dead past. The life histories of Galileo, Rembrandt, El Greco, Renoir, and Cézanne furnish examples of the imaginative insight surviving onslaughts of contemporaries who blindly accepted the unqualified sovereignty of the past. The work of these creators shows what their contemporary assailants never came to know at all, that a tradition survives because it embodies the spirit of highly endowed individuals fully and freely alive to the forces in the age that give it individuality and distinction.

Translate this blind clinging to the past, and its opposite, the reacting of a creature alive with all his senses and mind to the world about him, into the terms of the perceptive process as it has been described, and we find stated one of the most fundamental problems of education and also the method of approach to its solution. Both the problem and its solution stem from the universal human tendency to confuse *recognition* with perception, a static condition with a dynamic process. Recognition is the servant of the dead past because it takes in only what is already familiar in any object. If perception ends with recognition, instead of merely beginning with it, no connection is made between sense-stimuli and the background of accumulated experiences, and the process is halted before it can develop that uninterrupted reaction between the object, the senses, and the mind, which constitutes real living. What happens is identification, reference of the object or situation to a stereotype preserved in the mind as a model.

The perception which leads to discrimination is no such abortive process and reaches no such dead ends. It begins only when some observed trait or attribute, impinging upon the senses, stimulates the individual's accumulated store of meanings to absorb the new material and to undergo itself a process of reconstruction. The vitality, the dynamic character, of the reaction is evidenced by the familiar warmth and glow pervasive of the whole self when a new experience is born—when one learns to swim, sees the dénouement of a skilfully presented drama, the form of a painter's individual expression of human character or of the contemporary scene. The warmth and glow are as positive and as real as they are when experienced in front of a fire on a cold day; in each case they result from, point to, an actual expenditure of energy. It is the expenditure of energy which makes perception difficult; the effortless, automatic process of recognition is easy, but it fails to generate the warmth of being alive.

Thus far our outline of the nature of perception has assumed that there is no difference between the process as it takes place in our contact with a painting, a part of the world of esthetic enjoyment, and with, for example, an automobile, an object which serves its purpose when it transports us from one place to another. The process in each case *is* identical; even though the *qualities* perceived are not the same, the two categories, esthetic and practical, are not mutually exclusive. A painting which is a work of art may also be a congruous object of furniture in a room; an automobile, by both the form of its structure and its efficient performance in travel, may be the source of esthetic pleasure. The prevalent tendency to confine esthetic enjoyment to what are termed works of art has no sound psychological foundation; it rests rather upon the erroneous assumptions that esthetic quality is something superimposed upon material, and that there is a fundamental difference between the perception of the artist as he creates and the beholder's perception of the esthetic form of the finished product.

To dispose of this misconception we need only reflect upon two such widely separate experiences as that of an epicure taking his dinner and that of a sculptor modeling a statue. The epicure may supply sharp appetite, sound digestion, a knowledge of what constitutes good cooking; and the dinner may provide the best quality of food, irreproachable cooking, agreeable companionship, and a setting satisfactory to the most cultivated taste. The meaning of dinner, however, consists not merely of properly prepared food placed in front of a hungry person, but of a series of interrelated transactions between food and consumer.

If the series of these mutually affecting elements unfolds harmoniously, their orderly progress and the gourmet's perception of them flow in a composite whole and become a definite esthetic experience, infinitely more exciting and more fully satisfying than the mere appeasement of hunger. The whole experience has a unity arising out of a pervasive excellence intrinsic not only to each of the subjective and objective components but also to the specific relationships between them: the epicure's background of culture appreciating the art and science of the cook, the personal qualities of the companions, the attributes of the setting, etc.

Let a break occur—a sudden indisposition of the diner, a dish badly seasoned or served, an impertinent remark of a companion—and the clash brings disorder in the sequence of events and interrelationships; the epicure's enjoyment of the meal is interrupted, and the esthetic quality of the experience aborted. The connected links which would have organized the parts of the dinner in a harmonious ensemble have been severed by episodes, the incongruity of which destroys the pervasive satisfying quality of the dinner as a whole. The quality of excellence flowing smoothly through the courses of the successful dinner was the decisive factor in the epicure's enjoyment. His background of culture and his acute senses, by their interaction with the environment, created that unity and quality which made the orderly dinner a satisfying experience, authentically esthetic, in contrast to the revolting experience of the disordered meal. The value of the dinner as a human experience depended, therefore, as much upon the creative process as it took place in the epicure's personality as upon conditions external to him.

The sculptor's modeling of a statue, though it creates a form more capable of objective verification, differs in no essential point from the experience of the epicure. The sculptor too makes use of an external material, clay or marble, that must have qualities capable of satisfying his need for expression; otherwise, his esthetic feelings would lie fallow and his frustration be as poignant as the cry of the body for food. He too has criteria of excellence which prescribe the qualities of the material and the manner of its organization which will make it answer his purpose; the organic connection between these subjective and objective factors is likewise vital for his esthetic experience.

As the sculptor works, his job is to perceive and, if necessary, alter and correct, the relationships between the feeling he wishes to embody in the clay and the effect obtained by the way he handles his material. At every movement of his hand, his eyes inform his mind just how far the external object has traveled toward the fulfilment of his conception. Every action upon the material is inevitably directed by what the sculptor saw, felt and did in all his preceding activity, and at the same time it is colored with the qualities the finished form has taken in his imagination. At each step it is the perception of relationships between what the hand has done and what the mind holds which guides and controls the continuous unfolding of the process in its subjective and objective aspects, in the reciprocal interaction and the concurrent development of both the original conception and the material object created. Only when the sculptor has achieved an orderly balance between what he has in mind and what the object reveals to have been done, does the creative process come to an end and the experience yield satisfaction.

Adventitious and irrelevant details apart, a common esthetic strand enters into the perceptions of both the epicure and the sculptor. As each progresses in his experience he perceives a set of *immediately felt relationships* between subject and object, and his series of perceptions proceeds to its conclusion in an orderly manner with no irreparable break in the continuity of the quality of the components. The epicure no less than the sculptor is a creator because he perceives the quality of the relationships that makes the experience a fully satisfying consummation and unity, and hence a dominantly esthetic experience.

The esthetic strand in all human activities consists precisely in this perception of immediately felt relationships of subject and object, and of parts to each other and to the whole. This type of perception is the *sine qua non* of the art of the painter, sculptor, writer and musician, as it is also of the art of the baseball player, the golfer, the epicure, or of any one enjoying intelligent social intercourse. The prerequisites in each case are alert senses trained to perceive significant objective attributes, and an unobstructed interpretation of these data by the background of stored meanings. The new values are incorporated in the accumulated experiences and serve as a guide to the individual's future activities.

Progress in learning to see pictures as records of enriched experience is of necessity slow, even when interest is genuine and application wholehearted. A set of habits essentially new and of a very special character must be gradually built up to supplant those ingrained in us by our adjustments to other phases of life. Progress has begun when the beholder, pausing for reflection, becomes conscious that his senses are feeding upon the objective traits of the painting, that the nutriment furnished is stirring his imagination, and that a *feeling* of warmth pervades his whole organism.

The word "feeling" is italicized in order to emphasize the fact that Nature herself furnishes experiential evidence that the perceptive process is not a cold intellectual affair, fundamentally different in character from the emotion that takes possession of a person when a work of art is appreciated. This warmth *is* the emotional factor productive of the consciousness of heightened vitality characteristic of every genuine experience. Heat is always the product of the expenditure of energy, whether in a stove, a dynamo, or a living body. A live animal attains to experience because of his alert interaction with the world, and the energy expended is always manifested. When feeling reaches the degree of warmth attendant upon esthetic experience, it is the organism's shout of victory proclaiming that something vital to it has attained fulfilment, that the forces of the individual have joined combat with and vanquished those of the external world. But a shout of victory is never the whole body of the experience: it is merely the outward sign of emotion born of the entire experience and, for the moment, preponderant over its other aspects. Consciousness, in other words, abstracts the esthetic strand from the composite whole and endows the total fabric of experience with a specific flavor.

The emphasis by many writers upon emotion as the chief, sometimes as the exclusive, characteristic of the enjoyment of art is largely responsible for the prevalent gush of sentiment so obstructive to genuine appreciation. It is easier and more natural for a large proportion of humanity to gush than it is to impose upon itself work in a field that holds no real interest for it. Gush is a mere explosion of disembodied feelings: the ghost of experience wandering aimlessly in an alien world of material objects. An *expression* of emotion is part of, inseparably connected with, the objective factors that gave it birth.* It acquires a very substantial body when it becomes an integral part of both the object or situation and the mind of the percipient, as it must if these factors have interacted sufficiently to produce perception in its true sense.

Excess of emotion is unabsorbed feeling; it spills over into a vacuum and inhibits the process of perception, thereby preventing any production of the material of experience.† Emotion of this sort is quite a different thing from the excitement about subject-matter that penetrates to the store of accumulated meanings of experiences and uses them as fuel for the fire which warms every vital experience. Emotion is abiding only when it has an abode, a body; when it is feeling *about something,* to which it is so organically bound that the two are inseparable. Gush, sentimentalism, is free-floating emotion, unattached to anything; when emitted in the presence of a work of art, it lacks any specific relevance to its object. Its quality, in other words, is the very antithesis of that which makes feeling esthetic.

Another pitfall in the development of esthetic discrimination lies in confusing technical skill with the meaning of the picture as an expression of the artist's experience. A painter may possess a high degree of technical skill and still remain a mere craftsman, utterly incapable of creating a work of art. Mere recognition of such skill is as far removed from genuine understanding of painting, and is quite as irrelevant to it, as sentimentalism. Mere technical skill and the outpouring of excessive emotion, are kindred vices in that each is a dis-located phase of a totality, usurping a sovereign rôle. Thus emphasized and isolated, technique loses its

---

* "It takes the wine-press as well as the grapes to express juice, and it takes environing and resisting objects as well as internal emotion and impulsion to constitute an *expression* of emotion." John Dewey, "Art as Experience," p. 64, Minton, Balch & Co., New York, 1934.

† A sentimentalist is one "whose physiological complexion involves more poignant emotion than his ideas can absorb." George Santayana, "Reason in Art," p. 64, Charles Scribner's Sons, New York, 1917.

appropriate function as an instrument for expression, and becomes itself an expression of vanity and manual dexterity, and hence of dull perception and stupidity. Technique thus masquerading as art is mere virtuosity, an isolated set of muscular adjustments— in extreme cases a mechanistic avalanche which sweeps away all the essentials that make a picture significant. Sensory stimulation, if present, either falls dead upon mind or calls forth for repro- duction a stereotyped formula. In this mechanical performance, perception is either aborted or still-born, degraded into mere recognition of already known facts which perforce leaves the trained observer cold.

In its proper instrumental function, technique represents a set of adjusted muscular activities controlled by what the mind of the painter undergoes under the stimulation of the senses. It is an integral part of a process which links together the sensory stimulation, the imagination, and the hand's movements in a single, continuously unfolding operation, the activity of which never ceases until the created object has absorbed the feelings inherent in the experience. Creative production, in other words, is organi- cally integrated with esthetic perception. Attention to technique, therefore, in the study as well as in the painting of pictures, is to be restricted to ascertaining the part which it plays as a strictly subordinate instrument of artistic expression.

From the foregoing account of the nature of perception, it is apparent that esthetic quality is not confined to our perception of works of art, but pervades a large part of ordinary practical life. We have seen that there is no essential difference between perception as it takes place in the producer of works of art and in the non-producer who is able to grasp the experience which a work of art expresses. What the personality of the artist under- went in producing the object is duplicated in the creative act of any person who perceives the meaning of the object.

The significant difference between the artist and the layman is that the former is infinitely more sensitive to the esthetic pos- sibilities of particular things, and this sensitivity guides his per- ceptions as well as his embodiment of them in objective forms. The work of art is thus a coherent record of the sensitivity and individuality of his perceptions; to read the record one must learn the language, share the artist's perceptions and experience. The basic problem of learning to see, therefore, centers inevitably around the knowledge of what to look for, and how to interpret it when found. What must be sought in works of art is their form, and this is to be interpreted as the expression of a personality and an experience. The nature of expression in its relation to form is the topic to which we next turn.

CHAPTER III
EXPRESSION AND FORM

LIVING organisms, from the lowest to the highest, rarely find ready-made in the world the conditions indispensable to their continued existence and well-being; consequently, their greatest concern is to rectify the discrepancy, to establish the conditions which will provide them with what they require. This is the process of adjustment to environment in which all life fundamentally consists, and which finds expression in the attitudes or acts of the live creature. Man, indeed, is truly alive only in so far as he keeps aware of the possibilities and chances offered him by the environment to attain the equilibrium needed for his life progress; in this sense only, may he be justly called a live animal. The adjustment in question is a process in which the two factors, live animal and environment, are in a constant state of activity upon one another; and expression is a record of these activities, whether it be embodied in an artist's work or revealed in the behavior of a lost dog tracing his way back home from a great distance.

The adjustment between the animal and his environment is made possible by the fact that the world as a rule presents opportunities and resources as well as menaces; if it is wholly hostile, as it is to a man overtaken by an avalanche, no adjustment is possible. Adjustment, in other words, is not only to, but *by means of* the environment; the living being can do nothing except in so far as his energies engage with those which, actually or potentially, are already under way. He cannot even run away from danger unless the environment provides him with a sure footing and a place of refuge. The interaction between the live animal and his environment, through which a continuous and cumulative change is effected in both, constitutes, as we have seen, the actual process of experience. It begins with a felt discrepancy, proceeds with definite steps taken to establish harmony, and concludes, if the adjustment is successful, with an achieved equilibrium, a consummation in a sense of satisfaction or well-being. An experience, thus successfully consummated, expresses the nature both of the individual and of the situation itself.

Unless the impulse which begins and animates the process of adjustment is specifically directed to the conditions responsible for the breach of harmony, its expenditure of energy is futile, since the cause of the trouble remains unchanged. In a panic, we may run away from a fire which could easily be put out by pouring upon it the glass of water standing on a nearby table; in a fit of rage, we may stamp and shout, disregarding entirely the measures by which, if we composed our emotions and collected our energies, we could immediately dispose of the offending circumstances.

Only by an abuse of language can such outbursts be termed an expression of either emotion or personality; when they are over, the obstacles to adjustment remain unaffected, and the force which might have been used to rectify them has not been employed, but dissipated. Impulse, in a word, can be effective only in so far as it is from the start directed and controlled by an intelligent *purpose;* that is, in so far as it takes account, not of the fearsomeness or obstruction of the situation in general, but of the particular features which come between the individual and whatever end he may be striving for. Active effort, thus brought to bear upon the actual obstructions, institutes a new order of things propitious to the well-being previously threatened; a significant change is introduced into both the material situation and the active individual who has acquired a new adjustment, a harmonious relation to his environment. The relevance and adequacy of the reaction to the stimulus constitute it a genuine ex-pression, a pressing out or extraction of essential quality both in the living being and in the environment.

Expression, in the proper sense of the word, thus begins only when the purpose directing the expenditure of energies is to convert the obstacles into agencies contributing to the attainment of the needed adjustment. Purpose means an end forecast in consciousness through the help of meaningful images garnered from previous experiences and stored up as a background of funded knowledge. It remains at the stage of sheer imagination— therefore futile as expression—unless the individual uses it to direct his activities toward control of the situation by removal of the obstructions to adjustment.

When purpose is thus in command, the obstacles themselves

become active stimuli to that coördinated interplay of thought and action which constitutes intelligence, and the original impulse toward adjustment imparts to the specific measure taken an intense driving force. The process of adjustment, in the course of its forward movement, absorbs into itself the qualities of the external conditions acted upon, as well as those of the acting individual, and unifies them in the consummatory act expressive of the total situation or experience. In the practical world intelligent purpose thus finds its expression, achieves its end, by discovering the relevant qualities of an actual situation and in devising the measures which must be taken if the possibilities of the situation are to be realized. Neither the sensitivity of perception which discovers what the objective situation is, nor the sagacity which discloses how it can be changed into what is desired, is possible except through the use of meanings stored up from past experience: it is the discriminating use of these meanings which imparts effectiveness and reality to the expression.

Expression in art entails the same acuteness of perception and employment of relevant meanings as every other intelligent execution of purpose in the practical affairs of life. Like the "practical" man, the artist is moved by some object or situation to feel and to do. What he does is not an attempt to arrest or alter the course of natural events, but to depict them, to paint a picture, carve out a statue, write a poem or symphony. The art in his picture, statue, poem or music is a record of an experience, an expression of his sensitiveness, intelligence, feeling, and personal individuality.

The artist, stirred by some specific aspect of the world, reacting with his whole personality—his senses, habits of perception and interpretation, imagination, emotional attitudes and muscular adjustments—is impelled to extricate, to draw out from the object of his emotion the particular set of qualities and relationships that called forth his response, and to reincorporate them in a form of their own, in the process of which the work of art comes into being. The form of the work of art is thus literally ex-pressed from the original external stimulus as well as from the artist's personality and the clay, paint, musical tones or words used as a medium. As the process goes on, the artist's stir of excitement, at first directed upon the situation as a whole, is gradually differentiated as the separate aspects of the situation emerge one by one into attention, and as each of them assumes its individual place in the total form and its distinctive feeling-tone within the harmony of the whole.

These successive steps are never independent: each proceeds out of what has gone before, and paves the way for what is to come, while all are suffused with the general feeling characteristic of the impression as a whole. In the process, both the artist himself and the material on which he is working undergo a change. As the material is refined, clarified, purged of what is irrelevant, reshaped and more meaningfully unified, the artist's own feelings are transformed; the excitement which at first incited his activity expends itself in the work of perception and organization; mere intensity becomes enduring vitality; and eventually the sense of composure and peace, characteristic of all successful adjustments to life, supervenes. The end and fruition come when equilibrium is established between what the situation had im-pressed upon the artist and what he succeeded in ex-pressing from it through the use of his medium. Nature has thus been transformed through the interplay of forces between the artist and the external world; raw material has been given meaning by an intelligently directed purpose; the emotional content of the artist's experience is concretely embodied in the objective attributes of the created form.

The exploration and organization of subject-matter through which the artist executes his purpose of conferring upon it a definite form, always proceeds more or less tentatively. Until the end is reached, both the form to be achieved and the detailed handling of its components, remain indeterminate, and creative expression manifests itself, in imagination or in fact, as the qualities revealed to sense are taken account of, weighed, emphasized, slurred over, or distorted, as they are judged suitable or unsuitable to the office intended.

At the same time the design itself, the purpose, assumes more definite character; it is not something fixed from the start and imposed by force upon matter to which it is unadapted, but a way of ordering which ex-presses, draws out, the nature of the material itself, the subject-matter as well as the medium of expression. Both the projected form and its components thus undergo a process of investigation and canvassing, checked at every move; the process is not unlike the movements of a person entering a dark and unfamiliar room, littered with he knows not what, conscious only of a need to find a resting place. The inquiring, groping and testing continue until what is found answers the specific purpose in view, enters into the required relationship with what has gone before.

In the whole ordered set of relationships each part both determines and is determined by every other; *this thoroughgoing interdetermination of parts constitutes form in a work of art, as it does in a machine, an organism, or the intelligent execution of any purpose.* The fact that every detail of a work of art is shaped with reference to a specific purpose, establishes unity of an artistic form, and the realization of the purpose by such objective means makes its form perceptible to a qualified observer. The individuality of the form arises from the fact that it is the expression of a unique personality; conversely, the artist's personality, his distinctive individuality, are revealed by the objective qualities of the form itself and by nothing else. Form is thus a book of record of the artist's mind and soul, and the medium through which he publishes his experience and communicates it to the world.

Form in a painting is a harmonious merging of the plastic means —color, line, light and space—through which the artist gives expression to his experience, and it is so permeated with his own personality that its meaning is all its own. A successfully painted landscape, compared with the scene depicted, reveals what the artist has done to and with the original components of the subject-matter—trees, houses, earth and sky—to make them and the nexus of their relationships expressive of the distinctive way in which he sees them, the very specific meaning with which his senses, his feelings, his background and active impulses, endow them.

This meaning is objective; it is a version of the natural scene itself, but the extraction of it, the revelation of what the natural scene essentially is, is an act of creation, possible only to one who has the artist's specific endowment, his trained perceptions, and the funded meanings which his past experience has stored up. In his painting, therefore, nothing remains as it was in its original condition: color, line, surface-texture, the shape, degree of voluminousness and distribution of masses, are all altered, sometimes even to the point of gross distortion, in the process of their incorporation in the new form created by the artist. This penetration to essentials, and the reorganization of mere fact to make it expressive of an experience, is what distinguishes art from every form of imitation and photography. The artist does not meaninglessly repeat what already exists: in one and the same act he shows what *it* really is, and what *he* is.

This creative transformation of natural appearance by artistic insight may be termed *drawing,* if the word be understood not in the arbitrarily limited sense usually given it, but as the whole intricate process of drawing out what is essential in any given subject-matter.* Every exciting object contains a mass of detail a large part of which has no relevancy to what the artist feels in perceiving the object; on the other hand, what is significant in it for artistic expression may be far from obvious. Expression, that is to say, involves selection, emphasis, and the addition of material which only the artist can discover and supply. The drawing out of what is fundamental and significant is therefore the essence of the expressive act, and it involves all the aspects of the thing depicted, the color, illumination and spatial arrangement, as well as the line. A landscape, a figure, or a still-life drawn in this manner not only represents the essentials of the subject-matter as it occurred in nature, which any spectator is free to interpret differently, but it conveys to the trained beholder a record of life and nature, enriched by what the artist's mind and spirit have drawn out, and by what his funded experience has fed to his imagination. Drawing in the full sense, in other words, *is* expression.

The abiding appeal of art to human beings springs from the presence in it of the characteristics which lend interest and poignancy to life itself: movement, contrast, rhythm, symmetry, coherence of parts, unity of form and meaning, and individuality of purpose, are common to nature and art. The regular recurrence of night and day, of the seasons of the year, the systole and diastole of the heart, are natural rhythms to which we are all subject and which profoundly affect our lives. The alternation of these rhythms in nature lends contrast and movement to life, as their repetition and interdependence, their interweaving and dovetailing, lend unity; they thus provide both variety and unity, the indispensable conditions of satisfactory living.

In the world of actuality, however, the harmonious adjustment of natural rhythms to human purposes is only occasional, and it constantly tends to give way to monotonous repetition or to chaotic disorder, either of which is destructive to the individual's well-being. The artist, therefore, deliberately modifies his subject-matter to make rhythm ubiquitous, and at the same time he discards, in the interest of variety and contrast, the mechanical uniformity characteristic of many natural rhythms. The pervasiveness of rhythm is one of the most important agencies of unification;

* See Barnes and de Mazia, "The Art of Henri-Matisse," p. 80, Charles Scribner's Sons, New York, 1933, for a fuller account of drawing.

understood in the widest sense, as embracing color, lighting, shape and mass as well as line, and also such general qualities as grace, charm or power, rhythm establishes unity, the reciprocal determination of every part by every other and by the form as a whole.

In making rhythm more definite and pervasive than it is in the natural world, art brings to a conclusion a tendency which, as Professor Dewey points out, is manifested in all perception. The eye reports things and events to the mind, and the mind interprets them in a series of pulse-beat waves, through which what is seen is gradually unfolded. The details, that is to say, do not enter consciousness simultaneously but as a progressive series, in which contrast between the parts is emphasized along with the common relationship to the whole which maintains unity. When perception has the fulness characteristic of genuine experience, it has a definite form with distinctive movement, rhythm, variety, and balance, and is already well advanced on the road to art; art, indeed, may be regarded as simply the consummation of the striving toward fulness and order in perception, and as its objective record. Art thus contains the values of experience in a purified and heightened form. The keenness of the artist's perception, the intensity of his feelings, the vitality and reality of his experience, in a word, blend every part of the authentic work of art in a continuous rhythmic flow, which springs out of and coördinates the rhythms and contrasts of every detail.

The inherence of rhythm, contrast, symmetry and balance in the organic unity of all the parts of a form, as distinguished from their factitious superposition, is the criterion by which genuine artistic expression may be differentiated from its simulacrum. The importance of this differentiation in any intelligent study of art may be appreciated by a brief glance at this aspect of Renoir's work, prior to our detailed survey of his paintings. Rhythm in Renoir is an element pervasively ingrained in the structural form of the picture, a continuous ebb and flow of all its constituents. The outstanding rhythmic feature is in itself a composite of numerous factors which, in turn, are organized in a great variety of subsidiary rhythms and, by an ever-expanding set of relationships, reënforce and increase the significance of the total form.

Often in Renoir these infinitely varied and intricately intertwined series of rhythms bear striking similarity of quality, extending at times to a close correspondence in structure, to the rhythmic sequence of themes and variations in Beethoven's symphonies. This kinship can be readily perceived by a trained observer tracing with his finger the rhythms in Renoir's *"Noirmoutier"* (201),* for example, as he listens to the second movement of Beethoven's Fifth Symphony. In both the painting and the music the rhythmic movement, a swinging lilt, is extremely fluid, powerful, colorful; if picked up at any point in its course, it develops constantly in variety of content and in mode of expression; each addition to the prevailing rhythm punctuates the basic underlying movement with refreshing throbs of new meaningful units. It is a powerful, all-pervasive rhythmic surge that stirs the percipient's whole personality to sympathetic vibration.

Renoir's rhythm is never a mere repetition, it is a varied recurrence of elements with modifications usually in more than one of their components. The variations not only create rhythms of their own, but enter into the rhythmic corporate body of all the main plastic elements; that is, through their immediately felt influences upon their context, they become dynamically related to the other rhythms and also to the pervasive feeling of life and force distinctive of the composition as a whole. So thoroughgoing is the unity resulting from the rhythmic interpenetration of all the constituents, and so continuous is the transformation of each by every other, that only upon analysis can the rhythms be separated from the other aspects of the formal structure. In the whole painting there is no break in the compositional continuity of the rhythmic movement: each interval between punctuations or accents is in itself a unit of subtle rhythms and contrasts. Composition, in other words, is an uninterrupted progressive sequence of rhythmic contrasts in color, line, light, space, mass and pattern. Renoir's own glow of vitality is communicated to the spectator as the latter's own energies are reorganized by the constantly varied and ever-widening pulsating rhythm which feeds his mind and stirs it to activity. In short, the part played by rhythm in Renoir's form is organic, growing out of the basic design and inseparable from it.

The fact that rhythm, contrast, variety, symmetry and balance are so vitally important in esthetic expression makes them also the principal means through which the surface-effects of art are manufactured. The stock in trade of all such manufacturers consists mainly of rhythms mechanically imposed upon subject-matter, and

---

* This number and all similar documentation by numerals, throughout the book, refer to the "Catalogue Data," listed in the Appendix, p. 441.

distributed throughout the composition in accordance with shop-worn formulas, to obtain balance.*

A simulation of rhythm by units which monotonously repeat one another in the way they are constructed and placed, is far from the rhythmic contrast that effectively recalls and organizes the specta-tor's store of accumulated meanings. The manufactured rhythms, in any field of art expression, in their failure to renew or even sustain the original sense-stimulus, differ in no essentials from the ticktack of a clock, or the monotonous rows of horizontal and ver-tical bars in a rail fence. Reaction to them is barren of significant meanings: at best the senses are titillated, as by the repetitive pat-terns of sound in jazz music, instead of being made to convey to the entire personality the compelling and profound human values expressed in genuinely creative esthetic forms.

The difference between the rhythms in Renoir's work or Bee-thoven's and those in manufactured concoctions can be detected at once by the trained observer; in the former the interplay of rhythms and contrasts constitutes the very substance of the construction and are the very means by which the depth and significance of the artist's experience is conveyed to the spectator. The contrast be-tween the manufactured rhythms and those of Renoir is that between a pattern of lines, colors and masses factitiously arranged and barren of meaningful content, and a rhythmic expression loaded with significant meaning.

What is true of the rhythms in manufactured art is true also of their arbitrary distribution throughout the composition in order to obtain a symmetrical appearance; the symmetry thus speciously secured is merely a physical equilibration of quantities and ex-panses: it is on the same esthetic level as that which the grocer obtains when he weighs a pound of sugar. The only sort of bal-ance that counts esthetically is the symmetry arising from the intrinsic *qualities* of the balanced units themselves. Professor Dewey calls attention to the fact that symmetry is itself a phase of rhythm and can be separated from it only on reflection.†

* E.g., the paintings of Thomas Benton; the poetry of Edgar Guest; the sculpture of George Barnard; the music of Vincent Lopez.

† "Symmetry and rhythm are the same thing felt with the difference of emphasis that is due to attentive interest. When intervals that define rest and relative fulfilment are the traits that especially characterize perception, we are aware of symmetry. When we are concerned with movement, the comings and goings rather than arrivals, rhythm stands out. But in every case, symmetry, since it is the equilibrium of counteracting energies, in-volves rhythm, while rhythm occurs only when movement is spaced by places of rest, and hence involves measure." John Dewey, "Art as Experience," pp. 178-179, Minton, Balch & Co., New York, 1934.

Symmetry, in short, is bound up with, is a product of, the organization of rhythms; it is one of the media through which expression of experience attains to esthetic status; and in all genuine art, symmetry, no less than its constituent rhythms and the dynamic movement they engender, is a quality emerging spontaneously from the form, not imposed upon it from without. Thus in all fully expressive works of art, contrast, which forms the basis of drama, and rhythm, which conduces to unity, are the two variable qualities, by the interplay of which symmetry and balance are established and form unified.

Because art embodies these universal qualities of life and nature, great works of art call forth in the sensitive percipient a wide range of human values over and above those which attach to the treatment of particular subject-matter. Indeed, works of art are great in proportion as they possess the power not only to impart the enhanced vitality characteristic of all genuine immediate experience, but to revive the feelings stored up from scattered experiences of the distant past. Thus art has the unique quality of containing within itself an epitome, a condensation, of the values of innumerable phases of life that cannot find expression through any other medium. Painting and music call up visible and audible images loaded with the "hushed reverberations" of past vital experiences in the everyday world, gone beyond recall except for the magic of pictorial and musical forms. The recalled emotion is all the richer, fuller, more moving, for having all the discordant concomitant factors of the original experience refined away and only a purified residue retained. The condensation and clarification of the meanings of the earlier experiences make the emotional content all the more poignant.

This capacity of art-forms to express the universal qualities of things, limited in range only by that of the perceiver's background of experience, rests upon the same psychological basis as the normal human tendency to transfer the values of one form of experience to that of another and different field. The determining part played by these transferred values in all forms of art-expression warrants restating here a detailed account of the matter as it appeared in another of our books: *

Human beings always and necessarily interpret the present, the given, in terms of the past. The fact is a truism as regards intel-

* Barnes and de Mazia, "The Art of Henri-Matisse," pp. 30-31, Charles Scribner's Sons, New York, 1933.

lectual apprehensions: we understand anything only in so far as we identify it, place it in a context of familiar meanings; but what is not so generally realized is that this intellectual apprehension is accompanied by an imaginative or metaphorical extension of meaning which imports into the experience of the here and now at least a part of the emotional aura, the heat and glow, of our past sensations and feelings. Sometimes, especially when the importunity of practical necessities is relaxed and the situation is propitious to flights of fancy, as on a steamer passing within sight of land off the coast of the Riviera, material objects may attract to themselves swarms of images, and serve as the figures in fantastic dramas. Fleecy clouds sailing over the sky often remind us of animals, persons, buildings; as they move and change, we may interpret their movement and change according to our fancy, and weave narratives about them. A portion of the cloud may detach itself and remind us of the spire or façade of a cathedral; or starting from faint or vague resemblances, we may see in it an elephant's trunk, a shining silver river, or the broad surface of a cliff. Or it may be a living figure moving in stately grace to the melody of a minuet which our memory has cherished for years.

Reveries of this sort are only the extreme development of a tendency to figurative perception which is present in all persons at all times. We say of a man that he is adamant, or soft, or a fox, and the emotional quality conveyed by the figure of speech, no less than our purely intellectual estimate, pervades and determines our attitude toward him. We feel in a Cézanne the qualities of a solidly constructed building; a Renoir picture of a girl recalls a rose in a garden or a morning in June. In short, there is scarcely an object or situation in life, or in art—the mirror of life—not fraught with emotional associations for which its objective qualities give no demonstrable ground.

Often the recall is not of memories and feelings as separate and distinguishable psychological facts, but of what Santayana calls the "hushed reverberations" of the original experience: vague thrills, obscure likings and dislikings, a sense of importance or triviality, of which we can no more bring to mind the basis than we can explicitly state the evidence which underlies many of our most fundamental beliefs. As with intellectual beliefs, there are in our minds in solution a vast number of emotional attitudes, feelings ready to be reëxcited when the proper stimulus arrives, and more than anything else it is these forms, this residue of experience, which, deeper, fuller and richer than in the mind of the ordinary man, constitute the artist's capital. What is called the magic of the artist resides in his ability to transfer these values from one field of experience to another, to attach them to the objects of our common life, and by his imaginative insight make these objects poignant and momentous. Far from being the exotic flower which "practical" people look at askance, art is an essential and vital part of life in that it reveals, expresses, the meaning, the universal significance and emotional import of innumerable facts and experiences which without it would be flat and commonplace.

This chapter may be briefly summarized as follows: every living being is constantly expressing itself by adjustment to its environment, an adjustment in the course of which both the organism and the environment are changed. The expression which constitutes art consists of both a more penetrating perception and a more thoroughgoing rhythmic organization of the material of the objective world. The qualities of real things are drawn out and resynthesized in a form which adds, to the values actually present in the reality, a whole range of others which the artist transfers from remote realms of experience. Art is thus a clearer, more luminous, and imaginatively richer version of the world of nature.

Every worthwhile artist, like any other normally developing human being, passes through stages of infancy, adolescence and maturity of personality and of expression. Consequently, the full significance of his life's work, his contribution to the traditions of art and to human experience, can be revealed and judged only by approaching the study of his form with the knowledge of the principles of the developing process through which personality and insight continuously grow. The next chapter will examine the significant factors in development and growth.

CHAPTER IV
EXPERIENCE AND GROWTH

THERE is a widespread impression that experience is something which, with the passage of time, happens to every one, that exposure to objective conditions automatically generates the ability to perceive and understand them. Thus a man who has spent twenty years in a profession is usually said to be "experienced" in it, irrespective of the qualities of mind, the habits of observation and reflection, that have directed his practice of it. Modern psychology and logic have made it abundantly clear that no such inevitable generation of experience takes place; not only objective conditions but active interest, alert senses, an open mind, a store of knowledge already in hand, and systematic reflection on the part of the individual, are the indispensable conditions of any discriminating sensitiveness to the world about him. What is inevitable in their absence is a counterfeit of attention, a mechanical set of habits, and the prematurely fossilized mind which, as William James says, makes the majority of human beings incapable of growth after the age of twenty-five.

The organic connection between growth and experience is obvious in every aspect of experience itself: all the activities which enter into it have their function and meaning only as instruments of growth, and the reality of the experience as a whole is destroyed when the continuity of growth is broken. Except in so far as the organism utilizes the situations in which it is placed as food out of which to build up a constantly more robust and individualized personality, its perceptions, purposes and achievements, either intellectual or esthetic, are without substance or significance. A survey of the various levels and types of experience will show the continuous interaction with environment and resulting growth to be essential to them all.

We have seen in Chapter II that perception furnishes the material of experience through a process of active intercourse of the individual with his environment. Every living being is constantly undergoing stimulation from some external object, responding, and again undergoing, in its entire organism, the effects of the response. That such constant interaction with the surroundings is the first condition of growth is revealed by the most striking feature in the behavior of the lower animals. An animal is constantly observing, investigating, and actively doing something about the things going on in his vicinity. His activities may be limited in scope, but they are never half-hearted or perfunctory; he is, in a word, *interested* in his environment, and his interest shows itself both in a constant attentiveness to it and in an equally constant expenditure of energy to adjust himself to it. A dog which greets the arrival of a stranger by growling, that of an acquaintance by wagging his tail, is testifying both to his interest and to his discrimination, and the obvious limitations of his world and his reactions do not in the least affect the genuineness of his interest, the definiteness of his response, or the reality of his experience.

The behavior of even very young children exhibits the same unjaded interest, manifesting itself in spontaneous curiosity, appropriate responsiveness, and freedom from affectation. It shows also, and even more clearly, the *ability to learn* which is always present when experience is real, and which becomes more and more important as the test of such reality as life reaches higher levels. This will be apparent if we consider the familiar instance of a baby's grasping a flaming object and thereby burning himself. The baby may repeat the act again and again without having a genuine experience: not until he connects what he did with what happened to him as a result of his act, does he grasp the meaning; that is, the experience, that fire burns. Experience, in other words, involves not only doing and undergoing but perception of the relation between the two—and this, in a word, defines thinking. Such perception endows situations and the acts which they prompt with meaning: a flame (touched) means a burn; and the perception of meaning constitutes experience.

The simplest reflex action thus makes apparent the fact that two conditions are essential to experience—interest, manifesting itself by active attention and specific response, and grasp of meaning. In so far as a situation does not incite some one to do something positive and appropriate, he has no experience of it because he is not really alive to it at all. The action, even though nothing more than an unconscious adjustment of the organism to the situation, is always positive and appropriate. With the perception of the consequence of action, the meaning of the situation is revealed: the

organism has fed on its environment and enriched its own substance. Mind is merely the store of accumulated meanings remain-
ing from past experience, and it grows by adding to that store new
meanings, likewise born of the uninterrupted interaction of individual and environment.

In mature life, intelligence consists in the explicit use of one's
store of accumulated meanings, and this is likewise a dual process
of doing and undergoing, with reciprocal and continued interaction
between the two phases. The problem for reflection is always set
by a situation which as a whole is unfamiliar, so that no habitual
course of action can serve as a response, but not too unfamiliar to
be recognized as having a bearing upon our interests. The fact
that it is not altogether strange means that our past experience can
furnish us with suggestions about it, and the test of intelligence is
found in the way in which such suggestions are used. If they
amount to no more than guesses, means for bringing the inquiry to
an immediate end, not only is any action premature and exposed to
the risk of practical disaster, but the opportunity for growth is lost.

If, in contrast, the suggestion is treated as a hypothesis, which
as its implications are developed points to additional observations
which will justify its acceptance or rejection, we avoid as much as
possible the danger of practical loss, and at the same time turn the
situation to our intellectual advantage. Often a number of hypotheses may call for consideration before we can reach a conclusion,
and the final decision may be a compromise between conflicting
hypotheses, but when it is attained the action supervening has
acquired a new status: it is no longer mere trial and error, but
experience. Whether the action itself succeeds or fails, it brings
illumination, and its results are thus available for the interpretation of similar situations in the future. The reality of experience
is thus attested in reflective as in spontaneous behavior by the fact
that the continuity of development is maintained: the organism has
been nourished by the objective situation, in and through the process of amplifying its own store of meanings, its mind.

Another factor of the utmost importance in the process by which
the matter of experience is assimilated to yield fresh insight, is the
ability to perceive analogies between things superficially different.
No problem is solvable by any one who lacks a fund of knowledge
out of which suggestions or hypotheses may arise, but even when
this is present individuals differ enormously in the degree to which
they can avail themselves of it for the interpretation of unfamiliar

situations. The extremely literal-minded or habit-bound can take in a situation only if it repeats practically point for point one already encountered. Their past experiences can be revived only as wholes; such are the persons who are unable to give an accurate and succinct statement of anything, or to tell the simplest story without adding a multitude of irrelevant details. Lacking the capacity to select, reject and eliminate, they are helpless in the presence of complexity, and their development is arrested by problems which to the intellectually resourceful would be a challenge and stimulus to growth.

At the other extreme are those who can detect very slight resemblances and in so doing discover the indispensable clue to the solution of a problem. All interpretation of really formidable novelty requires this ability to discriminate between the essential and the adventitious, and to carry away from experience a grasp of generalized connections applicable to innumerable things which need have no obvious common quality. Experience thus requires, in addition to living interest and a reflective habit of mind, an ability to look beneath the surface and distinguish what is fundamental from what is trivial.

Interest, perception of meaning, the use of suggested meanings as hypotheses, and a penetrating discrimination of essentials, together with a background of meanings retained from the past, are thus necessary for that continuous active interplay of forces between the individual and environment which alone constitutes experience. These activities, operating in every aspect of the individual's behavior, so expand and relate it to its context of absent, past and future conditions that action is no longer a response to a single fact, but to the totality of the situation. These factors in experience are distinguishable, but not isolable: in the absence of any one of them the continuity is broken between the individual and his environment, he fails to function as a complete organism, and the supply of nourishment required for his continued growth is suspended. If, for example, interest is not wedded to reflection and action, it speedily becomes emotional indulgence, and this, as our account of perception has shown, has no fruit in experience; and reflection itself, if not checked by experiment, is nothing more than idle speculation, a form of day-dreaming. Experience, in a word, is an organic whole, and is arrested or perverted the moment the reciprocal interaction of its elements is interrupted, and its supply of food from the objective world thereby cut off.

This statement of the nature of experience, in its application to practical affairs and science, would probably not be disputed by any well-informed person. It is almost universally supposed, however, that in esthetic creation intellectual processes have little or no part to play: that the effort in practical affairs to determine, by painstaking observation, elaboration of hypotheses, and recognition of objective connections, exactly what the facts of the situation *are*, is in esthetic creation replaced by something more emotional and "intuitive," often called "inspiration." As we shall see further on in this chapter, the idea of inspiration corresponds to an important phase or aspect of growth, but the aspect is as characteristic of intellectual growth as of esthetic, and the belief that artistic creation and reflective thought are in any sense opposed is a radical error, fatal to adequate understanding of either.* Far from being opposed, they are in psychological essence the same: the fundamental fact in both is interpretation of an objective situation in the light of the individual's whole personality and background; in both, this interpretation is made under the spur of specific interests, controlled by the purposes of the organism as a whole, and directed to action. In other words, genuine experience in reasoning and in artistic creation is a continuous process, each using the problems which arise and the material furnished by the past as food for an ever-renewed growth, and resulting in a constant reorganization both in the individual and in the world.

As already noted in the preceding chapter, all the elements or phases characteristic of practical and intellectual experience are also present in the esthetic: without interest and a store of accumulated meanings, both of them involving all the activities of

*... the idea that the artist does not think as intently and penetratingly as a scientific inquirer is absurd. A painter must consciously undergo the effect of his every brush stroke or he will not be aware of what he is doing and where his work is going. Moreover, he has to see each particular connection of doing and undergoing in relation to the whole that he desires to produce. To apprehend such relations is to think, and is one of the most exacting modes of thought. The difference between the pictures of different painters is due quite as much to differences of capacity to carry on this thought as it is to differences of sensitivity to bare color and to differences in dexterity of execution.... To think effectively in terms of relations of qualities is as severe a demand upon thought as to think in terms of symbols, verbal and mathematical. Indeed, since words are easily manipulated in mechanical ways, the production of a work of genuine art probably demands more intelligence than does most of the so-called thinking that goes on among those who pride themselves on being "intellectuals." John Dewey, "Art as Experience," pp. 45-46, Minton, Balch & Co., New York, 1934.

the organism as a whole, no such thing as esthetic expression could exist. Just as the physician detects symptoms to which the layman is blind, the artist too sees more than the man whose eyes have not been opened by specific training and active experiment. What the artist sees is, for example, more numerous shades of color, interrelations of volume and space, sequences and rhythms of line, but these things are as far from being divined intuitively or spontaneously composed into a single whole, as are the indications of health or disease.

Like the scientist, the artist is able to see only because he has learned to see: the traditions of art play exactly the same part in stimulating and directing his activities of mind and body, and in nourishing his growth, that the facts and principles of science do for the physicist's or chemist's. Indeed, each of the traditions of art may be described as a systemized way of seeing, in which particular aspects or qualities of the visible world are selected and arranged in a characteristic type of organization. To have mastered the traditions means therefore to have seen the objective things about us from many points of view, to have acquired a rich store of material for the esthetic interpretation of reality; and this is precisely the same thing as to have an ample supply of possible meanings for the interpretation of a practical difficulty or scientific problem.

The use in science of suggested meanings as hypotheses to guide observation is paralleled in artistic creation by the artist's use of traditions tentatively or experimentally, following them not as rules or laws to bind his own seeing, but as suggestions, means of illumination, to be adhered to in so far as they reveal what he as an individual wishes to express, but discarded or modified whenever they are irrelevant to his purpose. So used, in balanced coördination with the particular object or scene which provides the problem of seeing and the opportunity of growth, the traditions feed his esthetic activity and give it direction and meaning; otherwise, they are mere blinders, limiting his vision and stunting his growth. The distinction is that between authentic art and academicism, and illustrates once more the difference between true experience, in which interest, knowledge, and all the powers of mind and body coöperate to produce a personal achievement, and the meaningless repetition of undigested formulas which constitutes the entire stock in trade of academic painters.

The ability to discover analogies between things superficially very different, to utilize the essence of an experience in a new context, appears in art in the ability to extract from a tradition the elements responsible for its basic significance and to make of them instruments for the creation of a new form which need have little or no obvious resemblance to its prototype. This is what characterizes all profoundly creative art, such as Cézanne's, or, as we shall see in detail, Renoir's. A painter who is able to distinguish in the traditions what is essential from what is adventitious has at his command an immensely extended range of values: he can observe his world with an incomparably more penetrating insight than one who has no choice but to see things, in the main, as they have always been seen. He can, in other words, nourish his experience from all the resources of the past, incorporating its richness into the very fiber of his personality without compromising his own integrity; if he retains unimpaired his capacity for growth throughout a long career, his work may then come to be an epitome of all the most significant values of tradition, made fresh, distinctive and personal by the completeness with which everything irrelevant to his own vision is eliminated.

The vital importance in art of a constantly increasing capital of esthetic meanings, may be illustrated by a comparison of Monet's work with Renoir's. Because Monet's sensitivity and interest were practically restricted to the field of out-of-door light-and-color effects, each new impact upon his senses called forth a type of reaction similar to previous reactions; selection and interpretation took place each time according to the monotonous dictates of his fixed set of habits and limited background, and correspondingly, failed to enrich the latter by expanding the boundaries of his vision.

Renoir too was interested in the impressionistic interpretation of nature and in Monet's technical method of expressing it; but the impact upon his senses, and his interpretation of what was being done by his contemporaries, instead of limiting his field of vision, quickened his sense of perception and broadened his insight. Thus the impressionistic form itself, in Renoir's hands, acquired a richer meaning because his keener perception and greater freedom of receptivity had discovered in it fuller possibilities than were ever suspected by its originators.

A set of landscapes by Monet offers great variety in subject-matter, especially in the character of illumination at different times of the day; but the essential quality expressive of the interaction of the scene with the man's personality is monotonously alike in all. Monet, in other words, was awake to only certain phases of life beyond which his specialized vision seldom reached; Renoir, on the other hand, was continuously unfolding in his perception of Nature; he consistently inquired for, discovered, selected, established, organized and expressed new pictorial effects, connections, relationships, values and meanings, all reflecting a wide field of life activities, and a profound assimilation of the great traditions of painting. In contrast to Monet, Renoir could paint the very same spot of landscape a number of times and each version would reveal an essentially different ramification of his spirit and feelings.

An understanding of the fact that the process of creation is essentially the same in art, in science, in philosophy and in all intelligent living, makes it possible to see in each, the type of development or growth which occurs in cases of "inspiration." All art, as Santayana observes, is automatic, but this in no way implies that it occurs as a spontaneous sudden birth, without a long period of gestation. What automatic means here is that the experience which a work of art records cannot be consciously planned for in advance: that often, after a long series of fruitless efforts, the artist is visited by a flash of insight, a burst of inspiration, and that because of the absence of deliberate design on his own part, he may think of his vision as something which has come to him, rather than as something which he has produced.

This absence of conscious contrivance, however, which is characteristic of all art of the first rank, becomes intelligible as soon as we understand that mind and conscious reflection are not at all the same thing. The mind is a system of meanings, each of them the indelible record of an experience, and its growth consists in a more precise definition and a more fully organic interconnection of these meanings as a result of interaction with the environment. This growth may and in fact largely does go on without explicit awareness of it on our part, and sometimes when we finally do become aware of it we find that our personality has been changed to its depths, that our changed attitude makes us see a vast number of things in a totally new light.

A familiar form of this is religious conversion, but it occurs also throughout the whole range of experience, intellectual as well as esthetic. Its explanation is what William James calls "subconscious incubation," a germination so gradual that we do not realize that it has taken place until it is almost or quite complete. The suddenness of our realization, however, does not in the least indicate that the change itself was sudden. There has been no breach of continuity, no interruption of the steady assimilation of appropriate nutriment from the environment which can alone make growth possible, and when the new insight bursts upon us, analysis can always discover its relation to all that we have done and undergone. Interest, the system of habits and meanings which constitute the individual's real though often unconscious personality, have all left their mark upon it; they are bred into its substance, and in their absence it would never have been forthcoming.

Religious conversion, indeed, is only an exaggerated form of an experience which every one has constantly. We often find that the solution of our problems does not come as a result of a single uninterrupted process of thought, beginning with a difficulty or perplexity and proceeding forth to a conclusion; instead, after a long course of observation and reflection, we may remain completely at sea. The process may be repeated over and over without yielding a satisfactory conclusion; suddenly, however, perhaps when we are not thinking about it at all, what we have been looking for flashes upon us. Clearly, in the interval something has gone on, but it has been below the threshold of consciousness, and we know it only by its results.

On a more extended scale, the changes in our attitudes toward people largely take place in the same fashion. Often no question is definitely raised, but after a lengthy association we wake up some day to find that an infatuation has been outgrown, or an aversion changed into respect. The final result represents a long-continued summation of stimuli upon a mass of piled-up observations the significance of which was not felt at the moment, but which when assimilated grew into a final and dramatic alteration of our whole attitude and disposition of mind.

Growth or development, however continuous in essence, thus shows an alternation of rapid and obvious advances with pauses; the pauses are periods not of stagnation but of gestation, in which the activity of the organism continues unabated but takes the form of preparation for a new variety of expression. Indeed, the absence of such pauses is likely to point, not to uninterrupted development, but to the fact that the individual has reached the limit of his growth early, and is therefore unable to attain any more profound ordering of his experience. Haydn and Matisse are artists who, for all their ability, remain at approximately the same level once their maturity is reached: Beethoven and Renoir, in contrast, develop not only in technical mastery but also by advancing constantly to more exalted realms of experience and to higher levels of personality.

Since advances of this kind cannot possibly be planned beforehand, and yet represent the most important order of development, deliberation or conscious reflection is only one, and not the most vital, phase of that growth of mind and body which takes place when a living organism, by the operation of all its powers, draws nutriment from its world. It follows that in the profound thinker, as well as in the creative artist, the most significant part of growth takes place during the periods of gestation, when his subconscious is in control; that his experience too is basically a matter of active commerce with environment, and that his explicit reflection is instrumental to making an adjustment of his whole personality to the objective world. His emotions are deeper than his reasoning, and they determine the purposes which his conscious intelligence devises means to carry out.

This conclusion is of the utmost importance for the understanding of both art and intellectual activity.* Modern psychology, in showing the essential identity of experience in all its forms and phases, has revealed the possibility of analysis of art by the same means which have proved so fruitful in science. Such analysis, in fact, is indispensable to any real understanding of art or participation in the artist's experience. However little the artist is capable of formulating abstractly the purposes which animate his activity or the principles which guide it, their operation is demonstrable in the inherent rationality of his work, which is an orderly, coherent creation out of the material of experience, the culmination of a continuous growth which has drawn nutriment from all that he has done and that has happened to him. Conversely, a profound and living philosophy is first and foremost the reaction of a living being, fully alive to his environment and participating with his whole mind and body in all its activities.

As little as the artist, can the philosopher always identify the true basis in experience of much that enters into his world: the sources of his nutriment are too varied, subtle and elusive to be brought completely into consciousness. Largely because of this elusiveness, it is vital that they be perceived and made intelligible;

* See John Dewey, "Art and Education," p. 63, Barnes Foundation Press, Merion, Pa., 1929.

it is only in the light of them that we can hope to share his experience and judge of the validity of its result. The artist, like the philosopher, invites us to enter into his mind and view his world. If we are to accept his invitation to share what is offered we must feed our mind and grow through the active and unremitting enlistment of all our powers in the attainment of discriminating insight into what he has to show.

In the foregoing chapters we have considered the general principles underlying all perception, expression, experience and growth; in what follows we shall see how the same principles are specifically exemplified in the work of Renoir. In the range of his knowledge and experience, the vigor and penetration of his mind, the significance of the values at his command, Renoir challenges comparison with the profoundest and most astute thinkers. It is impossible to understand this important fact unless we see its roots in his entire personality, and in the environment and traditions by which it was nourished. To understand it best, one must see that the basic reason for his greatness was an enormous innate capacity to learn continuously as he grew in years and practiced his art. From the very beginning of his career his endowment enabled him to grasp what was significant in the life about him and in the traditions of the past and to incorporate the findings in his own expression. The successive stages of his painting reveal an ever-expanding personality embodied in the new and highly individual forms.

The purpose of the chapters which follow is to point out, in the objective qualities of the work of his successive periods, the identifying marks of this continued development of his whole personality and the progressively increasing fulness of its expression.

BOOK II

DEVELOPMENT OF RENOIR'S FORM

CHAPTER I
DEVELOPMENT OF RENOIR'S FORM

THE EARLIEST WORK *

PAINTING in France in the 1860's, when Renoir's career began, had made extensive progress in its emancipation from the pseudo-classicism of David and Ingres, which still controlled academic circles. The chief figures in the advance toward a more natural artistic expression had been Delacroix, Daumier, the painters of the Barbizon school, and Courbet, Manet and Monet. Delacroix's interest in the bright, rich and deep color of the Venetians and Rubens, had found a natural instrument in Constable's method of color-division; Daumier had revived Rembrandt's use of chiaro-scuro, made it a new means of rendering solid mass by color, and combined it with his own terse, vigorous and highly expressive drawing. The Barbizon school had taken painting out of doors, and given the effect of nature as actually seen, not merely as imagined in the studio. Courbet, resuscitating the naturalism of the Dutch and Spanish masters, had formulated a style of painting adapted to emphasis upon the unadorned reality of familiar things. Manet had added an even more penetrating eye for essentials, shown in his exceedingly simplified and generalized drawing, to which he added a new luminosity in the paint itself. Claude Monet, utilizing these contributions of Manet, devoted himself to pictur-ing the effects of actual sunlight falling upon colored surfaces at various angles and in varying degrees of intensity. The joint influence of Manet and Monet resulted in the elimination of shadows or their replacement by bright color, and in investment of the surface-colors themselves with a degree of effulgence pre-viously unrealized. This type of painting came to be known as impressionism.

These traditions furnished Renoir with natural points of de-

* Throughout the book the symbol "c." (circa) will precede the date of Renoir's undated pictures; the omission of "c." will indicate that the date appears on the painting itself.

47

parture, and they were nearly always qualified to some extent by his innate affinity with the spirit of eighteenth century French painting. The Barbizon influence can be identified in the painting of landscapes,* especially in the unappealing greens and in the modification of Corot's silvery light.†‡Courbet's is by far the major influence in Renoir's work of the sixties and very early seventies; ‡ it appears in the color-scheme of dark tones, the relatively tight linear drawing, the hardness of textures and the accentuation of light and shadow in modeling flesh.§ All are significantly modified in the best work of the period, chiefly by creative adaptations of Manet's characteristics.‖ The result is that Renoir's color is more luminous than Courbet's, it is richer, more varied and more sensitively related, more glowing and fuller of vitality; black-and-white contrasts are more lustrous; modeling is more colorful; pattern of brush strokes is more perceptible; drawing is simplified and less tight, and it yields a less literal, a more imaginative rendering of textures.‖

Even at this early stage, Renoir's especial interest in modeling solid volumes by means of structural color enables him to adapt Manet's contributions to a wider range of plastic relationships. Renoir's execution, though as yet less skilful than either Courbet's or Manet's, contains the promise of eventual greater richness and colorfulness. In its totality this early Renoir form resembles Courbet's most closely, but it is more complex, richer, and more thoroughly integrated. Nevertheless, Renoir was not yet fully able to discard from his borrowings whatever is adventitious and preserve only their essential values. The silvery light in landscape is as yet incompletely fused with color and retains some of the

* E.g., Renoir's *"Barges on the Seine"* (14) of c. 1869.
† E.g., Renoir's *"Lise"* (9) and *"Mr. and Mrs. Sisley"* (10), both of c. 1868.
‡ E.g., *"Easter Flowers"* (1) of 1864, *"Diana, the Huntress"* (4) of c. 1866-1867, *"Lise"* (5) of 1867, *"Boy with Cat"* (7) of 1868, *"Alfred Sisley"* (8) of c. 1868, *"Lise"* (9) of c. 1868, *"Mr. and Mrs. Sisley"* (10) of c. 1868, *"In Summer"* (11) of c. 1868-1869, *"Bather with Griffon"* (16) of 1870, *"Woman's Portrait"* (18) of 1870, *"Head of Madame Maître"* (22) of c. 1871.
§ Cf., e.g., Courbet's *"Spring"* (588) and *"Young Bather"* (591) with Renoir's *"Diana, the Huntress"* (4) cf c. 1866-1867, and *"Bather with Griffon"* (16) of 1870. The latter two are obvious exercises in constructing duplications of Courbet's form.
‖ E.g., *"Lise"* (5), *"Boy with Cat"* (7), *"Lise"* (9), *"Mr. and Mrs. Sisley"* (10), and *"In Summer"* (11).

monotony and mechanical character of Corot's;* and a number
of the devices by which space is indicated are inadequately supported by subtle relations of color and light † which subsequently
do so much to bind together volumes and spatial intervals.
Another sign of immaturity in Renoir's early work is the feeling of the paint itself, although even at this stage his control of
the medium was greater than that of the majority of important
painters. From this feeling of paint arises the wooden or metallic
quality of some of the areas, for example, the collar and the hat
in *"Lise"* (9) ; however, there is no such confusion of values as
sometimes arises from Cézanne's piling up of pigment.‡ A more
important deficiency than this lack of control of his medium was
Renoir's imperfect fusion of the separate plastic means and traditions; that is, color, line, light and space, as well as the individual
areas of the picture, play their particular part more obviously than
in Renoir's mature paintings; similarly, the contributions of his
predecessors and contemporaries bear more definite and unmistakable marks of their source. Like all great art, Renoir's painting
at each stage of his career drew upon the heritage of the past,
but as his stature increased, what he took from the traditions underwent constantly more radical transformation, became
more and more completely his own, until in his latest and greatest
period only a highly discriminating observer can recognize the
subtle essences of traditional derivations. No such discrimination
is needed to grasp the relation between an early Renoir and a
typical Courbet; the importance of the early work, therefore, resides chiefly in the way the traditions are shown in process of
transformation to a form which is more decorative, of greater
delicacy and colorfulness, of fuller plastic organization, and more
spontaneous human appeal than in the prototypes.

Renoir's earliest work, immature as it is, shows unmistakably
that he was endowed by nature with the prime requisites of a great
artist: the ability to unify his pictures and to put upon them the
mark of his own individuality even when traditional forms are
closely adhered to. This is convincingly demonstrated in his
"Mademoiselle Romaine Lancaux" (2), dated 1864, in which a

* E.g., *"Lise"* (5), *"Lise"* (9), *"Mr. and Mrs. Sisley"* (10).
† E.g., in *"Lise"* (9), the sharp contour of the hat brim, and the obvious
contrast made by the blue streamer against the color of the flesh, and also
by the shadow under the chin with the color of the face and neck.
‡ E.g., Cézanne's *"Bathers"* (617), especially the relation between the
arms of the main standing figure and the background.

Corot type of picture assumes a new form in a composition unified largely through color-quality and relationships individual to Renoir.* Again, his *"Boy with Cat"* (7), of 1868, is a Velásquez-Goya-Courbet-Manet theme endowed with richer plastic content by means of a color-organization which for individuality and abstract feeling of power is scarcely to be excelled by the work of even the greatest of old masters. Another picture of about the same year, *"Mr. and Mrs. Sisley"* (10) reworks characteristics of Corot, Courbet and Manet in a strong plastic organization imbued with Renoir's own feeling for subtle relationships. His early ability to draw with color—the most difficult task of a painter—is shown in *"Rowboat"* (6), a picture of the late sixties.

Great as these achievements are, especially for a beginner, they illuminate largely the psychology of relative immaturity. In spite of the individuality and power of the color-organization in *"Boy with Cat"* and in *"Mr. and Mrs. Sisley"* the general plastic content of the form remains very close to that of other painters; the successful use of color in drawing and in effecting compositional unity in *"Rowboat"* appears in only a part of the picture: the composition as a whole is one of disparate parts. In other words, Renoir's efforts to attain unity in an individual manner were successful in these pictures only intermittently. This is in accord with the principle that all growth results from experience, from doing and undergoing; Renoir's learning by trial-and-error in this early period enabled him to grow further and further away from this youthful reliance chiefly upon traditions, and toward his own individual expression.

The 1870-1874 Period †

The transition from a close adherence to traditional forms to a more individual expression took place between 1870 and 1874. Some of Renoir's pictures painted during these five years show a direct influence of Delacroix, but this influence is not, as critics

* Cf., e.g., Corot's *"Woman with the Pearl"* (570).
† E.g., *"Bather with Griffon"* (16) of 1870, *"Odalisque"* (17) of 1870, *"Capitaine Darras"* (19) of 1871, *"Madame Maître"* (20) of 1871, *"Still-Life with Bouquet"* (21) of 1871, *"Henriot Family"* (23) of c. 1871, *"Canoeists at Chatou"* (24) of 1872, *"Harem"* (25) of 1872, *"Pont-Neuf"* (26) of 1872, *"Breakfast"* (27) of c. 1872, *"Young Woman with Rose"* (28) of c. 1872, *"Landscape"* (29) of 1873, *"La Grenouillère"* (31) of c. 1873, *"Dancer"* (32) of 1874, *"Opera Box"* (34) of 1874, *"Path in the Field"* (36) of c. 1874-1875.

habitually claim, fundamental in the determination of his mature form. It seems to have two aspects: one in which the original as a whole is practically reproduced; * the other aspect is revealed in those rare pictures of this and later periods in which either the color is heavy, or it lacks internal illumination, or else the inter-penetration of tones is mechanical or the color-scheme is Oriental in general feeling.† Aside from certain pictures of the early seven-ties, there is no such specific vestige of the influence of Dela-croix on the totality of his form as, for example, there is of Manet's and Courbet's. After the mid-seventies the Delacroix in-fluence is so extremely generalized that it is practically negligible; on the rare occasions in which it is perceptibly present ‡ it injects qualities alien to the form best expressive of Renoir's personality.

The majority of his pictures of 1870-1874, while still leaning heavily upon the forms of other painters, attain to individuality through the introduction of significant changes which also fore-cast the more personal characteristics of his later and fully matured expression. These pictures show that Renoir is feeling his way toward a realization of his own powers, much as a child learns to stand upon its own feet and to move of its own volition. *"Madame Maître"* (20), dated 1871, has the feeling of an early Monet in its general technique and heavy pigment, but the composition is more ingenious, more organically integrated and the color is richer, more solid and better lighted.§ *"Henriot Family"* (23) of c. 1871, in which Renoir attains to the extremely fluid drawing character-istic of his best work of the mid-seventies, presents a Boucher surface-quality and coral-tinged pearly color-scheme enhanced in decorative and expressive values by the more comprehensive com-positional rôle played by color.‖ *"Pont-Neuf"* (26), of 1872, is in general a compositional theme of Pissarro's strengthened by firmer drawing, a more varied use of technique, and a better realization

---

* Cf., e.g., Delacroix's *"Algerian Women"* (571), *"Odalisque"* (573) and *"Study of Reclining Woman"* (574) with Renoir's *"Odalisque"* (17) of 1870, *"Capitaine Darras"* (19) of 1871, *"Still-Life with Bouquet"* (21) of 1871, *"Harem"* (25) of 1872 and *"Young Woman with Rose"* (28) of c. 1872.

† E.g., *"Girl with Cat"* (38) of c. 1874-1876, *"Madame Choquet"* (42) of 1875, *"Mademoiselle Charpentier, Seated"* (58) of 1876, *"Bouquet before Mirror"* (65) of c. 1876, *"Madame Georges Charpentier"* (78) of c. 1877-1878.

‡ E.g., *"Mesdemoiselles Cahen d'Anvers"* (117) of 1881 and *"Algerian Woman"* (123) of c. 1881.

§ Cf., e.g., Monet's *"Madame Monet Embroidering"* (631).

‖ Cf., e.g., Boucher's *"Sleeping Shepherdess"* (518).

of color- light- and space-relationships.* In this picture, as in *"Canoeists at Chatou"* (24), of the same date, any suggestion of plagiarism is precluded by the fact that the traditional forms drawn upon are changed radically by advances in drawing, color and technique.

In both pictures appears the foundation of the blue-green-ivory color-scheme which Renoir elaborated in the mid-seventies. The landscape in *"Canoeists at Chatou"* is similar to Monet in brush-work, patches of accentuated sunlight, and juxtaposed color-spots; these traits, however, are only incidental to Renoir's experiment with bright, vivid, daringly contrasted colors through which he breaks away from the somber color-scheme and general influence of Courbet, and achieves more fluid † drawing and a wider range of colors.‡ The influence of Manet appears in the drawing of the figures and boats but the brush strokes are more generalized and the colors are brighter and more varied.§ These varied colors are intermingled by brush strokes to produce the type of color-chords ‖ to which Renoir's subsequent surfaces owe much of their distinction and individuality. Renoir, in short, has thrown off the shackles of Courbet, devised the fluid drawing and rich color-chords which became part of his permanent working capital, and has utilized Monet's brushwork and areas of sunlight as means of organizing a color-ensemble which, in the next period of his work, he used creatively in some of his important pictures.¶

The form of *"Canoeists at Chatou,"* however, is still only an experimental step toward his mature form of the mid-seventies: the color, lacking internal luminosity, is merely bright, not rich and juicy, with an appearance of superficial tinsel, instead of depth, organic structure and glow; color-movement and compositional organization are obtained mainly by the facile means of pattern and contrast of direction of brushwork, instead of by flow

---

* Cf., e.g., Pissarro's *"Crystal Palace"* (593).

† Drawing is said to be fluid when color flows over the line of demarcation between adjacent objects and is accompanied by a lowered degree of sharpness in the line itself. Such drawing, when successfully executed, in no way obscures the distinction between the objects delineated. "Fluid" drawing is also described as "loose."

‡ Cf., e.g., Monet's *"La Grenouillère"* (628).

§ Cf., e.g., Manet's *"Tarring the Boat"* (609).

‖ A "color-chord" is a small area in which two or more juxtaposed colors overflow into each other: for example, red and an adjacent blue with reciprocal interpenetration constitute a "color-chord."

¶ Cf., e.g., *"Two Women in Park"* (44) of 1875, *"Moulin de la Galette"* (62) of 1876.

of color through organic relationships; the superficial sparkle is speciously obtained: light is concentrated in spots on bright color sharply contrasted with areas of darker and dull color, instead of pervading both bright and dark colors to provide commensurate degree of illumination to both.* These defects, largely technical, are the natural results of trial and error in the novel and complicated experiments.†

Similar but less pronounced defects in the relation of light and color appear in *"Breakfast"* (27), of c. 1872, another and more ambitious experimental venture of the period. Progress toward the form of the mid-seventies appears in a nearer approach to the typical blue-green-ivory color-scheme and better internal illumination of color, as well as greater variety of traditional features. Here Renoir obtains, through a more individual technique, a synthesis of elements from Titian,‡ Tintoretto,§ Correggio,|| the seventeenth century Dutch painters,¶ Chardin ** and Goya,†† in a patterned composition of interlocking planes, with more fluid drawing and more luminous color than those in the prototypes.‡‡ Light and color are better integrated than in *"Canoeists at Chatou"* but are still far short of the degree of unity achieved in the mid-seventies, and the occasional crudity in handling pigment is still apparent.

Still other indications of Renoir's growth toward individuality are offered by *"La Grenouillère"* (31), painted about 1873, in which a Corot motif is transformed by fluid drawing, modified impressionistic technique, and bright colors. The general color-scheme, dominated by dark green, is enlivened by considerable

---

* Cf., e.g., *"Bougival"* (166) of 1888, *"Pont-Aven"* (206) of c. 1892, and *"Picnic"* (211) of c. 1893, in which the pervasion of light illuminates the whole canvas.

† For further analytical data see Appendix, p. 382.

‡ E.g., the still-life in Titian's *"Disciples at Emmaüs"* (350).

§ E.g., the still-life in Tintoretto's *"Two Prophets"* (394).

|| E.g., the modeling of St. Sebastian in Correggio's *"Marriage of St. Catherine"* (378), and of Mercury in *"Venus, Mercury and Cupid"* (379).

¶ E.g., the accentuated highlights in Juriaan van Streek's *"Still-Life"* (468).

** E.g., the modeling and space-composition in Chardin's *"Bottle of Olives"* (497), *"Still-Life"* (503), *"Study of Still-Life"* (504), and *"Various Utensils"* (505).

†† E.g., the reflected light on the edge of dark garments in Goya's *"Don José Alvarez de Toledo y Gonzaga, El Duque de Alba"* (545). *"Duques de Osuna and their Children"* (547), and *"Family of Carlos IV"* (548).

‡‡ See chapter "Renoir and the Eighteenth Century French Tradition," p. 201.

areas of bright soft yellows, and punctuated by spots of red and orange. Fluid drawing and a pervasive silvery atmospheric suffusion coöperate to establish a delicate continuous color-movement which links all parts of the picture in a smoothly flowing compositional unity. The spirit of figures in landscape is rendered in a form which combines the peaceful lyricism of Corot * with the charm and delicacy of the French eighteenth century painters.† The form represents an advance over that of *"Canoeists at Chatou"* in the use of all the plastic means and in finesse of execution: heaviness and stridency of color are replaced by a soft, gentle, but positive pervasive glow born of a better integration of color and light; space-composition is less conventional and of higher esthetic status; the form as a whole is better organized and is fuller and more delicately expressive.‡

Another picture of 1873, *"Landscape"* (29), displays additional evidence of Renoir's extensive experimentation at this period with the forms of his contemporaries and immediate predecessors. It contains motifs from Corot, Daubigny and Jongkind transformed by Renoir's distinctive brushwork and his more effulgent color. A Daubigny sky is made more dramatic by a treatment of clouds in the Jongkind style of light-and-dark contrasts,§ the Barbizon-like trees are decidedly more solid, the green fields are brighter and more luminous than those of Corot or Daubigny, and the entire landscape is more clean-cut and positive.|| The ensemble is extraordinarily rich and solidly colorful in spite of the limited palette of greens and yellows; and the contrasts and striking patterns achieved by the distribution of the varied tones are far more dramatic and decorative than those in any of the forms upon which Renoir drew. This picture marks an important stage in Renoir's development in that the novel use of small and unaccentuated brush strokes containing varied loads of pigment results in contrasts between relatively uniform and actively patterned areas, and in that this technique contributes much to the patterns and variation

---

* E.g., Corot's *"Landscape"* (564) and *"Marcoussis: Road across Fields"* (565).
† E.g., Lancret's *"Spring"* (492).
‡ Compare with *"Le Cannet"* (225) of c. 1902 or *"Two Figures in Lane"* (237) of c. 1906 in which Renoir again reinterprets the Corot form as a whole in the terms of the more fluid drawing with color characteristic of his late work.
§ Cf., e.g., Daubigny's *"On the Seine"* (580) ; Jongkind's *"Marine"* (592).
|| Cf., e.g., Corot's *"Marcoussis: Road across Fields"* (565).

of surfaces in some of the best pictures of the mid-seventies.* A transitional stage in the development of this feature is seen in the Louvre landscape, *"Path in the Field"* (36), probably of c. 1874-1875, in the more pronounced contrast between areas of generalized brushwork and those patterned with brush strokes of different pigment-content.

The year 1874 seems to have been the culminating point of Renoir's preoccupation with traditional forms as material for expressions which, as a whole, bear close resemblance to the prototypes. The apotheosis of this period is represented by *"Dancer"* (32) and *"Opera Box"* (34), both of 1874, which rank in general quality with the best of his later work. These two important pictures differ from Renoir's work of the preceding period, in taking as their point of departure a composite old-master form, with little specific recourse to traits of the Barbizon school, Courbet, or the impressionists.

"Opera Box" is essentially a Venetian picture in general form, composition and, more particularly, quality of color, even though each of these features is modified by types of drawing and relationships of light and color originated by Renoir. The color has the rich, sumptuous, warm, glowing quality, and the smooth appealing surface of Titian at his best.† As in Titian, the color in *"Opera Box"* is muted, that is, not lighted internally to give the brightness, vividness, sparkle and life of Renoir's typical color. Other influences which modify the basic Venetian form are those of Velásquez and, to a lesser extent, Delacroix and Manet. The actual colors used—black, dull silver-white, and wine-rose—make up a typical Velásquez color-ensemble,‡ and the loose, fluid, solidly structural color of the textiles derives also from Velásquez. All these are given direction by influences which reached Renoir from Velásquez through Manet, namely, the more pronounced black-and-white contrasts, the deep, luminous black, the generalized brushwork, the flattening of volumes, and, in the flowers, the terse epigrammatic drawing and modeling. The muted illumination of the color, and the yellowish-ivory undertone of the flesh, are obviously an outgrowth of the Venetian glow as Delacroix modified it by reducing the quantity of brown. The influence of Courbet, so

---

* E.g., *"Two Women in Park"* (44).
† E.g., Titian's *"Lavinia"* (355) and *"Woman's Portrait: La Bella"* (370).
‡ E.g., Velásquez' *"Don Juan de Austria"* (442) and *"Infanta Marguerite"* (446).

outstanding in Renoir's preceding work, has now gone into solution and is only vaguely discernible.

Notwithstanding this basic derivation of the form as a whole from the old masters, *"Opera Box"* has a very strong flavor of Renoir's individuality. None of the original traits is merely duplicated; each of them, in fact, is actually enhanced by Renoir's imagination and skill: the color is richer, deeper, more lustrous, more convincing, varied and alive than in the best work of Titian or Velásquez, and it is more subtly used in drawing, modeling and space-composition. Indeed, the whole form is more fluid, more ingeniously composed and better integrated than theirs.* Perhaps the most potent of the factors operative in the transformation of the Venetian form into a Renoir expression is that composite of innate qualities which make of Renoir a natural heir to the spirit of the eighteenth century French tradition. *"Opera Box,"* in other words, is a Venetian picture given a form typically French, which Renoir develops, with vast enrichment, from that of Watteau, Lancret, Boucher and Fragonard. Renoir's development between his earlier work and *"Opera Box"* consists in augmented depth, solidity and richness of color,† ampler resources in drawing, modeling and painting of flesh,‡ more ingenious integration of disparate factors in a more picturesque composition,§ and in an enormous increase in technical skill.‖ Compared with pictures of corresponding importance painted two years later,¶ the main plastic defect of the picture is its color: it is duller because of the deficiency of light-content, it has less structural solidity, less originality, and is used less imaginatively and with less economy of means in all its functions.**

The foundation of the form of *"Dancer"* (32), of 1874, is also that of an old master, Velásquez. The full-length figure in a con-

---

* Cf., e.g., Titian's *"Alfonso da Ferrara and Laura di Dianti"* (346); Velásquez' *"Infanta Marguerite"* (446) or *"Infanta María Teresa, when Three Years Old"* (447).

† Cf., e.g., the quality of the black or of the color of flesh-shadows in *"Mr. and Mrs. Sisley"* (10) of c. 1868.

‡ Cf., e.g., *"Mr. and Mrs. Sisley"* (10) or *"Bather with Griffon"* (16) of 1870.

§ Cf., e.g., conventionality of composition, and disunity of figure and background in *"Bather with Griffon"* (16).

‖ Cf., e.g., the painting of transparent textiles with that in *"Lise"* (5) of 1867.

¶ E.g., *"Torso"* (52) of c. 1875 and *"Mademoiselle Jeanne Durand-Ruel"* (59) of 1876.

** For further analytical data on *"Opera Box,"* see Appendix, pp. 385-388.

tinuous sheetlike setting that embraces foreground and subtly receding distance, is a typical Velásquez compositional arrangement.* Also as in Velásquez, tonal gradations within a relatively monochrome color-scheme establish subtle spatial relationships between all parts of the composition and envelop the figure in circumambient space. The delicate poised movement of the dancer, the rendering of textiles, and the pervasive bluish silver-gray which is the key of the color-scheme, are borrowings from the same master. Each of these derivations is adequately changed by Renoir's adaptations from Courbet, Degas and Manet, all of whom were themselves deeply indebted to Velásquez. The flesh, for example, is Courbet's version of Velásquez' surface, texture, and muted color, modified by Renoir's more subtle modeling in which contours are fluid and shadows are practically abolished. Degas' influence appears in the more dextrous and simplified drawing, which makes more sensitive Velásquez' poised movement; Renoir has rendered this movement more convincingly and with more graceful daintiness than either Velásquez or Degas, by a looser, more fluid, and plastically fuller drawing in which line, light and color are fused in a more expressive unit.

An important factor in this extremely expressive drawing is the extraordinarily effective brushwork which, while based on Manet's, is more generalized, less obtrusive, and directed to a wider range of specific plastic purposes. This subtle and skilful brushwork makes the dancer's skirt more fluffy and floating, and the shoes, hair, handkerchief and ribbons infinitely more delicate and more real than any corresponding passages in Velásquez, Goya, Manet or Degas.† Subtle brushwork also draws the dancer's left arm and the space behind and around it by an uninterrupted flow of color from the volume into the space.

The form as a whole advances upon its prototypes in plastic richness and fulness in that the drawing is done primarily by color, in contrast to the emphasis upon line in Velásquez and Degas, upon surface-effects in Goya, and upon pattern of technique in Manet. The picture's chief claim to distinction as a landmark in Renoir's plastic development lies in the fact that drawing by means of fluid color, noted in restricted areas in *"Row Boat"* (6)

* E.g., Velásquez' *"Pablo de Valladolid"* (449).
† Cf., e.g., Velásquez *"Infanta Doña Margarita de Austria"* (445) or *"Infanta María Teresa, when Three Years Old"* (447); Goya's *"Doña Tadea Arias de Enríquez"* (544); Manet's *"Eva Gonzalès"* (603); Degas' *"Dancers Practicing at the Bar"* (612) or *"Four Dancers on Stage"* (613).

58   THE ART OF RENOIR

of the late sixties, has progressed to include the main compositional factors. Space, for example, is rendered by the continuous flow of color over contour, and this practice, in his work after 1890, was extended to all-inclusive compositional activity, with richer, brighter and more deeply structural color.*

"Dancer," in comparison with Renoir's work of the four succeeding years, has drawbacks similar to those in *"Opera Box"* (34) : it is less original in basic conception, the color is dull because of lack of internal luminosity, and the gray, while delicate, is comparatively cold, hard and little varied in tone by other colors. These deficiencies may be appreciated by a comparison with *"Mademoiselle Jeanne Durand-Ruel"* (59) of 1876, in which an equally predominating delicate gray is warm and rich, and the surface has the mellow, luminous quality of pearl.

1875-1877—RENOIR ATTAINS TO MATURITY †

After 1874 Renoir's form is no longer based upon traditional wholes as it is in the two pictures just discussed, but is a new organization of his own gradually accumulated elaborations of individual traditional traits, so changed by personal modifications that they become positive creations. The growth in the later paintings consists of great originality, fertility and scope in the imaginative use of plastic ideas; ‡ color, for example, is more individual to Renoir and it plays more diversified rôles in compositions in which more complex plastic problems are solved in a great variety of original ways.

This form at its best, as in *"Mademoiselle Jeanne Durand-Ruel"* (59) of 1876 and *"Torso"* (52) of about a year earlier, no longer shows any trace of imperfect assimilation of traditions, and the method of integration of the plastic means is more personal. The

* Cf., e.g., *"Promenade"* (236) of c. 1906, or *"Nude with Castanets"* (287) of c. 1916.
† E.g., *"Reader"* (40) of c. 1874-1876, *"Mademoiselle Legrand"* (43) of 1875, *"Two Women in Park"* (44) of 1875, *"House in Woods"* (48) of c. 1875, *"Torso"* (52) of c. 1875, *"Girl in Striped Dress"* (54) of c. 1875-1876, *"Child with Watering Can"* (56) of 1876, *"Girl with Jumping Rope"* (57) of 1876, *"Mademoiselle Jeanne Durand-Ruel"* (59) of 1876, *"Moulin de la Galette"* (61 and 62) of 1876, *"Swing"* (63) of 1876, *"Madame Henriot"* (69) of c. 1876, *"After the Concert"* (73) of c. 1877, *"Woman Crocheting"* (76) of c. 1877.
‡ Cf., e.g., *"Mademoiselle Jeanne Durand-Ruel"* (59) of 1876 with *"Dancer"* (32) of 1874.

form which is only hinted at in the late sixties and early seventies *
is here realized: a suffusion of much richer color pervades the
canvas and softens the transition between one area and another;
contour is a loosely defined division between juxtaposed color-
areas which maintains the linear demarcation, and at the same time
imparts to the whole picture the feeling of fluidity and graceful
delicacy. The exquisite poised movement of the figure in *"Torso"*
is achieved, as in *"Dancer"* (32) of 1874, by such subtle relations
between color, light, spatial depth and degree of voluminousness
that the color-contrasts are largely relations of tone, and the flow
of harmonious color is never interrupted by violent transitions of
color or sharply defined line. The plastic advance in *"Torso"* over
"Dancer" is indicated by the more important activities of color and
line: color is brighter, richer, more luminous, more varied and
more solidly structural, and the rhythmic progression of linear
flow between foreground and background not only knits together
a more intricate and higher type of composition, but emphasizes
the quality of fluidity and delicacy in every part of it.

What the aggregate of these separate and gradually developed
plastic advances signify as marks of Renoir's growth, becomes
apparent from a comparison between *"Torso"* and his early *"Lise"*
(9). In *"Lise"* the shadows in the flesh are of a rather monotonous
grayish-brown and are sharply juxtaposed with almost uniform
patches of brownish pink; in *"Torso"* the shadows are of many
delicate tints of green and blue, which flow into and merge with
the pink of the flesh, thus making of the entire face a rich color-
chord of intermingled delicate tones. This difference between compartmental organization and continuous flow of color appears in
every part of the two pictures, and extends to all their plastic
components, with the result that figure and background in the
earlier painting lack the complete merging, the inseparable pictorial unity, which they have in *"Torso."* In *"Lise,"* light, line,
color and space work more or less independently as entities, that
is, they do not work so harmoniously as indissoluble units as they
do in *"Torso."* This advance is brought about mainly by a finer
sensitivity for relationships and by a richer, more varied and more
personal color, which exercises more diverse compositional functions. Furthermore, the fluidity of color and its impregnation with
light, produce a color-light suffusion which, by its extension to all
parts of the canvas, aids materially in unifying the composition. A

* Cf., e.g., *"Lise"* (9) of c. 1868, or *"Breakfast"* (27) of c. 1872.

luminous pearly blue that permeates this suffusion is the means
by which Renoir has enriched the dull silver-gray circumambient
atmosphere common in Corot.

The contrast between the immature and the mature Renoir is
still more striking when the pictures of the late sixties and those
of the mid-seventies are compared from the point of view of their
decorative and expressive aspects. In the earlier works * these two
aspects are more isolated and hence each is relatively superficial;
consequently, expression tends more toward literal illustration, and
decoration toward obvious pattern. Though the figures are alive
and penetratingly characterized, the sharper distinction between
foreground and background, together with the more abrupt transition between one area and another, results in a more pronounced
pattern in which the expressive values are less organically blended.
This treatment tends to blur the distinction between the plastically
essential and non-essential. In contrast to this, the delicate movement of rich color in the best work of the mid-seventies embraces
foreground and background, brings them into compositional equilibrium, and the pervasive drama of contrasts binds every element
to every other.† Traditional forms used by Renoir in the earlier
periods are still evident, but they have lost their separable identity,
and have been made instrumental to ends more decorative, picturesque and expressive, chiefly by the power of rich, varied, subtly
related color. The fusion of values and traditions in a lyric poetry
extracted from commonplace subject-matter represents in every
detail a personal vision which is entirely and uniquely Renoir's
own.

The typical form of the middle seventies has in general a characteristic color-scheme of blue, green and ivory, the totality of
which is pervaded with a pearly quality. This color-scheme appears
in two forms: sometimes one or more of the colors dominate both
light and dark tones to give a relatively monochrome appearance; ‡
more often, the distinction between light and dark is greater, and

* E.g., *"Lise"* (5) of 1867, *"Lise"* (9) of c. 1868 and *"Artist's Father"*
(13) of 1869.
† E.g., *"Torso"* (52), *"Girl with Jumping Rope"* (57), *"Mademoiselle
Jeanne Durand-Ruel"* (59), *"Madame Henriot"* (69), *"After the Concert"* (73), *"Woman Crocheting"* (76).
‡ E.g., *"Woman in Blue"* (53), *"Mademoiselle Jeanne Durand-Ruel"* (59),
"Madame Henriot" (69) and *"Madame Henriot in the Field"* (70). The
monochrome tendency is anticipated in *"Henriot Family"* (23) of c. 1871
and in *"Dancer"* (32) of 1874.

the effect is one of color-and-tone contrasts in broad areas.* A feature common to both forms is the accentuation of small notes of black, red and yellow, which often establish or heighten local contrasts without altering the essential blue-green-ivory whole, its pearly tonality or monochrome effect. The pattern formed by the areas of light and dark colors is now a more important factor in the design than in the earlier work because of the more fluid use of color in drawing. All the areas have a loose contour: none is separated from neighboring areas by clean-cut lines of demarcation, nor, with rare exceptions, is there any sharp contour defining the objects within any one of them. This fluidity of drawing results partly from Renoir's adaptation of Manet's and Monet's free brushwork and partly from the actual flow of color over contour. These areas of light and dark are still much more definitely contrasted than in Renoir's later work, but color is already so active in both the light and the dark that the contrasts are always felt also as color-relations. The pattern of dramatic contrasts is richer than in the previous work and the areas of colored light have a larger range of compositional activity: sometimes they are large, delicately voluminous units; † sometimes they are small and form a highly accentuated pattern of quasi-superposed islands of light alternating with either islands or ill-defined areas of shadow; ‡ at other times one outstanding large area of the composition is intensely illuminated and functions like the light element in chiaroscuro,§ sometimes it is so fully pervaded with variegated color that it acts as a glowing iridescent focal mass.‖

---

* E.g., *"Woman at Spring"* (37), *"Two Women in Park"* (44), *"Torso"* (52), *"Girl with Jumping Rope"* (57), *"Swing"* (63), *"After the Concert"* (73) and *"Woman Crocheting"* (76). This aspect is anticipated to some extent in *"Breakfast"* (27) of c. 1872.

† E.g., *"Torso"* (52).

‡ In the mid-seventies, Renoir was fond of painting out-of-door scenes in shadow, and patterned by small islands of sunlight filtering through foliage. These islands of light appear already in *"Henriot Family"* (23) of c. 1871, and are an elaboration of similar areas of sunlight used to represent detail in the landscapes of Claude le Lorrain, the Barbizon painters, and the impressionists. Renoir, disregarding realistic representation, puts more color into the sunlighted areas and organizes them in an all-over diapered pattern, thus enhancing the decorative value of the ensemble —cf., e.g., Renoir's *"Girl in Striped Dress"* (54), *"Moulin de la Galette"* (62) and *"Swing"* (63), with Claude le Lorrain's *"Seapiece"* (453), Corot's *"Road to Méry, near La Ferté-sous-Jouarre"* (566) or *"Spinner"* (567), and Monet's *"Luncheon"* (630).

§ E.g., *"Woman Crocheting"* (76).

‖ E.g., *"Reader"* (40) and *"Young Girl Sewing"* (41).

The increased and more significant use, in the mid-seventies, of these areas of light and dark, resulting as it does from more active color and more fluid drawing, inevitably entails other consequences. Color is now so definitely an integral part of the areas of both light and dark that the contrasts are felt not as merely between light and dark but as contrasts between positive colors. Color also enters more fully into the drawing than ever before, by so varying and enriching the Manet-like brush strokes that they are more effective instruments both for drawing out the essence of what is presented, and for lending it decorative charm. These general characteristics are emphasized in individual pictures as the design, and especially as the particular traditions employed, require. As a result the specific technique of drawing, modeling and compositional unification varies from picture to picture, but these variations do not obscure the essential identity of the mid-seventies' form. In the whole group the illustrative value, the presentation of scenes and episodes having universal human significance and appeal, is not only richer in itself than in Renoir's earlier work but is embedded in an organization of greater plastic strength and decorative content.

Renoir's modification and enrichment of Manet's technique and of the luminous quality of his paint show a parallel advance. Manet's resort to brushwork is so incessant as to make it stereotyped and largely to destroy its usefulness for emphasis; Renoir's brushwork is more varied and more discriminating not only in departing from Manet's monotonous pattern of broad strokes, but often in introducing at various parts of the design small, narrow, ribbonlike brush strokes not unlike Monet's in general form but much less individually accentuated. Renoir's color is more solid than either Manet's or Monet's, so that the brushwork has more varied and complex compositional functions and creates rich color-chords which enhance expression and add decorative appeal.* Manet frequently renders light by areas of comparatively uniform and definitely white paint; Renoir's infusion of rich color brings his light more completely into the organization of the picture, and correspondingly extends its compositional scope.† Renoir's paint-

* Cf., e.g., Renoir's *"Two Women in Park"* (44) with Manet's *"Tarring the Boat"* (609) and Monet's *"Girl in Garden"* (625), or Renoir's *"Woman Crocheting"* (76) with Manet's *"Mademoiselle Voisin"* (606) and Monet's *"Monsieur Cogneret"* (632).

† Cf., e.g., Renoir's *"Torso"* (52) with Manet's *"Mademoiselle Voisin"* (606).

ing, always more fluid and graceful than Manet's, is thus also more subtle, dignified and real: for him technical devices are always instrumental to plastic ends, never, as too often with Manet, pretexts for self-display.

The general features of this period—blue-green-ivory color-scheme, patterns of broad areas and of light-dark contrasts, and frequent use of perceptible technique—are related differently and used in varying proportion and degree of emphasis in different pictures, and usually even in the same picture, in the modeling, drawing, and compositional unification. The modeling generally lacks that precise indication of continuous rise and fall of illumination which is the common traditional practice, but the patterns of subtle light-shadow contrasts and of delicate and varied brush strokes secure an adequate degree of three-dimensional solidity which varies according to the design from an extremely delicate lightness * to firm solidity.† The fusion of color, light and technique eliminates actual or independent line from drawing, and the infiltration of color from area to area, or tonal approximation of color in adjacent areas, preserves recognizable identity of shape and texture of objects. Drawing of this type is not only highly decorative but firm, sure, and very expressive, surpassing in these respects the work of Renoir's earlier periods. It is even more subtle and delicate than the best Venetian drawing.‡

Compositional distribution of masses is always diversified with many elements of contrast; space is rendered as a rule by subtle indications, and reduced in depth; pattern of light and color is usually the most active agent of organization; comparatively simple means, though they are varied and often very subtle, suffice to knit foreground and background in compositional unity. These means include succession in space of patterned planes,§ rhythmic repetition of color-areas ‖ or of islands of light,¶ the inclusion of both figure and setting in a continuous transition of light,** or in a

* E.g., *"Torso"* (52), *"Girl with Jumping Rope"* (57), *"Mademoiselle Jeanne Durand-Ruel"* (59), *"Madame Henriot"* (69).

† E.g., *"After the Concert"* (73), in which both firm solidity and delicate lightness are realized in different units.

‡ Cf., e.g., Giorgione's *"Sleeping Venus"* (344) or Titian's *"Venus and Adonis"* (365).

§ E.g., *"Two Women in Park"* (44).

‖ E.g., *"Woman at Spring"* (37), *"Mademoiselle Legrand"* (43), *"Girl with Jumping Rope"* (57).

¶ E.g., *"Moulin de la Galette"* (61 and 62) and *"Swing"* (63).

** E.g., *"Woman at Spring"* (37), *"Reader"* (40), *"Young Girl Sewing"* (41), *"Woman Crocheting"* (76).

smooth flow of all the plastic units.* The setting is often conceived as a screen against which the comparatively flattened figure or figures are set, but the interflow of color, light and line provides the necessary advance and recession to prevent either foreground or background from appearing as a mere flat surface.†

All of these pictures of the middle 1870's attest the truth of Renoir's statement that he learned to express himself mainly by systematic study of the old masters in the Louvre. Each represents one or more aspects of the vision of his artistic ancestors used as a point of departure for a versatile and ingenious creation of new forms. In effecting this transformation he utilized, as we have noted, a number of contemporary practices, but only after modifications of his own which adapted them to a form more radically different from the impressionistic than was his earlier work in that style.‡

In his best painting at this stage all the borrowings are integrally assimilated in his own color-scheme, drawing, modeling and space-composition. Each of the pictures has its own distinctive color-form and set of decorative and expressive values, and makes a definite selection from the traditions. In each the traditional elements are modified and combined in harmony with both the individual form of the picture and the general characteristics of the middle seventies. Within the period itself, there are marks of growth in Renoir's power of assimilation and creative transformation. The lesser light-content of the color in *"Woman at Spring"* (37) than in *"Torso"* (52) and *"Mademoiselle Jeanne Durand-Ruel"* (59) marks a transitional stage between the muted color in *"Dancer"* (32) of 1874 and the more luminous and solid color in the typical pictures of 1875 and 1876; *"Madame Choquet"* (42) and *"Mademoiselle Legrand"* (43) are crude and banal; the superficial color and speciously employed technique in *"Child with Watering Can"* (56) give the effect of an overcolored illustration, not far removed from a chromo in quality. These defects have been overcome in *"Reader"* (40), *"Torso,"* *"Mademoiselle Jeanne Durand-Ruel"* and *"Madame Henriot"* (69), by a perfection of technique which has brought the contributions of antecedent

* E.g., *"Torso"* (52), *"Mademoiselle Jeanne Durand-Ruel"* (59), *"Madame Henriot"* (69).

† E.g., *"Woman at Spring"* (37), *"Girl with Jumping Rope"* (57), *"Mademoiselle Jeanne Durand-Ruel"* (59).

‡ Cf., e.g., *"Two Women in Park"* (44) of 1875 with *"Canoeists at Chatou"* (24) of 1872.

painters so completely into solution that their origin can be stated only in the most general terms. The flexibility of this form of the middle seventies appears from the diversity of traditional traits which Renoir incorporates in individual pictures. In *"Torso,"* for example, Venetian features in the painting of flesh are indissolubly merged with qualities and characteristics derived from Velásquez, Goya, Courbet and Manet. Renoir's transformations have refined away the painty texture of Velásquez and Goya, the heaviness of Courbet, and the flashy virtuosity of Manet.* In *"Woman Crocheting"* (76), technique, color-chords and a pattern of light and shadow reinterpret in enriched form Titian's rendering of flesh,† the Dutch and Goya's renderings of textiles,‡ and Rembrandt's use of chiaroscuro.§ In reworking these traditional forms, Renoir relies, especially in the treatment of the background, upon a new modification of impressionistic technique, a deviation from the usual broad strokes of the mid-seventies toward the well-defined, small, narrow and more swirling brush strokes characteristic of his work at the end of the seventies.‖ The individual brush strokes are as yet ill defined; their pattern is less pronounced, and the vibration of color and light which they impart to the surface is not so determining a factor in the total design as in the later pictures.

"Reader" (40) and *"Young Girl Sewing"* (41) are Renoir versions of the Vermeer type of picture in which the plastic problem is concerned with an accentuated pattern embracing both direct light and reflected light.¶ By saturating the light with richly variegated color, Renoir makes of the light-pattern an ensemble of shimmering, glistening, sparkling color-chords which give to the textures more substantial structure and greatly increased decorative appeal. In *"Girl with Jumping Rope"* (57), color achieves a personal interpretation of Velásquez' subtle space-relationships and color-contrasts,** and tempers the light, filmy textiles of Goya with

* Cf., e.g., Velásquez' *"Lady with Fan"* (448) or *"Venus and Cupid"* (451), Goya's *"Doña Isabel Cobos de Porcel"* (543) or *"Maja Nude"* (552), Courbet's *"Nude"* (585), and the nude in Manet's *"Picnic"* (608).
† Cf., e.g., the hands in Titian's *"Man with Glove"* (357). Also see chapter "Renoir and the Venetians," p. 180.
‡ Cf., e.g., Vermeer's *"Lacemaker"* (466), Goya's *"Doctor Galos"* (542) or *"Don Luis María de Cistue, as a Child"* (546).
§ Cf., e.g., Rembrandt's *"Man with Stick"* (457).
‖ E.g., *"Jeanne Samary"* (72), *"Pourville"* (80), *"Madame Murer"* (87).
¶ Cf., e.g., Vermeer's *"Cook"* (464), *"Girl Reading Letter"* (465), *"Lacemaker"* (466) or *"Woman with Pearl Necklace"* (467).
** Cf., e.g., Velásquez' *"Infanta Marguerite"* (446).

eighteenth century French delicacy.* In *"Mademoiselle Jeanne Durand-Ruel"* (59), Renoir expresses the charm of childhood by converting the weightiness of Venetian structural color into a daintiness and delicacy as exquisite as, but more real than, that of Lancret, Boucher or Fragonard.† In *"Girl in Striped Dress"* (54), the two versions of *"Moulin de la Galette"* (61 and 62), and *"Swing"* (63), Manet's brush strokes and Monet's patterns of light are enriched by more active color-reënforcement in well-defined islands of light.

"After the Concert" (73) offers an interweaving of three principal traditional themes, each endowed with more luminous and richer color and surface-quality. The delicate volumes and porcelain-like surface of Boucher and Fragonard appear in the painting of the two women at the left; ‡ the subtle space-volume relationships throughout the picture are reminiscent of Chardin at his best; § Venetian solid color is recalled by the painting of the woman's head at the upper right ‖ and by the surface of the wall,¶ and the latter includes modifications by Daumier both of the Venetian color itself and of the Venetian surface-quality.**

At the opposite pole to this solid color stand the extremely light almost evanescent pastel tones in *"Madame Henriot"* (69), through which, in practically a monochrome of light pearly blue, Renoir carries eighteenth century French painting to an apotheosis of delicacy, daintiness and charm.†† The extreme finesse of execution gives the picture an ethereal imponderability; it seems to have been breathed upon the canvas, yet in no other painting has Renoir realized more convincingly, with equal economy of means, the essentials of human character and the textural feeling of flesh and dainty fabrics. More completely than in any other picture of this

---

* Cf., e.g., Goya's *"Doctor Galos"* (542) or *"Juanita Mazarredo"* (550), Fragonard's *"Boy as Pierrot"* (532).
† Cf., e.g., Lancret's *"Mademoiselle Camargo Dancing"* (489), Boucher's *"Marquise de Pompadour"* (512), Fragonard's *"Boy as Pierrot"* (532).
‡ Cf., e.g., Boucher's *"Sleeping Shepherdess"* (518), Fragonard's *"Woman Undressing"* (538).
§ E.g., Chardin's *"Grace before Meal"* (499) and *"Various Utensils"* (505).
‖ Cf., e.g., Tintoretto's *"Head of a Man"* (386) or *"Vincenzo Morosini"* (396).
¶ Cf., e.g., the architecture in Titian's *"Venetian Family"* (364) or the well in Tintoretto's *"Woman of Samaria"* (397).
** Cf., e.g., Daumier's *"Ribalds"* (578).
†† Cf., e.g., Perronneau's *"Girl with Cat"* (526) or *"Mademoiselle Huquier"* (527), Boze's *"Comtesse de Provence"* (540) or *"Lady's Portrait"* (541).

period, the lightness of eighteenth century French painting is converted by fluid color-drawing into a floating ethereal delicacy.

Renoir's rendering of landscape in the mid-seventies is well represented by *"Two Women in Park"* (44) of 1875, and *"House in Woods"* (48) of c. 1875. The typical blue-green-ivory color-scheme is somewhat modified by the introduction of more yellow in the lighted parts of the landscape, and the technique is more definitely impressionistic than in the pictures of the mid-seventies thus far discussed. These landscapes display an advance upon Pissarro, Sisley and Monet in a number of important points: * their compositional organization is richer and more firmly integrated; masses are more convincingly constructed in solid color; the pattern of brush strokes conjoined with more luminous and forceful color results in increased decorative value as well as more robust structure and more vivid colorful atmospheric glow; the light is more deeply ingrained in the color, more definitely organized and focussed and more vividly patterned through its alternation with areas of rich dark color. This use of light is a blending of the impressionistic with effects of the Dutch,† the Barbizon painters ‡ and Manet,§ but it acquires added reality and charm from Renoir's own feeling for color in all its plastic functions.

To sum up the pictures of the mid-seventies: as a group they display a distinctive color-gamut predominantly blue, green and ivory; fluid color-drawing and loose contours; luminous structural color, frequently applied in accentuated brush strokes, and resulting in clearly marked contrasts and patterns of broad areas of light and dark. The color is more fluid and the color-chords are richer and more numerous than in the earlier paintings; the drawing and brushwork are more colorful than Manet's and serve more varied decorative, expressive and compositional ends. The form is characterized by subtlety of means and delicacy of effect, and at its best it represents a perfectly balanced and executed expression of artistic personality. It is an advance over that of the late sixties and early seventies in its more thorough assimilation of all the traditional influences and technical means, by which a vision both deeper and more characteristically Renoir's own is given embodi-

---

* Cf., e.g., Pissarro's *"Garden"* (594), Sisley's *"River Scene with Ducks"* (616), Monet's *"House Boat"* (626).

† E.g., Jacob van Ruisdael's *"Road"* (462), Hobbema's *"Watermill"* (469).

‡ E.g., Diaz' *"Road"* (577), Daubigny's *"Sunset on the Oise"* (581).

§ E.g., Manet's *"Tarring the Boat"* (609).

ment in a form of higher plastic status. No sooner, however, was this stage of Renoir's development attained than a new series of experiments began, the first manifestations of which were an incorporation in his form of a greater variety of color, a diminution of sharpness of contrast between areas of light and dark, and a more comprehensive use of the impressionists' vision and technique as a whole.

EXPERIMENTS IN 1877 AND 1878

As material for the experiments of this period, Renoir selected some of the features of the mid-seventies form; these features, and the changes introduced into them in the mid-seventies, fall into three categories. First, the blue-green-ivory color-scheme of pervasive pearly tonality is vivified by a more liberal use of other colors;* second, light is more evenly distributed throughout the canvas and tends to establish a closer parity of light-content in the areas of light and dark colors; † third, more extensive use is made of narrow, ribbonlike, somewhat swirling brush strokes than of the generalized broad brushwork.‡ When this third variation is accentuated, the form of the painting differs so much in general appearance from the typical form of the period that it may be said to represent a type in itself.§ The majority of these pictures are small and most of the execution is in narrow brush strokes, often criss-cross and apparently haphazard, the pattern of which makes the ensemble appear as a spontaneous, freely drawn but well-executed sketch. This style of brushwork clearly represents experimentation with the technique of Pissarro, Sisley and Monet which, a year or two later, was incorporated in pictures quite close in general appearance to those of his contemporary impressionists.‖

* E.g., coral tones in *"Moulin de la Galette"* (62) of 1876 and *"Swing"* (63) of 1876, positive red in *"Reader"* (40) of c. 1874-1876, *"Child with Watering Can"* (56) of 1876, and *"Mademoiselle Muller"* (60) of 1876.
† E.g., *"Girl with Cat"* (38) of c. 1874-1876, *"Mademoiselle Jeanne Durand-Ruel"* (59) of 1876, *"Madame Henriot"* (69) of c. 1876.
‡ E.g., *"Reader"* (40) of c. 1874-1876, *"Moss Roses"* (50) of c. 1875, *"Child with Watering Can"* (56) of 1876, *"Mademoiselle Charpentier, Seated"* (58) of 1876, *"Woman Crocheting"* (76) of c. 1877.
§ E.g., *"Beautiful Season: Conversation"* (45), *"Beautiful Season: Promenade"* (46) of c. 1875, *"At the Milliner's"* (64) of c. 1876, *"Head of Woman and Flowers"* (71) of 1877, *"In the Studio"* (74) of c. 1877.
‖ E.g., Pissarro-pointillist in *"Spring Landscape"* (75) of c. 1877 and *"Picking Flowers"* (85) of c. 1878, Monet in *"Margot"* (84) of c. 1878 and *"Madame Murer"* (87) of c. 1878-1879, Seurat in *"Woman with Veil"* (77) of c. 1877.

"Jeanne Samary" (72), dated 1877, illustrates the significant changes in Renoir's development and modifications of the form of the mid-seventies. The palette is more varied, the light pervades the canvas more completely, and the thin brush strokes pattern the surface, promote the interpenetration of color and formation of color-chords, and also carry the light-and-color vibrations through dark and lighted areas alike. Thus, in point of color and technique, the picture indicates a transition from the 1875-1876 form of, for example, *"Two Women in Park"* (44), to the fuller plastic expression represented in *"Pourville"* (80) of 1878. It lacks the accentuated light and dark contrasts of the earlier work, and in comparison with *"Pourville,"* the color is not so rich, the modulations are not so subtle, the textures not so mellow and velvety, and there is less finesse and delicacy in the execution.

The presence of a large area of red in *"Jeanne Samary"* introduces a different effect in the total color-organization than that which the use of a contrasting color has upon the typical mid-seventies' palette of blue, green and ivory. In the 1876 *"Mademoiselle Muller"* (60), for instance, a mahogany red does not materially affect the identity of the characteristic color-scheme of the period; the red in *"Jeanne Samary,"* by its brightness, the size and placing of the area in which it occurs, and by its penetration through pattern of technique into the other colors, becomes the key-note of a richer and brighter palette and of a new type of color-organization in which interpenetration of tones gives way to interplay of more positive multicolored units.

This extension and perfection of resources throws additional light upon the process of Renoir's growth: his form of this period, like that of the earlier years of the seventies, grew not only out of his own prior technique and use of traditions, but out of a constant absorption of new material from the traditions and his environment, and a long-continued experimentation with the technical means of reworking this material. As his assimilation of material and his technical mastery increase, the sources from which he draws and the means employed to individualize the material become less and less evident, until they disappear as separate entities and are recognizable only as traces in the integral unity of the new form.

Renoir's experimentation with small brush strokes in certain pictures of the mid-seventies was one of the principal means of the growth in knowledge and technical skill revealed by *"Pour-*

ville" of 1878. In this the pattern of technique fuses with a more varied and better integrated palette and becomes an organic part of a more fully expressive form: the feeling of graceful foliage, for example, is conveyed more directly by color-relations and less by pattern than in the earlier pictures.* The essential features of this growth as a whole may be illustrated by a comparison between *"Pourville"* and the two pictures of the mid-seventies, *"House in Woods"* (48) and *"Two Women in Park."* In the earlier paintings, thick impasto and the vigor and boldness in the use of brushwork make the drama comparatively obvious; in *"Pourville"* everything, even the texture of the pigment, is delicate, the surface is creamy and velvety, and the drama is subtle. Parallel with this increase in refinement goes an increase in range of resources, in color-scheme, subtlety of relationships, and in depth of human values. The areas of dark and light blue-green, which interlock throughout the picture, are felt more directly as color, less as pattern of light and dark, and their relations are more organic. The contrast between types of drawing present in each of the two earlier landscapes reappears in *"Pourville,"* in which the foreground is done with brush strokes, and the surface of the background is smooth, with much irradiation; but the sharpness of the contrast is diminished by the unobtrusiveness of the brushwork and by a continuous flow of color throughout the picture.

The fundamental change in the color-scheme of *"Pourville"* from that of the landscapes of the middle seventies resides in the use and function of the reds and yellows. In *"Pourville"* these two colors become more organic parts of the color-scheme than they are in the landscapes of the preceding period, and by their penetration into other colors they establish a greater fluidity of the color-organization. In addition they contribute to a pervasive and luminous lavender suffusion, the overtones of which bring together parts of the picture apparently different in hue, and not only increase the variety and subtlety of color, but add to Corot's filmy, silvery atmosphere a richer color and a delicate mother-of-pearl surface. The impressionistic technique here, because of finer color-relationships, is likewise more fully assimilated to the form than in Renoir's earlier pictures, in that it works in finer coördination with color to give a greater variety of decorative and expressive values through color-relationships. In the coral wall, for example,

* Cf., e.g., *"Two Women in Park"* (44) of 1875.

color-relationships produce the floating lightness and delicate porcelain quality of the French eighteenth century painters, in a form
less hard than Boucher's, looser than Lancret's or Fragonard's and
richer and more fluid than Watteau's, which it most resembles.*
Here again Renoir shows how firmly his art is based on that of the
eighteenth century French tradition, and how much he has added
to its decorative and expressive content.

"*Pourville*," to sum up, is an advance over "*House in Woods*"
and "*Two Women in Park*" primarily because the colors function
more as an organic whole and work in closer coördination with
technique. This results in drawing of greater plastic fulness, compositional unity of higher status, and a richer and wider range of
expressive values. The gain in Renoir's artistic stature is revealed
by the increase of both technical proficiency and imaginative scope.

The increased colorfulness in "*Pourville*," due to a more varied
and fully integrated color-ensemble, reaches the highwater mark
of the period in "*Café Scene*" (81) of c. 1878 and in "*Two Little
Circus Girls*" (99) of about the same date. The form in "*Café
Scene*" represents a perfect fusion of rich, varied, delicate and
charming decorative color, convincing expression of human values,
and technical means so unobtrusive as to be practically impercep-
tible. The colors are more varied than in "*Pourville*," the reds and
yellows are more numerous and more active, and all of the colors
intermingle so freely that the entire enamel-like surface is a continuous rich color-chord. This free interpenetration of color causes
background and figures to melt into each other and form a firmly
knit unity in which all areas are on a par in color-quality. The
plastic advance over "*Pourville*" consists in a further elimination
of perceptible brushwork, a more variegated palette, and an all-
inclusive extension of the color-chords and smooth enamel surface
which appear only in certain areas in "*Pourville*." The resulting
enhancement of the eighteenth century French qualities of daintiness, charm and delicacy is even greater than in "*Pourville*."

"*Café Scene*" is also very significant in its revelation of Renoir's
development from the period of the mid-seventies, and in its antici-
pation of further growth in the eighties. The flesh is of a more
natural tone than in the earlier pictures, and the blue-green of its

---

* Cf., e.g., Watteau's "*Pastoral*" (481), the church spire in Lancret's
"*Summer*" (493), Boucher's "*Mill*" (513), the house in front of the castle in
Boucher's "*Pastoral*" (516), Fragonard's "*Bathers*" (531).

shadows in the mid-seventies has almost disappeared, so that the one-piece effect * of the surface and modeling is closer to that of the early eighties than to the patterned flesh in the mid-seventies.† The color no longer overflows from one area into adjacent areas, and contours are consequently more precise, though they lack the incisive sharpness of the eighties.‡ The areas of blue, so prominent in the mid-seventies, are reduced in extent and made organic parts of a more multicolored ensemble, and the earlier pattern of brush strokes is replaced by a smooth, even surface enlivened by modulations of tone which produce rich color-chords.§ The smooth, even surface of the pigment, in conjunction with the richer color-content, converts the pearly quality of the mid-seventies into a colorful mother-of-pearl surface, a premonition of the heavier and harder porcelainlike surfaces of the eighties.‖ The faces are less masklike than in earlier years of the same decade ¶ and tend toward the continued roundness of those belonging to the later period.**

"*Two Little Circus Girls*" (99), one of the most novel and successful color-organizations of Renoir's entire career, illustrates even more fully than "*Café Scene*" the expansion of the mid-seventies' form by means of the increased palette of the late seventies. The picture may be termed a symphony in yellow, for the tonal variations of that color, extending from deep orange to the color of pale straw, are interwoven in the ensemble to form a harmonious unity dominated by yellow. The largest area of this principal color is the circus ring which occupies more than three-fourths of the canvas and is mottled by subtle nuances of blue, coral, green and lavender that vary and enliven the surface without changing the prevailing yellow tone. The dominance of yellow is increased by the lemon

---

* By *one-piece effect* is meant an unbroken continuity of surface, free from pronounced recessions and projections.

† Cf., e.g., "*Torso*" (52) of c. 1875, "*Dance in the City*" (135) or "*Sailor Boy*" (141) of 1883.

‡ Cf., e.g., the earlier "*Torso*" (52) or "*Girl with Jumping Rope*" (57), the later "*Blond Bather*" (131), "*Girl Plaiting Hair*" (165) or "*Head of Girl*" (173).

§ Cf., e.g., "*Torso*" (52), "*Girl with Jumping Rope*" (57) or "*Mademoiselle Jeanne Durand-Ruel*" (59).

‖ Cf., e.g., the earlier "*Torso*" (52), the later "*Head of Girl*" (173) or "*Bather*" (181).

¶ Cf., e.g., "*Torso*" (52), "*Girl with Jumping Rope*" (57) or "*Mademoiselle Jeanne Durand-Ruel*" (59).

** E.g., "*Dance in the City*" (135), "*Dance in the Country*" (136), "*Head of Girl*" (173).

color of the shoes, hair ribbons and spangles on the costumes, and by the orange balls enclosed in the girl's arms and scattered on the floor. As subtly contrasting colors to the prevailing yellow are the coral-lavender tones of the flesh, the delicate blue of the girls' garments, the small areas of the spectators' bluish-black clothing, the bright red border of the wall, and the color of the wall proper, which varies from slate-blue to coral-blue. An all-inclusive luminosity brightens the whole picture and creates a pearly tonality which pervades the ensemble, tempers the sharpness of color-contrasts and provides a substratum of uniformity of color-quality which is one of the main agents in tying the organization into a unity of extraordinarily harmonious nuances, tones and positive colors, each varied and enriched by subtle and charming color-chords.

Working hand in hand with this color-quality as a unifying factor is the drawing which is loose and fluid to a degree not exceeded in even the best pictures of the mid-seventies. No definitely linear contour exists anywhere except around the face seen in profile: all the rest of the contours are fluid, some of the edges are ragged and the color flows freely over into the adjacent space. This loose drawing coöperating with the subtle and pervasive pearly tonality causes all the tones to melt into an all-inclusive color-fluidity, a fluidity which enables Renoir to obtain with the prevailing yellow a general effect corresponding to the relative monochrome and the general color-suffusion achieved, in a number of his fine pictures of the earlier seventies, with gray and pearl.*

The flesh also is changed from that of the mid-seventies by the enlarged palette and by a different use of shadows in the modeling. Its color is somewhat more naturalistic, is permeated with delicate coral-lavender tones, the color-chords are more prevalent and more varied, and the smoothly painted mother-of-pearl, enamel-like surface is thus more colorful. The figures are less three-dimensional than in most of Renoir's work of the mid-seventies and the prevalent blue-green shadows of that period are practically absent; the few shadows used in modeling are in general bluish lavender or yellow-green.

The picture is as interesting for what it forecasts as for what it shows in marks of progress over the form of the preceding period. The flesh in color, texture, surface, and the hint of pink accents on the contour of fingers, ears and nostrils, represents a

* E.g., "Henriot Family" (23).

74 THE ART OF RENOIR

definite stride toward Renoir's flesh-painting of the early eighties.* The absence of perceptible brushwork, of patterns in modeling and of an accentuated compositional pattern of light and dark areas, and the presence of smooth, evenly painted surface, are all premonitions of the work of the early eighties. The drawing, more fluid than in the mid-seventies, represents just the happy medium between the firmness characteristic of the fulness, freedom and spontaneity of expression of the earlier form, and the looseness of the flaccid, inexpressive drawing which is responsible for Renoir's bad pictures of 1879. Color also is midway in richness and luminosity between that of the mid-seventies and the free intermingling of nuances of more effulgent color productive of the richer and more varied color-chords in his work of 1879.†

RENOIR'S FALL FROM GRACE IN 1879 ‡

The experimentation which brought forth some of the highest achievements of Renoir up to the year 1878, resulted, also, in some of the weakest paintings ever produced by him. Because of a decline in the integration of color with the other plastic elements, qualities which are virtues in the fine work of the mid-seventies become vices in the weak pictures painted in 1879. The fall from grace in, for example, *"At La Grenouillère"* (89), *"Bohemian"* (90) and *"Rose Trees at Wargemont"* (94), can be traced in its successive stages. Its beginnings are apparent in *"Mussel Fishers at Berneval"* (93).

This painting is superb in many of its details—in its richness and quality of color, in its fluid drawing, in the prevalence of color-chords and in the sensuous appeal of its organization as a decorative form; it has a smooth, evenly painted enamel-like surface, and a delicacy, lightness and charm, comparable to some of Renoir's finest versions of eighteenth century painting.§ The illustrative value is also of a very high order: all the persons are alive and intent on what they are doing, and we are very precisely informed concerning their individuality. All these attributes, em-

* E.g., *"Mother and Child"* (118).
† E.g., *"Dreamer"* (91), *"Mussel Fishers at Berneval"* (93).
‡ E.g., *"After Luncheon"* (88), *"At La Grenouillère"* (89), *"Bohemian"* (90), *"Marine: the Wave"* (92), *"Mussel Fishers at Berneval"* (93), *"Rose Trees at Wargemont"* (94) *"Wargemont"* (95), all of 1879, *"Fête of Pan"* (96) of c. 1879.
§ E.g., *"Café Scene"* (81).

bodied in what is practically a single, extremely rich color-chord that embraces the whole canvas, give the picture a very high place as decorative colored illustration. The organization, however, is weak, because this overcharge of decorative and illustrative content leads the expression toward prettiness and sweetness; in other words, Renoir's efforts to perfect the eighteenth century French form led him to overstep the mark and lean toward the softness and inanity of Greuze. Nevertheless, the form is of much higher plastic status than Greuze's, or even the best work of Fragonard.*

"*After Luncheon*" (88) shows another aspect of the deterioration, especially in the drawing of the blouse of the seated woman. Light and color in this unit fail to reënforce each other; light delicatizes the color but it neither illuminates it from within nor imparts structural solidity. The result is that both the woman's blouse and her body appear relatively unsubstantial.†

A more advanced deterioration of form is perceptible in other Renoirs of this period, and for the reasons that the drawing is still weaker and more flabby and the internal luminosity of color more deficient.‡ Their lack of fineness in color-relations makes individual units diffuse and unsubstantial, and the total organization flaccid and obviously incoherent. The basic fault is the failure of color to weld together all plastic factors in a well-integrated organization. The loose drawing by means of fluid color which in "*Pourville*" (80), of 1878, renders convincingly the spirit of landscape, now brings forth superficial, unconvincing decorative illustration. The elements of drawing are disintegrated and as a result the plastic units are soft, volumes are cottony or pulpy, sometimes really amorphous, and their spatial intervals are blurred and indefinite. The suffusion instead of being as in "*Pourville*" an all-pervasive factor carrying the color of one area over into the other in both two- and three-dimensional space, appears detached and resembles a curtain of smoky vapor emanating from the ground. In short, all the factors which make "*Pourville*" one of the most perfect examples of Renoir's power as a colorist and organizer up to the present stage are individually in evidence, but they lack the harmonious relationships between one another that are final determinants of plastic unity.

* Cf., e.g., Greuze's "*Broken Pitcher*" (528) or "*Dairy Maid*" (529), Fragonard's "*Boy as Pierrot*" (532) or "*Music Lesson*" (535).
† For analytical data see Appendix, pp. 399-400.
‡ E.g., "*At La Grenouillère*" (89), "*Marine: the Wave*" (92), "*Rose Trees at Wargemont*" (94), "*Wargemont*" (95), "*Fête of Pan*" (96).

The lowest depth to which Renoir fell at this period appears in *"Bohemian"* (90). The drawing is so loose that it becomes flabby and the objects drawn lose much of their substance and are confused with the surrounding space.* The figure is adequately three-dimensional, but its deficient content of color-solidity, and the lack of integration of the color-areas, overaccentuate the vividness of the color and give a flashy theatrical quality to the ensemble. The best that can be said of the picture is that it is a highly decorative, brightly colored, extremely vivid illustration.

THE EXOTIC INTERLUDE 1880-1887

Much of Renoir's work between 1880 and 1887 seems so different from that of the preceding and subsequent periods that it stands out somewhat as an excrescence upon the organic structure of his work as a whole. Our discussion has shown that there was no break in the continuity of his development between 1870 and 1878, and that in 1879 he had lost the capacity to find nourishment in the forces of his environment. The influences upon him, and the work resulting from them between 1880 and 1887, were in essence alien to what had gone before.† This period of unrest had lasted for three years before Renoir himself became conscious of it; several years later, he gave expression to it in this statement to Vollard: "Toward 1883 there occurred what seemed to be a break in my work. I had traveled as far as impressionism was capable of taking me and I realized the fact that I could neither paint nor draw. In a word I was in an impasse."

This confession, from a man of Renoir's dynamic energy and one who painted as easily, freely and spontaneously as most persons breathe, gives some idea of the depth of his discomfiture. His relentless, and perhaps unconscious, efforts to regain an adjustment to the world by a change in environment took the form of sojourns in Brittany, Africa, Italy and the Isles of

* This feeble and flabby drawing is reminiscent of Fragonard's in *"Bacchante Asleep"* (530).
† Exception to this must be made in the case of a few pictures painted between 1879 and 1881—e.g., *"Sleeping Girl with Cat"* (106) of 1880 and *"Luncheon of the Boatmen"* (116) of 1881—which retain the general appearance of the mid-seventies' color-scheme and patterned organization of broad light and dark areas; the smooth surface and precious quality of the paint, of pronounced eighteenth century feeling, also reveal the kinship with some of the good pictures of the mid-seventies.

Guernsey and Jersey, all between 1879 and 1883. The study of the development of his painting during the decade beginning with 1880 reveals the evidence of the alien experiences, as well as the colossal struggle which ended in converting them into forces contributory to the formation of the more profound Renoir who emerged. During the period he not only produced numerous fine pictures but added to his working capital assets of constructive and lasting value. He converted, for example, the dazzling Oriental glare of the 1880-1882 pictures into a balanced union of color and light, which after 1883, served a constantly increasing range of compositional purposes.

The years extending from 1880 to 1887 inclusive constitute an exotic interlude within which occur several styles of work, each with its own characteristics and clearly discernible influences. The first of these phases, from 1880 to 1883, is dominated by Oriental color-and-light effects; the work of 1883-1884 occasionally shows distinctive marks of the influence of Cézanne; that of 1885-1887 bears witness to Renoir's concentrated efforts to materialize in painting his reactions in Italy to ancient Greek sculpture and early Italian frescoes.

THE PAINTINGS OF 1880-1883 *

The most striking and outstanding characteristic of Renoir's paintings of 1880-1883 is an emphasis upon light much greater than in any of his previous work. The reason for this is to be found in his sojourn in Algiers in 1879, where he made the acquaintance of tropical landscape, in which brilliant light, pouring

* E.g., *"At the Concert"* (100), *"Girl with Falcon"* (101), *"Mademoiselle Grimpel with Blue Ribbon"* (102), *"Mademoiselle Grimpel with Red Ribbon"* (103), *"Mademoiselle Irène Cahen d'Anvers"* (104)—all of 1880; *"Bather, Back Turned"* (107), *"Naiad"* (108), *"Nude"* (109), *"Nude"* (110) —all of c. 1880; *"Experimental Garden at Algiers"* (111) of c. 1880-1881; *"Capodimonte-Sorrento"* (112), *"Chestnut Tree in Bloom"* (113), *"Flowerpiece"* (114), *"Fruit of the Midi"* (115), *"Mesdemoiselles Cahen d'Anvers"* (117), *"Mother and Child"* (118), *"On the Terrace"* (119), *"Railroad Bridge at Chatou"* (120), *"Venice"* (121), *"Vesuvius"* (122)—all of 1881; *"Algerian Woman"* (123), *"Boating at Bougival"* (124), *"Gondola on the Grand Canal"* (125), *"St. Mark's Church"* (126)—all of c. 1881; *"Ali"* (127) and *"Madame Lériaux"* (128), both of 1882; *"Beach Scene, Guernsey"* (130) and *"Blond Bather"* (131) of c. 1882; *"By the Seashore"* (133), *"Child in White"* (134), *"Dance in the City"* (135), *"Dance in the Country"* (136), *"Girl with Parasol"* (137), *"Madame Caillebotte with Dog"* (138), *"Madame Clapisson"* (139), *"Sailor Boy"* (141)—all of 1883.

down upon bright exotic colors, gives to the scene a hot strident glare very different from anything to be seen in a northern climate. It was natural that at first Renoir should be so possessed by his reaction to this brilliant color and dazzling light that he elaborated and emphasized their obvious and striking aspects.* As time passed, his more organic assimilation of these decorative qualities of light and color enabled him to use them as instruments in the construction of fuller and more expressive forms.† The best pictures of this 1880-1883 period ‡ show this assimilation of light and color as organic parts of his form: light deluges the picture without overaccentuation in any part of the canvas and without impairing the compositional activity of the color-light pattern. Light enters into color and, by enriching it and making it more solid, increases its expressiveness with no diminution of decorative value.

This fusion of light and color in the successful pictures of 1880-1883, becomes an integral part of the drawing, the rendering of textural qualities, and of the composition as a whole. In the less successful pictures of the period,§ although the union of light with numerous and vivid colors renders with verisimilitude actual scenes of brilliant sunshine, the light is integrated less firmly in the structure of color than before. Consequently, masses lack the solidity and conviction, as well as the depth of color, which they had in the best pictures of 1875-1878. Plastic strength is thus relatively sacrificed to illustration and rather obvious or superposed decorative effects.

As regards the use of light, these 1880-1883 pictures are divisible into two main classes: in one the light is focalized, in the other it is more evenly disseminated throughout the canvas. Each type of organization is a partial reversion to a form previously used. The first is similar to that of the mid-seventies in its color-pattern of contrasting broad areas of light and dark, but is greatly modified by the focal emphasis upon light.‖ The second continues the per-

---

* E.g., *"Girl with Falcon"* (101).
† Cf., e.g., *"Dance in the Country"* (136) with *"Girl with Falcon"* (101).
‡ E.g., *"Capodimonte-Sorrento"* (112), *"Mother and Child"* (118), *"Beach Scene, Guernsey"* (130), *"By the Seashore"* (133), *"Dance in the City"* (135), *"Dance in the Country"* (136).
§ E.g., *"On the Terrace"* (119).
‖ E.g., *"At the Concert"* (100), *"Mademoiselle Grimpel with Blue Ribbon"* (102), *"Mademoiselle Grimpel with Red Ribbon"* (103), *"Mademoiselle Irène Cahen d'Anvers"* (104), *"Child in White"* (134), *"Madame Clapisson"* (139). The 1884 *"Bust of Girl"* (143) also belongs to this category.

vasive light and colorfulness of the best pictures of the late seventies, but the more intense light and the brighter and more exotic color upon which it impinges, increase the total luminosity and vividness of the color-ensemble.* When, in either of these groups, light is emphasized to the point of overaccentuation, the form is disintegrated, the color-ensemble has a superficial quality, and the general effect is tawdry and unreal.† This unsuccessful illumination prevails in numerous portraits of 1880 and 1881 and yields flashy light-and-dark contrasts and a general melodramatic effect in spite of the usually skilful technical execution.‡

From the form in which focalized areas of light are set off by adjacent dark colors, emerged also a type of nudes in landscape distinct from all other Renoir figure-compositions.§ Its novelty consists partly in the color-scheme into which enter the flesh-tones of the figure and the dark purple-mahogany and deep bluish-greens of the landscape, partly in the contrast of light and dark between the brilliantly illuminated figure and the relatively somber setting; taken together the two characteristics establish a form new in Renoir's treatment of this type of subject-matter.‖

In this new form, as in the flashy portraits of the period, contrast between figure and background is further emphasized by differences in technique: the pattern of brushwork is relatively absorbed in the one-piece texture of the flesh, while in the setting it is pronounced and generally of broad Manet-like strokes which produce a sense of lively movement. Drawing tends more decidedly toward looseness and interpenetration of color at the contour than in the portraits, sometimes even to the point of weakening the structure of the plastic units ¶ and recalling in some measure the diffuse effects of 1879. When the drawing is firm and expressive and the

* E.g., *"Mother and Child"* (118), *"Beach Scene, Guernsey"* (130), *"Madame Caillebotte with Dog"* (138).

† E.g., *"Girl with Falcon"* (101), *"Mademoiselle Grimpel with Red Ribbon"* (103), *"Flowerpiece"* (114), *"Fruit of the Midi"* (115), *"On the Terrace"* (119), *"Vesuvius"* (122), *"Algerian Woman"* (123), *"Gondola on the Grand Canal"* (125), *"St. Mark's Church"* (126), *"Ali"* (127), *"Madame Lériaux"* (128).

‡ E.g., *"At the Concert"* (100), *"Mademoiselle Grimpel with Blue Ribbon"* (102), *"Mademoiselle Grimpel with Red Ribbon"* (103), *"Mesdemoiselles Cahen d'Anvers"* (117).

§ E.g., *"Bather, Back Turned"* (107), *"Naiad"* (108) and *"Nude"* (109).

‖ The general effect of these compositions suggests a source of derivation in the type of eighteenth century painting represented by Watteau's *"Jupiter and Antiope"* (479A).

¶ E.g., *"Nude"* (109).

light is properly merged with color,* this new type of picture compares favorably in plastic strength with the best of Renoir's work of the mid-seventies, with which, indeed, it has many points in common.

Another result of Renoir's African experience was the introduction of new and brighter colors into his palette, and these are as important as light in determining the identity of the 1880-1883 form. The blues and greens of his earlier periods persist, as do also the effects of pastel quality not uncommon in the mid-seventies; but a series of intense reds and yellows are used so assertively and in such relations that their exotic overtones set the key to the color-scheme and give it a pronounced Oriental feeling. The scarlet, carmine, orange and positive shades of yellow of this Oriental scheme, flooded by light which sometimes seems dazzling, increase the decorative force but often result also in a glitter, a surface-quality of tinsel which impairs solidity and plastic strength.†

When colors with the quality of pastel are used in combination with the Oriental effects the bright colors generally lose their stridency and at the same time the pastel-quality is increased in strength and sensuous appeal by the more vivid colors.‡ The emphatic Oriental color-scheme gives to some of the work of this period a superficial resemblance to Delacroix's, quite different from the positive similarity in those of his paintings of the seventies in which Delacroix's form as a whole supplies a point of departure.§ The overemphasis upon the Oriental color-scheme disappears as Renoir learned by trial and error to assimilate the novel experience; and, in new and properly subordinated forms, this color-scheme or elements from it recur in pictures painted throughout the rest of his career.‖

Renoir's landscapes of the early eighties vary widely in esthetic value because of the different degree to which the bright exotic

* E.g., *"Bather, Back Turned"* (107), *"Naiad"* (108).
† E.g., *"Girl with Falcon"* (101), *"Flowerpiece"* (114), *"Vesuvius"* (122), *"Algerian Woman"* (123) and *"Madame Lériaux"* (128).
‡ E.g., *"Mother and Child"* (118) and *"Beach Scene, Guernsey"* (130).
§ Cf., e.g., *"Girl with Falcon"* (101), *"Algerian Woman"* (123) and *"Ali"* (127) of the early eighties, with *"Odalisque"* (17), *"Capitaine Darras"* (19), *"Harem"* (25) and *"Young Woman with Rose"* (28) of the early seventies.
‖ E.g., *"Mt. Ste. Victoire"* (175) of 1889, *"Girls at Piano"* (203) of c. 1892, *"Bathers in Forest"* (216) of c. 1897, *"Writing Lesson"* (234) of c. 1905, *"Bathing Group"* (285) of 1916, and *"Standing Odalisque"* (295) of c. 1917-1919.

color, the intense sunlight and the modified impressionistic technique are integrated in the total form.* *"Gondola on the Grand Canal"* (125), for example, by its overemphasis both on light and on bright color, acquires in spite of a fair degree of structural color, a banal Turneresque superficiality and quality of tinsel. *"Venice"* (121) shows a better integration of Oriental color and the flood of sunlight in a form more definitely Renoiresque than impressionistic. A still better union of the same factors is attained in *"Capodimonte-Sorrento"* (112), in which the Oriental color is sublimated and blended with the hot sunlight to render convincingly the spirit of place. In this picture, part of the particular effect is due to the introduction of a lavender-purple reminiscent of Sisley.† The lavender is not of the same tone nor does it have the same relationships to the other colors as in Renoir's previous work. It is more localized and more vivid than in *"Pourville"* (80) of 1878, for example, and, because of its association with intense sunlight and an accentuated pattern of small brush strokes, it contributes to an effect closer to that in Sisley, from which it is differentiated, however, by its permeation with the exotic Oriental overtones.

The lavender in Renoir's work of 1880-1883 is significant for two reasons: first, by its reënforcement of the Oriental color-form it creates color-organizations of great flexibility in varied renderings of the spirit of landscape; second, Renoir's experimental use of it at this period was largely the source of its subsequent diverse compositional functions during the mid-eighties. *"Chestnut Tree in Bloom"* (113), of 1881, and *"Boating at Bougival"* (124), of c. 1881, offer examples of two different color-schemes, each saturated with lavender, and each adapted to a different and specific effect in landscape. A flood of light in *"Boating at Bougival"* playing upon colored surfaces extensively tinged with lavender, forms a bright, vibrating atmosphere very much as in the impressionists, but with a heightened colorfulness, a better reënforcement of color by light, and a richer and more varied pattern. The design embodies the feeling of gentle colorful movement in trees,

---

* E.g., *"Capodimonte-Sorrento"* (112), *"Chestnut Tree in Bloom"* (113), *"Railroad Bridge at Chatou"* (120), *"Venice"* (121), *"Vesuvius"* (122), *"Boating at Bougival"* (124), *"Gondola on the Grand Canal"* (125), *"Beach Scene, Guernsey"* (130).

† E.g., Sisley's *"Edge of the Forest in Spring"* (614) and *"River Scene with Ducks"* (616).

sky, water, ground, figures and atmosphere, and everything in
the picture is light, delicate, floating and sparkling.

"*Chestnut Tree in Bloom*" presents a color-scheme more
weighty, deeper and darker, a different type of composition, and
another variation of impressionistic technique. Lavender, by its association with these other factors, contributes to the rendering of
a phase of landscape evocative of a different set of human values:
the accentuation of bushes and foliage as individual masses is
in striking contrast to the succession, in "*Boating at Bougival,*"
of objects rendered more flatly and in shallower space. Color has
a deep glow and the sunshine seems to emerge from the individual
units, while in "*Boating at Bougival*" the color has a more positive sparkle and the sunshine bathes the whole surface with relative uniformity. Thick impasto in alternation with spots of bare
canvas gives less uniformity of surface and color than in "*Boating
at Bougival,*" and aids materially in making bushes and clumps of
foliage embody the feeling of small bouquets, in harmony with the
bouquet-effect of the picture as a whole.

The loose, fluid drawing of the period extending from 1872
through 1879 gives way, in the early eighties, to a comparatively
sharp linear drawing more akin to that which prevailed before
1871. Its character is, however, radically changed by the introduction of many of the advances in color and technique evolved by
Renoir during the intervening decade. The drawing is more clean-
cut than in the earlier type, the contour is sharper, and the colors
in adjacent areas are in more positive contrasts.* Sometimes the
drawing has an apparent looseness due to the breaking up of color-
areas by brush strokes into color-chords but, in comparison with
the really loose fluid drawing of the 1872-1879 pictures, there is
much less intermingling of brush strokes between adjacent color-
compartments.† This is true even of the landscapes of the period
in which the continuous pattern of brush strokes establishes apparent continuity of color, but conveys no such feeling of actual
fluidity of color as in his landscapes of the seventies.‡ Because

---

* Cf., e.g., "*Nude*" (110) of c. 1880 with "*Bather with Griffon*" (16) of
1870.
  † Cf., e.g., "*Mother and Child*" (118) of 1881 with "*Torso*" (52) of
c. 1875.
    ‡ Cf., e.g., the following early eighties' landscapes: "*Experimental Garden
at Algiers*" (111), "*Capodimonte-Sorrento*" (112), "*Chestnut Tree in
Bloom*" (113), "*Railroad Bridge at Chatou*" (120), "*Boating at Bougival*"
(124), "*Beach Scene, Guernsey*" (130) and "*Near Mentone*" (140) with
"*Two Women in Park*" (44) of 1875 and "*Pourville*" (80) of 1878

of the emphasis upon the boundaries of areas, especially to be noted in the contour of figures, the drawing as a whole is decidedly sharper and the composition more obviously patterned and decorative than in any of Renoir's prior work.

This increase in decorative emphasis is due to the fact that concurrently with Renoir's ornamental use of Oriental color and light, there appears in the eighties an unmistakable transcription into his form of specific traits of the eighteenth century French tradition. From this source Renoir selected as material for experiment a number of distinct features: the smooth mother-of-pearl surface; the relatively dry pigment; the clean-cut drawing; the delicate one-piece type of modeling; the fluid, linear, ornamental rhythms; the light, often pearly, tonality; the exotic texture of flesh; and the distinctive types of subject-matter—nudes, dancing figures, etc. Indeed, his work during the entire 1880-1887 period bears closer resemblance to the Boucher-Watteau-Fragonard form than at any stage of his career.* In *"On the Terrace"* (119), *"Beach Scene, Guernsey"* (130) and *"Blond Bather"* (131) of the early eighties, French eighteenth century traits are emphasized particularly in the painting of flesh. The essential characteristics of his figure-painting in 1883 †—the smooth enamel-like flesh and the flat one-piece modeling—are obtained by a resynthesis of the elements of the sharply linear drawing of the earlier eighties, and these characteristics, in turn, became foundation-stones in the form of 1885-1887.‡ This is another instance of the underlying continuity of Renoir's development, of the fact already commented upon, that his pictures of all periods preserve vestiges of the past and show anticipations of the future.

The clean-cut contour of the figures in the 1880-1883 pictures is as yet seldom used to emphasize their three-dimensional quality, as it is in the mid-eighties, but serves mainly to accentuate the illustrative and decorative phases of the design. Indeed, the simplified modeling in the 1880-1883 period renders volumes so unemphatic that they function less as masses than as relatively uniform areas of color in an all-inclusive ornamental pattern. While sharp linear drawing and flat modeling apply to the 1880-1883 pictures as a whole, it is nevertheless precisely the departures

---

* For details see chapter "Renoir and the Eighteenth Century French Tradition," p. 203.
† E.g., *"Dance in the City"* (135), *"Sailor Boy"* (141).
‡ E.g., *"Woman with Fan"* (160) of 1886.

from this general rule that confer individuality upon the outstanding fine achievements of these years. A brief study of these aspects
in four typical pictures—*"Dance in the City"* (135), *"Dance in
the Country"* (136), *"Girl with Parasol"* (137), and *"Sailor Boy"*
(141), all dated 1883—will illustrate the point.

The drawing of the setting in each is loose, fluid and generalized,
while that of the figures is sharp, with varying degree of linear
emphasis. The figures in the first two of the pictures are more
three-dimensional than those of the second two, but all four
have in greater or less degree the flattened faces characteristic
of the period. Similarly, variations in the flesh-painting also affect
the particular design of each picture. The flesh has none of the
concentration of thick impasto on highlights so common in Renoir's
earlier work; * instead, its surface is smooth like that of porcelain
and its texture is harder than heretofore. The dry, whitish pigment
pervasively toned with light pink, lacks the earlier definite internal
patterns of color or of light-and-shadow, so that the volumes of
face, hands and legs remain rather flat and have a one-piece effect;
the volumes, however, are not so flat as in his typical work of
the preceding two years,† nor so three-dimensional as in most of
the paintings of the mid-eighties.‡

Variations in general appearance are brought about by different
color-and-light content of the complexion and by the degree of
precision of linear contour. The flesh in *"Girl with Parasol"* is
warmer in tone, slightly more nuanced in color and more solid
than that in *"Sailor Boy"*; in *"Dance in the City"* it has more of
the color, surface and texture of ivory; the woman's complexion in
"Dance in the Country" is more naturalistic, and the man's face
is tinged with vague and slight shadows. The varying interrelationships between sharpness of linear contour, light and shadow,
light-content of color, and texture of pigment, establish the differences in drawing, modeling and general painting of flesh that
give widely different individuality to each of these pictures. The
man's head in *"Dance in the Country,"* for example, is almost
Courbetesque in solidity and general character, while the cameo-
like head of the woman in *"Dance in the City"* is strongly reminis-

---

* E.g., *"Reader"* (40) of c. 1874-1876, *"Young Girl Sewing"* (41) of
c. 1874-1876, *"Two Women in Park"* (44) of 1875.
† Cf., e.g., *"On the Terrace"* (119) or *"Beach Scene, Guernsey"* (130).
‡ Cf., e.g., *"Washerwoman and Baby"* (163) or *"Bathers"* (164).

cent of both François Clouet * and the eighteenth century French painters.†

An important factor in the creation of one of the most characteristic traits of the period, the continuous one-piece surface of the flesh, is the use of light. Shadows, which by their relations to areas of light produced the patterns in the flesh of the mid-seventies, became less and less pronounced between 1877 and 1882, and are practically eliminated in most of the 1883 pictures. This more even distribution of light throughout the flesh is undoubtedly an adaptation of the extensive diffusion of light which, as already noted, resulted from Renoir's experiments with the hot Algerian sunlight and bright color. The one-piece effect in the flesh continues through the eighties, but after 1883 it helps to model volumes which have accentuated three-dimensionality ‡ and, at the end of the decade, the one-piece effect of the masses is achieved by the aid of Renoir's earlier patterns of shadow and pronounced highlights.§ The point here is that, as is constant in Renoir's progress, outstanding creations of one period are made instruments in the development of characteristic traits of later periods.

The technique of the 1883 pictures likewise has well-defined characteristics, so varied and adapted as to help give identity to each design. A striking feature of the technique is the contrast between areas differently executed, with its attendant compositional function and picturesque effect. The setting, for example, in *"Dance in the City," "Dance in the Country," "Girl with Parasol"* and *"Sailor Boy,"* done in perceptible broad brush strokes in variegated and contrasting colors, brings into relief the more smoothly painted figures. Throughout the canvas the pigment, thicker in general than previously, is smooth, even when patterned by brush strokes, except in certain areas in which variegated color in small brush strokes of raised pigment form superposed patterns which greatly enhance the total decorative value.‖ These superposed

* Cf., e.g., François Clouet's *"Woman's Head"* (382) or *"Elisabeth d'Autriche"* (383).

† Cf., e.g., the profiled head in Boucher's *"Diana at the Bath"* (508) or in *"Venus and Vulcan"* (522).

‡ E.g., *"Bathers"* (164) of 1887, and *"Bather"* (181) of the late eighties.

§ E.g., *"Girl with Marguerites"* (179) of c. 1889, *"Girl Reading"* (195) of c. 1890.

‖ E.g., the highlighted folds in the dress of the woman in *"Dance in the City"* (135), the foliage in the upper background and the floral motifs on the woman's dress in *"Dance in the Country"* (136), the red bush in *"Girl with Parasol"* (137), the middle section of the landscape at the left in *"Sailor Boy"* (141).

decorative units are the crystallization of Renoir's previous experiments with decorative brushwork and diversified color;* they form definite entities employed extensively and deliberately throughout the rest of his career as compositional agents with more and more comprehensive function.† They seldom impair plastic organization, since they are as a rule adequately ballasted by expressive values and are condensations or summaries of the general decorative scheme, not intrusions of an alien element, as they so often are even in the best work of the Venetians.‡

The general color-quality of the 1883 pictures results from a harmonious adjustment between the assertive Oriental feeling of Renoir's color-scheme of 1880-1882 and his quieter and less directly illuminated colors of 1875-1878. His blue, ivory and green of the mid-seventies recur in the work of 1883, but as organic parts of a greatly increased palette which acquires a distinctive identity from the presence of more reds and yellows and of a much higher degree of internal illumination in all the colors. The stridency and factitiousness of the Oriental quality, accentuated in many of the 1880-1882 pictures, here gives way to a pervasive freshness in all the colors, and decoration is better merged with expression. The Oriental feeling, in other words, has been engrafted upon the earlier color-scheme, but in such a degree of sublimation that the assertive red and yellow overtones are tempered by extensive areas of blue, green and ivory. The extreme diminution in assertiveness of the overtones naturally accentuates the color-areas and thus adds clean-cutness to the color-pattern and vividness to the composition.

Within the general form of these 1883 pictures, emphasis in each upon one or more of the plastic features just discussed results in a distinctive, individual design. *"Sailor Boy"* shows the Oriental quality only vaguely, in the glow of bright color in the upper background; its landscape is impressionistic, but it is less pronouncedly illustrative than in the earlier eighties,§ and the color-

---

* Cf., e.g., the flower in *"Head of Margot"* (86) of c. 1878-1879, the bowl and the dress in *"Mother and Child"* (118) of 1881, the foreground in *"Beach Scene, Guernsey"* (130) of c. 1882.

† E.g., the woman's blouse in *"Artist's Family"* (214) of 1896, the pink drapery in *"Bathers in Forest"* (216) of c. 1897, and the orange highlights on trees in *"Bathing Group"* (285) of 1916.

‡ Cf., e.g., Paolo Veronese's superposed decorative units on the textiles in *"Burning of Sodom"* (401).

§ Cf., e.g., *"On the Terrace"* (119) or *"Beach Scene, Guernsey"* (130).

scheme in the figure is close to that of the mid-seventies.*
"Girl with Parasol" combines impressionistic brushwork and light
with the textural qualities and technique which in the 1870's hark
back to Goya and Manet,† and with notes of Oriental color in the
landscape-foreground and in the parasol.

Both *"Dance in the Country"* and *"Dance in the City"* are characterized by an emphasis upon space-composition, complex and
elaborate in the former, extremely simple in the latter; in both,
the contrasts of color and technique are more effective than in
"Sailor Boy" and *"Girl with Parasol,"* and more generalized
brushwork makes the technique less obvious. The absence of accentuated pattern of brush strokes contributes to color-organizations which differ not only from those in *"Sailor Boy"* and *"Girl
with Parasol,"* but from each other. In *"Dance in the Country"*
emphasis is upon the variety, brightness and contrast of the colors,
in *"Dance in the City,"* upon large simply patterned areas rendered in fewer and less vividly contrasted colors. In each rendering
of the dance, the marvelously fresh colors and the vividness of
their contrasts coöperate with the subtlety of the varied and unusual space-composition to establish a firm foundation for striking
illustrative values in a plastic form stronger than that of any
other picture of this period. The abstract feeling of dance is
superbly realized in designs of different plastic type, each peculiarly
fitted to the specific expression aimed at: the preponderantly
vertical arrangement of few, simple, large units in *"Dance in the
City"* is admirably adapted to the placid, dignified movement; in
the other picture, a large number of more varied units of bright,
vivid, gay colors in curvilinear areas express fully the lively
abandon of a swirling country dance.‡

When the 1880-1883 form is resolved into its basic plastic essentials, the fact emerges that the typical pictures of the period have
in common, bright light and color, precise line in drawing, smooth
and hard surface, modified impressionistic technique, and emphasis
upon illustration and decoration. While these pictures come within
the category of decorative illustrations, some of them § also rank
in fulness of expression and strength of plastic form with Renoir's
best work of any antecedent period.

* Cf., e.g., *"After the Concert"* (73), *"Woman Crocheting"* (76).
† Cf., e.g., *"Girl with Jumping Rope"* (57).
‡ For further details see Appendix, p. 408.
§ E.g., *"Dance in the City"* (135) and *"Dance in the Country"* (136).

THE FORM OF 1884

An outstanding feature of much of Renoir's work of the next of these exotic years, that of 1884,* is the cumulative effect of the influence of Cézanne, a natural result of the admiration Renoir had for that artist.† Earlier manifestations of this influence appear in Renoir's *"Fruit of the Midi"* (115) of 1881, and *"Apples in Dish"* (132) of 1883, with their Cézanne type of modeling and drawing by hatchings of color, and their accentuation of dynamic relations between three-dimensional volumes and spatial intervals. By 1884 the Cézanne influence, which had been sporadic in the years 1881-1883, was manifested more frequently, sometimes in patches of organized brushwork, at other times in an increase in solidity and weight of color, and a somewhat greater emphasis upon three-dimensionality of volumes. The most important and lasting of these influences was the technique of brush strokes organized in patches, which function as planes. This technique is, however, stamped indelibly with a Renoir individuality by the way it is used in connection with color and texture of surface. Indeed, the influences of Cézanne consist mainly of giving direction to tendencies which were evident in Renoir's work before his association with Cézanne; that is, in 1884, Renoir's bright vivid color of the early eighties and his brushwork of accentuated narrow strokes of the mid-seventies, are definitely organized in a form which shows the influence of Cézanne.

The color in the 1884 pictures is generally in the high key of the early eighties, and often has in addition the bright, pale, dry, delicate appearance of pastel, an effect which is reënforced by the technique of long, narrow, more or less parallel brush strokes which simulate the striated surface of work in crayon or pastel.‡ The pastel-effects extend sometimes to the whole picture; § at other times they occur only in certain sections, in which they function as factors in a dramatic color-contrast.‖ The high degree of light-content of the color is responsible for an iridescence

* E.g., *"Children at Wargemont"* (144), *"Girl in Field"* (145), *"Madame Renoir at the Gate"* (146), *"Grape Gatherers Resting"* (147), *"Madame Renoir"* (148), *"Summer"* (150), *"Three Pears"* (151).
† Renoir painted Cézanne's portrait—*"Paul Cézanne"* (105)—in 1880.
‡ E.g., *"Girl in Field"* (145), *"Grape Gatherers Resting"* (147), *"Madame Renoir"* (148), *"Summer"* (150).
§ E.g., *"Girl in Field"* (145), *"Grape Gatherers Resting"* (147), *"Summer"* (150).
‖ E.g., *"Children at Wargemont"* (144).

which is sometimes sparkling * and at other times relatively muted.† Each of the characteristics of the technique and color-quality in Renoir's work of 1884 reappears in more or less modi-fied form in his paintings of all subsequent periods.‡

The emphasis upon long, narrow, parallel brush strokes, each loaded with more pigment than heretofore, creates a rough and rugged surface striated with ridges of thick paint and bristle marks, in contrast to the smooth, polished surface in the 1879-1883 pic-tures. Viewed from a distance the texture of the pigment lacks the unctuous quality present in the majority of Renoir's work prior to 1880. The new technique is obviously a composite of several of his previously used devices: the small narrow brush strokes in some of his pictures of the mid-seventies; § the high-lights of thick impasto used at various times between 1872 and 1879; ‖ the superposed decorations present in their incipiency in *"Mother and Child"* (118) of 1881, and in their fully matured form in the typical pictures of 1883.¶ Still another factor in the genesis of this striated surface is Renoir's work in actual pastel and crayon during the early eighties: ** each of these materials, even when used conventionally, lends itself naturally to a surface striated and patterned by strokes.††

The principal identifying mark of the technique in the pictures of 1884 is the orderly arrangement of the strokes in patches which sometimes extend in different directions throughout the canvas ‡‡ and at other times are parallel but, because of change in their color, give the appearance of extending in opposite direc-

---

* E.g., *"Grape Gatherers Resting"* (147) and *"Summer"* (150).
† E.g., *"Girl in Field"* (145).
‡ E.g., *"Pasture along the Seine"* (197) of c. 1890, *"Picnic"* (211) of c. 1893, *"Bathers in Forest"* (216) of c. 1897, *"View of Cagnes"* (222) of the early 1900's.
§ E.g., *"Beautiful Season: Conversation"* (45) and *"Beautiful Season: Promenade"* (46) of c. 1875, *"At the Milliner's"* (64) of c. 1876, *"Jeanne Samary"* (72) of 1877.
‖ E.g., *"Breakfast"* (27), *"Two Women in Park"* (44), *"After Lunch-eon"* (88), *"Two Little Circus Girls"* (99).
¶ E.g., *"Dance in the City"* (135), *"Dance in the Country"* (136), *"Girl with Parasol"* (137), and *"Sailor Boy"* (141).
** E.g., *"Paul Cézanne"* (105) and *"Young Girl with Bonnet"* (129).
†† The technique of pastel lending itself to long thin striations is illus-trated by Degas' *"At the Milliner's"* (611). In Manet's *"In a Boat"* (604) the woman's dress is painted by means of long, ribbonlike, parallel strokes also recalling the effect of the pastel technique.
‡‡ E.g., *"Girl in Field"* (145).

tions.* Each patch is of a same general color throughout but takes on variety by differences of tone in the constituent brush strokes. The distinctive general effect of these pictures is that of an accentuated color-pattern different from either the criss-cross brush strokes and shimmering surface of some of the mid-seventies' pictures † or the definite pattern of contrasting broad color-areas of the early eighties.‡

A prior suggestion in Renoir's work of this technique appears in *"Nude"* (110) of c. 1880, in the long, parallel, ribbonlike strokes in the background-setting; but the paint is thin, the color is less varied, the brush strokes are confined to small sections of the canvas and are used for purposes of contrast; the strokes are neither organized in patches nor used as a means to knit together the composition, as they are in the typical Renoirs of 1884. A step nearer to this matured technique is represented in part of the landscape-setting of *"Girl with Parasol"* (137) of 1883, in which the brush strokes tend to form a pattern of patches; in a few areas in *"Sailor Boy"* (141), also of 1883, the brush strokes are definitely organized in patches. The difference is that in these two pictures the colors within the patches are weightier and more varied than in the 1884 work, the patches are not such definite planes, and their pattern se˙ves primarily as a contrasting and decorative setting for the figures. In short, what are incidental factors in the earlier work are in the 1884 pictures definitely organized as a formal unit which becomes the outstanding characteristic of the period; it is the main factor in a new and distinctive type of decoration, and one of the most active agents in unifying the composition.

Emphasis or diminution of one or more elements of this technical unit produces, within the general form of 1884, individual designs that vary in color-quality, compositional pattern, drawing and general expression. Variations in degree of emphasis upon the perceptibility of the patches and of the individual brush strokes in *"Girl in Field"* (145) are responsible for the lively sense of movement in the accentuated color-pattern of the landscape as well as for the feeling of the peaceful repose of the figure. The accentuated striæ of heavily loaded brush strokes in *"Grape Gatherers Resting"* (147) impart the appearance of crayon to the

* E.g., *"Summer"* (150).
† Cf., e.g., *"Beautiful Season: Conversation"* (45), *"Beautiful Season: Promenade"* (46) or *"Jeanne Samary"* (72).
‡ Cf., e.g., *"Dance in the Country"* (136).

surface, while the curvilinear trend of the elongated brush strokes engenders the very graceful movement that pervades the whole composition. *"Summer"* (150) with its rather vaguely defined patches and brush strokes, and its profusion of bright and varied colors saturated with light, renders by its unaccentuated pattern and its luminous, sparkling sunlight and delicate haze, the spirit of a colorful landscape on a hot midsummer day. In *"Three Pears"* (151) the patches are organized as compact planes which model the pieces of fruit in pronounced three-dimensional volumes closely resembling Cézanne's. They differ from the latter in that the patches are less rigid, actual line is absent from contour of objects, and the color-scheme is one of Renoir's adaptations of the Oriental effects.*

The technique in *"Children at Wargemont"* (144), by far the most important picture of 1884 and one of the most complex and successful of all Renoir's plastic organizations, has undergone a radical change. The brushwork resembles Cézanne's but in a different way than does the technique in most of Renoir's other pictures of 1884; that is, the brush strokes run in the same direction throughout several adjacent areas of different colors.† The difference from Cézanne and from Renoir's general work of 1884 is that the patterns of accentuated patches and of individual brush strokes are replaced by a continuous unbroken surface. The marks of the bristles, still perceptible in the thick impasto, give the characteristic rugged surface of the period, but it is an even ruggedness which from a distance imparts to the surface a one-piece effect and thus aids in unifying the accentuated pattern of large sharply contrasted color-areas.

The colors in *"Children at Wargemont"* retain the suffusion of light, the pastel-effect and the Oriental feeling common to Renoir's work of 1884. But the palette has been increased, and the pastel and the Oriental effects are so interrelated and fused, and so intimately affected by the technique, that a new and distinctive quality pervades the color-organization. Sunlight bathes the whole picture and makes most of the colors extremely luminous, while the brushing and modulation by light cause the nuances of each tone to interpenetrate, thus converting the individual areas into a series of rich but subtle color-chords. Literally innumerable shades of blue, red, green, white, yellow, brown,

* Cf., e.g., Cézanne's *"Still-Life"* (622A).
† Cf., e.g., Cézanne's *"Bathers, Five Nudes"* (618).

lavender and orange, produce by their relationships a color-organization unique even in Renoir.

As a decorative illustration carried to a high degree of expression, this picture is equalled, among those of approximately the same period, only by *"Dance in the City"* (135) and *"Dance in the Country"* (136) of 1883. It exceeds both of the latter in complexity of plastic problems and in the novelty and ingenuity of their solution. The complexity is due to Renoir's purpose to construct a composition of space-and-volume relationships that involve numerous traditional forms, and to accomplish it in a new manner, by the two most characteristic and individual factors of his form of the period, color-quality and technique. His solution of the general problem is aided considerably by ubiquitous patterned units of contrasting colors which serve as adjuncts in the compositional integration of volumes variously distributed in space. In some areas a few objects are scattered in a large expanse of space; in others many volumes are set in restricted space. The contrasts which are concerned primarily with space, and vary from the strikingly dramatic to the extremely subtle, involve also line, light and color as active participants in the drawing and modeling of the units, and in their decorative and expressive content.

The interaction of all these factors results in a plastic form which, as already noted, represents decorative illustration with a high degree of expressive value. With all the liveliness and exotic quality of the daring color-adventure, the picture embodies a feeling of the imperturbable placidity of harmonious family life. All of the figures are thoroughly alive, intent upon what they are doing, and the natural charm of childhood is most convincingly realized. An exotic textural quality is present in practically all the objects: the substance of flesh, for example, is more like that of papier-mâché dolls than human flesh. This imaginative use of exotic color and texture, instead of detracting from the essential realism of the scene or from the esthetic strength of the form, adds piquancy and picturesqueness to both.*

CRYSTALLIZATION OF THE 1885-1887 FORM

The cumulative results of the conflict which arose in Renoir's personality in 1879 are clearly manifested in his figure painting

* For further analytical data see Appendix, pp. 409-412.

of the period extending from 1885 to 1887.* The growth in the intervening years was gradual and we have shown in individual pictures the evolution of the traits which in their ensemble give the 1885-1887 form its distinctive identity. In the mid-eighties the tendencies of the preceding five years are modified by the introduction of a number of novel features, and a new form appears that marks a strange phase in Renoir's career. Although some of its features are present in the earlier work, the total form as a distinct entity is not anticipated by anything previously done by Renoir, and after its culmination in the 1887 *"Bathers"* (164) and *"Girl Plaiting Hair"* (165), of about the same year, in which all the means are brought definitely into conformity with its distinctive type of design, Renoir abandons it as a whole.

The fundamental characteristics of this 1885-1887 form are as follows: sculptural one-piece modeling, light coral-toned flesh with lavender in shadows, extreme diminution of highlights, unaccented shadows, composition of masses in deep space, pale and light tonality, hard and smooth surface, sharp contour, abundance of linear rhythms and a distinctive type of color. This color is in general dry, arid, and of fresco-quality, occasionally acid and harsh, and sometimes associated with terra cotta tones.

The fact that each of these qualities is hinted at in Renoir's work just subsequent to 1880 justifies the conclusion that the form of 1885-1887 was the cumulative product of his visits to Italy in 1881 and 1882. The sharp contour and the three-dimensional sculpturesque modeling, together with the frequent fresco-quality of the color and surface, are decidedly reminiscent of the classic statues and the Pompeiian and Renaissance frescoes which he observed in Italy.† Equally obvious is it that the decisive factors in changing these influences of classic art into a form fundamentally different are impressionism and, more especially, the spirit of eighteenth century French painting. From the start both these

---

* E.g., *"Bather Arranging Hair"* (152) of 1885, *"Mother Nursing Baby"* (155) of 1885, *"Redheaded Girl in Yellow Hat"* (157) of c. 1885, *"Mother, Child and Cat"* (159) of 1886, *"Woman with Fan"* (160) of 1886, *"Garden Scene"* (161) of c. 1886, *"Mother and Baby"* (162) of c. 1886, *"Washerwoman and Baby"* (163) of c. 1886, *"Bathers"* (164) of 1887, *"Girl Plaiting Hair"* (165) of c. 1887.

† The incisive line is often attributed to the influence of Ingres, but this view is fallacious: Ingres' line is almost exclusively an element in linear pattern, with color as a mere filler-in between contours; Renoir's line is an integral component of the color-organization and one of the means by which color is made an inseparable part of the three-dimensional volume—cf., e.g., Renoir's *"Bathers"* (164) of 1887 with Ingres' *"Turkish Bath"* (562).

traditions, as we have seen, were constantly at work in Renoir's painting, and each at times assumed the rôle of dominant influence in it. We have also seen that in his most characteristic work of each period impressionism has been so changed in detail and made an instrument to ends so new and individual, that the resulting formal reorganization is far beyond impressionism itself. In the process of this transformation the essential traits of eighteenth century French painting assume the ascendancy, while simultaneously undergoing progressive changes as they too become means to Renoir's own expression.* As a group the pictures of 1885-1887 display the bright general illumination of the previous period, impressionism is now drawn upon to render individual versions of the tapestry-quality of eighteenth century French painting, and the sublimated Oriental color-scheme is employed to fit the exigencies of particular designs.† The adaptation of the significant characteristics of the period to different plastic expressions may be illustrated by brief analytic studies of a few representative pictures.

In *"Mother Nursing Baby"* (155), the principal identifying elements of the type are formally combined but not in the thoroughgoing manner represented in *"Bathers"* (164) and *"Girl Plaiting Hair"* (165). The color in *"Mother Nursing Baby"* is more transparent and retains much of the fresh pastel-quality of the 1884 pictures, and the volumes, while well-rounded, are less weighty, solid and sculpturesque. The traits which link it definitely to the type under discussion are the dryness of color, the smooth porcelain-like surface with a feeling of fresco, and the incisive linear drawing which creates a profusion of fluid linear rhythms. These characteristics are amplified in four pictures, painted about a year later, in a more fully matured form: *"Woman with Fan"* (160), *"Garden Scene"* (161), *"Mother and Baby"* (162) and *"Washerwoman and Baby"* (163). All four are closely akin in color-scheme and color-quality, in linear clean-cutness and rhythmic patterns, and in enamel, mother-of-pearl surface reminiscent of the eighteenth century French painters. Variation in the emphasis upon each of

* See chapter "Renoir and the Eighteenth Century French Tradition," p. 204.
† Renoir's non-typical pictures of the period are few, relatively unimportant, and are in the main experiments with previous forms by means of new devices. For example, *"In the Garden"* (153) and *"Mademoiselle Chapuis with Hoop"* (154) repeat the form of the 1883 *"Girl with Parasol"* (137), slightly modified by more incisive contour, and more fully rounded volumes.

these features determines the identity of the individual designs which recall, though in different ways and in delicatized versions, fresco painting,* the work of eighteenth century French artists,† tapestry,‡ miniatures § and water colors.||

The sculpturesque feeling in *"Washerwoman and Baby"* is secondary to qualities of surface-, color-, and line-effects of classic Italian frescoes. The long parallel brush strokes in the background, a vestige of the technique which attained its maturity in the 1884 period, function, as at that time, as planes in the modeling and spatial setting of volumes, but they are smoothly applied in thinner impasto, restricted to fewer areas, and their color is more transparent and fluid. *"Mother and Baby"* of c. 1886 presents the same subject-matter as *"Mother Nursing Baby"* of 1885 in a firmer and stronger plastic organization; compared to *"Washerwoman and Baby"* the colors are paler, more delicate, less acid and less frescolike. The coral-toned complexion and smooth even surface of the paint are typical of the distinctive flesh-painting of the period, as represented in the perfected form in *"Bathers"* (164). The picture has none of the sculpturesque feeling of the period; the three-dimensional quality of the figures is adapted to the dainty and exquisitely rendered organization, which as a whole is like an extremely delicate tapestry.¶

The third of this series of 1886 pictures, *"Garden Scene"* (161), has a fresco-quality more deeply colorful than the other two, and is painted in thicker impasto. Its most prominent features are the colorful frescolike surface and the miniature-quality of the sharply drawn foliage, which recalls the decorative patterns in early French miniatures and tapestries, and also those in the frescoes in the

---

* Cf., e.g., Renoir's *"Washerwoman and Baby"* with Piero della Francesca's *"Reception of Queen of Sheba by Solomon"* (326) and Benozzo Gozzoli's *"Journey of the Magi"* (327); and Renoir's *"Garden Scene"* with the early French fresco *"Fishing Scene"* (320), and also with Niccolò di Tommaso's *"Temptation and Expulsion"* (318).

† Cf., e.g., Renoir's *"Washerwoman and Baby"* with Fragonard's *"Young Woman and Child"* (539); and Renoir's *"Woman with Fan"* with Boucher's *"Madame de Pompadour"* (511).

‡ Cf., e.g., Renoir's *"Garden Scene"* with the French tapestries *"Scene of Courtly Life"* (377) and *"Concert in the Open Air"* (381); and Renoir's *"Woman with Fan"* with the Gothic tapestry *"Woman with Falcon"* (324).

§ Cf., e.g., Renoir's *"Garden Scene"* with the French miniature *"Hares"* (323).

|| Cf., e.g., Renoir's *"Mother and Baby"* with Cézanne's *"Landscape"* (621).
¶ For analytical data see Appendix, pp. 413-414.

Chambre de la Garde-Robe at Avignon and in Niccolò di Tommaso's at Pistoia. A suggestion of Oriental color is present but
is dominated by the fresco-tapestry-miniature treatment.

In *"Woman with Fan,"* each of the specific features of the
period is made instrumental to a novel version of the Pisanello
type of clean-cut portraiture, in which the background is compositionally equalized with the figure by detailed presentation of its
components.* The novelty consists in transferring to this type of
portraiture the decorative values of tapestry and of fresco, in
about equal degree, and in impregnating the total form with the
spirit of the eighteenth century French tradition to an extent perhaps greater than in any other picture of this period. The delicate
tones of light blue, green, coral, and yellow with a suggestion of
terra cotta, have a uniform content of light and hence are equal in
color-value. This equality of light-color values, together with an
evenly applied pigment of approximately uniform thickness, imparts a precious, porcelain quality to the ensemble and a delicate
texture to the flesh reminiscent of a bisque doll.

The characteristic tendencies of the period attain their most
distinctive formal organization in *"Bathers"* (164) and *"Girl Plaiting Hair"* (165). The immediate and most lasting impression of
the first-named painting is a strong suggestion of French art of the
seventeenth and eighteenth centuries: the sculpturesque figures
recall the pose and movement of the figures in Girardon's *"Bath
of the Nymphs"* (461), and the chinalike texture of flesh, the
rhythmic gracefulness of the composition, and the general tapestry-
effect of the ensemble are closely akin to those features in Boucher's *"Diana at the Bath"* (508).

The composite effect of the color-organization is that of a succession of light, delicate, mostly pale tones of green, tan, coral,
pink, terra cotta, all more or less permeated with lavender, and
all practically equal in light-content, so that the ensemble is relatively uniform in tonality. This uniformity in color-light content
is responsible for an effect more like that of the pale colorfulness
of eighteenth century French tapestry than of the full-bodied
colorfulness of oil painting. The surface is mat and dry and the
general color has the feeling of extremely delicate pastel, especially in the distant landscape at the upper right, or of enamel

---

* E.g., Pisanello's *"Princess of the Este Family"* (322).

without its gloss. Renoir's usual all-enveloping light, and the dry hard surface of the period are here combined with a more uniformly sharp drawing in the figures than in his other work except in *"Woman with Fan"* and *"Girl Plaiting Hair."*

The accentuated sculpturesque character of the foreground figures is achieved by the incisive linear contour working in conjunction with very solid pigment and subtle light-shadow modeling. The modeling is done by a gradual transition from lavender shadows to light brownish-coral and tan, all of them in broad areas and of relatively equal degree of light-value. Highlights play little if any part in the modeling except in the rendering of hair. The figures, painted in uniformly thick smooth pigment, have the weight and texture, though not the gloss, of heavy chinaware, and they stand out collectively as a sculptured group against a pearly yellowish-green tapestrylike background more loosely drawn, less accentuatedly modeled, and executed in part by perceptible brushwork. The difference in color and in drawing and modeling between foreground and background establishes an adequate contrast between the two areas without detracting from the tapestry-effect of the picture as a whole. Nor is this general effect diminished by the fact that the composition is one of volumes in space with clean-cut intervals between the different masses, as well as between the component parts of these as they enter into rhythmic arabesque-formations.

The compositional arrangement is of a general traditional type much favored by Boucher * and used also in other pictures by Renoir: † the canvas is divided into two approximately equal sections, one of which is a compact grouping of large well-defined volumes, and the other an open area of receding space with small and unaccentuated masses. The interaction of volumes and space, weaving both sections of the canvas into a single compositional fabric, is felt as an integral part of the general tapestry-effect.

The picture represents the most systematic organization of the plastic features of the period, on a large scale. The relationship between figures and landscape is truly organic and the total design is of high decorative value. The rigidly stylistic appearance is a natural result of the studied execution, which extended over a

---

* E.g., Boucher's *"Diana at the Bath"* (508), *"Nest"* (514), *"Sleeping Shepherdess"* (518).

† E.g., *"La Grenouillère"* (31), *"By the Seashore"* (133), *"Children at Wargemont"* (144), *"Green Trees"* (194).

period of several years and involved many preliminary sketches. Natural too, therefore, is the absence of Renoir's usual spontaneity of expression.

"*Girl Plaiting Hair*" embodies even more completely the summation of the characteristics of the 1885-1887 type, since it includes a concentration of the traditional traits then utilized, and also carries to the last degree the exoticism prevalent all through the eighties. The most striking feature is the color-scheme, dominated by terra cotta tones recalling those of Egyptian mural paintings (307), Tanagra figures (310), early Greek vases (313), and Pompeiian frescoes (314). These tones appear also in other pictures of the period but are usually confined to small areas and dominated by other colors.* Here Renoir departs from type by using accentuated light-and-shadow modeling, and this in conjunction with the terra cotta tones and the incisive contour produces an extremely sculpturesque volume like smooth stone in surface and substance. This accentuation of solidity and three-dimensional quality in the figure, and an emphasis upon the identity of the individual units of foliage as well as of space, achieve the most forceful, dynamic composition of volumes in space to be found in any of Renoir's work up to this period.

An active pattern of numerous sharp, clean-cut linear elements coöperates with the other plastic factors to reproduce, in the whole picture, a vivid effect of tapestry, but with the typical two-dimensional quality of the tapestry extended to include accentuated volumes and deep space. This novel tapestry-pattern is the framework for a dramatic interplay of strange colors,† and for a dynamic composition of solid volumes with smooth, hard, marble-like surface. Pattern and color are united in a wealth of rhythmic relationships, in a form in which commensurate powerful decorative and exotic expressive values are merged in a unique ensemble of extraordinary bizarre effect. In spite of the pervasive exotic feeling, the figure is convincingly alive, and the foliage, space and textures likewise ring true as creations with their own high esthetic value.

---

* E.g., "*Woman with Fan*" (160), "*Garden Scene*" (161), "*Washerwoman and Baby*" (163). In "*Redheaded Girl in Yellow Hat*" (157) terra cotta tones also dominate the ensemble but because of the quality of the other colors the total effect is somewhat different from that in "*Girl Plaiting Hair*" (165).

† Green leaves, blue, pink and white garments, terra cotta flesh with green and blue highlights and shadows, deep mahogany hair.

The fact that the 1885-1887 form was not a natural and spontaneous expression of Renoir's personal interests as a whole, appears in the promptness with which it was abandoned after he had
realized its full possibilities. After 1887, the influences which
started in 1879 to alienate him from his natural preoccupation
with the aspects and events of the everyday world had spent their
force, and his efforts thereafter were more in accord with his
natural bent. The period of disquietude which ended in 1887 was,
however, productive of a new and much deeper insight and an
enormous growth in plastic resources. This is clearly apparent in
his subsequent use, in modified versions and various contexts, of
several basic features of the 1880-1887 period. What he had
learned from the experiments was utilized to enrich and make
more personal his handling of the plastic problem which engrossed
him from the late eighties until the end of his career, the problem
of organizing volumes in deep space. Indeed, perhaps the most
significant gain accruing from the whole of the 1880-1887 interlude was Renoir's capacity to render space-volume relationships
with more dynamic power.

LANDSCAPES OF 1888-1893

Very few landscapes were painted by Renoir in the years between 1885 and 1887, at the time he was engrossed in working out
the problem of placing sculpturesque figures in fresco- and tapestrylike settings; only after he had exhausted the possibilities of that
exotic adventure did he resume the painting of landscape. His
work of the late eighties and early nineties in this field elaborates
his use of impressionistic technique, of Oriental color, of pastel
tones, and of Venetian organization of volumes in deep space.
Though all of these appear in every picture, preëminent emphasis
upon each of them individually differentiates the group as a whole
into four general classes.

One type is represented mostly by landscapes painted in 1888 *
in which Renoir further developed his general landscape-form of
the late seventies and early eighties. This type of 1888 landscape
is characterized particularly by a use of the impressionistic technique in accentuated Pissarro-like short brush strokes of juicy

---

* E.g., *"Bougival"* (166), *"Girl with Sheaf of Grain"* (168), *"Red Boat,
Argenteuil"* (170), *"Sunset on the Seine at Argenteuil"* (171), *"Argenteuil
Bridge"* (172).

color, which produce a quivering pattern of small color-units, a sense of active movement, a rugged surface, and a vibrant color-and-light atmosphere. The difference between the earlier landscapes * and this type of 1888 is that, as a consequence of Renoir's experiments in the intervening years, these features have been given a higher degree of formal organization. The flood of sunlight, Oriental color and overtones, and the small brush strokes, which were primarily decorative surface-effects in the earlier work, are organically incorporated in the form and enhance its expressive values. This advance is accomplished chiefly by a more intimate fusion of light and color which makes volumes more solid, textures more convincing, space more essentially realistic, and the atmospheric glow richer, deeper and more pervasive. The form as a whole is of much higher status than that of the sunbathed landscapes by Monet and Pissarro which served as its model: the drawing is firmer and more expressive, and all of the factors, including the pattern of brush strokes, are more firmly integrated by enriched color-light qualities.†

A noticeable improvement over Renoir's previous versions of the same general form is his successful combination of the mid-seventies pattern of alternating light and dark areas with the all-embracing flood of sunlight characteristic of the early eighties. The drama of contrast between light and dark areas is heightened enormously by the increased glow of color in both; it ranges through all degrees of sharpness and subtlety, and embraces contrasts between areas in foreground and background differently colored and illuminated.‡ and between a focus of intensely vivid color and its patterned setting of bright color-areas; § it is diversified by types of movement varying from the sharply angular § to the arabesque.‡

Space-composition shows a corresponding advance over the earlier versions. The more solid color and more ingrained light, in combination with the activity of technique and pattern in heightening contrast, increase the dynamic power of the volume-space relationships. The form of this group of landscapes is still in the

---

* E.g., *"Spring Landscape"* (75), *"Picking Flowers"* (85), *"Capodimonte-Sorrento"* (112), *"Chestnut Tree in Bloom"* (113), *"Railroad Bridge at Chatou"* (120), *"Venice"* (121).
† Cf., e.g., Pissarro's *"Woman at the Well"* (595); Monet's *"Etretat"* (624) or *"Spring Trees by the Lake"* (633).
‡ E.g., *"Bougival"* (166).
§ E.g., *"Red Boat, Argenteuil"* (170).

class of decorative illustration but even as such it marks a step in Renoir's growth, in that the essentials of his earlier forms have assumed a wider reach of plastic functions.*

The second category of landscapes of the period under discussion represents Renoir's development of a theme uppermost in his work of 1885-1887—that is, the organization of solid volumes in dynamic spatial relationships.† During the years extending from 1888 to about 1893 he attacked this problem from many standpoints, each time utilizing one or more of his previous forms as a point of departure. In *"Landscape with Harvester"* (169), the technique and play of light upon colors are less perceptible than in the more definitely impressionistic pictures just discussed, and the contrast between light and dark color-areas is more subdued. A set of simplified and flattened masses, arranged in a quasi-arabesque pattern, is balanced by a series of fully rounded volumes built of solid structural color. By means of simplified drawing, a color-scheme of pastel tones blended with dark colors, and patterns of islands of light and of arabesques—all hinted at in his previous work—Renoir here attains to a personal form which embodies the majesty and infinity of Claude le Lorrain combined with an intime spirit of place like that in Constable and Corot.

The picture represents a step toward Renoir's distinctive version of the Venetian theme of color-volumes in space which he realized more fully a year later in *"Mt. Ste. Victoire"* (175). This fuller realization is attained by an expansion of two of Renoir's own earlier devices—modified impressionistic technique and Oriental color-scheme—to exercise more comprehensive compositional rôles than at any previous stage. The design of *"Mt. Ste. Victoire"* is monumental in conception, the integration of means assures complete plastic conviction, and the bright Oriental color, the opalescent atmosphere, and the shimmering iridescent light of the distant sky and mountain, add great decorative charm. Surface-effects which are primarily decorative in the landscapes of the early eighties ‡ have here become incidental to the development of the basic compositional theme, a pronounced processional movement of solid volumes in colorful space.

In the third type of landscapes of this period, Renoir shifts the

---

* See Analyses, p. 415.
† E.g., *"Landscape with Harvester"* (169) of 1888, *"Mt. Ste. Victoire"* (175) of 1889, *"Apple Vender"* (198) of c. 1890-1891, *"Noirmoutier"* (201) of 1892.
‡ E.g., *"Boating at Bougival"* (124) and *"Beach Scene, Guernsey"* (130).

primary emphasis to qualities of Oriental color and light, and obtains what are perhaps the most daring and bizarre color-ensembles of his entire career.* The movement of volumes in space, so outstanding in *"Mt. Ste. Victoire,"* is retained but that theme is subsidiary to his main purpose of setting exotic colors in daring contrasts and increasing the drama by an all-embracing flood of dazzling sunlight.

The fourth type of these landscapes is represented by pictures in which two sets of colors are used, one with the pastel quality of the 1884 work, the other a combination of positive colors dominated by deep greens or blues. These different sets of colors are used either in two main subdivisions of pale and positive colors to form definite contrasts,† or each set intermingles freely with the other throughout the canvas to constitute a more homogeneous color-light ensemble, with pattern of light and dark in small units.‡ Another feature of the 1884 work which reappears is the tendency of the brush strokes to assume, in parts of the canvas, the character of patches, but the organization of these is not so definitely patterned as in 1884.

To sum up, Renoir's growth in these landscapes of the late eighties and early nineties consisted less in an expansion of his repertoire of traditional forms than in a development of the possibilities of those which he had already acquired. As a group they present a great variety of plastic effects, each a highly individualized version of diverse traditional forms, realized by a distinctive union of the plastic means through the medium of appropriately adjusted technique.

Although all of these landscapes fall in the general class of impressionism, technique is utilized as an instrument to be varied and adjusted as the individual design requires; this variation and adjustment prevails also in the organization in deep space, the degree of structural color, and the adaptation of decorative patterns to expression. According to the design of each, Renoir alternates between solid volumes and flattened masses, loose and tight drawing, bright and subdued color-scheme, expanded and compact space, and between active or diminished pattern of brush strokes and of islands of light. The principal advance resides in the more

* E.g., *"Near Pont-Aven"* (204) of c. 1892.
† E.g., *"Varangeville"* (174) of c. 1888, *"Pasture along the Seine"* (197) of c. 1890, *"View from Montmartre"* (208) of c. 1892, *"Cagnes Landscape with Three Figures"* (209) of c. 1893.
‡ E.g., *"Pont-Aven"* (206) of c. 1892 and *"Picnic"* (211) of c. 1893.

comprehensive plastic function of color and in the expression of more profound human values.

Over and above the spirit of landscape embodied in all these designs, their decorative and expressive values comprise a wide range of variations: abstract feeling of intense drama in *"Bougival"* (166) ; more accentuated effects of linear and color-pattern in *"Red Boat, Argenteuil"* (170) ; processional movement of volumes in *"Mt. Ste. Victoire"* (175) ; relatively emphasized decorative pattern in *"Landscape with Harvester"* (169), *"Noir-moutier"* (201) and *"Picnic"* (211) ; decorative illustration in *"Apple Vender"* (198) ; and rugged reality in *"Pont-Aven"* (206). The progress over earlier periods is thus in imaginative conception as well as in depth of vision and in technical proficiency. The importance of these landscapes as factors in Renoir's development is indicated by the fact that his specific elaborations in them of the impressionistic technique, Oriental color, pastel tones and plastic organization of space-volume relationships, remain as abiding features of his work until the end of his life.

DISRUPTION OF THE 1885-1887 FORM

Renoir's figure-painting at the end of the eighties and during the early nineties represents a transition from his exotic form of 1885-1887 to one more expressive of his natural interest in the profound human values intrinsic to the scenes of everyday life. The reconstruction involved both a general disintegration of the mid-eighties' form and tentative steps in the new direction; only gradually, with perceptible and occasionally abortive effort, did Renoir find his way back to his natural vein and attain the maturity of his powers. The disintegration, and an unsuccessful attempt to break the shackles which had previously bound him, appear unmistakably in *"Daughters of Catulle Mendès"* (167) of 1888.

This picture, a laborious and almost flashy piece of skilful painting, is an assemblage rather than an organization of traits characteristic of the stages between 1880 and 1887. Its most striking feature is the unusual color-scheme in which the earlier Oriental feeling, the pastel-effect paramount in 1884, and the terra cotta tones of the 1885-1887 work assert themselves as such, without submitting to the reorganization indispensable to the creation of a new entity. The intense illumination of the figures repeats the spotlight effects of Renoir's inferior portraits of 1880,* and this, in combination with the tinsel-quality of color and the heavy impasto, produces a disagreeable metallic feeling in flesh and textiles. The technique of generalized brushing, long streaks and bristle marks, is only slightly different from that in the 1884 pictures. Compared to one of the best paintings of that year, *"Children at Wargemont"* (144), the technique not only fails to promote compositional unity but descends into a pervasive heaviness and the feeling of crude paint. The color-chords of the 1884 picture reappear in a richer version but they are mainly isolated decorative units, and the space-composition lacks the earlier fineness of relationships because of the failure of line, light and color to work in unison in the drawing and modeling and in the rendering of space. The form of the 1885-1887 period has disintegrated but Renoir has not as yet succeeded in recasting its components in a new formal organization.

REHABILITATION

Definite signs of rehabilitation appear in *"Bather"* (181), painted in the late eighties, in which features of several forms of the decade are organized by color to yield fine decorative and expressive values and very subtle compositional effects. The rich and varied color-scheme, with its array of blues, reds, orange-yellows, is Renoir's Oriental color-scheme adapted to the painting of flesh. Pastel effects banish the earlier tinsel and excess of overtones and sunlight, and conjoin with the Oriental colors to render flesh with brighter and more varied exotic color and a texture which has the heavy hardness of majolica. The bristle-marked brushwork of 1884 is in evidence throughout and also the sharp linear contour and the sculpturesque volumes of the 1885-1887 period. Solid modeling is accomplished by color of great structural quality, of bright vivid and contrasting tones arranged in patterns of light and dark.

Further steps toward Renoir's more natural expression of the early nineties appear in *"Head of Girl"* (173) of c. 1888 and *"Girl with Straw Hat"* (196) of c. 1890. Emphasis is still upon weight and solidity as in the 1885-1887 form, and surface and texture of flesh retain a certain amount of hardness but linear

* E.g., *"At the Concert"* (101), *"Mademoiselle Grimpel with Blue Ribbon"* (102), *"Mademoiselle Grimpel with Red Ribbon"* (103).

contour is less incisive, the figure is less obtrusively sculpturesque, and the lavender shadows are more firmly ingrained in the structure of the flesh. The accentuated highlights of the later periods begin to appear, and, in *"Girl with Straw Hat,"* the modeling is definitely of the light-and-shadow type. Color in both pictures is more varied and more deeply illuminated than in the 1880-1887 work and begins to acquire the effulgent iridescence which reaches its height in *"Bathers in Forest"* (216) of c. 1897. This increase in the decorative, expressive and compositional functions of color gives a new cast to the space-volume type of design that had developed in 1885-1887: volumes are now more solidly colorful and the intervals between them are felt more as positive color and less as mere distance between objects. While both designs are basically of the space-volume type, the effect of each ensemble is different because of variations in color, in degree of precision of contour, in activity of light and shadow in modeling and in accentuation of voluminousness. The form of *"Head of Girl"* remains closer to the work of the mid-eighties, while that of *"Girl with Straw Hat"* definitely forecasts the mature expression of the late nineties.*

Thoroughgoing disruption of the 1885-1887 form, combined with extensive reorganization, is apparent in *"Girl in Gray-Blue"* (176) of c. 1889, in which tight drawing and sculpturesque modeling have given place to looser contours and volumes interrupted by patterns of accentuated light and shadow. A general decorative pattern of stripes and ill-defined islands of colored light includes the figure as well as the background, and hence unites the two more definitely than in the 1885-1887 form. Lavender shadows, Oriental tones, and some of the 1884 pastel shades are emphasized but in more harmonious relations, and the lavender is given a more general and active function as part of the compositional pattern of stripes and bands.

In a group of pictures painted in the early nineties, the process of transformation is clearly shown.† As a whole they display no such clean-cut form of organization as that of 1885-1887, but rather an experimental variation of method yielding a more thoroughgo-

* See also analytical data, Appendix, p. 417.
† E.g., *"Brunette"* (183), *"Child Reading"* (184), *"Girl Reading"* (186), *"Girl with Glove"* (189), *"Girl with Pink Bonnet"* (190), all of the early nineties, *"Girl in Profile"* (202) of c. 1892, *"Girls at Piano"* (203) of c. 1892, *"Piano Lesson"* (205) of c. 1892, *"Two Girls Reading"* (207) of c. 1892, *"Head of Girl with Hat"* (210) of c. 1893.

ing and personal interpretation of means and traditions. More specifically, they elaborate the means by which Renoir was ultimately enabled to achieve an organization of volumes in deep space, of the same order and on the same monumental scale as the Venetians. Plastically, the 1885-1887 form was already Venetian in its preoccupation with composing solid masses in deep space, but because of the direct sculptural and eighteenth century influences at that time it was not until the nineties that Renoir came to make structural color the supreme instrument both in individual masses and in their compositional integration.

The new form involved the elimination of the exotic qualities of color and texture and the exaggeratedly sculpturesque modeling by which in the mid-eighties masses were given three-dimensional solidity. The process, as always with Renoir, consisted in a gradual modification of all the means previously employed—sharp contour, hard surface, lavender shadows, decorative patterns, tapestry-effects, as well as such earlier means as Oriental color-scheme and brilliant illumination, patterns of light and shadow, and impressionistic technique. None of these was discarded at once or entirely, but each was revised and reunited with the others in a new synthesis more congenial to Renoir, hence more expressive and plastically richer. This period of transition culminated in the 1897 "Bathers in Forest" (216) in which Renoir's fully mature personality went on record in an epic reinstatement and enrichment of all that was most valuable in the classic Venetian form.

The most significant aspect of Renoir's transformation of the 1885-1887 form was a change in drawing and modeling, through which hard tight line was replaced by fluid contour and more organic union of color and light in the achievement of solid volumes. An important factor in softening the contrast between face and background is a narrow band or strip of color within the contour of the face which sometimes plays the part of shadow * and sometimes—usually in profiled heads—appears as a band of light.†
In "Girl in Profile" (202) this band of light, in conjunction with comparatively gradual transition in a pattern of light and shadow mingled with color, lends a greater degree of voluminous and textural reality to the face than that in, for example, "Head of

* E.g., "Girl in Gray-Blue" (176), "Brunette" (183), "Girls' Heads" (187), "Girl with Pink Bonnet" (190).

† E.g., "Child Reading" (184), "Girl with Glove" (189), "Girl in Profile" (202), "Girls at Piano" (203), "Two Girls Reading" (207), "Head of Girl with Hat" (210).

Girl" (173) of c. 1888.* The line of light is looser in *"Child Reading"* (184) and *"Two Girls Reading"* (207), and in *"Girl with Glove"* (189) it is pink in tone and still more subtle, so that the elimination of sharp contour and the union of color and light in rendering volume are even more complete. In *"Head of Girl with Hat"* (210) the contour is looser still with a subtle interfusion of tones between the face and the background, and the two tend to flow into one another. A similar blending of light and color in three-dimensional structure is heightened in *"Girl Reading"* (186) by a pervasive rose suffusion. In *"Girls at Piano"* (203), though the contours are quite precise, modeling depends much less upon them than upon the perfect fusion of color and light, and especially upon the structural quality of the color.

This group of pictures as a whole thus shows a cumulative progress in the use of color in conjunction with light, by which the exotic porcelainlike surfaces and hard contours of 1885 are replaced by an even more real solidity, and in incomparably greater fidelity to the essential texture and feeling of things. Decoratively as well as expressively, Renoir is far in advance of his previous stage, and well on his way to the supreme achievements of the period in *"Bathers in Forest."*

Renoir's color-schemes throughout the early nineties also show a continuous advance upon those used in the early and mid-eighties. Both Oriental color and the lavender shadows of his earlier work reappear, but they are more completely integrated in the general plastic design and color-organization. Oriental colors and general brightness are very evident in *"Girl Reading"* (186), but the illumination is sufficiently controlled to eliminate all glare or quality of tinsel, while actually heightening the rich glow of the color. The light pastel shades and the abundant pink in *"Girls at Piano"* (203) are likewise permeated with generalized Oriental color but all the 1880-1882 assertiveness is replaced by the harmony of bright delicate tones. Throughout this period the color is more varied and brighter than in the seventies, but is free from the stridency and tendency to decorative overemphasis prevalent in the early eighties.

In the 1885-1887 period the total effect of the design, as we

* The change in modeling is forecasted in those pictures of the late eighties in which the accentuation of the contrasts between highlights and shadows emphasizes the three-dimensional quality of the volumes, as, e.g., *"Girl with Basket of Fish"* (177), *"Girl with Basket of Oranges"* (178), *"Girl with Marguerites"* (179), *"Nude Wading"* (182).

have seen, is highly patterned, and very often takes on the appearance of tapestry, as is the case also in much of the typical eighteenth century French painting. Renoir accomplishes this reinterpretation of tapestry-effects largely by means of impressionistic technique. Decorative patterning, often of a similar tapestry-character, persists throughout the nineties, but gradually becomes less artificial, more faithful to the intrinsic quality of what is depicted, so that the decorative and expressive aspects of it tend to coalesce. In *"Girl in Profile"* the background remains essentially a decorative setting but in *"Two Girls Reading"* the loose, floating, vaguely defined volumes of which it is composed have a much more generalized freer tapestry-feeling than in the mid-eighties. In *"Girl with Glove"* the reminiscence of tapestry is vaguer and more generalized still, and in *"Girls at Piano"* it is sublimated to the extreme and the paint is so smooth and evenly applied that there is only the slightest indication of the technical means by which the pattern is secured. Sometimes, as in *"Girl with Glove,"* the decided contrast between the actively patterned background and the more evenly painted figure is heightened by opposing colors in the two parts; but the general trend is toward a more uniform treatment and hence unification through equality of figure and setting. This tendency also reaches its consummation in *"Bathers in Forest"* in the activity, in every part of the canvas, of islands of iridescent light.

THE MID-NINETIES—FURTHER MARKS OF PROGRESS

The general transition is further illustrated by two pictures of the mid-nineties, *"Nude in Brook"* (213) of 1895 and *"Artist's Family"* (214) of 1896. In the 1895 picture the advance is in general looseness of contour, fluidity of color and drawing, and subtlety of relation between all the plastic means. The face is outlined, as in pictures of the early nineties, by a band of pinkish light; elsewhere the body is sometimes sharply differentiated from the background, as in the period of 1885-1887, sometimes so loosely defined that its color flows freely into the surrounding areas. The smooth even paint and mother-of-pearl quality of the flesh recall, in a more generalized form, the eighties, but the interpenetration of light and shadow produces a dappled surface more richly modulated in color and pattern. This dappled surface, in an infinite variety of specific forms and compositional functions,

reappears in most of Renoir's subsequent work; though it is anticipated in the Venetians, Renoir himself elaborated it out of his
earlier mother-of-pearl surface, modified here by an adaptation
of impressionistic technique.

The advance in the form of the picture as a whole is brought
about by the use of color, which is a more integral part than at any
earlier period of both the structure of the flesh itself and the
pattern of light and shadow, and hence achieves more effectually a
delicate but positive three-dimensional solidity, and convincing
textural reality. The previously used pink here pervades the flesh
more fully, and its varied tones are related to similarly varied tones
of lavender to form throughout the picture a series of rich patterns of more or less clearly defined shape. All these interrelated
tonal nuances, the light-and-shadow aspects of which are emphasized in varying degree, not only model the flesh and convey its
natural feeling more fully than hitherto, but they also form a succession of subtle color-contrasts decoratively much richer than the
comparatively monotonous porcelain or mother-of-pearl surfaces
of the eighties. In all parts of the canvas the colors, over and
above their activity as areas in a subtle color-pattern, perform
specific compositional functions; for example, unity between the
figure and setting is established by a rhythmic repetition, in the
background, of the colors and relationships of color which give
the figure its distinctive character.* The composition as an entity
resolves itself into a figure, embodying natural grace and charm,
set against a background of tapestrylike landscape, with light
soft-toned volumes floating rhythmically and gracefully in space.

"Artist's Family" is a composition of masses in deep space, similar in that respect to *"Nude in Brook,"* but more complex and in a
different and more extensive context of adaptations from Renoir's
previous periods. The design is based upon a thematic variation
of accentuated contrasts in all the plastic elements and means; for
example, the general contrast between a foreground of figures and
a background of landscape is heightened by contrasts between the
respective color-areas, in size, shape, spatial organization, degree
of voluminousness, drawing, technique and surface-quality. The
movement of volumes is similar in principle to that in *"Mt. Ste.
Victoire"* (175) of 1889, but the effect is totally different because of the emphasis upon contrast, which determines both the
form as a whole and the execution of all the masses and spatial

* For details see Appendix, pp. 422-423.

intervals. Each of the figures is a distinctive synthesis of features taken from Renoir's prior forms: in the boy, for example, the contour, a less incisive version of that in *"Sailor Boy"* (141) of 1883, is related to more structural color in the flesh, without the porcelainlike surface of the earlier picture. These modifications of antecedent features, as well as other changes in drawing, modeling and flesh-painting, all contribute to the theme of contrast. The picture as an ensemble combines in a novel form two types of composition previously used: the ordering of masses in realistic deep space * and the placing of a group of volumes against a screenlike background of generalized tapestry-quality.† The receding movement of the foreground masses is carried over through the brightly colored hat of the woman into the rhythm of vaguely defined delicate masses in the background and the silvery atmospheric suffusion of the landscape. This suffusion, a more colorful version of Corot's silvery atmosphere, together with the generalized impressionistic technique, imparts to the background a vague tapestry-quality without compromising its character as a delicately rendered natural landscape.

1897—An Epoch in Renoir's Career

"Bathers in Forest" (216), of c. 1897, marks an era in Renoir's progress. Not only is it different from any of his antecedent pictures, but it is his most thoroughgoing plastic reorganization of his more significant prior creations. It is particularly important in Renoir's development in that it represents a very personal interpretation of the highest type of Venetian design, and also because it clearly indicates the direction which he is to follow toward his still greater achievements of the years after 1900. The basic traditional forms upon which Renoir had drawn so abundantly in the past—classic sculpture, eighteenth century French painting, impressionism—are here more fully assimilated than ever before, and they are individualized by a set of plastic features which Renoir himself had largely developed: lavender shadows in modeling, fluid movement of volumes in space, voluminous arabesques, and islands of iridescent light. The organic fusion of the traditional elements with Renoir's own, results in a new, extremely powerful and distinctive form, in which solid, delicate, graceful

* E.g., *"Henriot Family"* (23) of c. 1871.
† E.g., *"Nude in Brook"* (213) of 1895.

volumes of light and color unite in a fluid, all-embracing rhythmic arabesque-movement through colorful atmosphere.

The plastic advance of this picture over Renoir's *"Bathers"* (164) of 1887 lies in the fact that all its color-volumes are more nearly on equal terms in the organization and play much more numerous compositional rôles. Unity is established by the glowing color, the fluid linear pattern, and especially by the rhythmic distribution of the volumes and their coördinated grouping in all parts of the canvas. Each iridescent figure, tree and mass of foliage not only assumes its natural position within the landscape, but moves in rhythmic relationship with all the other volumes and colorful spatial intervals.

The extraordinary decorative features are inseparable parts of the very groundwork of the composition and of its expressive content. The ubiquitous iridescent islands of light, for example, form an integral constituent of the color-ensemble, of the patterns of line, light and shadow, of spatial intervals, and of the substance and surface-texture of the volumes. Similarly, the graceful linear pattern which flows around each figure and unites it with every other, is indissolubly bound up with the large arabesque in space formed by the whole set of volumes—figures, trees, and bushes. This uninterrupted and unifying flow of volumes carries the arabesque-movement into the distant landscape and back again to the foreground; it is varied in its course to confer upon each part of the canvas its own individual kind and degree of movement; and it binds all sections of the picture into a single dynamic volume-and-space organization plastically superior to anything in the Venetians even at their best.* Renoir had previously achieved this general type of design, but in pictures much simpler in scope and without the wealth of plastic and profound human values here present.†

The technique is in the main impressionistic, as in the 1888 landscapes,‡ but it is more highly individualized and given a more extensive and important compositional rôle. For example, the deep rich blue dominating the color-ensemble is enlivened by small brush strokes of contrasting color which make of the blue suffusion a setting for the variegated pattern of extraordinarily rich

---

* Cf., e.g., Titian's *"Entombment"* (352) or Tintoretto's *"Origin of the Milky Way"* (388).
† Cf., e.g., *"Mt. Ste. Victoire"* (175) of 1889.
‡ E.g., *"Bougival"* (166), *"Red Boat, Argenteuil"* (170).

color-chords; the pervasive pattern of brush strokes in the background, with their varied tones of blue, green, red and lavender, simulate the stitchwork of tapestry; throughout the composition, brush strokes build up the solid color-volumes and at the same time, overlapping many of the contours, they soften the edges of objects and contribute to the floating movement of these volumes in space.

Renoir's prior modifications of the impressionistic and Venetian use of light are likewise carried further and endowed with new functions: they transform color into iridescent islands of resplendent and variegated color-chords which, as they move throughout the canvas and vary in luminosity and definitiveness of shape, largely determine the characteristic decorative pattern and general color-organization. The loose contour of the islands contributes to the general fluidity of the drawing, while by virtue of their relations of color and light they enter into the structure of flesh, trees and foliage, modeling each object to the required degree of three-dimensional solidity, and conferring upon each the appropriate textural feeling and surface-effect. Moreover, the iridescent units are so shaped, placed and drawn that they tend to coalesce into continuous sequences, and thus participate in the general compositional arabesque-movement of line, light, color, volumes and spatial intervals. In short, these color-light units, primarily decorative in his work of the early eighties,* have assumed not only more important individual part in drawing and modeling and in rendering the shimmer of atmospheric glow, but a more vital and organic rôle in the rhythmic construction of the dynamic three-dimensional composition.

The arabesque-formation is a motif used by many painters,† and by Renoir himself in his earlier work.‡ Here it is developed to become an integral part of the Venetian form at its best. One element of the general arabesque is the garlandlike plane of flattened foliage across the upper part of the picture; it is suspended like a curtain between foreground and background and extended into an arch by its relation to the branches and trunks of trees on either side. In decorative effect the arch so formed is not unlike that in Paolo Veronese's *"Unfaithfulness"* (408) ; in its

---

* Cf., e.g., *"Girl with Parasol"* (137) of 1883.
† E.g., Claude le Lorrain's *"Village Fête"* (454) and Corot's *"Dancing Nymphs"* (563).
‡ E.g., *"Noirmoutier"* (201) of 1892.

relation to the focus of light in the distance, it also recalls Claude le Lorrain and the Barbizon painters,* as well as Renoir's earlier use of the enframing motif in *"Noirmoutier"* (201) of 1892. In the present picture, however, it becomes a more complex and comprehensive feature; all the figures and most parts of the landscape form sets of volumes grouped and interrelated to repeat throughout the composition the enframing motif of the arch. The sequence of these volumes not only develops a pattern on the plane of the picture proper but at the same time it weaves, more completely than in the work of any previous painter, both the enclosing movement and the arabesque-formation in an all-embracing, intertwining and self-enframing organization.† This enframing motif, in other words, like the drawing, pattern of iridescent islands, and surface-quality, has been so extended in its scope that it unites foreground, middle ground and background, and forms an integral part of the main compositional theme, the arabesque-movement of solid volumes in colored space.

1900 AND AFTER: RENOIR'S EXPANSION OF THE VENETIAN FORM

The foregoing analysis shows that in 1897 Renoir had reached the stage at which he was able to make the Venetian form as a whole serve the process of his development, and to fuse with it what he had previously assimilated from other traditions. From the very start of his career Renoir's form is Venetian in the sense that it is based upon color, but the early pictures represent abstraction and utilization of particular details of the Venetian form, not its recreation and adaptation as a whole. In the pictures of the late sixties, Courbet's version of the Venetian form, which had served Renoir as his point of departure, influences the final result more obviously than do the original sources.‡ In *"Torso"* (52) of c. 1875, the resemblance to Titian is more in the methods employed, in the uses of glazes and loose contours, for instance, than in the quality of the final form. Again, in *"Woman Crocheting"* (76) of c. 1877, the color-chords, modeling and solidity of the hands,

---

* E.g., Claude le Lorrain's *"Landscape with Cattle"* (452) and Théodore Rousseau's *"Edge of Forest of Fontainebleau"* (579).
   † Cf., e.g., Giotto's *"Pietà"* (316), Botticelli's *"Pietà"* (339), Titian's *"Entombment"* (352).
   ‡ E.g., *"Lise"* (5), *"Lise"* (9), *"Mr. and Mrs. Sisley"* (10), *"In Summer"* (11).

recall those features in Titian, but the hands are only a single unit, and are combined with others in which Renoir interprets plastic elements from Rembrandt, Goya and Manet. During the eighties the Italian, including the Venetian, influences are fundamental in his form though these are strongly tempered by the lightness and delicacy characteristic of the eighteenth century French tradition. In the nineties the Venetian characteristics begin to assume outstanding importance, and are more frequently drawn upon than in the earlier periods.

After about 1900 the actual methods are farther from the Venetian but the form at its best contains the very essence of the Venetian tradition, the general qualities of solidity, fulness, richness, reality, dignity, depth and majesty, all of which are embodied in compositions characterized by dynamic relations between solid volumes of color and units of colorful space. Renoir's new form conveys likewise the feeling of life in broad fundamental terms and without recourse to the illustrative detail or decorative emphasis present in the previous stages. The massive solidity of the Venetians acquires the lightness, delicacy and charm always characteristic of Renoir; and at the same time the graceful, fluid linear contours of his earlier work become still looser, as they enter more organically into voluminous and convincing masses. This type of drawing is achieved mainly by color overflowing contour, and involves a further elimination of naturalistic detail and a less conventional demarcation of shapes, particularly noticeable in the rendering of eyes and lips.* The more complete fusion of line with color throughout the composition contributes much to an all-inclusive continuous sweep of solid color-volumes, moving in and out in deep space.

The expressive form of the pictures painted after 1900 has, in addition to the subtlety and charm of his earlier work, an intensity of conviction, an economy of means, a richness in plastic relations, which greatly augment its human appeal. The combination of greater richness of effects and increased economy of means results also in a high type of decorative organization: each of the pictures

---

* This more generalized drawing of facial features makes its appearance in Renoir's work of the late eighties. From the mid-nineties until the end of his career, the progressively increasing simplification results in quite characteristic distortions of the eyes and lips: eyes are usually accentuated dabs of blue or brown placed within the diffusely rendered socket; vaguely shaped lips are indicated by smears of color, most often a deep luscious red.

is not only a more convincing realization of profound human values but is also a richer, more glowing color-ensemble.

COLOR ASSUMES SUPREMACY—THE PREDOMINANCE OF ROSE-RED

In the opening years of the twentieth century this new form had matured and achieved distinctive identity, the study of which may begin with *"Promenade"* (236) of about 1906. This picture marks an advance over *"Bathers in Forest"* (216) in that color exercises an even more important compositional function and becomes also the instrument of a stronger, fuller type of drawing, modeling and spatial organization. The most important factor in this supremacy of color is the glowing rose-red, which dominates the flesh and assumes the particular sensuous quality and plastic function it has in most of Renoir's work of the latest period.

The red in the flesh of figures painted before *"Promenade"* is usually a note of contrast in the complexion, not the dominating factor in its tonality.* In this picture the red, concentrated in certain areas—the cheeks, lips and chin—radiates from them and forms a suffusion which permeates the shadows, lights and highlights, and thus determines the color of the whole flesh. The red suffusion is so pervasive that it prevails even over the colors in the shadows, whether brown, gray or lavender, and melts all the hues into one another by subtle gradations of its tone. As a result the volumes modeled by warm mellow color are more subtly rounded than at any previous stage, and in spite of the exotic color they are also more fleshlike in texture and feeling. This flesh-painting resembles that of Rubens only in the actual shades of color employed; in all plastic essentials it is radically different. Rubens' red lacks the mellowness and the subtlety of tonal gradations which this has, and it is only skin-deep, like a cosmetic; Renoir's is completely structural, and it conveys more fully than Rubens' and with richer decorative content, the textural quality, the glow and warmth of natural flesh. Renoir's flesh-painting is henceforth further in appearance from that in the eighteenth century French painters than before, although its kinship with that tradition never disappears.†

The gain in plastic strength and scope which accrues from

* Cf., e.g., *"Woman at Spring"* (37) of c. 1874-1875, *"Girl with Jumping Rope"* (57) of 1876 or *"Girl in Gray-Blue"* (176) of c. 1889.

† See chapter "Renoir and the Eighteenth Century French Tradition," pp. 208-209.

Renoir's new use of red in the present period may be seen by a comparison between the baby's arm in *"Promenade"* and the shoulder in *"Head of Girl with Hat"* (210) of about 1893. The flesh in both pictures is drawn and modeled by the interaction of light and shadow, color, and linear contour; the difference is that the red in the arm in *"Promenade"* is not only more fully structural, but its overtones dominate the highlights and shadows and convert them into integral parts of the general rose suffusion. The introduction of this decorative element as an inseparable part of the whole form of the arm naturally enriches its expressive value also.

Because of this advance in structural quality, color assumes a more active function in drawing and spatial organization, and these in turn become more comprehensive. The overtones of more solid color, in flowing across the borders of volumes, bestow upon the masses a more realistic three-dimensional quality, and at the same time actually define the units of space in which they are set. This drawing of volume and space by loose contour and overflow of color already appears in Renoir's work of the middle and late seventies * and of the nineties,† but because the earlier color has less structural solidity and less richness, neither the volumes nor the spatial intervals are so substantially defined as in the period after about 1900.

This dual function of color in determining, without perceptible line of demarcation, both the contour of a volume and the space by which the volume is encompassed, establishes the differences in appearance and structure between the baby's head in *"Promenade"* and the head in *"Girl in Profile"* (202) of c. 1892.‡ Each is seen in profile; in the earlier picture the head is less solid, its three-dimensional character is attained mainly by accentuated light and shadow and clean-cut outline, and only its visible half is felt to be fully rounded out, much as in the profile head in Boucher's *"Diana at the Bath"* (508) and *"Venus and Vulcan"* (522) upon which *"Girl in Profile"* may have been patterned. In *"Promenade"* the unseen half of the head also is felt to be solid, and to extend back and repose in a pocket of space that is actually born of tonal relationships in the unbroken flow of color. The effect in the earlier painting is that of a cameo against a screen; in *"Promenade"* a fully rounded Venetian type of mass seems to rest naturally in the

---

* E.g., *"Dancer"* (32), *"Torso"* (52), *"Mussel Fishers of Berneval"* (93).
† E.g., *"Head of Girl with Hat"* (210), *"Nude in Brook"* (213).
‡ Cf. also *"Woman and Child in Field"* (223) of the early 1900's with *"Nude in Brook"* (213) of 1895; or *"Nymphs"* (304) of c. 1918 with *"Girls at Piano"* (203) of c. 1892.

clearly defined and convincingly realized area of deep space around and back of it. The new set of relationships, establishing an indissoluble unity between the volume and the space, makes each of them a definite part of the other, without loss of identity in either.

This uninterrupted flow of color, which at one and the same time defines both volume and space, represents an enormous growth in Renoir's feeling for color-relations and a commensurate technical advance in establishing color as the prime factor in a fuller expression of human values. Indeed, the extension of this type of color-drawing to all compositional purposes is largely responsible for Renoir's enrichment of the Venetian tradition in every aspect.* Its development and elaboration continue throughout the rest of Renoir's life and it becomes perhaps the most important factor in the supreme compositional harmony and expressive force of his latest work.† This increase in the function of color, interpreted in the light of our analysis of the meaning of experience and growth, indicates that color preëminently stimulated Renoir's whole personality and enabled him to expand and systemize the whole store of meanings accumulated from his experience both as a painter and as an intelligent observer of life.

Renoir's imagination was at first impelled by this particular form of color-stimulus to use red in depicting objects of some other natural color.‡ Next he went on through the medium of red to give to color an ampler function by making it an organic part of types of drawing, modeling and composition of higher plastic status than ever before.§ After this goal had been reached, he succeeded in augmenting equally the plastic function of colors other than red.‖ Finally he arrived at a stage at which all the colors work in unison to do what red alone had done at the start.¶ As a result of this unity of action we find, after 1900, color playing a more comprehensive rôle than at any other time in the history of painting. Red, *per se,* was probably a mere incidental in the complicated process of growth: it is likely that any other color would have

---

* Sée chapter "Renoir and the Venetians," pp. 175-176.
† At times—e.g., *"Missia"* (235), *"Woman Reading"* (238), *"Girls in Garden"* (290)—the overflow of color in the adjoining space appears as a line which parallels and emphasizes the shape of the object, but unlike Tintoretto's use of line around volumes, Renoir's line is part and parcel of the continuity of color from volume to space.
‡ E.g., the flesh in *"Coco"* (229) of c. 1903.
§ E.g., *"Promenade"* (236) of c. 1906.
‖ E.g., blue in *"Antibes"* (269) of c. 1915-1917.
¶ E.g., *"Two Figures in Landscape"* (296) of c. 1917-1919.

served the same purpose. Renoir's predilection for red is revealed by the fact that in most of his late pictures red dominates the ensemble, even when, as often happens, other colors are physically present to the same extent as the red itself.*

The advance in Renoir's mastery of color in *"Promenade"* consists, as we have seen, in its more fully structural use, and in its extension over boundaries to unite objects and space in an unbroken color-continuity. Color, moreover, in its interaction with light produces overtones which coalesce and form a general suffusion. This suffusion dominates the flesh and renders the masses, intervals of space, and relations between space and volumes more imaginatively and with greater esthetic effect than at any previous stage of Renoir's work. In numerous other pictures of this period this type of drawing by color, and the resulting color-suffusion, is extended to the entire composition, usually in conjunction with a corresponding extension in the plastic rôle of the characteristic red. In all, plastic devices previously developed such as the pattern of brush strokes, Oriental color-effects, islands of light, dappled surface of flesh, and the effect of tapestry, are amplified in compositional scope by means of color, with resulting enrichment and reënforcement of the design as a whole. The diversified compositional purposes served by this advanced form of drawing and emphasis upon red are illustrated in a group of pictures painted in the decade beginning with 1900.

TYPES OF RED PICTURES †

These late red pictures present so many variations in design as to elude any systematic classification, but they fall into two main types. In the first, large areas of deep rich red alternate with other areas, equally large, of contrasting colors, but red notes in the other areas give rise to a suffusion which makes red overwhelmingly dominant in the total color-ensemble.‡ This suffusion, which determines the composite color-effect and is an important factor in the extremely fluid drawing, distinguishes pictures of the type in question from those of the Venetians and Rubens in which there are also large areas of red. In the second type, the red, instead of being

---

* E.g., *"Bathing Group"* (285) of 1916, *"Nymphs"* (304) of c. 1918.
† E.g., *"Coco"* (229) of c. 1903, *"Embroiderers"* (233) of c. 1904, *"Writing Lesson"* (234) of c. 1905, *"Missia"* (235) of c. 1906, *"Woman Sewing"* (256) of c. 1910.
‡ E.g., *"Coco"* (229) and *"Writing Lesson"* (234).

concentrated in large areas, filters into all parts of the canvas in the form of delicate tones, chiefly of rose.* The most important agent of this infiltration is light, which creates not only an extensively varied set of tonal gradations of red but also a generalized ruddy iridescence that contributes much to the dominance of that color. The swimming suffusion thus produced in each of the two types is, in principle, a version of the Venetian glow, enhanced in appeal by color more varied and more luminous, sparkling and alive.† The pictures of the second type are linked more definitely by their pearly tone, lightness and delicacy, with the eighteenth century French tradition.

These two general methods of employing red, and their use in fundamentally different compositions, may be illustrated by five pictures—*"Coco"* (229), *"Writing Lesson"* (234) and *"Woman Sewing"* (256), of the first general type mentioned, and *"Embroiderers"* (233) and *"Missia"* (235), of the second. In *"Coco,"* the red areas vary in shade from mahogany and reddish brown to lavender-pink, and are so distributed and interrelated that the area furthest in color from positive red functions as an element of contrast. The red, in other words, provides a theme of contrast in the design by the interplay of its greatly varied tones, each of which performs specific compositional activities. In the red background, for instance, Renoir reinterprets, with more nuances of color and space and much richer surface, Velásquez' subtle rendering of receding space.‡ This picture illustrates also the immense advance made by Renoir over Rubens in the use of the same color. In the latter's *"Baron Henri de Vicq"* (416), for example, the red is less varied in tone and less structural in function, and the large red area in the background, which sets off the head by vivid color-contrast, serves merely as a screen just back of the head instead of carrying the volume over continuously into the encompassing space.

The red in Renoir's *"Writing Lesson"* is primarily the instrument of a composition of emphatic and dramatic color-contrasts. The slight infusion of red in the large area of highly iridescent shimmering silver-green-blue, does not diminish the force of this area as an element of dramatic contrast in the color-composition

---

* E.g., *"Embroiderers"* (233) and *"Missia"* (235).
† See chapter "Renoir and the Venetians," pp. 169-171.
‡ Cf., e.g., Velásquez' *"Infanta Marguerite"* (446).

as a whole; nor does the large expanse of contrasting color deprive the picture of its predominantly red tonality.*

The ensemble in *"Woman Sewing"* is dominated by the extensive red background but the red differs from that in the last two pictures both in sensuous quality and in compositional function. A lavender-orange tone suffuses the whole picture as an enveloping atmosphere in which delicate, luminous, lightly rendered volumes gently move. The suffusion changes subtly from red to orange-red and to yellow, and each of these colors is tinged with nuances of lavender, sometimes so accentuated as to make an extremely dramatic contrast, such as that between the red background and the lavender-black hair, sometimes so attenuated that the contrast is very subtle, as it is between the pearly-lavender blouse and the pinkish-purple skirt. The extreme fluidity of the color, the very gradual transition from light to shadow and the light pastel and water color quality of the tones impart delicacy to the volumes, subtlety to space, filminess to the textiles, and an airy floating feeling to the all-inclusive lavender-rose suffusion. This painting is midway between the type in which the use of red in large areas suggests Rubens,† and that type in which qualities of eighteenth century painting predominate.‡

"Missia" (235) belongs to the second type of Renoir's red pictures, and in it the red is adapted to a compositional theme of rosette-formation of volumes in space. The fluidity of its rose suffusion and its delicate modulations with purple, orange and coral, spring from intimate interpenetration of color and light, and flow of color over contours. Its overtones spread throughout the composition and, by blending with the color-pattern, cause all its differently colored units to melt into a rose-red ensemble. The blending of multi-colored units is aided by a scarcely perceptible pattern of brush strokes which also produces a subtly dappled surface. These areas of iridescent dappled surface unite in a vibrant pattern, and this, in conjunction with the rhythmic movement of the volumes, transfers to the general rosette-organization the qualities of a flower or a bouquet.

"Embroiderers" (233) is also of the second group of red pictures and in it too the red is used in developing a rosette-motif as a compositional theme. The theme involves vivid contrasts in drawing,

---

* For analytical data see Appendix, p. 427.
† E.g., *"Coco"* (229) and *"Writing Lesson"* (234).
‡ E.g., *"Embroiderers"* (233) and *"Missia"* (235).

modeling, space-composition, pattern, technique and the traditional ideas drawn upon. The red, in addition to its agency in developing this theme, serves numerous other purposes: it tinges contrasting colors, enters into more or less pronounced patterns, builds up volumes, yields textural qualities of flesh and of stuffs, and conveys the illusion of space. A similar diversity prevails in the manner in which the rose-colored suffusion is obtained in the different parts of the picture: by admixture with much light in the background; by overtones of red and extremely loose drawing in the standing girl at the back; by intermingling of vague brush strokes in the blue area at the lower left. Not only do the individual tones of rose contrast with each other in hue and function, but the red in its entirety both tinges and contrasts with the two other predominating colors—blue and ivory—in the color-design. The interpenetration of these tones throughout the ensemble converts the entire canvas into what is practically a pattern of color-chords.

EXPANSION AFTER 1900 OF THE LANDSCAPE FORMS OF 1888-1893

Our discussion has shown that Renoir's landscapes painted between 1888 and 1893 represented an expansion of his work done in that field in the late seventies and early eighties, and that the development was accomplished by elaboration of his prior use of impressionistic technique, of Oriental color, pastel tones and the Venetian space-volume type of organization. After 1900 Renoir painted a large number of landscapes of this same general type, but color, in these, is not only more solidly structural than before, but by its flow over contour unites objects and space in an uninterrupted color-continuity. Color and light by their more intimate interaction than at any previous time produce a general color-suffusion which increases still further the all-embracing fluidity of rhythms, particularly those of volumes and space-intervals.

Here, as is common with Renoir, motifs previously used are reënforced in both their decorative and expressive aspects by a more comprehensive use of color. In *"Le Cannet"* (225) of c. 1902, the Corot form utilized by Renoir in the seventies has grown to the stature of a Venetian space-volume composition, mainly through the medium of more generalized drawing associated with richer and more solidly structural color.* In *"Woman and Child under*

* Cf., e.g., *"La Grenouillère"* (31) of c. 1873.

Tree" (255) of c. 1910, the enframing device employed in *"Noir-moutier"* (201) of 1892 is woven into still another organization of solidly colorful volume-space units with especial emphasis upon a contrast between a large expanse of colorful space and an area of compactly grouped volumes. In *"Girl at Gate"* (267) of c. 1914, an accentuated pattern of iridescent islands of light, together with a multicolored suffusion of pearly tones and bright red, becomes the medium through which loosely rendered volumes and spatial intervals are exploited in a very individual and highly picturesque manner. *"Farm House"* (288), of c. 1917-1919, is a symphony of moving color-volumes. The drawing is so generalized that only bare essentials of representation are hinted at; color flows over masses into space and vice versa, and creates an all-inclusive suffusion through which the masses of trees and foliage appear to revolve. The rhythmic flow of color-volumes is brought into equilibrium by the richly varied, centrally located house, the color-focus of the organization.

In practically all of these late landscapes Renoir uses one or more aspects of impressionistic technique, Oriental color-scheme, and fluid color-drawing.

DISTINCTIVE T PE OF LANDSCAPE AFTER 1900

After 1900 Renoir painted numerous landscapes in which the local characteristics of houses, trees and sunlight of the Midi are utilized in conjunction with islands of colored light to achieve a distinctive type of design.* The islands are more definitely shaped than heretofore and they function more specifically as planes of accentuated light related to planes of equally colorful shadows. These multicolored planes participate actively in the drawing and modeling, and by their interaction produce a lively color-movement as well as an iridescence of surface. The sharpness of contrast between the different colors and between the light and shadow is responsible for a pattern of colored planes more dramatic and accentuated than usual, a new type of patterned design well fitted to embody the natural appearance and feeling of the sun-swept landscape and houses of the Midi. Renoir varies this general form by laying primary stress either upon the angular planes of the buildings or upon the curvilinear foliage of the trees and bushes,

* E.g., *"Cagnes"* (219), *"Houses at Cagnes"* (220), *"View of Cagnes"* (222), all of the early 1900's, and *"Garden of the Post Office at Cagnes"* (271) of c. 1915-1917.

so that the patterns range from a blocklike angularity suggestive of Cézanne's * to a general sinuous fluidity.†

The general type of color-pattern is differentiated in particular pictures by the predominance of one color over others, especially in the areas of multicolored shadow, and in a lesser degree in the rest of the picture.‡ The characteristic suffusion is born of the interaction of the color prevailing in the shadows with the overtones of light and color in the illuminated areas, and it is studded with notes of sparkling iridescence resulting from the permeation of the light-areas with various tones of pink, yellow, blue, tan, or green. A great amount of pinkish red filters into the prevailing color and brings these pictures within the general category of red paintings represented by *"Missia"* (235). The appealing color quality of the ensembles is due to a tempering of the bright colors, assertive overtones and brilliant sunlight of Renoir's Oriental color-scheme by the delicacy of the pastel effects attained in the 1884 period § and used in some of the landscapes of the late eighties and early nineties.||

PAINTING OF NUDES AFTER 1900 ¶

The painting of nudes, always a preoccupation of Renoir's, became after about 1900 a frequent medium for varied interpretations of the Venetian form, all executed with the economy of means characteristic of his late work and in a form very different from the nudes of his previous periods. The earlier flesh usually contained a greater variety of definitely contrasting colors—ivory, blue, pink, green, yellow, lavender-brown—which made up patterns.** In the later pictures the colors are more nearly tonal modifications of each other, such as lavender-pink and pinkish lavender, brownish red and reddish brown, and their relationships establish

* Cf., e.g., Renoir's *"Houses at Cagnes"* (220) with Cézanne's *"Gardanne"* (619).

† E.g., *"View of Cagnes"* (222) and *"Garden of the Post Office at Cagnes"* (271).

‡ In *"Houses at Cagnes"* (220), for example, the predominant color is golden yellow; in *"View of Cagnes"* (222) a delicate blue; in *"Garden of the Post Office at Cagnes"* (271) it is rose.

§ E.g., *"Grape Gatherers Resting"* (147) and *"Summer"* (150).

|| E.g., *"View from Montmartre"* (208).

¶ E.g., *"Judgment of Paris"* (240) of 1908, *"Bather Drying Herself"* (243) of c. 1909, *"Bust of Nude"* (244) of c. 1909, *"After the Bath"* (247) of 1910, *"Reclining Nude"* (252) of c. 1910, *"Nude, Back View"* (259) of c. 1911, *"Psyche"* (260) of c. 1911.

** E.g., *"Torso"* (52) of c. 1875, *"Nude in Brook"* (213) of 1895.

a gradual flow, a subtle rise and fall of tone, rather than a pattern of variously colored units.

The earlier ensemble, despite the greater number of colors, is less colorful and the flesh less realistic in feeling; the later flesh is more vivid and glowing, more varied in its decorative effect, and it has more of the natural feeling and textural quality of actual human flesh. This testifies to Renoir's greater command of color at the later stage, his ability to select just those tones and relations which, with lesser variety, lesser quantity of material, yield a more impressive final result. Not only flesh, but textiles and landscape also are rendered with increased effectiveness by the reduced palette of this period, as is apparent, for example, when the landscape-setting of Renoir's late nudes is compared with even so colorful a picture as the 1878 *"Pourville"* (80).

The great advance in the flesh-painting is due primarily to the more organic use of color. This is made strikingly evident by a comparison between the volume of the thigh in *"Nude in Brook"* (213) of 1895 and that in *"Nude, Back View"* (259) of c. 1911. The former is a solid cylindrical volume, the roundness and solidity of which are due largely to a pattern of light and shadow, and only partly to structural color. In the thigh of the later nude the part played by light and shadow is subsidiary to the action of color in building up the substance of the flesh, the full roundness of its volume, and its more natural textural appearance. Modulated and intermingled tones of rose and lavender are the major factors in creating a texture, solidity and weight which are felt as belonging inherently to the thigh as a thing in itself, apart from the perceiver's associative memory connecting it with the human body.

A parallel increase in essential realism appears even when the design embodies to a pronounced degree the exotic 1885-1887 frescolike surface and sculpturesque solidity or the eighteenth century French qualities. These qualities are much closer in the earlier work to what they were in the sources from which Renoir took them; in the late nudes they are more organically incorporated in the general color-organization, and hence greatly enriched.* As a

---

* Cf., e.g., the fresco-quality in *"After the Bath"* (247) of 1910 and *"Caryatids"* (248 and 249) of c. 1910 with that in *"Washerwoman and Baby"* (163) of c. 1886; the sculpturesque solidity in *"Bust of Nude"* (244) of c. 1909 with that in *"Bathers"* (164) of 1887; and also the eighteenth century delicacy and grace in *"Gabrielle Arising"* (245) of c. 1909 with that in *"Woman with Fan"* (160) of 1886.

result of this growth, qualities which in the earlier period were primarily bizarre decorations have acquired full expressive conviction, while their exoticism has been replaced by the abstract feeling of voluptuousness, conveyed by means of color. Renoir's form, in brief, has become fully Venetian in plastic status.

These late nudes exemplify Renoir's intense interest at this period in the forms of the great Venetians—Giorgione, Titian and Paolo Veronese—and of classic sculpture as this was interpreted by Michelangelo, Raphael, Rubens, Poussin and the eighteenth century French painters. Throughout his entire late work Renoir levied upon all these sources, recreating what he took from them in forms richer in plastic content. From them came in germ the red, the lavender, the pronounced pattern of light, the loose fluid contours and the dappled surface, all of which are blended with his own earlier plastic devices, and transfigured in his new form. As an example of the way in which old means are turned to new uses, we may consider the overhanging mass of foliage which appears as a compositional feature in pictures belonging to various stages of his career. In the seventies and eighties, the plastic status of such masses is mainly that of decorative illustration; * in the paintings after 1900, the corresponding masses are more solid and voluminous and they have acquired a compositional function commensurate with the richer and fuller, though more generalized, character of the other components.

By his varied treatment of such units of foliage Renoir largely determines, in a distinctive series of designs, the particular identity of form in each; and conversely, in each organization the unit itself undergoes transmutation in all its aspects in accord with the design as a whole.† The masses of foliage, compared with those in Renoir's earlier work, are not only more assertive individual color-volumes and more expressive of the natural qualities of trees and leafage, but they are also more dynamically and integrally related to the other objects and the figure in which the space-composition is focussed. Compositional unity of figure and background is not of course new in Renoir's work, but the more fully expressive form

* E.g., *"Henriot Family"* (23), *"Meditation"* (49), *"Girl with Parasol"* (137).

† The following pictures are typical of the use of this foliage-unit: *"Judgment of Paris"* (240), *"Bather Drying Herself"* (243), *"Bust of Nude"* (244), *"After the Bath"* (247), *"Reclining Nude"* (252), *"Nude, Back View"* (259), *"Psyche"* (260).

which it takes here points not to a change in this or that plastic feature, but to an actual enlargement in the scope of the design upon which individuality is thus conferred.

Each of the pictures into which the foliage-unit enters represents a different version of the Venetian type of dynamic space-composition; that is, in each the essentials of the Venetian form are varied, as is also the use of red and any other plastic factor taken from the past; consequently, while all are Venetian in essence, each contains its own creative combination of traditional traits. *"Judgment of Paris"* (240), although probably inspired by Rubens' composition of similar title in the London National Gallery (430), represents a type in which Rubens' version of the Renaissance form is definitely subsidiary to Renoir's adaptation of elements more suggestive of Poussin, Claude le Lorrain and the eighteenth century painters. It is closer than the other Renoirs of this type to both the Venetian and the eighteenth century French traditions; for example, the intensity of the red is diminished to the point that the flesh has a suggestion of the familiar brown of the Venetians; also the extreme delicacy and fluidity of the composition recalls the general feeling of the work of Fragonard, Boucher and Watteau.*

"After the Bath" (247) embodies in the general Venetian form the surface-quality of the Florentine fresco-painters, the classic feeling of Michelangelo and Raphael, and the swirling surging movement of Tintoretto and Rubens; † *"Nude, Back View"* (259) presents an individual version of elements taken from Giorgione, Titian, Tintoretto, Rubens and Claude le Lorrain;‡ *"Bust of Nude"* (244) is a novel combination of features characteristic of classic sculpture, the Venetians and Rubens; § *"Psyche"* (260) is a reintegration of the colorfulness, voluptuousness and swirl of Ru-

---

* For kindred analytical data see Appendix, p. 428.

† Cf., e.g., Giotto's *"Scenes from Life of St. Francis"* (317), Piero della Francesca's *"Reception of Queen of Sheba by Solomon"* (326), Benozzo Gozzoli's *"Journey of the Magi"* (327), Michelangelo's *"Original Sin"* (341), Raphael's *"Madonna: Belle Jardinière"* (374), Tintoretto's *"Susannah at the Bath"* (392), Rubens' *"Bathsheba at the Spring"* (417) or *"Ixion Deceived by Juno"* (429).

‡ Cf., e.g., Giorgione's *"Concert in the Open Air"* (343), Titian's *"Nymph and Shepherd"* (359) or *"Venus and Adonis"* (365), Tintoretto's *"Susannah at the Bath"* (392), Rubens' *"Rape of Leucippus' Daughter"* (432), Claude le Lorrain's *"Landscape with Cattle"* (452).

§ Cf., e.g., *"Venus of Milo"* (312), Giorgione's *"Concert in the Open Air"* (343), Rubens' *"Rape of Leucippus' Daughter"* (432).

bens; * *"Reclining Nude"* (252) recalls the classic feeling of Giorgione and Titian brought nearer to earth in a more real and lifelike expression, and with the dynamic relations between volumes and space enhanced in esthetic appeal by the gentle sweeping movement in figure and background; † *"Bather Drying Herself"* (243) carries Venetian flesh-painting to infinitely greater heights of color than in any other picture of this series or in the Venetians themselves, in a design which combines, in an original fashion, Titian's drawing with Tintoretto's dramatic rhythms.‡ In all of these pictures, Renoir does with the Venetian form what the Venetians had done with the Florentine: he brings it closer to everyday life, and yet does not lose the poetry or epic quality of the originals.

STILL-LIFE AND GENRE PICTURES AFTER 1900

Renoir's still-lifes § and genre paintings || of the late period under discussion, like his figure compositions, are versions of the Venetian form expressed in Renoir's own idiom, but with elements taken from other traditions, more particularly Chardin and the Dutch. The features derived from the Dutch, Chardin and Manet, which in *"Breakfast"* (27) of c. 1872 were separately identifiable,¶ are now inextricably welded in the form; for example, the pattern of highlights which, as in Chardin,** contributes to the compositional relationships of volumes in deep space, is now more strongly bolstered up by color, more intimately blended with it and more deeply wrought into the substance of each object. Similarly, in comparison with the prototypes in the traditions and with his own

* Cf., e.g., Rubens' *"Ixion Deceived by Juno"* (429), *"Peace and War"* (431), *"Rape of Leucippus' Daughter"* (432).
† Cf., e.g., Giorgione's *"Sleeping Venus"* (344), Titian's *"Venus and Organ Player"* (368).
‡ Cf., e.g., Titian's *"Venus and Adonis"* (365), Tintoretto's *"Susannah at the Bath"* (392).
§ E.g., *"Strawberries and Almonds"* (221) of the early 1900's, *"Fruit on White Cloth"* (241) of c. 1908, *"Apple and Pear"* (242) of c. 1909, *"Fruit"* (250) of c. 1910, *"Two Pomegranates"* (254) of c. 1910, *"Apples"* (262) of c. 1911-1912, *"Bananas and Oranges"* (264) of c. 1913, and *"Fruit and Cup"* (265) of c. 1913.
|| E.g., *"Tea Time"* (257) of 1911, *"Cup of Chocolate"* (263) of c. 1912, *"At the Café"* (266) of c. 1914.
¶ See chapter "Renoir and the Eighteenth Century French Tradition," p. 208.
** E.g., Chardin's *"Bottle of Olives"* (497), *"Still-Life"* (503), *"Study of Still-Life"* (504).

earlier works, Renoir renders more convincingly the textural surface-qualities characteristic of Dutch still-life. His late color has become so completely structural that it gives reality to attributes of subject-matter which Dutch painting renders imitatively by play of light and color upon the surface.* A like advance toward a fuller expression results from an expansion of the function of the Manet-like brush strokes: the color which they carry and the pattern which they form, are now so fully integrated in the form that the decorative color-pattern is a firmly organic part of the Venetian type of composition of solid color-volumes in colored space.

Compared to Renoir's earlier versions of similar subject-matter each unit in this late form, whether volume, spatial interval, or patch of light, has both a more positive individuality and a more active plastic function; that is, all factors are more nearly equivalent compositionally and the form as a whole is more decorative as well as more fully expressive. This added richness and strength arises mainly from the fluid drawing by juicy, luscious, glowing, structural color, which reënforces and binds together every part and aspect of the form. A feeling of eighteenth century French delicacy pervades the design and adds charm to its robust strength.

Within this group of still-life and genre paintings, widely varied use of the plastic means creates as diversified a range of pictorial effects as those in the figure-pieces. In *"Apples"* (262), depth of color reënforced by a weighty pervasive color-suffusion makes the objects ponderous as well as solid, and their progression through space is felt as a throbbing sequence of weighty, full-bodied colorful masses. Contrasting with the latter, *"Fruit"* (250) is less ponderous, the glow of color assumes more of the nature and function of light, and the compositional sequence is a slow diagonal sweep or downward flow. The identity of the form is due mainly to the clean-cut space with its preponderant content of light, as distinct from the vivid atmospheric glow and deeper overtones which fill the space in the preceding picture. Another variation upon the same general type of design is realized in *"Fruit and Cup"* (265) through an adaptation of the familiar Oriental color-scheme which imparts an exotic color-intensity and brightness. In these still-lifes in general, the plastic, decorative and expressive values are so richly concentrated in each unit and at the same time so closely woven into a network of relationships that the plastic value

---

* E.g., Pieter de Hooch's *"Interior of a Dutch House"* (463), Juriaan van Streek's *"Still-Life"* (468).

or identity of each part of the subject-matter heightens the power and fulness of the form as a whole.

"Cup of Chocolate" (263), a genre picture of about the same period as the still-lifes, shows the same Venetian principle of volume-space organization but on a larger scale and with a different range of human values. The plastic identity and spatial distinctness of the individual units are even more emphasized than in the pictures just discussed: the bunch of violets, the chocolate pot, the cup-and-saucer and the component parts of the figure, are each a solid colorful unit, with clear identity and well-defined position in space; and this motif is echoed in the background-drapery by the volumes of its folds separated by bands of subtly rendered space. The intricate relationships between these variegated color-volumes, spaced at greatly diversified intervals, engender a pulsating movement of color which embraces still-life, figure and background. The form in its entirety conveys the intentness, reflectiveness and repose of the figure, and the intimacy, charm and essential reality of a familiar episode of everyday life, enriched by the poetry of Renoir's own vision.*

Another adaptation of the Venetian tradition to a version of the Dutch genre scene is illustrated by *"Tea Time"* (257). Here the main compositional theme is one of dramatic contrasts in the placing of volumes, the color-areas, the patterns, and the use of light. The specific character of the design is determined chiefly by a very dramatic pattern of streaks of highlights, which intensifies the contrasts between the large areas of green, ivory and red in the color-pattern. The highlights extend in deep space and in all directions and are an enriched adaptation of Renoir's familiar islands of light to a particular rendering of textiles and foliage. This very active pattern of variously colored highlights, while extraordinarily decorative, is fundamentally a colorful reëxpression of Tintoretto's dramatic patterns of color, light and line, combined with the textural quality and sheen of stuffs in Terborch and the eighteenth century French painters in a form which conveys the human feeling associated with genre scenes, and the abstract values of dynamic space-composition.

The part played by the large area of vivid red in the color-organization recalls the dramatic effect achieved by the use of a similar color-focus in *"Red Boat, Argenteuil"* (170) of 1888 and *"Girl with Glove"* (189) of the early nineties. The plastic advance

* See also Analysis, pp. 429-430.

in *"Tea Time"* is that the red unit itself and every other part of the color-pattern is a more positive, solid volume, and is placed more definitely in three-dimensional space.

Color-Suffusion

Our discussion has shown that Renoir's ability to make color serve an ever-increasing variety of functions had reached, in the early years of the present century, the stage of development wherein color is the very substance of volumes and spatial setting. Color takes command, as it were, of the total design by becoming the agent of coördination of all the plastic means and compositional factors. The ubiquitousness of the color, its brightness and its fusion as an integral part of light, result in a wealth of multi-colored overtones which coalesce and form an all-embracing color-suffusion. A color-suffusion, by virtue of its intrinsic character, has always a certain amount of decorative, expressive and compositional value. Decorative, because it spreads a large quantity of color over the canvas; expressive, because it gives to the objects which it envelops certain aspects which materially exist—fluidity, softness, floating quality, enclosure in a surrounding medium, mysterious or magical character; compositional, because of the color continuity which it establishes between units diversely shaped, patterned, colored and located.

Color-suffusion is not in itself a novelty: it had been used by the Venetians, Claude le Lorrain, Poussin, the Barbizon painters, the impressionists; in fact, it is these traditional forms that provide points of departure for many of Renoir's own designs. Even in his early work color-suffusion played an important part as one of the instruments of compositional unity, whether as a set of over-tones,* interpenetrating colors,† or as predominance of one color over the others.‡ As his form developed the suffusion became more and more an integral part of drawing, modeling and space-composition, and a decisive factor in determining the individuality of each design.§ After about 1910, at the apogee of his career, the color-suffusion becomes one of the principal agents in the thorough-

---

* E.g., *"Capodimonte-Sorrento"* (112).
† E.g., *"Pourville"* (80).
‡ E.g., *"Torso"* (52) and *"Mademoiselle Jeanne Durand-Ruel"* (59).
§ Cf., e.g., *"Bathing Group"* (285) of 1916 with *"Bathers in Forest"* (216) of c. 1897, and *"Bathers"* (164) of 1887.

going plastic integration of Renoir's individual interpretations of numerous traditional forms.

The elements basic to each of the methods employed earlier are recognizable as vestigial traces in the new synthesis which constitutes the fully matured suffusion. The overtones which emanate from the volumes are themselves organized as quasi-solid color-masses which fill the surrounding space with a radiant, richly colorful atmosphere. Space thus becomes positive color and has almost the substantiality of tangible material.* The colored units of space echo the substantial solidity of the volumes themselves and both volume and space arrive at approximate compositional parity; because of this parity the Venetian type of dynamic space-composition achieves a more complex, a more rhythmic and a more continuous color-movement than in even the best work of Giorgione, Titian or Tintoretto.† The suffusion, in other words, is an entity with many-sided aspects, each of which exercises varied plastic, expressive, decorative and compositional functions in different pictures. A study of Renoir's work in the last decade of his life resolves itself largely into a differentiation of the various ways in which the color-suffusion, related to his fluid generalized color-drawing, acquires constructive activity and functions in its own right.

The gradual development by which Renoir's color-suffusion passed from its early simplicity to its eventual multiplicity of compositional functions was due chiefly to the increased expressiveness of drawing attendant upon looser contour, freer interflow of color between volume and space, and more extensive elimination of representative detail. Technically, this was accomplished by confining the function of brush strokes to the rendering of essentials, and by using thin washes of pigment which by their interpenetration produce an uninterrupted flow of multicolored tones from area to area. In *"Antibes"* (269) of c. 1915-1917, for example, a single brush stroke draws simultaneously parts of two adjacent bushes and carries the color of one bush over into that of the other. The widespread adoption of this technique naturally brings about interpenetration of color and extends the suffusion to all parts of the canvas.

Color-suffusion often determines not only the general character

* A corresponding effect in music is the orchestral "color" of Beethoven or César Franck.
† See also chapter "Renoir and the Venetians," pp. 170-172.

of a picture but also its distinctive individuality. For instance, the preponderance of blue in the suffusion in *"Girl in Landscape"* (268) and *"Antibes"* establishes a common color-theme, but in each picture the blue suffusion fulfills a different plastic purpose: as a swimming pearly atmosphere in *"Antibes"* it renders the epic grandeur and majesty of Claude le Lorrain with greatly increased decorative value; in *"Girl in Landscape"* it participates in the design by contributing to the specific character of a figure in repose, to the generalization of the landscape-setting, and to the merging of figure and background in a composite rhythmic pattern of voluminous bands of fluid color.

The ways in which color-suffusion gives new meaning and distinction to plastic devices evolved earlier in Renoir's career may be illustrated by a brief study of the color-scheme in two late paintings, *"Woman with Black Hair"* (261) and *"Fruit and Bonbonnière"* (270), each representing a sublimated version of the Oriental color-scheme. In the latter, the glowing iridescent suffusion, while dominated by the blue, contains also intermingled contrasting overtones of orange, yellow and red, which emanate from the large area occupied by the fruit. These Oriental color-effects, mainly decorative in their earlier status, are here an organic part of the structure of the solid volumes and of the all-inclusive atmospheric glow.* The suffusion in *"Woman with Black Hair"* is dominated more by a single tone, bright red, and is dramatically punctuated by a large area of black and a vivid pattern of effulgent highlights. The suffusion here becomes a medium for rendering a color-effect reminiscent of Delacroix, but with more convincing realization of volumes, space, flesh and textiles, and a more complete integration of the decorative pattern in the form as a whole, than in either the work of Delacroix or Renoir's earlier effects reminiscent of Delacroix.† Everything in the picture is illuminated and knit together by a circumambient glow of rich, forceful, warm color, and the alternating accentuation and diminution of the density of the suffusion contributes rhythm, variety, contrast and movement to the pronounced pattern of color-areas.

The color-suffusion in *"Woman Resting Near Tree"* (284) of about c. 1915-1917, and especially in *"Woman in Muslin Dress"* (298) of c. 1917-1919, is one of the principal agents by which

---

* Cf., e.g., *"Fruit of the Midi"* (115) of 1881.
† Cf., e.g., Delacroix's *"Algerian Women"* (571) and also Renoir's *"Girl with Falcon"* (101) of 1880.

Renoir carries decorative values to heights never before attained in the traditions of painting. The first-named of these pictures offers a good example of the interaction of loose drawing, islands of light and contrasting styles of technical execution, to bring about a suffusion which reënforces the active movement of color. The distinctive feature of the space-composition is a cascade-movement of curvilinear color-masses which involves all the components of figure and landscape. The continuity of this all-pervasive rhythm is aided by the uninterrupted flow of luminous, glowing and iridescent color which builds up both the delicate but solid volumes and the atmosphere which envelops them. The richness of the color-suffusion—its juiciness, sparkle, warmth and glow—derives mainly from the use of effulgent islands of light which, interspersed with bright colorful shadows, yield a succession of rich color-chords. These iridescent islands are executed by technical means of considerable variety—washes of pigment, interpenetrating brush strokes, thick impasto. This variety, together with the changing solidity of the volumes and intensity of the color in the suffusion, vivifies the pervasive, rhythmic, drooping movement and these factors unite to render the abstract feeling of a woman at rest in a richly colorful landscape on a warm summer day.

The same principles of color-organization by loose drawing, fluid color, iridescent islands and suffusion are specifically adapted in *"Woman in Muslin Dress"* to a new type of space-composition, and yield a totally different esthetic effect. In the picture previously discussed, the compositional emphasis upon movement of volumes involves pronounced contrasts between figure and background in color, technique and degree of solidity; in *"Woman in Muslin Dress"* less variety in treatment and technique makes the contrasts so subtle that foreground and background melt into a continuous uniformity of positive colorfulness, without accentuation of either area. So complete is the fusion of all the plastic means and details of subject-matter that objects primarily expressive—face and arms, for example—blend inseparably with such decorative features as patterns of stripes and bands, and acquire an equal decorative value. Each volume floats into colorful space and is an organic part of the bright bouquet of delicate, variegated, flowerlike units.

This particular type of color-design necessitates extreme distortion of natural appearances; in the pattern of the background-drapery, for example, the decorative floral motifs appear as light color-volumes detached from the texture of the fabric and suspended in the swimming atmosphere surrounding the figure. Non-naturalistic spatial setting of volumes to this extent constitutes a compositional novelty probably unprecedented in Occidental painting.* They serve as a compositional bridge between the units of light-and-color in the setting and the more pronounced islands of colorful light which depict the flowers in the hat and other decorative details of the dress. These floral ornaments thus establish a rhythmic garlandlike sequence of delicate color-volumes which float in free colorful space, envelop the figure and by their overtones increase the density and richness of the color-suffusion.

The whole canvas is effulgent, it shimmers with iridescent areas and resplendent color-chords. The unaccentuated play of light and dark, and the loose contour of the decorative motifs temper the conspicuousness of the components of the general pattern and re-enforce the fluid continuity of the color. From the figure and garments the bright glowing color overflows into the setting, and the all-embracing exuberant suffusion imparts to the whole picture the appearance of an effulgent variegated bouquet. Red dominates the color-scheme to a degree unparalleled, probably, even in any other Renoir, and its infinite range of tonal modulations together with varied color-notes of Oriental effect are chiefly responsible for the extraordinarily bizarre sensuous quality of the color-ensemble. In spite of the great wealth of decorative detail, and the attendant reduction in weight and definition of the units, the volumes and spatial intervals preserve their individual identity, and the decorative splendor of the figure and its rich and brightly colorful garments leaves unimpaired their essential reality.

Perhaps no more characteristic Renoir decorative form exists than this, nor one that reëmbodies more richly, or with greater imaginative force, what was bequeathed by the Venetians. The color *per se* is richer and more luminous than Venetian color, the more extensive interpenetration of its tones creates a wealth of surface decorative values unequaled in any Venetian painting, and the ensemble diffuses a glow more organic, more pervasive, richer in tonal variations and compositionally more effective, than that in any of the Venetians. The golden brown of the Venetians is here transformed into a bright, vivid and luminous rose-madder.†

---

* Cf., Pisanello's *"Princess of the Este Family"* (322), Hindu-Persian miniature *"Head Servant"* (412), Chinese fresco *"Priest's Portrait"* (319).
† Cf., e.g., Titian's *"Lavinia"* (355) or *"Woman's Portrait: La Bella"* (370).

The accentuated stripes of light and color represent an enormous advance in decorative value over their prototypes in Titian, Tintoretto and Paolo Veronese.*

Space also is enriched in esthetic importance, with no loss either of its own reality or of the identity of its enclosed volumes, by Renoir's characteristic floating lightness and delicacy; for instance, the garlandlike unit, which binds foreground and background, is suspended in compressed space and thus establishes an original version of the traditional dynamic organization of volumes in deep space. Practically all the components of this garland are iridescent motifs, so that the unit as a whole is not only a set of ordered volumes in space, but also an integral part of the general composition of effulgent color-patches. All the elements borrowed from the Venetians are endowed with a light delicate surface-quality reminiscent of the eighteenth century French painters,† but decoratively richer and more deeply expressive of the textural reality of natural things. This enriched surface, which embraces the entire canvas, participates also in unifying the composition.

ABSTRACT AND TRANSFERRED VALUES OBTAINED BY EPITOMIZED DRAWING

We have seen that at about 1900 Renoir achieved an important increase in the compositional function of color, chiefly by so loosening contours that color flows over into space and thereby causes volumes and adjoining spaces to interpenetrate and form a composite color-unit. After about 1910 this type of drawing frequently assumes a marked twofold activity: it entails such an elimination of representative detail that the extremely simplified objects are reduced to their fundamental abstract essentials and by a massive overflow of color it also increases the intensity of the color-suffusion.‡

From the very start of Renoir's career his drawing became

* Cf., e.g., Titian's *"Venetian Family"* (364), Tintoretto's *"Paradise"* (389) or *"Venetian Senator"* (395), Paolo Veronese's *"Baptism of Christ"* (400) or *"Burning of Sodom"* (401).

† E.g., Watteau's *"Buck"* (473), Lancret's *"Actors of Italian Comedy"* (485) or *"Music Lesson"* (490), Pater's *"Comedians in a Park"* (494), Boucher's *"Madame de Pompadour"* (511).

‡ E.g., *"Landscape with Woman and Dog"* (275), *"Figure in Garden"* (289), *"Riviera Landscape"* (294), *"Two Figures in Landscape"* (296), *"Woman in Landscape"* (297).

stronger as he learned to eliminate unnecessary representative, illustrative and decorative detail; as he progressed in singling out the essential qualities of things, his drawing acquired a greater and greater degree of expressiveness. At the latest stage of his work he has become so superlatively skilled in abstracting essentials, and also in bringing the epitomized drawing of every part of the composition into harmony with that of the whole, that he can, at will, either depict clearly recognizable subject-matter,* or strip away all but the barest marks of identification.† The latter type of drawing preëminently characterizes the crowning epoch of Renoir's career.

This terse pregnant drawing, applied to all parts of the composition, involves generalization of the entire design and carries Renoir's previous interpretations of the Venetian form to a still more exalted plastic status. The increase in technical proficiency is enormous: in the earlier work, for example, the primary purpose of brush strokes was to render individual volumes and their shapes; now it is to individualize the form in its entirety, with such a degree of generalization that the identity of the components, as such, plays a very minor rôle. In other words, Renoir develops Manet's simplified drawing to the supreme height, in that color brings out the quintessence of the whole design. Compared to any of his previous work, these late pictures show a more organic unity, a more fluid coalescence of parts into the whole, in a form at the very pinnacle of plastic fulness. The expression embodies a much more profound vision, and a range of human values at a higher level than ever before. This is achieved fundamentally by color-power: color, of deep and rich sensuous appeal, renders the abstract values of things through the medium of an organized color-form.

An outstanding characteristic of most of these pictures is that they convey to a much greater extent than at any previous period values transferred from other realms of experience. The general effect of a figure in a landscape-setting, for example, may be that

---

* E.g., *"Woman Resting Near Tree"* (284) and *"Woman in Muslin Dress"* (298).
† E.g., *"Landscape with Two Women"* (274), *"Landscape with Woman and Dog"* (275), *"Two Girls among Bushes"* (282), *"Woman at Rest in Landscape"* (283), *"Figure in Garden"* (289), *"Landscape with Figure in Yellow"* (291), *"Riviera Landscape"* (294), *"Two Figures in Landscape"* (296), *"Woman in Landscape"* (297).

of ancient stained glass,* an effulgent multicolored mosaic,† a rich Oriental rug,‡ a kaleidoscopic rain of color,§ or the many forked flames of exploding fireworks.‖ While these transferred values speak in their own right, their principal function is to enhance the human appeal intrinsic to the particular subject-matter presented. Renoir's versatility and ingenuity in these respects may be appreciated by a study of varied designs illustrative of his vision and skill at this stage of his career.

The individual colors in *"Woman in Landscape"* (297)—greens, yellows, reds, lavenders, blues—are juicy, luscious, rich, deep and glowing, and so too is the pervasive multicolored glow of the suffusion. A vast number of small brush strokes form an all-over pattern of color-light units and add sparkle to the general effulgent glow. The individual brush strokes, by their relationships in color and tone, appear to interpenetrate in deep space, and thus make up a pattern which forms an integral part of the structure of solid color-volumes. The drawing and modeling weave the color and pattern of brush strokes into the very fabric of the volumes themselves, while the interpenetration of the brush strokes carries color over contours and fills the intervening space with a glowing and scintillating suffusion. Through this highly generalized drawing—an enormous advance over Renoir's previous use of the impressionistic technique—the whole set of volumes and spatial intervals are merged in a closely knit unity of which the sparkling glow is an inseparable part. Volumes, spatial intervals, patterns, the iridescence and the suffusion, are all on substantially the same level of compositional activity. The figure, for example, preserving its recognizable human identity, is not accentuated as such, but is primarily a focus in the color-organization, in which the other masses and the spatial intervals are no less important compositionally. The organization conveys, besides the human values of a figure in a landscape, the transferred values of tapestry, mosaic, stained glass, precious stones, a variegated bouquet, all impregnated with shimmering, effulgent, sparkling color.

Similar subject-matter in *"Two Figures in Landscape"* (296),

---

* E.g., *"Two Figures in Landscape"* (296) and *"Woman in Landscape"* (297).
† E.g., *"Woman in Landscape"* (297).
‡ E.g., *"Landscape with Woman and Dog"* (275) and *"Riviera Landscape"* (294).
§ E.g., *"In the Orchard"* (273).
‖ E.g., *"Figure in Garden"* (289).

executed in a different technique and with a different degree of solidity, is converted into a form which embodies, within very small dimensions (9½″x12″), the feelings associated with a large surging movement of volumes in a wide expanse of landscape. These effects, common to the best work of Claude le Lorrain, Poussin and the great Venetians, are here glorified by Renoir's brighter, more luscious and more luminous color.* Volumes of jewel-like color swim in a circumambient mother-of-pearl atmosphere, and every part of the composition—the volumes themselves, the space in which they move, and their enveloping atmosphere—is rendered by subtle and delicate color and technique. The brush strokes, small, short and only slightly contrasting in color, tend to reduce the pattern of the composition to uniformity, and this, in conjunction with the all-pervasive color-suffusion, causes the delicate volumes and spatial intervals to melt into one another. The picture suggests a hill of autumn foliage seen from a distance, but of more than natural delicacy and fluidity. The richness, depth and luminosity of the color recall the shimmer of the best stained glass,† or of colorful early mosaics. These transferred values are incidental to the majesty of the expansive landscape, the reposefulness of the figures, and the extremely dynamic movement in deep space, uncompromised by the extraordinary lightness and delicacy with which everything is rendered. This is expression of the highest artistic rank: a plastic organization embodying the feelings of epic grandeur and peace, but in combinations of color never encountered in nature.

"*Landscape with Woman and Dog*" (275) renders the local effects of a garden of tropical richness under the hot summer sunshine of the Riviera. Light, space and volumes are accordingly saturated with deep, rich, juicy, glowing color, which makes the objects solid, the atmosphere weighty, and every plastic unit of the picture positive and forceful. The solidly constructed woman sits placidly in the chair, the colorfully substantial dog is fast asleep, the strongly built house rests firmly on the ground and its massive walls are deluged with hot colorful sunlight. Multicolored bushes and trees rise gracefully from the ground into variedly colored space that sweeps away to the deep azure sky.

---

* Cf., e.g., Claude le Lorrain's "*Landscape with Cattle*" (452), Poussin's "*Summer, Ruth and Boaz*" (440), and Titian's "*Bacchus and Ariadne*" (347).
† E.g., Chartres Cathedral "*Tree of Jesse*" (315).

The picture represents a convincing plastic realization of the spirit
of place: a luxuriant garden, and the lassitude, repose, peace of a
summer afternoon in the Midi. With less reliance upon illustrative detail, Renoir, by a more comprehensive use of color, gives to
a form reminiscent of Constable's a fulness of expression and a
content of esthetic value incomparably greater than in the prototype.

A figure reposing in a peaceful colorful landscape of the Midi
is also the subject of *"Riviera Landscape"* (294), but the dynamic
space-composition is of a totally different type from that in the
preceding pictures. Generalization in this reaches such a degree
that individual volumes coalesce into a single large undulating
plane, the uniformity of which is somewhat broken by contrasts
of color, technique and pattern. This large plane sweeps upward
and backward between two trees—one in the extreme left foreground and one in the upper right distance—the spreading foliage
of which forms an arabesque and enframes the expanse of land
and sea. A similar theme of gradually receding landscape with
distant sea, enclosed in an arabesque of trees, is found in *"Noirmoutier"* (201) of 1892; in the present version, the drawing is
much more generalized, and the arabesque-pattern, less assertive
as a unit, merges on more equal terms with the all-embracing
atmosphere of rich, luscious, effulgent overtones. This color-suffusion, dominated by tones of lavender, rose and coral, is variegated
by Oriental notes in the delicate floating foliage of the trees and
the subtly iridescent islands of light. Thus Corot's delicate silvery
atmosphere is transformed by the yellows, reds and blues of the
Oriental color-scheme, in relationships that give to the lavender-
rose suffusion its distinctive character. The suffusion is what
chiefly conveys the abstract feeling of a placid colorful landscape
seen through the mist on a hot summer day. The picture, besides
conveying the spirit of local place, also suggests a rich delicate
Oriental rug, a series of gently smoldering rose-colored flames, a
succession of rainbows.

In *"Figure in Garden"* (289) the theme of flames assumes the
chief compositional status, with many variations in the manner of
its development and in its fund of associated ideas. Indeed, the
whole composition is a congeries of multicolored tongues of fire;
the loosely drawn plants in the foreground resemble a bouquet on
fire, from the individual flowers of which shoot up greatly variegated flames; the full-length figure, garbed in bright vivid red,

suggests a sharp undulating tongue of flame; the red bush near the center is like a bed of hot coals in a grate; the large green-and-yellow clumps of foliage on the left recall the feeling of exploding multicolored rockets. The idea of conflagration is completed by the all-pervasive swimming suffusion of bright shimmering color and light which echoes throughout the composition the flickering effects of the bushes, figure and foliage. The color-movement, in which three-dimensional space filled with color plays as important a part as do the volumes, takes the form of a large wind-blown arabesque organized as a continuous enframing garland. Similar instances of the garland-motif in Renoir's earlier work * formed a subsidiary part of the composition; now it constitutes the framework of the whole organization, and is basically interwoven with the rhythmic sequence of volumes and spatial intervals throughout the depth as well as the surface of the picture. The garlandlike swirl and the transferred values of flames enhance enormously the human values intrinsic to the subject-matter.

VARIATIONS IN FIGURE-LANDSCAPE RELATIONSHIPS

The foregoing group of pictures represent a type of design in which the figure is compositionally on a par with the objects in the landscape and is the focal point in the color-organization. In another series of late pictures, similar subject-matter is rendered with the relations between figure and landscape differently emphasized.† The landscape is very broadly treated and is primarily a setting for the figure; the figure remains focal in the color-organization, but functions principally as the volume about which the components of the landscape form subsidiary interrelated units in a composition of color-masses in a many-hued atmosphere. The figure in *"Woman on Hillside"* (299), for instance, is a solid weighty volume from which the vague and more lightly painted landscape extends uninterruptedly in all directions in an ordered series of alternate masses and intervals of space, each reduced in voluminousness and rendered as units of contrasting color in an accentuated pattern.

The contrast between figure and setting results from differences in degree of generalization: the drawing is more detailed in the

* E.g., *"Pourville"* (80) of 1878, *"Noirmoutier"* (201) of 1892, *"Artist's Family"* (214) of 1896.

† E.g., *"Reapers"* (278), *"Woman on Hillside"* (299).

figure and the color more solid; in the setting, simplification is carried to such an extreme that the individual units fuse in an iridescent continuous pattern of elongated oval shapes. This contrast is heightened by the rugged impasto in the figure and the thin washes of color in the setting, and it determines also the space-composition: the figure is a crisply drawn, definitely patterned volume precisely located in space, and is surrounded by delicate, less patterned, vaguely defined volumes and spatial intervals immersed in a swimming colorful suffusion. The distribution of light follows the same plan: it reaches its maximum of concentration on the figure, and is proportionately reduced in the landscape, the oval units of which it converts into subtly iridescent islands. This pattern of light accentuates the rhythmic throb of the color and of the volumes and spatial intervals as they radiate in all directions from the decentered figure which serves as a focal mass. A series of rich color-chords in both figure and landscape participate in establishing the decorative parity of all parts of the picture.

The compositional importance of light in these late pictures is further illustrated in *"Reapers"* (278). The suffusion here has scarcely a suggestion of haze: it is a clear, extraordinarily luminous and delicate atmosphere bathing the whole picture with bright colorful sunlight. The suffusion is felt primarily as illumination, in part because of the lightness, delicacy and pastel-quality of the bright vivid colors, and in part also because of the overtones of higher light-content than would arise from heavier or darker colors. This luminous, delicate, clear but positive suffusion is produced by the same type of generalized drawing, interpenetrating brush strokes and fluid color-washes as in the other paintings of this period.

This emphasis upon an all-inclusive flood of sunlight in a bright vivid color-ensemble preoccupied Renoir, as we have seen, from the time of his sojourn in Algiers in the early eighties, and quickly assumed an important and comprehensive compositional rôle. At the late stage of its development represented in *"Reapers,"* the color-content of the sunlight is fuller, and the suffusion discharges with great effectiveness a wider range of compositional functions. The sunlight is no longer, as in *"Beach Scene, Guernsey"* (130) of c. 1882, a glare cast upon objects from outside, but is a suffusion of color welling up from within them. Color is a more integral part of the drawing and structure both of individual things and of the design as a whole. This more organic generalized drawing purges illustration and decoration of superfluities, and contributes much to a plastic form expressive of human experience in its abstract essentials.

Varied Treatment of Figures in Interior Scenes

The operation of color to bind figure and setting into a continuous organization of volumes and spaces, is further illustrated by a group of interior scenes in which a figure, often a nude, is placed in a room filled with bright colorful objects.* Variations in drawing, in space-volume relationships, in degree of three-dimensional quality, and in intensity of color-suffusion, determine in each picture the distinctive compositional function of the figure and the setting.

In *"Reclining Odalisque"* (293) the floral ornaments of the multicolored drapery in the background appear as solid color-masses detached from the fabric and floating in free space, compositionally on the same footing as the head and other volumes of the woman's body. Overtones and the flow of color across loose contours create a suffusion and, by extending the substance of volumes into space, make each volume and its adjoining space part of each other. This type of drawing, described in detail in the discussion of *"Promenade"* (236),† is here carried to an extreme degree in all areas of the picture, and joins figure and background in an unbroken continuity. The actual interpenetration of parts of the figure and background makes all the units more interdependent, both individually and as elements in the whole composition, than in Renoir's earlier work. The detached floral ornaments, for example, give the impression of receding from the woman's body as much as they project from the background-drapery; the color, densely packed in space at the rear, gives to the blue portion of the drapery the appearance of a large ornament enveloping the head; a pillow in the left foreground which functions as a mass balancing the detached floral motifs in the upper right background, may also be interpreted as an extension forward of the volumes of the woman's body. These departures from realism establish a type of composition plastically akin to that in *"Woman in Muslin Dress"* (298),‡ with the difference that in *"Reclining Odalisque"* space and volumes as

* E.g., *"Seated Nude"* (279), *"Seated Odalisque"* (280), *"Nude on Couch"* (292), *"Reclining Odalisque"* (293).
† See pp. 115-117.
‡ See pp. 133-134.

such are more accentuated, the pattern of iridescent highlights is more emphatic, the color more sparkling, and the technique more varied by the alternation of streaks of thick impasto with thin color-washes. These modifications produce a sharper pattern than in *"Woman in Muslin Dress,"* they vivify the contrasts, enliven the color-movement and intensify the jewel-like sparkle of surface.

Figure and setting in *"Seated Nude"* (279) and *"Seated Odalisque"* (280) are differently related to each other than in the picture just studied: instead of forming an unbroken continuity, figure and setting preserve each their separate identity, and are organically related by rhythmic repetition in the background of the constituent volumes of the figure. This is essentially the form of organization which Renoir used early in his career, but it is now enriched by the greater activity of color in all its functions. The two pictures under discussion are differentiated from each other chiefly by the specific way in which the setting in each is related to the figure.*

FORMAL DECORATIVE ORGANIZATION

As Renoir approached the end of his career, he became more and more interested in increasing the esthetic fulness of deliberately planned formal decorative organizations. In most cases the decorative values have an adequate expressive balance, so that the more profound human values are in fact enhanced by the ornamental aspects of the form. At times, however, as in *"Standing Odalisque"* (295) of c. 1917-1919, and also in his large *"Nymphs"* (304) of c. 1918, his obvious purpose was to minimize expressive values in the interest of more purely decorative organization.

The outstanding features in *"Standing Odalisque"* are the sensuous quality and the strikingly Oriental character of extraordinarily bright, vivid, exotic colors, daringly contrasted and charged with light in a degree unusual even for Renoir. The subject-matter is similar to that in the last two pictures discussed, but greater emphasis upon the decorative aspects of color and still looser drawing bring the figure and the setting to compositional equality in an accentuatedly decorative design. One of the chief agents in this equalization is the all-pervasive suffusion of exotic overtones saturated with light. The intense light and exotic color in every part of the canvas produce a richly nuanced set of contrasting color-

* For details see Appendix, p. 431.

units organized in multicolored areas. In its pattern of daring, vivid, exotic colors the painting is like a Matisse, but the color is richer, deeper and of greater sensuous appeal, and its pattern is fluid rather than compartmental, and therefore more subtle than Matisse's.* The color conveys the feeling of voluptuousness intrinsic to the subject-matter.

"Nymphs" is also primarily a decorative organization, although expression is sufficiently maintained to remove the picture from the category of pure decoration. It also falls within that group of Renoir's latest paintings in which figures and settings are practically equivalent compositionally. Every part of the picture is rendered with especial emphasis as a decorative unit, each is a varied accentuation of the familiar islands of light, and all are merged in a pronounced pattern of effulgent multicolored areas dominated by red. While essentially decorative in function, the ubiquitous islands of colored light which determine the character of the accentuated pattern participate also in the drawing and modeling of objects and in the definition of space, and are firmly integrated in the total compositional unity.

Every component of the organization is essentially color: contrast and drama, ranging from the almost strident to the extremely subtle, is chiefly a matter of color-relations; indeed, there is no line, light or unit of space except as it is perceived as one of the aspects of color. The primary decorative status of the picture does not involve a ruthless sacrifice of expression; in fact, its fundamentally decorative value is actually enhanced by the part contributed by the color-light units to the expression of human values: the figures are alive and voluptuous, the textiles are adequately real, and the landscape with its clear atmosphere and dynamic volume-space relationships conveys the feeling of an open-air scene with the lyricism of nature. However, the expression of many aspects of familiar objects of the everyday world is reduced relatively to their interpretation in terms of sensuous color and accentuated pattern, and this brings the compositional scope of the picture within the limited plastic orbit of decoration.

THE APOTHEOSIS

Most of the characteristics of Renoir's late work attain their highest point of development in *"Bathing Group"* (285) of 1916.

* Cf., e.g., Matisse's *"Reclining Odalisque"* (637).

This picture though painted three years before his death represents the apotheosis of his art, the culmination of his steady growth
in profundity of imaginative insight, in resources and in technical
skill. The design is a fusion of two late types already discussed:
one in which all the objects are generalized and have an equal
compositional status in the form as a whole; * the other in which
the components are primarily individual units in an organization
of volumes in space.†

Color attains to the highest levels of sensuous quality and active
movement: every object is constructed of deep, rich, luscious,
voluptuous color, and the richly variegated organization is resplendent with shimmering color-chords, and has the exuberance, the
glamour of a glorified bouquet, studded with sparkling jewels. A
delicate many-toned rose-red dominates the ensemble and its areas
interlock with large areas of green and blue to form a three-colored
general pattern which is interspersed with areas of iridescent light
and color. These iridescent units are less accentuated as elements of
pattern than are usually Renoir's islands of colored light; they merge
more completely with the total form and the ubiquitous multicolored glow.

The large areas of red are concentrated in the figures, in which
the highlights and shadows, also tonal variations of red, are part
of a well-defined decorative pattern which embraces the whole
composition. The most important rôle of these tonal variations
consists in providing numerous nuances of rose for definitely expressive purposes: they dominate the suffusion as well as the
color-organization in general; they help to model, illuminate and
establish textural quality in the flesh; they participate in the varied
union of color, line, light and space by which Renoir, in drawing
the nudes, incorporates in them the static grace of early Greek
sculpture,‡ the solidity of the Venetians,§ the voluptuousness of
Rubens,‖ and the delicacy and charm of the eighteenth century
French painters.¶ Monotony is avoided by great variety in the

* Cf. the background figures and their setting with, e.g., *"Two Figures
in Landscape"* (296).
† Cf. the foreground masses with, e.g., the composition of *"Reclining
Nude"* (252), or *"Cup of Chocolate"* (263).
‡ E.g., *"Three Fates?"* (309), *"Standing Figure"* (311).
§ E.g., Giorgione's *"Concert in the Open Air"* (343) and *"Sleeping Venus"*
(344).
‖ E.g., Rubens' *"Judgment of Paris"* (430).
¶ E.g., Lancret's *"Actors of Italian Comedy"* (485), Boucher's *"Diana
at the Bath"* (508).

rose tones and the number of their contrasts with other and equally positive colors. The all-pervasiveness of these contrasts produces an active and moving color-drama, which is one of the distinguishing traits of the design.*

The high esthetic value of the picture springs from the fact that color is in supreme command everywhere: line, space and light have no independent identity except as aspects of color; hence, the indissoluble oneness of all the individual plastic units in a single, highly decorative and expressive form. An important factor in this unification is the all-pervasive luminous and richly colorful suffusion which radiates from the ubiquitous iridescent units. The suffusion, like the design as a whole, is an epitome of Renoir's earlier forms of the same feature, stripped to basic essentials and made instrumental to an infinitely greater variety of plastic functions. The technical means by which the suffusion is achieved are likewise condensations of devices previously employed; in parts of the sky, for example, the suffusion is executed by delicate color-washes flowing into one another and producing the subtle effect of glazes. Elsewhere the suffusion arises from color-chords created by the interpenetration of brush strokes in contiguous areas, and it is varied in richness in proportion to the degree of contrast between the constituent colors of the areas. It is varied also in content of luminosity by the quantity of light that filters into the overtones and intensifies their glow.

Variations in the density of the suffusion are due mainly to the specific adaptation of color to diversified types of drawing; that is, when color overflows from volumes into space, the distinctive character of the volume, whether dense and solid or light and delicate, is transmitted to the enveloping suffusion. The solid color which draws the large standing nude, for instance, is carried into the adjacent space and creates a suffusion of corresponding color-density. Conversely, the colors of the two small loosely drawn nudes in the center of the picture intermingle with adjoining delicate washes of color and form overtones which impart lightness, delicacy and translucency to the encompassing suffusion. Again, the hat and garment in the lower left corner, as well as the adjacent space, are drawn by the interplay of brush strokes of variegated, contrasting and iridescent colors, a type of drawing which brings forth a suffusion of a density midway between that of the two other areas described above. Thus, throughout the whole can-

* For details see Appendix, pp. 431-432.

vas, variations of drawing adjusted to different uses and aspects of color cause the suffusion to become alternately more and less dense, fluid and colorful, and these contrasts contribute to the extraordinary color-drama of the design.

Correspondingly, drawing, modeling, color, technique, light, space and composition, all contribute to and are affected by the many-phased plastic activities of the suffusion. This coördination and fusion of all plastic factors reach a high degree of intricacy, individuality and perfection in the compositional organization of *"Bathing Group."* Any one of the individual units may be selected as a focal point and corresponding units will be found elsewhere in the picture to balance it and establish equilibrium. Moreover, these subsidiary groupings flow into one another in a continuous movement that embraces every plastic factor in the entire composition. The unity thus established is between a wealth of plastic relationships greater than in any of Renoir's previous paintings, and the technical skill in execution represents the climax of his powers.*

Whatever the plan of compositional analysis, the organization overlaps that disclosed by other possible plans: consequently, all schemes of organization are aspects of a complex set of relationships that blend in a single harmonious effect. The chief agent of unification is color, and this too has its own plan of organization: a theme of red against a setting of blue, green and yellow, with which it interlocks. The distribution of these various areas results in a very novel color-pattern which establishes an essential continuity and equilibrium in the color-ensemble by an unbroken flow of colorful volumes and spaces. The color-pattern is unaccentuated as such because the loose contour of its units and the rich overtones of the suffusion produce an extreme general fluidity; the pattern, in other words, like all the other plastic factors, blends in the total form of the picture as do the individual themes of a symphony in the musical effect of the whole. Unity of this sort is the result of an uninterrupted interplay of qualities common to all the objects in the composition: movement, fluidity, delicacy, grace, convincing reality, all of them imbued with the characteristic individuality of Renoir's latest stage of development.

From the traditions drawn upon, Renoir here strips away more fully than ever before all that is irrelevant to his purpose and enhances the value of the originals by a more imaginative inter-

---

* For details see Appendix, pp. 432-433.

pretation of their essentials. The arcadian, elysian feeling of Giorgione or Titian, for example, is realized with greater richness and voluptuousness, with an added jewel-like sparkle of color and with more of the living reality of the actual world, less of the conventional classic idealization of figures and landscape.* Renoir's suffusion is richer and more colorful than the glow of the Venetians and it has a more varied compositional activity. His drawing is looser, broader, more generalized than in any of the Venetians, it is as fundamentally based upon color, is equally expressive, and infinitely more decorative.

The derivations from Rubens—bright voluptuous color, swirl of masses and feeling of drama—become by virtue of more structural color incomparably richer as decoration and expressive of deeper and more significant human values. Similarly, the daintiness, the delicacy, grace and charm of the eighteenth century French painters, always so apparent in Renoir's work, acquire greater strength from the more vigorous drawing and deeper, richer, more solid color, and are set in a more comprehensive and more firmly integrated composition.

The basic esthetic effects of ancient Greek sculpture † appear in each of the two large figures in the left foreground, and are rendered in terms wholly intrinsic to painting: the solid three-dimensional figures with the textural feeling of natural flesh are realized by color which draws and models the volumes, builds up the structure of the flesh, fills space and forms the substance of fluid contour, light and shadow. This constitutes an enormous advance in plastic strength over the sculpturesque effects of such Renaissance painters as Mantegna, Signorelli, Michelangelo and Raphael which depended upon the more literal and imitative methods of sharp line and accentuated light and shade.‡ Figures in the work of these Italians lack structural color and are often like volumes of stone isolated from each other in their surrounding space; Renoir's are not only more lifelike in themselves, but they are unified with their context by the uninterrupted interflow of

---

*Cf., e.g., Giorgione's *"Concert in the Open Air"* (343) or *"Sleeping Venus"* (344), Titian's *"Christ and the Magdalene"* (348).
† E.g., *"Three Fates?"* (309) and *"Standing Figure"* (311).
‡ Cf., e.g., Mantegna's *"Parnassus"* (332) or *"St. Sebastian"* (333), Signorelli's *"Hell—Paradise"* (336), Michelangelo's *"Original Sin and Expulsion from Eden"* (342), Raphael's *"Descent from the Cross"* (372) or *"Transfiguration"* (375).

color between volumes and space. Renoir's interpretation is an organic merging of the simplicity, grace and dignity of classic Greek sculpture with an enriched version of the fundamental values of the Venetians, Rubens and the French painters of the eighteenth century. The variedly proportioned combination of traditional elements determines the plastic identity of each unit, and the contrast between individual units is one of the main sources of the all-pervasive drama. In the reclining figure in the foreground, for example, are united the fluidity and grace of Tanagra sculpture, the flowing voluminous quality of the Elgin marbles, the structural color of Titian, and the voluptuousness of Rubens, all indissolubly fused in a new and characteristic Renoir form. The rich color and convincing reality of the garments of the seated figure on the right combine elements from the seventeenth century Dutch tradition with simplifications like Manet's and color-qualities of Tintoretto, Paolo Veronese, Rubens, Lancret, Pater and Watteau. All of these traits bear the imprint of Renoir's individual drawing, by which rich, sparkling and extensive color-chords form highly decorative iridescent areas and impart reality to textiles. In the clothed standing figure at the right, a motif from Delacroix is transformed and enriched, mainly by generalized drawing and a sublimated version of the Oriental color-scheme.* In the nude on the right the voluptuousness of Rubens' flesh is enhanced by color more solid, more effulgent, and of greater sensuous appeal,† and the form acquires an added value by recalling Girardon's interpretation of ancient Greek sculpture.‡ The hat and drapery in the left corner contain in solution the essential qualities of Manet's form § and the delicacy of eighteenth century French painting, similarly enriched by Renoir's distinctive color. The sky is reminiscent of Giotto in color-quality ‖ and of Tintoretto in dramatic treatment.¶ Finally, the landscape as a whole has the splendor and majesty, the lyric and mystical quality of Giorgione, Poussin and Claude le Lorrain, at their best, rendered with the technique

* Cf., e.g., Delacroix's *"Algerian Women"* (571) or *"Triumph of St. Michael"* (575).
† Cf., e.g., Rubens' *"Rape of Leucippus' Daughter"* (432).
‡ Cf., e.g., Girardon's *"Bath of the Nymphs"* (461).
§ Cf., e.g., the woman's hat in Manet's *"In a Boat"* (604).
‖ Cf., e.g., Giotto's *"Scenes from Life of St. Francis"* (317).
¶ Cf., e.g., Tintoretto's *"St. George and the Dragon"* (391).

and the more vivid and luminous color which Renoir himself had developed.*

All these diverse combinations of traditional elements are adapted to the fundamental principle of the design—the uninterrupted fluid movement of volumes in space. The volumes are varied in degree of massiveness, the spatial intervals in density of color, and the resulting contrasts exercise a cumulative effect upon the pervasive theme of drama.

The form embodies an abstract of the subject-matter, of the traditions upon which Renoir drew, and of the forms developed by him during his long career; it conveys not only the profound human values inherent in each of these sources, but also a great wealth of values transferred from other realms of experience. The exalted status of *"Bathing Group,"* in comparison with any of Renoir's previous work, is the natural result of his progress in command of his medium and in range and depth of imaginative insight. He has attained to the vision of the great artists of the past, the Greeks, Giorgione, Titian, Tintoretto, Rubens, the Dutch, the French painters of the eighteenth century, as well as of Manet, Monet and Sisley, and has given to them all a meaning of his own. In short, the essential and moving qualities of nature, already enriched for us by these artists, gain an extensive range of new values from Renoir's very individual interpretation of them.

CONCLUSION

In its continuity, its basically uninterrupted progress both in range and depth, Renoir's career is a superlative example of all the essential characteristics of the process of growth. Nothing is ever included in his mature paintings that he has not made genuinely his own, and nothing, once assimilated, is lost. We have seen how Courbet's essential realism, the simplified drawing and brushwork of Manet, impressionistic illumination, loose drawing, structural color, reappear from period to period, forming at each a part of a definite and unified design, but given a richer meaning, a more comprehensive plastic function, as the designs themselves assume greater significance and value. Islands of light, arabesque-formations, the Oriental color-scheme, tapestry surface-effects, are

---

* Cf., e.g., Giorgione's *"Concert in the Open Air"* (343) or *"Sleeping Venus"* (344), Poussin's *"Summer, Ruth and Boaz"* (440), Claude le Lorrain's *"Landscape with Cattle"* (452).

a few instances of devices which pass gradually from a rôle primarily illustrative or decorative to one of full plastic expression. Even the exotic form of the eighties bequeathed its essential values to the compositions which constitute the supreme achievements of his career.

In the course of his development, Renoir enriched not only his own form, but the traditions of painting as a whole. Thus Manet's drawing, his elimination of non-essentials, his generalizations and tersely expressive brush strokes, acquire in Renoir's hands a deeper significance: they are united with richer and more structural color in volumes that are more solid and set in deeper space, and thus are made an instrument for effects altogether beyond Manet's powers. The characteristic qualities of the French eighteenth century painting are purged of their frequent artificiality and occasional triviality, and combined with a power and universal human appeal of which Watteau, Lancret, Boucher and Fragonard have comparatively little. Even the Venetian tradition is given a new and richer meaning: the full measure of its plastic expressiveness is regained, its accidents and archaic aspects are stripped away, and it is given a decorative setting more opulent than anything in Giorgione, Titian, Tintoretto or Paolo Veronese; Renoir's vision, in a word, reveals a wealth of unsuspected values in the great art of all time.

SUMMARY

The foregoing account of Renoir's development as a creative artist illustrates all the aspects of esthetic vision, expression and form, experience and growth, described in the early chapters. It was pointed out in these chapters that the conditions indispensable to a living experience are a constant intercourse between the organism and its environment, animated by active interest, and guided by a fund of meanings in which the results of previous experience are recorded. The resulting assimilation of new meanings by which personality is enriched and fresh experience made possible, constitutes growth. Experience, in other words, means a process of feeding upon objective conditions, and growth means being nourished by them. We have seen at each stage of Renoir's development an inherent acuteness or penetration of mind which enabled him to find nourishment in the traditions of painting and in all aspects of the world about him. His growth to progressively higher levels of artistic creation was clearly due to his capacity to use the meanings embodied in his previous forms not as hard and fast rules for interpretation and action, but as working hypotheses, instruments for investigation, to be accepted only in so far as they are useful for the specific purposes in which he as an individual was interested. During each of his successive periods his growth is characterized by the reorganization of his personality as a whole, changes in its fundamental attitudes and point of view. The fact that when these changes are complete the process of active expression is resumed at a new and higher level, may be made clear by recalling the successive stages in the development of his form.

Beginning his work in the 1860's, Renoir naturally nourished himself first upon the traditions which were then most influential, and the influences which appeared in his pictures at the start were those of the Barbizon school, Courbet and Manet.* His spontaneous interest in the everyday life going on all about him made these realistic painters his natural guides, but his initiative and independence kept him from taking any of them as a model. The major influence in his pictures of the late sixties and early seventies, for example, was obviously that of Courbet, as their color-scheme, drawing and modeling, their relative tightness and

---

* Another influence, that of Delacroix, was of relatively minor importance.

hardness, show ; but these qualities are all modified by the simplified drawing, perceptible brushwork and luminosity of color taken from Manet, and by the silvery atmosphere derived from Corot. All these contributions, however, are significantly changed by Renoir's color, which is of finer sensuous quality and more structural in its functions. Renoir, in other words, had used the ways of seeing embodied in Courbet's, Manet's and Corot's painting as working hypotheses, and he adopted them only in so far as he found them useful instruments for his own reactions to the objective world. What he fed upon in the work of his predecessors and in his own environment is brought into fruitful relationship, and thus made a part of the tissue of his own personality. Simultaneously, his great natural aptitude for execution, his gifts as a craftsman, made it easy for him to put down in paint what he had learned to see. From the start, in other words, the process of active and meaningful response to environment took place in him, and it was this facility of adjustment, this ability to experiment readily with what the world and the traditions suggested to him, that made his development so continuous and so far-reaching in its eventual scope.

His pictures of the late sixties and early seventies, however rich in promise, were the work of a young and immature mind, as yet unable to eliminate wholly from what he borrowed the things which were not appropriate to his own purposes. This lack of complete unity in Renoir's own personal vision, an incomplete assimilation of the things he had fed upon is, of course, a part of the nature of immaturity. In 1874, for example, he painted such important pictures as *"Dancer"* (32) and *"Opera Box"* (34) which, while they show marked individuality in the interpretation of traditional forms, still contain no radical departure from those forms as a whole.

His pictures of 1875-1877 are the mark of a more developed personality : in them we see the record of an experience which has more completely digested the material provided by its environment and added that material to the tissue built up in its earlier process of growth. The influences of other artists are now less obvious, more overlaid with Renoir's own achievements. *"Torso"* (52) of c. 1875, for example, compared to *"Lise"* (9) of c. 1868 shows more continuous unity between the color, light, line and space, between the different areas in the picture, between expression and decoration. All this indicates a more organic assimilation of the traditions and of the matter furnished by the subject itself. It indicates also the wider range of material fed upon: the Venetian tradition is utilized more directly, the French eighteenth century tradition appears more prominently as an unmistakable source of many of the effects, and other individual painters, Velásquez, Rembrandt, Vermeer, Chardin, Goya, Daumier, for example, are drawn upon as occasion requires. Renoir, in other words, has transcended the influences of his immediate environment and found sources of nutriment in the more remote past; at the same time he has learned to select and reject more discriminatingly, so that he never takes over any form as a whole in the degree that he did in his earlier work. The looser line, the richer, brighter and compositionally more effective color, the less conventional, more subtle use of light-shadow contrasts, the greater general delicacy, subtlety, singleness of effect, all testify to his growth in richness of resources and artistic individuality.

A commensurate growth in craftsmanship is apparent in the elimination of the feeling of paint and the hardness of surface: as Renoir's eye and mind have learned to see more, his hand has learned to execute more precisely and effectively, without intrusion of the irrelevant physical features of the pigment itself. The new and more fully characteristic form is a logical development of that which has been superseded: its color-scheme of blue, green and ivory is a natural outgrowth of the subdued colors of the earlier period, and the general distinctness of areas as light and dark is an expansion of Courbet's light-dark contrasts and Manet's black-and-white effects, as these are reflected in *"Lise"* (5).

The landscapes of this period show more fully than do the figure-pieces and genre scenes the use of a way of seeing and of a technique destined to be of the utmost importance throughout Renoir's career—the impressionistic. He draws extensively upon the perceptible brushwork, juxtaposed color-spots and direct sunlight of the impressionists, but as usual the experience to which they are means is basically his own, as shown by the richer, more active color and the more complete compositional unity. The union of color and light is more intimate than in any of the impressionists, and in certain areas of the pictures it gives rise to what we have termed "islands of light," one of the plastic devices most constantly used, with ever-increasing scope, throughout Renoir's career.

The stage of growth attained by Renoir in the 1875-1877 period represents not only a more organic assimilation of plastic materials and traditions, but a finer grasp and a wider range of human and abstract values as well. The much greater continuity between all the areas and aspects of his pictures of this period indicates his realization of the value of harmony or unity in every field of experience, including those not directly related to art at all. In our material surroundings, our practical undertakings, our human relationships, we all crave an adjustment of particular things and acts to each other, and to the wholes of which they are parts, which shall eliminate jarring discords, disruptive conflicts, and the intrusion of irrelevancies of any sort. This does not mean monotony, the absence of contrast or surprise, but it does mean the subordination of differences or contrasts to a general unity of effect. The principle of unity, in other words, is applicable not only to art but to life as a whole. At this period, Renoir's merging of color, line, light and space in a continuous flow, the absence from it of any trace of disjointedness or overemphasis, is not only in itself a realization of complete unity, but a promise of the deeper and fuller unity which Renoir achieves in the final period of his career.

At the end of the seventies, Renoir enriched his characteristic form of the decade by a more varied and richer color-scheme, and especially by an increasing use of red which prefigured his later color-effects. The next important stage of his development, however, is of the type in which there is an apparent, though only an apparent, break in continuity. Up to this point there is a practically unbroken advance in the same direction: his personality, while increasing its stature through the use of a wider variety of material and a more complete assimilation of it, shows no alteration of essential interests. Then, in 1879, we encounter the amazing fact that after a steady progressive growth in vision and resources, and only a year or two after the production of some of the finest pictures of his whole career, he also painted his very worst. To regain the spontaneity of expression characteristic of his work prior to this date took him nearly a decade.

This crisis in Renoir's career was undoubtedly due to the fact that the environment which had previously stimulated the whole of his personality to full and natural expression now failed as a source of nutriment and crippled his powers. He had seen in it and recorded essentially all that his instruments of vision, the traditions as yet at his command, could show him. To continue in that environment, with those traditions, meant merely to repeat what he had already done, but what could no longer enlist his interests and powers, and consequently between 1879 and 1882 he painted a considerable number of pictures which were comparatively disorganized. His old habits failed him and left him unattuned to his world, and though four years passed before he became fully conscious of his maladjustment, it showed itself unmistakably in the restlessness which his wanderings in various parts of the world strove to appease. During these years he made lengthy stays in several widely separated provinces of France and in Africa and Italy. A study of the pictures of the period discloses a constant struggle on Renoir's part to reconcile a vast amount of new and foreign material with the knowledge and experience which constituted his background at the time the crisis occurred.

This reconciliation, the organic assimilation of the new material, proceeded gradually and slowly. It involved the reforging of Renoir's instruments of perception, a recasting and enrichment of his mind by an added store of meanings from traditions, and a synthesis of these with meanings which had served him previously. Such a reorganization of his entire individuality was necessarily laborious, and attended by constant partial failures—pictures in which the union of means was imperfect, and which expressed fragmentary or superficial aspects of his artistic personality. These unsuccessful ventures, however, were not abortive, they represent Renoir's exploration of a wider world and a partial incorporation into the structure of his mind of what he discovered there—an incorporation that was destined to be complete in his final form. This period, in other words, is not one of purposeless trifling or suspended animation, but a period of growth in the deeper regions of his personality, a growth without which the ultimate flowering of his genius could never have taken place.

Renoir's trips to Algiers in 1879 and to Italy in the early eighties supplied him with the material of a new environment and, by opening sources of nutrition previously inaccessible to him, introduced into his experience elements qualitatively new. The African sun, which transfigures everything on which it shines, opened his eyes to a world of more vivid, intense and fiery colors and lights than anything he had previously seen. This acquaintance with Oriental color and light gave a new impetus to his growth, and shifted, though it did not deflect, its direction. The essential continuity between this and the preceding stage is shown by the fact that when he came to express his new vision he had an instrument ready to his hand, in the impressionistic technique as he had already modified it. The imperfect assimilation of the new and old at this stage appears primarily in overaccentuation of light, its incomplete integration with color and form which is responsible for the decorative-illustrative status of such pictures as *"Vesuvius"* (122) and *"Gondola on the Grand Canal"* (125). The hot bright light and color in these paintings reproduce with great fidelity the appearance of sunlight upon vividly colored surfaces, and their intrinsic appeal adds a decorative value to the picture, but their integration into a single esthetic tissue is less complete than that of the subtler effects in his best pictures of the seventies. The sharper line of the period likewise enables him, as sharp line always does, to reproduce with ease and accuracy the natural appearances of figures, and to construct patterns more obvious than those in his best work; the rather porcelainlike surface provides added embellishment, though it detracts to some extent from textural realism. In spite of this relative superficiality, the pictures of the early eighties have a specific positive individuality, which expresses Renoir's interpretation of the world as he had come to see it, and they mark a definite step in the development of the rich glowing color and light which eventually produced forms incomparably richer, both decoratively and expressively, than those of the seventies.

In 1884, the cumulative effects of his acquaintance with Cézanne, and of a great admiration for that artist's work, begin to appear more definitely in Renoir's painting. This influence is most in evidence in the use of small groups of parallel brush strokes, organized in patches of solid color, which function as planes in the drawing and modeling and are the characteristic feature of dynamic composition of volumes in space. In most cases the Cézanne influences are associated with color-schemes in which pastel effects play an important part.

The work of 1885-1887 shows in various ways that the experience expressed in it had drawn upon Renoir's own earlier forms, and at the same time introduced a new traditional source of nourishment—the classic sculpture and frescoes which he had seen during his Italian trip. The continuity with the early eighties is evident in the general sharp line and hard surface, as well as in the occasional use of the Oriental color-scheme; but the even more incisive line and harder surface are now combined with a sculpturesque modeling of volumes in deep space to give much of the effect of actual statues. Continuity with the seventies is preserved by the constant presence of impressionistic brushwork and of eighteenth century French influences, but these too are changed: the eighteenth century influence is primarily that of Boucher, and the brushwork is combined with it largely to produce a tapestry-quality in backgrounds. The general bright light in *"Bathers"* (164) of 1887 is not the realistic illumination of either the seventies or such landscapes of the early eighties as *"Beach Scene, Guernsey"* (130), and the general decorative emphasis, while never carried to the point of plastic unreality, does lessen the naturalness, the complete conviction, of the 1875-1877 form at its best. However, the sculpturesque form and the deep space contain the promise of the great Venetian compositions of Renoir's late years and, though he has not yet succeeded in giving them an equivalent so fully in terms of painting as he does eventually, the general continuity between these pictures and his latest work is indisputable.

By 1887, Renoir had completed his exploration of new fields of experience and tradition, and was prepared to return to his natural vein of expression. He had absorbed his new material and continued the development of the general form—organization of volumes in three-dimensional space—which was to be carried further in his greatest work, but the systematic integration of materials and means in that form remained to be accomplished. Hence the decade following is also a period of incubation, though its goal is more clearly prefigured than in the preceding years. The work of organization progressed rapidly in his landscapes and, already in 1889 in *"Mt. Ste. Victoire"* (175), dynamic composition of masses in deep space is achieved, though with less richness and structural reality of color, less organic color-continuity between volumes and space, and a far simpler compositional organization than in the late pictures. In figure-painting the fusion of elements from previous periods went on more slowly, so that even such successful paintings as *"Nude in Brook"* (213) and *"Artist's Family"* (214) of 1895 and 1896, still remain in fact in the incubative stage. It is only in 1897, in *"Bathers in Forest"* (216), that a new form of organization is completely achieved, and that a considerable number of the distinctive features of the late form are definitely established. In it there is a fully dynamic Venetian space-composition, an inclusion of figures and landscape in a continuous movement of line, light and color in deep space.

This picture is a comprehensive summing up of practically everything that has gone before: its ubiquitous islands of iridescent colored light, its compositional arabesques, its highly decorative surface and rendering of textural qualities, combined with a realization of solidity by structural color, its color-scheme, fluid line, intimate union of color and light in modeling, and its technique—all grow directly out of what Renoir had previously developed. There is, indeed, scarcely any plastic device or tradition earlier employed which is not in some manner or degree represented, but all are used as means to more comprehensive compositional ends. The form as a whole is new and belongs essentially to that of the period to come.

The period after 1900 is that of Renoir's supreme plastic achievement, the complete realization by color of the movement of volumes in deep space, with both space and volumes built out of structural color, and made a single whole by the continuity of the color. In the opening years of the twentieth century, the drawing of volumes and spatial intervals by extension of color over contours, which makes of the two a single indissoluble unity, is accomplished, and the use of Renoir's characteristic red is begun. The basic factors in the post-1900 form have thus definitely come into being. The plastic and compositional function of color reaches its logical conclusion and its highest degree of perfection in the suffusion of color which characterizes all the late pictures, and becomes more important each year until the very end of Renoir's life. What above all distinguishes these late pictures is their growth in power, and in the range and depth of both human and traditional values expressed. As the youthful Renoir of 1868 was able, with all his natural gifts, to absorb only a relatively small part of the values which tradition and the objective world provided, so the Renoir of the seventies and eighties could assimilate from the past and from the environment chiefly the qualities of grace, charm, lightness, delicacy, subtlety. After 1900 the whole fiber of his personality has become more robust: in his growth he has nourished himself so extensively, assimilated so completely all that he had absorbed, acquired so unerring an eye for essentials, that with the utmost economy of means he can attain effects on the most epic scale.

This gain in power is not accompanied by any loss of the significant earlier values: the lightness and delicacy of his early work is still present in the extreme finesse with which everything is conceived and executed. The vividness and glow of the red, the luminosity of the color-suffusion, reproduce in an intensified form the early Oriental color-scheme, without its garishness and superficial glitter. Compared with even so late a picture as *"Bathers in Forest"* (216) of 1897, Renoir's work after 1900 shows a higher and finer grade of plastic integration: decoration and illustration no longer have any existence except as aspects of full plastic expression; and separate areas, masses and spatial intervals are more tightly knit together by a more continuous interflow of color, light and line between them all. The basis of everything is color, fused with light to draw solid volumes and deep space filled with a glowing luminous color-suffusion, to render textural quality, decorate surfaces, and organize the composition as a whole. While basically Venetian, this form is enriched by the essentials of all the great traditions of plastic art, from Greek sculpture to impressionism: impressionism, indeed, furnishes a large part of the fundamental technique for Renoir's work of all periods.

Renoir's resourcefulness, his imagination, is shown in the way in which he is able to apply his final form to the most diverse subject-matter—figure-pieces, portraits, still-lifes, genre scenes, and landscapes—giving a penetrating presentation of their essential qualities, endowing them with human values which testify to the range and depth of his personality, and incorporating them in a form of incomparable decorative splendor. His growth, in other words, has not been along any single line or in any one dimension; his personality has not, like Cézanne's, attained power by specialization in a highly restricted plastic field; his vision is synoptic, all-inclusive, and is matched by a skill in execution which can render anything whatever without the least sign of effort or strain. To every great tradition upon which he has drawn Renoir has added something new, personal, and of distinguished value; he has achieved a union of expressive force and decorative richness unprecedented in plastic art.

BOOK III
RENOIR AND THE TRADITIONS

CHAPTER I
RENOIR AND THE VENETIANS

In the course of our chapter on Renoir's development, we have repeatedly asserted that Renoir carried Venetian painting to greater decorative heights and made it more expressive of significant human values than did the Venetians themselves. The evidence sustaining this claim is present in the demonstrable plastic content and formal organization of his pictures. We have seen that Renoir's work shows a more varied and imaginative use of means, draws on more sources, avoids stereotypes more completely and creates more new forms than Giorgione's, Titian's, Tintoretto's, or Paolo Veronese's. In addition to its plastic form, a work of art embodies human values, and the depth and significance of these must be judged by a criterion which the spectator's background determines.

To understand Renoir's superiority to the great Venetians, we must consider the factors which control our fundamental attitudes to experience—the habits of thought, feeling and will which basically characterize individuals as well as periods of time. In the light of such an understanding, it will become apparent that much of the admiration for the Renaissance painters is generated by associated, and basically irrelevant, ideas. This is certainly true also in some measure of specialists in art. Preoccupation with subject-matter, in other words, and more specifically with the values of supernatural religion, explains a great part of the popular appeal of these old masters, and is the unconscious reason why conventionally minded critics assign them a supreme position in art. Their importance is indubitable, but the objective qualities which make them important are present also, and in even higher degree, in Renoir, and in him are purged of the irrelevant associations which detract from essential esthetic value.

As we have seen in Chapter III, all human activities, including art, spring from the individual's effort to adjust himself to his world and the world to himself. Over and above the specific acts by which he deals with situations as they arise, an individual may

163

steadfastly confront reality as it has been scientifically ascertained to be, he may face the facts of the human situation as they objectively exist; or he may ignore or deny the hostile and painful aspects of the world, and palm off upon himself a more agreeable, comforting, exhilarating substitute. This is the psychological process known as "flight from reality" which appears most flagrantly in the dreams of the opium-addict and the delusions of the insane, but which also animates the systems of assumption and belief in which human beings, individually and collectively, find consolation for their limited powers and frustrated purposes.

Social, political and national myths come under this head, but humanity's most important compensatory device has been supernatural religion, which assures man that the universe is controlled by a deity or deities whose assistance can be enlisted in the gratification of his desires. From the crude superstitions of savages to the more refined cosmologies of civilized peoples, all religions alike assure their followers supernatural assistance from on high. They also provide, as a rule, a mass of legends and myths, stories about the lives of the gods, saints and heroes, that may have a high degree of human and poetic appeal, and that often provide a means of entertainment and enjoyment apart from any promise of miraculous intervention in time of need.

The subject-matter of the classic Italian painting was, apart from portraiture, drawn almost exclusively from such sources, Christian and pagan, and was therefore from the start shaped to provide substitute-satisfaction for human wants. By many, indeed, the story told in the pictures was taken as literally true, a revelation of what had actually happened; but even when it was recognized to be fictitious, it encouraged distraction from the plastic qualities. No doubt a certain number of observers, naturally sensitive to color, line, composition, felt the plastic qualities in the pictures, even when they could not analyze them, and such observers did secure a relevant esthetic experience; but the experience was genuine only in so far as it was a specific response to the plastic qualities in question and was not overweighted with the associated ideas of the subject-matter.

In all the ages before science reached its maturity, people inevitably found their adjustment to the world through magic, mythology and religion. Lacking the precise and detailed information about human nature and the objective world which science has since supplied, they were powerless to reconstruct experience in fact, and had no choice but to do so in fancy and by faith. The world has moved away from religion by the road of science, but the habits which long ages of religious belief ingrained deeply in the human mind still persist much more widely than is usually realized. They profoundly affect the attitudes, sentiments, ways of feeling and thinking, of many people who suppose themselves to have outgrown religion completely.

The immense vogue of such a painter as Titian, which in the eyes of many makes it seem a sacrilege to regard any modern painter as his equal, is unquestionably due to the "cultural lag" which we have just described, to the operation of unconscious survivals from the past. There is in addition, of course, the effect of prestige, the respect which it is almost impossible not to pay to works of art which have been revered for centuries. Prestige and the general human preference for a version of things which flatters our instinctive desires thus combine to draw a veil between the observer and the work of art that makes impossible the inter-related doing and undergoing which alone constitutes experience. The old masters are valued, consequently, by a vast majority of spectators and even by critics, for qualities which are totally ir-relevant to their plastic excellence and which indeed may easily become a positive detriment to their esthetic value.

The foregoing does not imply that in the modern world religion is an excrescence upon art, or that the two are irrelevant. On the contrary, there is an important respect in which they are identical, so that the religious values in Giorgione and Titian are in part legitimate and relevant to their artistic value. Religion has two aspects: it is an imaginary means of control by supernatural pow-ers, and it also is a mystical experience, a conviction of essential oneness with the world. The first may now justly be stigmatized as a relic of superstition; the second stands upon a very different footing, and represents a legitimate demand of human nature. When an artist has shown us a vision of things which profoundly stirs our emotions, calls all our interests into harmonious play, which strips from material things all the accidents, irrelevancies, discrepancies with which they are usually encumbered, he has re-built the world according to the heart's desire, and the sense of mystical union ceases to be illusory, and becomes a realization of substantial fact.

This function of art has been stated by Professor Dewey in the following words: "A work of art elicits and accentuates this quality of being a whole and of belonging to the larger, all-inclusive, whole which is the universe in which we live. This fact, I think, is the explanation of that feeling of exquisite intelligibility and clarity we have in the presence of an object that is experienced with esthetic intensity. It explains also the religious feeling that accompanies intense esthetic perception. We are, as it were, introduced into a world beyond this world which is nevertheless the deeper reality of the world in which we live in our ordinary experiences. We are carried out beyond ourselves to find ourselves." *

Religion, in brief, contains two aspects, one valid, the other invalid. As mythology, it presents us with a picture of the world which intelligent people know to be untrue, which supplies consolation and compensation at the cost of deadened senses and a stupefied mind. The consolation is short-lived and precarious, it is at the mercy of circumstances, and at every moment objective fact threatens to destroy it and replace it by a sense of disillusioned futility. A mysticism which takes its stand upon the real world, not refusing to recognize that world as it actually is, but finding within it the objective qualities which satisfy a cultivated mind and senses, has the stability, the permanence, the integral relationship to the rest of experience, which supernaturalism lacks. There is no breach of continuity between it and the other activities by which we find adjustment to the world, whether by such practical means as planting fields or building houses, or such intellectual means as scientific or historical research. These activities also yield, in addition to their practical consequences, an immediate warmth of satisfaction, a sense of assured mastery, a perception of ordered relations, which are characteristic of the esthetic and mystical experiences.

We are now in a position to state the exact relationship between Renoir and the great Venetians. In so far as the Venetians realized the sense of union with the world by actual objective means, their religious and mystical effects are legitimate. In part, however, their paintings do depend upon a flight into a different world, a kind of Garden of Eden or Elysian Fields, and to this extent their effects are irrelevant, and involve a recourse to myths now discredited. Renoir has all the objective plastic equivalents of awe, peace, majesty, that the Venetians have, and more. No Venetian painting has the plastic content of his late small *"Two Figures in Landscape"* (296), for example. He has the further very great advan-

* John Dewey, "Art as Experience," p. 195, Minton, Balch & Co., New York, 1934.

tage that his pictures, while they present human action with the fullest essential realism, have no associated story such as that of Titian's *"Entombment"* (352) or *"Bacchus and Ariadne"* (347) to distract attention into realms of fancy. Finally, his painting represents in the highest degree the discovery of human and mystical value in the world we actually live in. There is not the slightest smack of otherworldliness in his painting: he transfigures the world without ever abandoning it. It is in finding the supreme values of experience in the particular scenes and events of everyday life that he shows his unparalleled power of insight and imagination.

The plastic relationship of Renoir to the Venetians and his superiority to them, remains to be shown in detail. At each period of his development, as we have already seen, he makes an individual and creative use of the great traditions, but of all the traditions it was the Venetian which offered the most fertile soil for Renoir's form to take root in, draw sustenance from, and grow. Renoir's Venetian origin is constantly apparent, and the other traditions from which he drew, those of Rubens, for example, the French eighteenth century, Velásquez and Goya, were themselves largely outgrowths of the Venetian. A comparison of his painting with that of Giorgione, Titian, Tintoretto and Paolo Veronese will show how fundamentally his form was based upon theirs, what he specifically added in expressing the very different materials and scale of values of his own era, and how greatly, in plastic and human content, he advanced upon them.

COLOR

The outstanding characteristic which links Renoir more closely to the Venetians than to any other predecessor is his color. As in the Venetians, color is the foundation of his form, in that all the other plastic means are aspects of color; like theirs, too, his color enters into and builds up the structure of objects, it is rich, sensuously pleasing and highly decorative, and it is the most active agent in unifying the composition and determining its character. A point by point comparison of each of these aspects of color in the two forms will show that Renoir extends the decorative, structural and compositional value of color to a level unattained by any of the Venetians.

The primacy of color in design is more definite and assured in

Renoir : line, light, space, are much more integral parts of his total color-form, than in the Venetians. In the latter the patterns of line, for example, of light, and of light-and-dark, are more readily perceived as separate entities, and their individual contributions to drawing, modeling and composition, while convergent in their effects, are more or less independent of each other and of color. The corresponding patterns in Renoir are so completely integrated as color-units in the composite form that their function as pattern *per se* is entirely subsidiary.* A proof of this is the fact that in photographic reproduction Venetian paintings lose less effects of spatial organization, less three-dimensionality of volumes, and less movement and drama, than do Renoir's.

The structural solidity of objects and their location in space in the Venetians is obtained by the conjoint action of color, contrasts of light and shade, and linear and aerial perspective, with great help from the means other than color. Structural solidity in the masses in Renoir's mature work, and their spatial organization, depend less upon patterns of light and shadow and effects of perspective; they are obtained primarily by color-relations which at one and the same time build up the structure of the object and define the space in which it is located. The solidity in the Venetians is usually that of dense weighty masses, whatever the natural character of the object depicted; Renoir's color conveys more of the specific structure, texture, degree of solidity, massiveness and weight of the particular objects. Furthermore, the intrinsic quality of his color and its more extensive and varied relationships endow the volumes—however massive and weighty they may be—with a feeling of lightness, delicacy and fluidity. Thus, with no loss of the feeling of reality, Renoir's use of color increases the content of expressive qualities.†

The greater richness and decorative quality of Renoir's color over that of the Venetians is due to several factors: the higher tonality in which he works; the dominance in his palette of colors which have greater immediate sensuous appeal; the color-chords and color-patterns resulting from his more subtle blending and adjustment of contrasting color-units; the iridescent surface; and the

* Cf., e.g., Renoir's *"Bathing Group"* (285) with Giorgione's *"Concert in the Open Air"* (343) and Titian's *"Bacchus and Ariadne"* (347).

† Cf., e.g., Renoir's *"Reclining Nude"* (252) with Giorgione's *"Sleeping Venus"* (344) and with Titian's *"Venus and Organ Player"* (368), or Renoir's *"After the Bath"* (247) with Tintoretto's *"Susannah at the Bath"* (393).

fluid juicy quality of the pigment itself. Apart from these general differences in the sensuous aspect of color, Renoir's ensembles, even when dominated by a single color, are variegated and enlivened by eloquent contrasts, vivid color-accents and -focuses, and patterns of positive color. In the Venetian color-ensembles the browns and yellows so pervade and dominate the blues, reds, greens, that these are relatively absorbed or submerged and lose much of their effectiveness as elements of contrast.*

The difference between Venetian color and Renoir's, in both its expressive and its decorative aspects, is naturally attended by a very marked corresponding difference in its compositional function. The characteristic Venetian space-composition consists of an organized sequence of accentuated color-volumes and spatial intervals filled with color, and this is also the foundation of Renoir's composition; but he shifts the emphasis from the activity of volumes and intervals as such to the determining function of color itself. The identity of volumes and spatial intervals is retained, as is also the dynamic relationship between them, but the primacy of the color in constructing the units and in endowing them with their distinctive characteristics, places color on an equal footing with the sequence of volumes and intervals in establishing rhythm, balance and compositional organization.†

LIGHT

Renoir's light is also based upon the Venetian; that is, light is in itself color, it enriches color, it helps to draw and model objects and is deeply embedded in their substance, and it is a constituent of the overtones which produce a pervasive atmospheric suffusion and glow. As with the Venetians, the light is often organized in a compositional three-dimensional pattern focussed in a distant concentration of the glow.

Renoir's adaptations of each of these aspects of the Venetian use of light attain new plastic heights mainly because of a more imaginative employment of color and a more complete integration of color and light. Not only is Renoir's light more saturated with color and his color richer and more variegated, but this colorful

---

* Cf., e.g., Renoir's "Bathing Group" (285) with Titian's "Bacchus and Ariadne" (347) and Giorgione's "Concert in the Open Air" (343).
† Cf., e.g., Renoir's "Girls in Garden" (290) with Giorgione's "Tempest" (345), Titian's "Christ and the Magdalene" (348) and Tintoretto's "St. George and the Dragon" (391).

light filters through the entire canvas and eliminates the more obvious Venetian dramatic contrast between illuminated and non-illuminated colors. Thus infusing bright and dark colors alike, Renoir's light emphasizes the individuality of every hue, adds sparkle to highlighted areas, increases the intensity of positive colors, and raises the pitch of the whole color-ensemble. It replaces the heaviness, density and somberness of the Venetian shadows by lively, internally luminous color, and makes color and tone alike more homogeneous, so that every plastic unit may be described as either colorful light or luminous color. The striking difference between Renoir's pervasive glow and sparkle and the muted Venetian glow arises from the more positive enrichment of Renoir's color by light, and from the uninterrupted sequence of color-and-light modulations which lends a glowing depth and a shimmering surface to every part of his canvas.

Renoir's light, in uniting with color to build up structure, substance and mass, is adjusted to the varying quality and function of the color: it is felt to penetrate into the substance of the color-volumes and to saturate it with as much delicacy, subtlety and lightness as does the color and as is necessitated by the specific character of particular volumes. This more organic illumination of color, and greater variety in the proportion of light and color in individual units, are the means by which Renoir extends the possibilities of Venetian structural color; through them he adapts the color and light to varying degrees of voluminousness and weight, as well as to the textural differences which distinguish a piece of fruit, a wall, a human body, a fold of drapery. These qualities in the Venetians differ but little in degree because of the limited variation in the proportion of the color- and light-factors out of which their substance is built.

Renoir's more flexible and organic blending of color and light also makes his adaptation of the Venetian glow more pervasive and richer, with an array of decorative, expressive and compositional functions totally unobtainable with its relatively monotonous proto-type. The latter contains proportionately more light than color, and is usually dominated by a single brownish-golden tone throughout the picture. In spite of what it contributes to compositional organization and to expression and decoration, its uniformity often becomes monotonous and suggests mechanism. Renoir's suffusion, in contrast, is multicolored and radiant, shimmering and effulgent, and it varies in degree of intensity, colorfulness and activity even within a single picture. The Venetian glow appears chiefly in large, rather well-defined areas, which are thus set in contrast to the areas of shadow. Renoir's pervades all parts of the picture, so that even the deepest shadows are usually internally glowing and sparkling; thus it becomes a more organic part of the form and establishes an all-embracing, intricate and organic network of unified plastic relationships.*

There is also an enormous difference in the color-quality of the two types of atmospheric suffusion. The heaviness of Venetian color necessarily extends to the space and saturates it with an atmosphere of relatively uniform weight. Renoir's light, transparent, delicate suffusion carries the varied color-and-light content of the substance of volumes into the spatial intervals, and thus converts them into quasi-voluminous units which echo plastically the delicacy and the colorfulness as well as the solidity of the masses themselves.

The superiority of Renoir's suffusion is largely due to the all-pervasive color-chords, which endow it with a rich and variegated content of color and light; it actually changes in color and degree of luminosity as it moves throughout the picture while the Venetian glow, as we have seen, is relatively monochromatic. In Titian's *"Bacchus and Ariadne"* (347), for instance, although the tone of the glow varies from a deep bronze in the foreground to a lighter greenish-yellow in the sky, the essential similarity in undertone produces a rather monotonous continuity, without the color-variety which Renoir's suffusion has even when it too is dominated by a single color.† Renoir, moreover, is able to make even sharply contrasting colors participate in the suffusion and contribute to its unifying action. Particularly in his work after 1900, the atmospheric glow is saturated with the intermingling luminous overtones of extremely varied, iridescent and sparkling color-units. Through Renoir's more imaginative blending of color and light, the uniform, relatively adventitious, not to say mechanical and technical, device of the Venetian glow is thus converted into a means for obtaining plastic results of an importance and range far beyond anything in even the best work of the Venetians.

Like his color-and-light suffusion, Renoir's organization of units of concentrated light in a compositional pattern focussed in a distant glow, is more varied and more subtly graduated in content

* See chapter "Development of Renoir's Form," pp. 130-135.
† Cf., e.g., *"Bathing Group"* (285).

of color and light than are corresponding Venetian light-patterns.* The distant focus of the glow in the latter is more a concentration of colored light than, as in Renoir, of multicolored units saturated with light; examples are the grayish-blue light in the distance of Titian's *"Bacchus and Ariadne,"* the golden-yellow light in his *"Christ and the Magdalene"* (348), and the greenish golden-yellow light in Tintoretto's *"St. George and the Dragon"* (391). Moreover the drama in these pictures is made comparatively specious by the rather abrupt contrast in tone between the light-pattern itself and the surrounding dark areas.

The corresponding drama in Renoir is plastically as effective and esthetically more moving because of the more deeply organic interpenetration and interrelation of light and color: the tonal gradation, from the highlighted to the most deeply toned areas, is essentially a modulation of color and only secondarily one of light, and thus the drama is charged with the subtlety, delicacy, richness and effulgence characteristic of Renoir's color. Here again, Renoir's finer feeling for relationships of color and light enables him to make the Venetian focalized light-pattern more flexible and to augment greatly all its plastic functions.

In Renoir, as in the best of the Venetians, the light-pattern related to the distant focus contributes much to the specific expression of the composition. In his *"Bathers in Forest"* (216), for example, as in Titian's *"Bacchus and Ariadne,"* the distant focus brings into equilibrium the general pattern of light; in Renoir's *"Two Figures in Landscape"* (296), as in Titian's *"Christ and the Magdalene,"* the glow at the horizon extends unbrokenly throughout the sky, and its mystic lyric quality is in harmony with the calm, fluid, lyric drama of the total picture. In each of the Titians the drama is obtained by the obvious accentuation of the pattern of light, and remains therefore comparatively extraneous to the form as a whole. In the Renoirs, the light-pattern and the distant focus work in a more equal unison with color, and the drama, as a more organic part of the total color-form, is of a higher plastic status.†

---

*Cf., e.g., Renoir's *"Bathers in Forest"* (216), *"Bathing Group"* (285) or *"Two Figures in Landscape"* (296) with Titian's *"Bacchus and Ariadne"* (347), *"Christ and the Magdalene"* (348), *"Disciples of Emmaüs"* (350), *"Entombment"* (352) or *"Jupiter and Antiope"* (354), and with Tintoretto's *"St. George and the Dragon"* (391).

†Cf., also, from the same viewpoint, Renoir's *"Bathing Group"* (285) with Tintoretto's *"St. George and the Dragon"* (391).

DRAWING

Renoir's drawing is also derived from the Venetians at their best, primarily because, like theirs, it is a composite of all the plastic factors, with each of its components an aspect of color. Other points of similarity are that contours are generally fluid, with color overflowing the boundaries of areas, and that consequently the volumes seem to melt into adjacent space and a continuous flow of color includes all parts of the composition. In both forms too, this fluid drawing is conducive to subordination of illustrative details to expressive essentials.

This similarity of Renoir's drawing to that of the Venetians is only in fundamental character, for he wrought radical changes in each of the elements. The most important advance is in his better fusion of the individual components of drawing. Line, light, color and space, in the Venetians, are each more easily separable as entities in the patterns, and also in what they contribute individually to the drawing of particular units and of the design as a whole. A result of Renoir's more organic synthesis of the plastic elements is a greater delicacy and subtlety in the interrelation of the components and the individual units, a delicacy and a subtlety which inevitably extend to the form as a whole.

Nothing in Titian has the fulness of expression as the drawing of the hands in Renoir's *"Woman Crocheting"* (76). Here, as usually in Renoir's best work, color-relations build up the structure and draw out its essential characteristics, while Venetian drawing relies more upon linear effects and pattern of light and dark as such. The Venetian lines consist of the boundaries of color-areas, in conjunction with the contrasts in light-content of the color. Although these factors of light and line are rendered in color, it is primarily the linear character of the color and the contrast in content of light that define the shape and volume of objects and also their position in space. In Renoir, on the contrary, the specific qualities of the linear effects and patterns of light and dark, and the respective functions they fulfill in the drawing, are due primarily to both the intrinsic quality of their own color and its relationships with the color of adjacent units.

Furthermore, in contrast to the Venetians' frequent use of a broad dark line around contour to affirm the shape of the object and help locate it in space, Renoir, except for his exotic work of the eighties, dispenses with exact contour or actual line. When occasionally an accentuated outline does appear, its color participates in the drawing as much if not more than its linear character.* The result of this relative absence of linear demarcation between areas is a more ready and constant interflow of color between them, so that their edges are suggested by subtle modulations of color rather than precisely defined. The color of the objects, thus expanded, as it were, beyond its natural boundaries, increases the massiveness of the volumes, and also establishes a fluid color-movement which makes them seem to melt into space without losing their separate individuality.

No such interpenetration of color occurs in Venetian drawing: its fluidity is attained by an approximation in tone of the contrasting color of adjacent areas, and by tonal gradations within the individual color-areas themselves; that is, the color changes in tone within each of the contrasting areas, and changes in hue as it passes the area's boundary. The colors of the juxtaposed shadows of the two contrasting areas have thus a tonal quality in common, usually the characteristic pervasive Venetian brown. Continuity of color is therefore established primarily through affinity of tone, and the effect is consequently more monotonous and less decorative than Renoir's intermingling of actual colors.

The shortcomings noted in Venetian drawing appear very strikingly even in its highest type, represented by Titian's *"Christ and the Magdalene"* (348). The color here seems in places to flow freely from one area to another, but close inspection reveals slightly ragged boundaries of areas, due perhaps to an uneven superposition of layers or glazes of color. In the two adjacent color-areas at the junction of the Christ's legs in this Titian, the relative activity of tone and color in the drawing is clearly apparent: the two areas are very near in tone, the brown shadow in each having the same degree of dark-content, so that the shaded area of one leg actually continues uninterruptedly over into the shaded area of the other with just sufficient gradation of tone to differentiate each. But even supreme instances of Venetian color-fluidity such as this or as the fine adjustment of color-relations in the fluidly drawn, deep, rich draperies of the Magdalene in the same picture, lack the color-fluidity and color-richness of Renoir's mature drawing. Corresponding units in Renoir are drawn with much greater fluidity, and by brighter and more varied colors, the nuances of which inter-

---

* E.g., *"Missia"* (235), *"Woman Reading"* (238), and *"Girls in Garden"* (290).

mingle freely, so that the total effect is incomparably richer.*

It is obvious, therefore, that Renoir's development of Venetian drawing is due primarily to an enhancement of the sensuous quality of color and to its more meaningful relationships, and not merely to its flow over contour. The best confirmatory evidence of the fact is offered by a comparison of the activity of color in his mature drawing with occasional passages in Venetian drawing in which actual line of contour is replaced by a continuous flow of modulated color. In the face of the baby satyr in Titian's *"Bacchus and Ariadne,"* for example, the features and contour are loose to the extreme, but again it is tonal gradations rather than variations of color which give form to the unit; the face in Renoir's *"Claude in Arab Shirt"* (232), in contrast, is drawn by constantly varied modulations of deep, rich and delicate color, and hence is more richly decorative and expressive. Again, in Titian's *"Mother and Child"* (358) the prevailing extremely loose contour is inadequately supported by structural color, so that the masses lack solidity and their texture is soft and flabby. Contour equally loose in Renoir's *"Maternity"* (303) is obtained by relationships of color which reenforce its structural quality, and the flow of color across boundaries contributes to the plastic qualities of both the volumes and the surrounding space, as well as to the color-continuity of the entire composition.†

The full significance of this enhancement of Venetian drawing which Renoir accomplished by increasing the plastic function of color, can be realized only when its two main achievements, each of monumental importance, are grasped. The first of these is the addition of an uninterrupted, all-inclusive sequence of rich variegated color-chords to the fluid continuous Venetian space-composition. The second consists in an even greater fluidity of color, which relieves the Venetian type of drawing still further of irrelevant details, adds values much more fully expressive of the basic qualities of life and nature, and at the same time incorporates them in a richer decorative organization.

Renoir's drawing is not only more broadly generalized, but it reveals more specifically the qualities distinctive of various objects

---

* Cf., e.g., *"Bathing Group"* (285).

† For further illustration of the superior reënforcing effect of Renoir's color in drawing, compare also Renoir's late still-lifes such as *"Fruit and Bonbonnière"* (270) or *"Pomegranate and Figs"* (277) with the still-life objects on the table in Titian's *"Disciples at Emmaüs"* (350) or with the loosely drawn loaf of bread in Tintoretto's *"Two Prophets"* (394).

and textiles. Applied to the subject-matter of our actual world, it replaces the Venetian sumptuousness and magnificence with a convincing realization of the homely and familiar aspects of everyday persons and events, with a great gain in universal human appeal. His figures, for example, are realized in terms of everyday experience, and they fit naturally into a setting which likewise carries its own appealing associations; the expression is moving and convincing because it is the world of nature and people as we know them. A similar transition in the scale of human values is represented by the accomplishments of the Venetians in replacing the austerity of the Florentines by an expression of magnificence and splendor. Renoir in turn built upon the Venetian foundation a new edifice which reveals and embodies the intrinsic intimacy and charm of everyday affairs. Titian's statelier but also less flexible form, like the themes which he employed, expressed the spirit of his age, its comparative pretentiousness and remoteness; Renoir's is an expression of his own time, secure in its command of its world and finding there a poignancy and poetry sufficient for its needs.

MODELING

Renoir's modeling also stems from the Venetians', in which structural color unites with subtle gradations of light and shadow to yield full three-dimensional solidity and the textural quality of objects. He adopted in addition the Venetian technique of glazes, an important means in the rendering of many specific qualities. Since his constructive use of Venetian modeling is particularly evident in the rendering of flesh and textiles, a comparative study of these features in his work and the Venetians will illustrate the transformation which Renoir achieved, and will also make more specific his adaptation of Venetian color, light and drawing. The transformation was gradual and at the start, as we have seen in the chapter "Development of Renoir's Form," its point of departure was less the Venetians themselves than the versions of their form current in Renoir's own youth. We shall therefore trace its course through the successive stages of his career.

FLESH-PAINTING

The flesh-painting in most of Renoir's work of the 1868-1870 period is allied to the Venetians chiefly through the medium of

Courbet's version of that form.* The general tonality of the mono-chrome complexion is more brownish gray and old ivory, as in Courbet, than golden, as in the Venetians; the shadows are dense and often blackish green, the contour firmer and relatively sharper, the volumes more solid and full-bodied and of heavier texture, and the pigment more weighty. Renoir eliminates Courbet's relative coarseness from these characteristics, and not only restores much of the Venetian fineness of relationship but anticipates the delicacy, subtlety, lightness and luminosity of his later reinterpretations of the Venetians.

Other versions of Venetian flesh-painting which Renoir builds upon in the early stage of his development are those of Velásquez and Delacroix. In *"Young Woman with Rose"* (28), in *"Dancer"* (32) and in *"Opera Box"* (34), the flesh has, along with the lesser illumination of color responsible for the muted quality in Renais-sance painters, the light, slightly yellow, ivory undertone more directly reminiscent of Velásquez and Delacroix. In the first-named of these Renoirs, the flesh is tinged by the typical Venetian brown, but play of light upon color links it to Delacroix.† In *"Dancer"* a Velásquez ivory-gray appears in the flesh but lightness of touch and delicate color supersede Velásquez' feeling of crude paint. The draw-ing and painting of the flesh follow more closely Velásquez' version of the Venetian form as it was transmitted by Courbet and Degas, but very few shadows are used and they are of delicate tones and restricted in area. Moreover, the modulations of tone within the relatively monochromatic complexion are more subtle and varied than in Degas, Courbet or even Velásquez at his best.‡

The flesh of the woman in *"Opera Box"* is dominated by a Velásquez-Delacroix ivory; it also recalls Velásquez in its simpli-fied rendering and in the focal part it plays in the patterned, rich black-and-white ensemble; but Velásquez' flesh, even at its best, lacks the deep glow, the feeling of internal life already present in the flesh of this early Renoir.§ The face and chest of the woman

---

* Cf., e.g., *"Mr. and Mrs. Sisley"* (10) or *"Bather with Griffon"* (16) with Courbet's *"Nude"* (585), the nude and the woman with the shawl in *"Painter's Studio"* (586), *"Spring"* (588), *"Wounded Man"* (590) or *"Young Bather"* (591).

† Cf., e.g., Delacroix's *"Death of Sardanapalus"* (572) or *"Study of Reclining Woman"* (574).

‡ Cf., e.g., Velásquez' *"Infanta Marguerite"* (446), Courbet's *"Nude"* (585), Degas' *"After the Bath"* (610).

§ Cf., e.g., Velásquez' *"Infanta Marguerite"* (446) or *"Lady with Fan"* (448).

have the typical smooth Venetian modeling and drawing, but shadows are fewer than in the Venetians, much more restricted in area, and extremely reduced in tonal depth.* They are of light transparent greenish-blues, only slightly contrasting with the ivory of the lighted areas. These delicately colored shadows, their extremely subtle contrasts with the lighter portions of the flesh, and the simplified modeling and drawing of facial features, are all forerunners of Renoir's later and more constructive modifications of Venetian flesh-painting. His flesh-painting, at this period, in short, while leaning toward the old traditional type and still lacking the delicacy and the rich colorfulness of the best of his mid-seventies work, already represents a delicatized lightened version of the Venetian.

As Renoir emerges from his formative period, his absorption of other traditional forms enables him to utilize many of their traits in his reinterpretation of Venetian flesh-painting. At successive periods he concentrates upon the French painting of the eighteenth century, the early Italian frescoes and, still later, upon certain features of Rubens. During each of these respective periods the new influence competes with the Venetian and flavors it, but not sufficiently to compromise its status as the essential foundation of Renoir's flesh-painting.

The flesh-painting in *"Torso"* (52) of c. 1875 is an instance of Renoir's recreation of the Venetian form, still at an early stage, through the influence of a number of other traditions. When compared with Giorgione's *"Sleeping Venus"* (344) which well represents the highest type of Venetian flesh-painting, the figure in *"Torso"* shows both basic resemblances and basic differences. The color of the Venus is somewhat darker and more yellowish than natural flesh and of a tone midway between the usually heavier browns of Titian or Tintoretto and the lighter ivory in *"Torso."* Light pervades the color and imbues it with an internal warmth and glow, but the glow is muted, less bright and luminous than Renoir's.

In both paintings, the figure is modeled with extraordinary fineness of relationships: there are no accentuated highlights and very few shadows, and the greenish-blue tones as they proceed toward the lighter portions of the flesh are modulated with extreme subtlety. Delicate interrelations of light and shadow in the model-

* Cf., e.g., Titian's *"Alfonso da Ferrara and Laura di Dianti"* (346).

ing of the breast, for instance, render, in each picture, a real, solid and subtly rounded volume with smooth and fluid one-piece surface. As painting, the Renoir excels the Giorgione in that its less heavy pigment gives a greater degree of transparency and textural delicacy to the flesh. Renoir's flesh excels Giorgione's also because of its variegated sequence of delicate color-chords formed by differently colored lights and shadows. The corresponding intermingling of color in the Giorgione produces a rather uniform general color-mottling.

As a result of the greater transparency, fluidity and delicacy of the glazes in the Renoir, the colors flow freely from one area to another and establish a series of tonal relationships which render contours more subtly and effectively than does the line in the Giorgione. No actual line separates the body and its setting in *"Torso,"* yet the two parts are clearly defined and differentiated in color, texture, shape and position in space; in the Giorgione the contour on the left side of the figure, from the shoulder down along the whole outer outline of the arm, is more facilely rendered by a concentration of shadow which has the appearance of a dark broad actual line.

The smooth subtle one-piece modeling and the delicately loose contour in *"Torso"* suggest also a comparison with corresponding plastic characteristics, occasionally found in Titian; for example, in the female figures in *"Jupiter and Antiope"* (354) and *"Venus and Adonis"* (365). Here the flesh is modeled in the manner of the Giorgione just discussed, by a subtle adjustment of color and tone at contours to yield the typically Venetian loose but firm color-drawing, and without resort to Titian's usual contrast between extensive heavy shadows and large areas of light. This type of flesh-painting, rather rare in Titian, shows the characteristic Venetian weighty color with brownish tonality and muted glow, reliance upon linear contour as an aid to modeling,* and general heaviness of form. None of these appears in the flesh in *"Torso"*; instead, the color is lighter, more positive, delicate, and internally luminous;

---

* E.g., in Titian's *"Jupiter and Antiope,"* at a distance the concentration of the shadow along the contour of the reclining nude forms a definite continuous brown line. In Renoir's *"Torso,"* contour reveals no line, but a subtle differentiation in tone between the flesh and the area back of it distinguishes object and background as convincingly as in the Titian. This is obviously a question of degree of skill in the manipulation of color.

fluid contour is established by subtle color-relations between the flesh and the setting, and the total form is light and dainty.

Technical changes in the use of color-glazes is largely responsible for these differences between Renoir and the Venetians. At the contour in Giorgione and Titian there is an abrupt change in the color of the glaze from that of the flesh itself to that of the broad dark outer line which both connects and separates figure and background; in *"Torso,"* the delicate glazes of the flesh, as they flow uninterruptedly over the contour, gradually and almost imperceptibly change their color to that of the setting; thus, subtle nuances of color soften outline, temper the contrast between the light flesh and the darker background, and increase their atmospheric continuity.

One of the most striking examples of Renoir's richer and at the same time more delicate version of Venetian flesh-painting is the hands in *"Woman Crocheting"* (76) of c. 1877. Compared with these, the hands in Titian's *"Man with Glove"* (357), and the right leg of Christ and the arms of the woman in *"Christ and the Magdalene"* (348), which represent Titian at his best, are of the usual Venetian light brown tone, differentiated with color-chords by subtle intermingling with greens, blues, pinks and ivories. The hands in the Renoir are drawn and modeled by much more diversified lights and colors interpenetrating and reënforcing each other in color-chords which render the structure of the flesh as solidly as Titian's, and with far greater sensuous appeal. Renoir's drawing is more fluid and delicate, and his color-chords are more active both individually and in the intricate set of color-relations which draw out the inherent nature of the hands and form their richly decorative surface. The variety of Titian's color-chords is much less and the prevailing golden brown of his flesh, for all its intrinsic richness, is monotonous in comparison with Renoir's variegated and constantly changing series of color-nuances.

The variegated surface in these Renoir hands invites a comparison also with Rembrandt's and Velásquez' flesh-painting, both derived from the Venetians. The coral tone of the hands in Rembrandt's *"Woman's Portrait"* (459) is a composite of light shades of green, blue, pink and yellow which suggests the color-chords in the Renoir hands. Renoir's color-chords, however, form a vibrating subtle pattern and thus add life and movement to the surface, while the corresponding chords in the Rembrandt are more continuous with each other in a one-piece, smoothly rounded and comparatively monotonous surface.

The hands in *"Woman Crocheting"* recall also, in their grace and delicacy of poised movement conveyed by color-drawing, the hands in Velásquez' *"Infanta Marguerite"* (446). These are a wonderful achievement of drawing which attains form and reality, but they lack the internal richness of Renoir's delicate juicy color-chords, as well as the subtlety which Renoir's color imparts to the drawing, and which enables him to render even more convincingly the essential nature of human hands. Velásquez' modeling depends more than Renoir's upon contrast of light and dark; not only is the contrast itself sharper, but neither the light nor the dark is felt so definitely as positive color.

Velásquez' painting of flesh is, in general, devoid of rich color-variations and internal life and, compared to Renoir's, usually has the tendency just noted to overaccentuation of light.* Even when Velásquez' tones of pink blend finely with light bluish or brownish shadows in a subtly variegated complexion,† the smooth even surface of the flesh, with its relative absence of pattern of color and of light-and-shadow, is conducive to monotony; the feeling of paint is almost always present, and often the texture resembles that of putty or plaster rather than of human flesh. His flesh-painting, even at its best, as in *"Infanta Marguerite"* and, in a heavier type, in *"Felipe IV"* (443), is never entirely free from this lack of quality in surface and texture. The flesh-painting in these portraits is essentially a resetting of Paolo Veronese's in a context of broader, more simplified drawing.‡ Into this Veronese-Velásquez form, Renoir, as we have seen, introduces a greater variety of patterns and more color in the blending of light and shadow. These changes increase the delicacy, subtlety and the solidity of the color and make it richer both decoratively and expressively. Renoir's departure in this respect is further from Velásquez than Velásquez' was from Paolo Veronese and the Venetians in general: it represents an increase of the function of

---

* Cf., e.g., Renoir's baby in *"Mother and Child"* (118) with Velásquez' *"Infanta Marguerite"* (446), and the hands in Renoir's *"Girl with Jumping Rope"* (57) with the right hand in Velásquez' *"Felipe IV, in his Youth"* (444).

† E.g., Velásquez' *"Infanta Doña Margarita de Austria"* (445) and *"Príncipe Don Baltasar Carlos"* (450).

‡ Cf., e.g., the woman at the left in Paolo Veronese's *"Wedding at Cana"* (411).

color in drawing, and hence is more individual and of greater plastic significance.*

A parallel evolution appears in the pictures in which Renoir
leans upon Tintoretto. Nothing in the flesh-painting of Giorgione,
Titian, Paolo Veronese or Velásquez, is comparable to the richly
patterned and variegated face at the upper right of the composition in Renoir's *"After the Concert"* (73) of c. 1877. Its closest
prototype is perhaps Tintoretto's *"Head of a Man"* (386) or
"Vincenzo Morosini" (396) in which the faces contain similar internal patterns, and the flesh is likewise richly and solidly colorful.
The color of the flesh in the Renoir is more glowingly illuminated
throughout, and the pattern, though looser, is also more pronounced; the areas of light and dark are reënforced by brighter,
more varied and more luminous color, which makes the pattern a
more integral part of the form.

Rembrandt also at times revised and enriched Tintoretto's flesh-
painting, mainly, as did Renoir, by making color play a more important part in the pattern.† The difference between the two
transcriptions is typically illustrated by the face in Rembrandt's
"Man with Stick" (457) and that of the woman at the extreme
right in Renoir's *"After the Concert."* The face in each has a
pattern of areas, with interpenetration of colors between them to
produce color-chords, but Renoir's pattern is more accentuated and
loosely drawn, and the complexion is more varied and nuanced with
brighter color. His light, more evenly distributed throughout the
whole face, makes the color more luminous than does Rembrandt's
sharp contrast of broad areas of light and dark. The features common to the flesh in each picture, deep structural color, pattern of
color-areas, very rich surface and positive color-chords, are in the
Renoir given an ampler decorative variety by his more delicate and
luminous color. Renoir's form is a more pictorial rendering of
flesh, a more personal interpretation of the Venetian tradition, and
it has none of the feeling of paint present in Rembrandt's color.

The outstanding features of Renoir's flesh-painting in the eighties—the smooth, relatively dry surface, the light-toned complexion,
the pinkish-white foundation, the one-piece modeling and the
exotic texture—are drawn less directly from Venetian sources than

---

* Cf. also Renoir's *"Girl with Jumping Rope"* (57) with Velásquez'
"Infanta Marguerite" (446) and *"Infanta Maria Teresa, when Three
Years Old"* (447).

† E.g., *"Dressed Beef"* (455), *"Hendrickje Stoffels"* (456), *"Man with
Stick"* (457), and the hands of *"Margaretha Trip"* (458).

those of any other period. They have their source in the reconstruction of Paolo Veronese's flesh-painting by the French painters
of the eighteenth century.*

As Renoir emerges from the exotic interlude of the 1880-1887
period, his flesh-painting reassumes its earlier lifelike quality, but
in a form which profits appreciably by his assimilation of the traditional aspects and methods upon which he drew during that interval. After the eighties it remains close to Paolo Veronese's in
which the complexion is lighter in tone, the substance less weighty,
and the surface usually more mottled than in the work of the
other Venetians. Paolo Veronese's shadows in general are also
much lighter in tone than Titian's or Tintoretto's and are more
often permeated by greenish or pinkish grays than by heavy golden
or greenish browns.† The complexion of his women and children,
with its tendency toward a whitish-pink cast with pinkish accents
on cheeks, knees, and other parts of the body, very decidedly forecasts the flesh-painting of Rubens and of the French eighteenth
century painters, Boucher and Fragonard, from whom Renoir derived many characteristics of his flesh-painting.‡

After about 1890, two essential new elements appear in Renoir's
rendering of flesh: the dappled surface and the rose-red suffusion.
They are new in the use which Renoir makes of them, and new
in their intrinsic individuality and fulness of decoration and expression, but in their origin they both hark back to the Venetian
tradition, the dappled surface more directly, the rose-red suffusion
by way of Rubens and the eighteenth century French painters.

The dappling of the flesh appears in Renoir's work during the
nineties, and remains a distinctive feature until the end of his
career.§ It takes the form of an all-over mottled pattern of small

* Cf., e.g., Paolo Veronese's *"Venetian Woman"* (409) with Lancret's
"Open Cage" (491) and Renoir's *"Woman with Fan"* (160) of 1886.

† Cf., e.g., Paolo Veronese's *"Happy Union"* (403) or *"Unfaithfulness"*
(408) with Titian's *"Bacchus and Ariadne"* (347) and Tintoretto's *"Origin
of the Milky Way"* (388) or *"St. George and the Dragon"* (391).

‡ Cf., e.g., Paolo Veronese's *"Mars and Venus United by Love"* (407)
with Rubens' *"St. Cecilia"* (434), Boucher's *"Three Graces"* (519), Fragonard's *"Bathers"* (531) or *"Young Woman and Child"* (539), and
with Renoir's *"Head of Girl with Hat"* (210) of c. 1893, *"Reclining Nude"*
(217) of c. 1910 and *"Caryatids"* (248 and 249) of c. 1910.

§ E.g., *"Nude in Brook"* (213) of 1895, *"Bathers in Forest"* (216) of
c. 1897, *"Bather with Legs Crossed"* (227) of c. 1902-1903, *"Missia"* (235)
of c. 1906, *"Woman Reading"* (238) of c. 1906, *"Bather Drying Herself"*
(243) of c. 1909, *"Bust of Nude"* (244) of c. 1909, *"Reclining Nude"*
(252) of c. 1910, *"Bathing Group"* (285) of 1916, *"Nymphs"* (304) of
c. 1918.

blurred areas of colorful light and shadow, so interrelated that neither the continuity of the surface nor the unity of the volume is disturbed. Sometimes the dappling is only slightly perceptible, as in *"Nude in Brook"* (213) ; sometimes as in *"Missia"* (235), it produces a delicate color-vibration and takes an active part in the subtle color-suffusion of the entire picture. In *"Caryatids"* (248 and 249), the components of the pattern are enlarged into ill-defined areas of light and shadow which dovetail and produce a fluid rhythmic pattern. At other times the dappling is so pronounced, as in *"Bust of Nude"* (244), as to be of paramount importance in the sculpturesque solidity as well as in the decorative appeal of the flesh. Renoir's dappled surface is a version in a new synthesis of his fluid mid-seventies' pattern of color-chords and of light and shade, which had practically disappeared from his flesh-painting during the eighties. Technically it is achieved by small dabs and brush strokes derived from the impressionists, but the resulting subtle interplay of colors and tones gives rise to decorative and expressive values which have no counterpart in the work of the impressionists.

The nearest traditional prototype to Renoir's dappled surface is the subtly patterned intermingling of color perceptible, in very varied degree of accentuation, in a number of the Venetian masters. The slightly dappled appearance of the flesh in the female figure in Titian's *"Perseus and Andromeda"* (361) and of that in *"Venus and Adonis"* (365) is due partly to a subtle pattern of unaccentuated semi-shadows melting smoothly into intervening loosely defined areas of light, and partly to the weave of the canvas itself, which gives a grainy surface to the paint. The latter characteristic, of frequent occurrence in the Venetians, is due to the effect of time, which has allowed the grain of the canvas to break through the impasto, thus converting it into a grainy or minutely pitted surface with infinitesimal pin-points of dark and light.* The effect is that of a generalized mottling rather than of Renoir's dappled pattern of distinguishable areas. Occasionally, however, as in *"Bather with Legs Crossed"* (227), Renoir's tonal variations of the flesh-color almost duplicate the effect of a surface worn by age.

A comparison between the dappled flesh in Renoir's *"Bather Drying Herself"* (243) and the woman's left shoulder in Titian's

* E.g., Titian's *"Mother and Child"* (358), *"Man and Child"* (356), *"Nymph and Shepherd"* (359) and *"Salome"* (362), Tintoretto's *"Origin of the Milky Way"* (388) and *"Young Venetian Girl"* (398).

"Alfonso da Ferrara and Laura di Dianti" (346) shows that Renoir not only emphasized the pattern by more positive constituents but also enriched and embellished the structure of the flesh by brighter, more varied and more deeply illuminated color. The intermingling of color in Renoir's dappled flesh may have had its source in the type of Venetian painting represented by the flesh in Titian's *"Venus and Music"* (367) and by textiles in Tintoretto's *"Two Prophets"* (394), in the garment of the man at the left. In these pictures the light and color of the mottled areas actually melt into each other and form a continuous homogeneous surface, relatively uniform in color and free from pattern. In Renoir's typical dappled flesh the units of color and light retain their identity as parts of a decorative pattern at the same time that their fluid intermingling blends them into a single composite form.*

Paolo Veronese's painting of flesh, especially in babies, cupids and women, offers a closer approach to Renoir's dappled surface than does Titian's or Tintoretto's. The individual units of his surface-mottling are larger than in the other Venetians,† and the greater number of colors, decidedly more varied in tone, which they contain produce a more contrasting dappled pattern within the general one-piece cast of the complexion.‡ Renoir, in addition to modifying these features in detail, gives to the dappled surface a different rôle in the composite form of the flesh. For example, Paolo Veronese's light and dark areas contribute to the modeling of the flesh, but their contribution is materially supported by the broad, dark, accentuated line of contour. Renoir dispenses with this line and makes the dappled surface an integral part of the volumes, obtaining by his superior integration the effect of solid volumes, fleshlike in texture and felt to be supported by a firm internal structure.§

The preceding discussion shows that the dappled surface in Venetian flesh-painting provides points of departure for Renoir's

---

* Cf., e.g., Renoir's *"Bust of Nude"* (244).

† Cf., e.g., the face of the woman at the extreme left in Paolo Veronese's *"Wedding at Cana"* (411) with the face in Tintoretto's *"Susannah at the Bath"* (393), from which type of flesh-painting Paolo Veronese's very likely originated.

‡ E.g., the woman's shoulder at the extreme left in Paolo Veronese's *"Feast at the House of Simon the Pharisee"* (402), *"Happy Union"* (403), *"Unfaithfulness"* (408), and the woman at the left in his *"Wedding at Cana"* (411).

§ Cf., e.g., Renoir's *"Bust of Nude"* (244) with Paolo Veronese's *"Unfaithfulness"* (408).

more imaginative drawing, light-and-shadow modeling, technique and color-modulation. The flesh-painting in his late work is a condensation of traditional methods in a form further from the original sources than at any previous stage of his career. At each period his drafts upon the Venetian characteristics were enriched by meaningful developments of his own loose fluid drawing, luminosity, colorfulness, grace, delicacy and decorative charm. After 1900 these qualities reach their maximum and his flesh-painting becomes exuberant in jewel-like iridescent color, extraordinarily voluptuous, fully expressive and individual in the highest degree. During the course of this growth the Venetian characteristics are overlaid with a wealth of qualities adapted by Renoir from the eighteenth century French painters, and these in turn are affected by qualities of drawing and sensuous color derived from Rubens whose influence appears in the preponderance of warm reddish-rose in the complexion, the swirling rhythms of the volumes, and the abstract voluptuousness of the flesh itself.*

An indication of Rubens' influence appears in the flesh-painting in some of Renoir's pictures of the early nineties, for example, *"Head of Girl with Hat"* (210). Here his earlier lavender or blue-green shadows are diminished, and the pink, concentrated on the cheek, tends to suffuse the entire flesh with a decided rose tonality.† No such pervasive pink or rose is found in the Venetians. In Titian the flesh is generally dominated by heavy tones of fulvous brown or tawny ivory in figures of men,‡ and usually by a lighter warm golden-ivory in the women.§ The slight suggestion of pink in the flesh of Venus in his *"Venus and Adonis"* (365) and in a few other female figures ‖ gives the complexion a light pinkish-ivory cast quite different from the actual red or rose in Rubens and Renoir. Titian's pink or red, when accentuated on cheeks, heels, toes, does not modify essentially the prevailing general

* Cf., e.g., Renoir's *"Bathing Group"* (285) with Rubens' *"Diana and her Nymphs Surprised by Satyrs"* (421).
† Rubens' influence is already vaguely suggested in the late seventies, e.g., in the rose tonality of the complexion in Renoir's *"Café Scene"* (81) and *"Dreamer"* (91).
‡ E.g., orange-bronze in *"Bacchus and Ariadne"* (347), a lighter yellowish bronze-brown in *"Disciples at Emmaüs"* (350), brownish ivory or light brown in *"Head of Man—Ariosto?"* (353), deep reddish bronze-brown in *"Jupiter and Antiope"* (354), brownish coral in *"Venetian Family"* (364), and a heavy yellow-tawny cast in *"Young Man in Black"* (371).
§ E.g., *"Jupiter and Antiope"* (354).
‖ E.g., in *"Danaë Receiving Rain of Gold"* (349), *"Venus and Organ Player"* (368), *"Venus Blindfolding Cupid"* (369).

brownish or tawny-ivory strain. Tintoretto's slight variations from Titian's flesh-color consist chiefly in a tendency toward rather more ruddy browns in the male figures * and toward a green or gray-golden cooler tonality in the female.†

Paolo Veronese, as we have already noted, inclines toward a general lightening of the color of the flesh and uses more pink,‡ thus approaching the effects which Rubens developed further and Renoir carried to fulness. Paolo Veronese's red or pink is concentrated in a series of subtly accentuated focuses on cheeks, knees, or thighs, from which it radiates and gradually merges with the general silver or lavender-gray tone of the surrounding flesh. These relatively accentuated areas of pink or red lend a somewhat rosy cast to the complexion much, in principle, as in Rubens. In fact, Rubens and also Boucher owe to Paolo Veronese much of the decorative quality to which Renoir added substance, reality and greater charm.§

Rubens' development of this aspect of Paolo Veronese's form is usually more imaginative and individual in his painting of female figures than of male. The flesh in the latter is generally very close to Titian's fulvous bronze-browns; when the flesh in his women is tinged with such browns, the areas of shadow are generally lightened in tone and restricted in expanse, much as in Paolo Veronese; ‖ however, in the painting of both men and women he sometimes flagrantly imitates and perverts Titian's browns in an over-dramatic contrast of light and dark.¶ Rubens frequently used pink accents in shadows often function as reflected light which, reenforced by pink in the middle tones, casts a rosy glow over the

* E.g., Tintoretto's "*Two Prophets*" (394) and "*Vincenzo Morosini*" (396).

† E.g., Tintoretto's "*Origin of the Milky Way*" (388), "*St. George and the Dragon*" (391) and "*Susannah at the Bath*" (393).

‡ E.g., Paolo Veronese's "*Happy Union*" (403), "*Unfaithfulness*" (408), "*Venetian Woman*" (409), "*Wedding at Cana*" (411). All these pictures show that the tendency was especially prevalent in the painting of women, babies, and cupids.

§ Cf., e.g., Paolo Veronese's "*Venetian Woman*" (409) with Rubens' "*Holy Family*" (426), "*Holy Family in Landscape*" (427), "*St. Cecilia*" (434), "*Susanne Fourment*" (435), with Boucher's "*Diana at the Bath*" (508), "*Sleeping Shepherdess*" (518), "*Venus*" (520), "*Venus Adorning Herself*" (521), and with Renoir's "*Missia*" (235) or "*Bather Drying Herself*" (243). Or else cf. Paolo Veronese's "*Happy Union*" (403) with Rubens' "*Apotheosis of William the Silent*" (415) or "*Romulus and Remus*" (433), with Boucher's "*Pan and Syrinx*" (515) and with Renoir's "*Bathing Group*" (285).

‖ E.g., Rubens' "*Diana and Callisto*" (420).

¶ E.g., Rubens' "*Adoration of the Kings*" (413).

yellowish or brownish complexion.* The rose glow comes partly also from one of the parallel broad bands of color which pattern and model the flesh, the outermost of which is frequently a strip of reddish reflected light.† Often in Boucher and Fragonard these red accents of Rubens' at the outlines are accentuated to become actual linear contour.‡

The pervasive rose of Renoir's flesh-painting is attained without any such specious and adventitious means; it is an inseparable part of the decorative pattern and substance of the flesh itself, and is due directly to the fusion of color and light. When, on rare occasions, Renoir uses either accentuated pink contours § or parallel broad bands of color, ‖ they are not, as in the prototypes, primarily decorative, almost mechanistic, patterns but integral parts of the expressive form.

A more positive influence of Rubens upon Renoir appears in the graceful flow of linear areas of color and light. The prototype of this is the moving rhythm of Venetian figures, which was accentuated by Rubens into a turbulent swirl, highly decorative in its linear flourishes but overdramatic and expressively superficial.¶ By a new type of drawing, developed from traits found in ancient Greek sculpture,** the work of Girardon †† and the paintings of Boucher ‡‡ and Fragonard,§§ Renoir converts Rubens' turbulent, jerky and predominantly linear swirl into a graceful, smoothly flowing, rhythmic movement of color, which embraces the whole

---

* E.g., Rubens' *"Horrors of War"* (428). A slight lavender tinge is sometimes present in Rubens' pink semi-shadows and occurs also occasionally in Paolo Veronese and more often in the eighteenth century French painters—e.g., Paolo Veronese's *"Baptism of Christ"* (400), Rubens' *"Annunciation"* (414) and *"David Playing on the Harp"* (419) and Boucher's *"Venus"* (520).

† E.g., Rubens' *"Annunciation"* (414) and *"Diana Returning from the Hunt"* (422).

‡ Cf., e.g., Rubens' *"Holy Family"* (426) with Boucher's *"Three Graces"* (519) and Fragonard's *"Bathers"* (531) or *"Young Woman and Child"* (539).

§ E.g., Renoir's *"Two Little Circus Girls"* (99), *"Mother and Child"* (118), *"Grape Gatherers Resting"* (147), *"Washerwoman and Baby"* (163).

‖ E.g., Renoir's *"Seated Nude"* (279), *"Nude with Castanets"* (287), *"Bathers"* (301).

¶ Cf., e.g., Rubens' *"Diana and her Nymphs Surprised by Satyrs"* (421) with Titian's *"Offering to the Goddess of Love"* (360).

** E.g., Greek *"Reclining Figure"* (308), *"Three Fates?"* (309), *"Standing Figure"* (311).

†† E.g., Girardon's *"Bath of the Nymphs"* (461).

‡‡ E.g., Boucher's *"Diana at the Bath"* (508) and *"Three Graces"* (519).

§§ E.g., Fragonard's *"Bathers"* (531) and *"Woman Undressing"* (538).

composition.* Rubens' swirling movement is confined to contours or individual component shapes, and rarely includes volumes as a whole, much less the entire composition. His color, moreover, has not the depth, the subtlety of tonal gradation, nor the mellowness of Renoir's, and hence the swirl itself lacks these qualities which are everywhere present in Renoir's more organic color-movement.

A similar refinement of exaggerated decoration into well-balanced plastic form is evident in Renoir's use of the other Rubens' traits in flesh-painting, color-chords and an extensive use of red. The color-chords in Rubens are more numerous and of brighter tone than in the Venetians generally, and they merely lie on the surface of the flesh. In this also Rubens derives from Paolo Veronese rather than from Titian or Tintoretto, and clearly forecasts the eighteenth century French painting.† Renoir utilizes the rich surface-quality of this type of Rubens' flesh-painting but avoids the decorative overemphasis by implanting the color-chords in the substance of the flesh itself, thus restoring the fundamental qualities of Venetian painting.‡

To a trained observer, the apparent similarity between the red of Rubens and that of Renoir means nothing more than that both painters had a predilection for pinks and reds in their depiction of flesh. One feels that the reaction to Rubens' red is due to the impact upon the senses of the color itself rather than to color as a stimulus to an intricate esthetic perception. The same color in Renoir also pleases the senses, but the percipient undergoes simultaneously a continually unfolding experience as he observes the organic participation of the red in the construction of the solidity and textural quality of a substance that has the feeling of human flesh enriched by the painter's imaginative interpretation.

With rare exceptions Rubens' flesh is like that of a mummy encased in a reddish or pink skin; color lends no vitality to its substance, and the fluidity of the volumes is conveyed not by their color but chiefly by the broken curve of their contour, often indicated by actual line. Renoir, in contrast, constructs the flesh, its contour and the space which the volumes occupy, each of color. In

---

* Cf., e.g., Renoir's *"Judgment of Paris"* (240), *"Bathing Group"* (285) or *"Bathers"* (301), with Rubens' *"Diana and her Nymphs Surprised by Satyrs"* (421).

† Cf., e.g., Rubens' *"Holy Family"* (425) with Paolo Veronese's *"Happy Union"* (403) and Boucher's *"Three Graces"* (519).

‡ E.g., Renoir's *"Nude with Castanets"* (287). Rubens, whose relatively literal drawing is basically Flemish, did not avail himself of these essential qualities of Venetian painting.

his *"Bathing Group"* (285), for instance, the texture of the flesh is in itself color, and the fluid streamline contours of the figures and also the space around them result from an uninterrupted flow of structural color from the figures into the space. Renoir, in other words, through his fusion of all the plastic means in drawing and modeling, endows the expressiveness of flesh with new significance and added decorative appeal.* Rubens fabricates a counterfeit of flesh mainly by superficial color and by a specious, undulating linear contour.

An exception to the foregoing indictment of Rubens must be made in the case of his most important painting, *"Judgment of Paris"* (430). Here, the figures are graceful and majestic, their curving contours are restrained and extremely rhythmic, and the flesh-painting, in its solidity, depth of color, graceful classic drawing and convincing textural quality, recalls that in Giorgione's *"Sleeping Venus"* (344). The pattern of light and dark derives from Titian's modeling, and the general complexion—a golden yellow with pinkish light tinging the pink-orange shadows—is allied to Paolo Veronese's. The texture of the flesh is more natural than in most Venetian painting, and it lacks Rubens' usual pronounced pinks and reds. The picture is in the main an extraordinarily fine version of the Venetian form at its best.

Renoir in 1908 also painted a *"Judgment of Paris"* (240), in which a similar classic feeling is imparted to the figures by fine adjustment of moving linear rhythms and graceful color-volumes. Renoir's version is the more delicate, and it has the fluid charm acquired from the eighteenth century French painters. A brownish tinge in the rose tones of the complexion brings the flesh closer in color to the Venetian than it is in Renoir's more typical late work.†
Not infrequently, however, in his flesh-painting after the nineties Renoir reverts to the browns of the Venetians, but their slight admixture in the pinks and reds does not destroy the preponderant rose or red tonality.‡ Conversely in the Venetians, with the exception of Paolo Veronese, the occasional rose or pink in the lighted parts of the flesh does not materially alter the brownish-ivory or golden-brown cast.§ Tones of brown or red are also asso-

---

* Cf., e.g., Rubens' *"David Playing on the Harp"* (419) or *"Holy Family in Landscape"* (427).
† Cf., e.g., *"Promenade"* (236) or *"Bathing Group"* (285).
‡ E.g., *"Artist's Family"* (214) and *"Cup of Chocolate"* (263).
§ E g., Titian's *"Danaë Receiving Rain of Gold"* (349), and the figure of Christ in Tintoretto's *"Woman of Samaria"* (397).

ciated in Rubens' painting of flesh, and the domination of one over the other varies greatly according to the extent of his departure from the Venetian prototypes.* We may now summarize in brief essentials Renoir's emancipation from the flesh-painting of the Venetians and of Rubens, and his conversion of their forms into something richer, fuller and more individual. Renoir's color is deeper than theirs and is pervaded by brighter and more mellow tones—especially pinks and reds in his late work; its higher and more inherent luminosity intensifies the colorfulness and adds an iridescent quality to the surface; its greater fluidity results in more subtle modeling, looser, more delicate, natural and spontaneous drawing, and a more continuous flow of the whole composition as rhythmic color-movement. All these extensions of the function of color produce decorative values far in excess of the best work of the Venetians and of Rubens; but much more than that, they permit a more complete integration of decoration and expression, a finer adjustment to each other, which enhances the esthetic value of the form as a whole. Renoir's flesh-painting transcends anything in Rubens or the Venetians in degree of voluptuousness, conviction of essentials, reality of texture, decorative charm and imaginative grasp of traditions and subject-matter.†

PAINTING OF TEXTILES

Painting of textiles in general resolves itself chiefly into the question of color-quality in the expression and decoration of textures and surfaces, and the question of the relationships of light, color and line in the drawing of folds. Renoir's painting of textiles stems chiefly from the Venetians and the eighteenth century French painters, but leaves no element of either tradition isolated or intact.

In order to appreciate Renoir's abstraction, condensation and ingenious re-creation of Venetian methods and effects in this field, it will be advantageous to indicate briefly the principal variations of the traditional form in the great Venetians. In Giovanni Bellini

---

* In Rubens' *"Adoration of the Kings"* (413) the unadjusted mixture of red and brown in the flesh of the men produces a feeling of raucous heaviness in the colors themselves and a jerky disharmony in their relationships.
  † Further, but less direct, relationships between Renoir's flesh-painting and the Venetian are discussed in the chapter "Renoir and the Eighteenth Century French Tradition," p. 209.

and some of his close followers the crest of folds is generally of the same color, in lighter tone, as that of the material itself, and these lighted areas are circumscribed in more or less well-defined shapes.* This manner of painting folds, together with the as yet incompletely structural color of the pre-Titian painters, often results, in the minor men, in an unreal and papery effect.† In this traditional type of drawing, Giorgione and Titian, by finer adjustments of color and light and greater solidity of color, increased the feeling of textural reality as well as the surface-appeal of the materials.‡ Renoir's use of this Giorgione-Titian merging of highlights with adjacent middle tones and shadows gives to his textiles the Venetian qualities of richness, depth, glow and textural reality, but his drawing is broader, more simplified, his color and patterns are more fluid, and the textiles themselves are more delicate in structure and lighter in weight.

These fundamental differences are perceptible even in Renoir's early work. The red-rose draperies in *"Opera Box"* (34), for example, by their tone, color-quality, velvety texture, and technical execution, bring to mind Titian's rendering of similar materials in *"Emperatriz Doña Isabel de Portugal"* (351), *"Danaë Receiving Rain of Gold"* (349) and *"Venus and Music"* (367), and also, and more particularly, Velásquez' simplified use of the same Titian form, as in *"Infanta Marguerite"* (446). Renoir's fabrics are of more delicate texture and more loosely drawn than either of these prototypes, and their opulent surface is free from Velásquez' dryness and feeling of paint. Velásquez' painting of stuffs, with its simplification of the Venetian form, retains an adequate degree of structural color, but usually fails to embellish the surface with either juicy pigment or interpenetrating colors; and these defects, as we have already noted, persist in Velásquez' traditional successor, Goya. Thus, any comparison between Renoir's and the Spanish versions of the Titian form reveals Renoir's better feeling for sensuous quality of color, for color-relations, and for use of paint.

* E.g., Gentile Bellini's (School of) *"Reception of a Venetian Ambassador at Cairo, in 1512"* (328), Giovanni Bellini's *"Madonna and Child"* (329) and *"Madonna of the Little Trees"* (330), Mantegna's *"Parnassus"* (332) and *"Wisdom Triumphing over the Vices"* (334), Carpaccio's *"St. Stephen Preaching at Jerusalem"* (340).

† E.g., Crivelli's *"Annunciation"* (331), Mantegna's *"Madonna and Child"* (335).

‡ E.g., Giorgione's *"Sleeping Venus"* (344), Titian's *"Christ and the Magdalene"* (348).

These points may be illustrated in Renoir's *"Girl with Jumping Rope"* (57), Velásquez' *"Infanta Doña Margarita de Austria"* 445)* and Goya's *"Doctor Galos"* (542).† The dress in both the Renoir and the Velásquez is a broad surface streaked with light, and the guimpe in the Renoir and the stock in the Goya each conveys the feeling of transparency and delicacy. The Velásquez and the Goya, however, bear marks of mechanical technique, monotonous color and painty surface which deprive the textures of richness, fully convincing reality, and colorful surface-charm. Renoir has delicatized the color-solidity of the Venetians and preserved the simplified drawing of Velásquez and the lightness of Goya in a form richer in color and more expressive of the character of textiles than that of either of the Spaniards.‡

Practically the same differences can be seen in comparing the transparent draperies in Renoir's *"Torso"* (52) and in Goya's *"Maja Nude"* (552). The covering of the pillow between the figure and left arm in the Goya is patterned by a technique of broad brush strokes similar to that in the Renoir. Goya's drawing here is taken practically entire from Velásquez; Renoir's is based upon both of them, but nobody before Renoir ever attained his variety of color, subtlety of relations, interpenetration of tones, luminosity of color, or reality of textiles, all rendered in good plastic terms instead of illustratively as by the other men. Renoir's superiority in the use of color to render the transparency of delicate fabrics is evident even in his pre-1870 stage. In *"Lise"* (5) of 1867 the woman's guimpe over her chest and right arm presents the natural color-quality and textural feeling of both the transparent fabric and the flesh beneath it. This creative achievement, though crude compared to Renoir's later work,§ places the picture

---

* Or Velásquez' *"Court Attendants"* (441), in which the painted surface of practically all the textiles is hard, resembles wood, alabaster, or plaster, and is devoid of sensuous appeal.

† Or Goya's *"Doña Tadea Arias de Enríquez"* (544).

‡ Cf. also Renoir's transparent materials in *"Dancer"* (32) or *"Torso"* (52) with the stock in Goya's *"Doctor Galos"* (542) or the dress in *"Doña Tadea Arias de Enríquez"* (544), and the textiles in Renoir's *"Opera Box"* (34) with those in Velásquez' *"Infanta Marguerite"* (446) and Goya's *"Maja Dressed"* (551) or *"Majas on the Balcony"* (553). Particularly in the latter, Goya's textiles are academic, painty and literal; while accurately representative, even though broadly drawn, they have an exotic character not connected with the essential feeling of textile, but rather an incongruous metallic quality.

§ Cf., e.g., *"Girl with Jumping Rope"* (57) of 1876, *"Promenade"* (236) of c. 1906 or *"Woman Sewing"* (256) of c. 1910.

far beyond Goya's *"Woman with Fan"* (554), for example, in which the corresponding effect is that of two superposed layers of paint which convey little if any feeling of either textile or flesh.*

Renoir's creative reinterpretation of Venetian textiles acquires additional distinction by the different function he assigns to patterns of light in the drawing of folds, and to the qualities which these patterns obtain from his color-drawing in general. The Venetians usually relied much on accentuated highlighted streaks to depict folds and on relations of light-pattern to color to convey the specific character of the textile. With this traditional method, Titian, Tintoretto, Paolo Veronese, each attained distinctive effects by modifying the shape and degree of emphasis of the patterns of light, and the manner in which they are related to color. These individual adaptations reached Renoir chiefly through Rubens, the eighteenth century French painters and Manet, but whatever the particular influence operative upon Renoir's fabrics at various stages of his career, the foundation of the method is always Venetian.

Titian's folds are sometimes vividly patterned with accentuated highlights which bring out the sheen of silky or velvety materials.†
These highlights appear generally as a single long streak or stripe of colorful light along the crest of the fold, which forms a dramatic contrast with the actual color of the material. This method acquired in Tintoretto's hands a more specific form: he accentuated the contrast of light and color by diminishing the width of the highlight and reducing the number of intermediary tones between it and the deepest color of the fold, not infrequently placing streaks of highlight directly upon the darkest area of the material, thus causing their pattern to stand out like flashes of lightning in a dark sky.‡ Paolo Veronese, in turn, by other shifts in emphasis upon the constituents of folds, obtained novel effects of sheen, which brought out chiefly the decorative surface-aspects of the textiles. His color is less structural than either Titian's or Tintoretto's, his highlights are relatively detached and more nearly mere

* Cf. also the sleeves in Renoir's *"Girl with Jumping Rope"* (57) with the transparent headdress of the figure at the right in Goya's *"Majas on the Balcony"* (553).

† E.g., Titian's *"Bacchus and Ariadne"* (347), *"Danaë Receiving Rain of Gold"* (349), *"Venetian Family"* (364), *"Venus and Love"* (366), and *"Venus and Music"* (367).

‡ E.g., Tintoretto's *"St. George and the Dragon"* (391).

ornamental additions. Their patterns are less powerfully dramatic than Tintoretto's, and the sheen of the material is often a superficial metallic glitter or gleam.* It was chiefly this, Paolo Veronese's form of the Venetian method and effects, which Rubens took over and transmitted to the eighteenth century painters.†

Renoir's accentuated patterns of highlight in streaks or stripes on the crest of folds are an enormous advance over the Venetian. His more subtle correlation of light and color in the highlights themselves, and between them and the actual color of the draperies, usually arrives at a finer type of expression and drama than in Titian and Tintoretto, and the patterns are of higher decorative value than those of Paolo Veronese.‡ The more active function of Renoir's color in rendering the fabrics enables him to abstract the essence of Titian's expressiveness, of Tintoretto's drama and of Paolo Veronese's decoration, and so to use all of these factors that they reënforce each other and yield fuller, more comprehensive plastic units. The highlights in Renoir are more colorful than in the Venetians, more intensely luminous, and more varied in color-content, in degree of light-accentuation, in technical execution and in their relations to adjacent colors. Furthermore, the greater fluidity of his color-drawing establishes a more gradual transition from the highlighted crest of the folds to the middle tones and shadows, and the more decorative quality of his color transforms the tonal transitions into subtle, uninterrupted sequences of rich, juicy, delicate and sparkling color-chords. In other words, the highlighted streaks are more deeply incorporated in the fabric, and also more integral parts of the total color-composition.

Even the best examples of Venetian textile-painting lack this subtle adjustment and subordination of everything to color, which give to Renoir's fabrics their distinctive character. One of the highest Venetian achievements in this respect is the red brocade

---

* E.g., Paolo Veronese's *"Burning of Sodom"* (401), *"Mars and Venus United by Love"* (407), *"Vision of St. Helena"* (410).

† Cf., e.g., Paolo Veronese's *"Baptism of Christ"* (400), *"Feast at the House of Simon the Pharisee"* (402) or *"Mars and Venus United by Love"* (407) with Rubens' *"Annunciation"* (414) or *"Garden of Love"* (423), and Watteau's *"Buck"* (473), *"Embarkation for Cythera"* (474) or *"Figures in Landscape"* (477).

‡ E.g., Renoir's *"Girl with Basket of Flowers"* (188), *"Writing Lesson"* (234), *"After the Bath"* (247), *"Tea Time"* (257), *"Girl on Balcony at Cagnes"* (258), *"Cup of Chocolate"* (263), *"Bathing Group"* (285), *"Reclining Odalisque"* (293), *"Woman in Muslin Dress"* (298).

on the figure at the extreme right in Titian's *"Entombment"* (352). This fabric is wonderfully rich in color, and its pronounced pattern of light, well related to the shadows and color, increases the decorative quality of the material and contributes to its textural conviction. Its interrelations of light and color, however, fall short of those in the garments in Renoir's *"Bathing Group"* (285). The light in the latter sparkles and glows with multicolored effervescent overtones, which charge the garments with a rich iridescence lacking in Titian's fabric. A similar difference is apparent in the richness and variety of color and light in the color-chords of the respective textiles: Titian's color-chords are produced mainly by the unevenness of the impasto in the individual tones, and the technique is mechanical; Renoir's are due primarily to the subtle interpenetration of a great variety of color nuances, and the technical means are more diversified.

The defects in Titian's relations of light and color in *"Entombment"* are not due primarily to the relatively restricted color-gamut, because the same faults appear also in those occasional pictures in which he multiplies colors and accentuates their contrast, in a manner forecasting the color-patterns in the fabrics of Tintoretto, El Greco and later painters. *"Trinity Receiving Charles V"* (363) is a Titian of this type. The woman near the center of this composition is dressed in a green garment elaborately patterned with many-colored stripes and bands, and this pattern is emphasized by a technique of long brush strokes, clean-cut in shape and direction, and modern in general appearance. The skirt of the seated woman in Renoir's *"Bathing Group"* also shows perceptible brush strokes, vivid color-contrasts and patterns of streaks and highlights. With all Titian's internal enrichment by linear pattern, variety and brightness of color, and decorative handling of technique, the area so painted represents hardly more than an ornamental surface-depiction of the drapery; in Renoir's fabric the sensuous quality of color and light and the decorative patterns are thoroughly organic elements of the substance itself.

Tintoretto also renders colorfully iridescent textiles as, *e.g.,* in some parts of *"Paradise"* (389); but they are still far removed from Renoir's stuffs in degree and quality of glow, effulgence and sparkle.* The same is true of Paolo Veronese, as may be seen by a comparison of the dress in his *"Vision of St. Helena"* (410)

* Cf., e.g., Renoir's *"Writing Lesson"* (234).

with the ivory satin garment in Renoir's *"Embroiderers"* (233).*
The highlights in the former are isolated strokes and dabs of ivory
and coral superposed upon a practically uniform brownish under-
layer. From a distance the effect is that of a silky material with
realistic rendering of its folds and sheen, but close inspection
reveals the superficiality of the sheen, its lack of structure, glow
and colorfulness, and the outstanding speciousness of its execution.
Renoir's method is an adaptation of Paolo Veronese's but his form
exhibits an organic union of color, light and pattern, which achieves
a fully convincing as well as highly decorative plastic expression
of real satin. His form here is a delicate version of his predecessor's, more akin to that of the eighteenth century French painters,
in general, and, because of the lively pattern of shadows, reminiscent especially of Pater.†

Another device which Renoir adopted from Paolo Veronese is
the accentuation of the pattern of highlights in textiles as a dramatic motif in the design. The Venetian is at his best in this
respect in *"Burning of Sodom"* (401), in which the dramatic light-
pattern in the dress of the second figure from the left is well
merged with the underlying color of the fabric; the result is a good
realization of the sheen and texture as well as an appealing decorative pattern. Compared to the corresponding mutual reënforcement of color and light in the satin dress in Renoir's *"Tea Time"*
(257), the rendering of the textiles in the Paolo Veronese falls far
short of Renoir's both expressively and decoratively, and the surface has a certain amount of the feeling of paint.

Another device from the same source upon which Renoir im-
proves is the superposition of a decorative surface-pattern of brush
strokes upon units of color and light. These patterns in Renoir
retain sufficient connection with the texture itself to make more
convincing the expression of its particular quality; in Paolo
Veronese they are usually so accentuated by the swirl of brush
strokes and abrupt contrast of color that they seem to jump out
from their context as more or less detached embellishments.‡
Renoir far excels Paolo Veronese also in the surface-quality of
silky textiles. The sheen on Paolo Veronese's fabrics is not only

* Cf. also the painting of the dress at the extreme left in Paolo Veronese's
"Feast at the House of Simon the Pharisee" (402).
† Cf., e.g., Pater's *"Comedians in a Park"* (494).
‡ Cf., e.g., Renoir's *"Mother and Child"* (118) or *"Bathing Group"* (285)
with the dress of the woman at the extreme left in Paolo Veronese's *"Burn-
ing of Sodom"* (401).

superficial but tends to have a hard metallic quality,* seen occasionally also in Tintoretto's work; † in Renoir the metallic sheen is an inseparable part of the texture and its surface has a jewel-like sparkle pervaded with delicate, rich and deeply glowing color.‡ What is primarily decoration in Paolo Veronese, in other words, becomes in Renoir a powerful reënforcement of the expression.

CONCLUSION

Our study of Renoir's relation to the Venetian tradition may now be summed up. In all important respects, his form originated in that tradition, rendered its essentials, developed its methods and possibilities, and advanced beyond it. In the process Renoir displayed unrivaled sagacity in picking out the specific traits in other traditions which could be used to qualify and supplement the Venetian, and a high order of imagination in adjusting means to ends and giving to all that he found in the traditions his own personal form. After 1900, as we have shown in the chapter "Development of Renoir's Form," the most important aspect of his final expression was the dynamic organization of solid volumes in space, which was fundamental also in the Venetian form, and which Renoir carried, as he did all the other aspects, to expressive and decorative heights never before attained in the history of painting.

In his development of the Venetian form, Renoir drew especially upon the painting of the eighteenth century in France. What he found in this tradition, and how he used it is the subject of the following chapter.

* E.g., Paolo Veronese's *"Holy Family"* (404) and *"Jesus Healing Peter's Mother-in-law"* (405).
† E.g., Tintoretto's *"Esther and Ahasuerus"* (385), *"Judith and Holofernes"* (387), *"Queen of Sheba and Solomon"* (390).
‡ E.g., the shoes in *"Grape Gatherers Resting"* (147), the skirt of *"Girl with Basket of Oranges"* (178), *"Girl with Basket of Flowers"* (188), the rose drapery in *"After the Bath"* (247), the hat, pillow and background-drapery in *"Seated Nude"* (279), the green part of the garment in *"Woman in Muslin Dress"* (298), *"Bathers"* (301), *"Seated Figure in Landscape"* (305).

CHAPTER II

RENOIR AND THE EIGHTEENTH CENTURY FRENCH TRADITION

THE profound influence exercised upon Renoir by his French predecessors, Watteau, Lancret, Boucher and Fragonard, is evidenced by the delicacy, grace, idyllic charm and poetic vision that mark Renoir's work throughout his entire career. His spiritual endowment was as purely French as that of any member of the eighteenth century group, and it is expressed in a form which is at one and the same time French, Venetian, and something new in the history of painting.

In Renoir's work the Venetian and French derivations not only invariably qualify each other, but their plastic qualities are greatly enhanced and the derived elements become cognate constituents in the new form. Renoir's Venetian drafts, reënforced by color which is more juicy, rich and solidly expressive, put greater substantiality into the delicacy of the eighteenth century form, and weld decoration more firmly with expression. Conversely, the expressive fulness characteristic of the Venetians acquires a new status by Renoir's assimilation of the delicacy and decorative charm of the earlier French form. The French influence is ever present in Renoir's work; at various stages of his development, it increases and decreases in degree of accentuation and enters his form under different aspects and in varying amounts of preponderancy over adaptations from other traditions, but it consistently commingles with and qualifies the Venetian traits.

The varied effects of the eighteenth century influence upon Renoir's work may be broadly subdivided into five stages corresponding successively with: Renoir's formative period up to the early seventies; the seventies up to 1878; the end of that decade; the exotic interlude of the eighties; and, finally, the gradually expansive growth from the early nineties to the culmination of his form in his latest compositions.

Renoir's early pictures, done under the direct influence of the

work of the painters in vogue at the moment—Velásquez,* Corot,†
Delacroix,‡ Courbet,§ Manet ‖—already bear sufficient marks of
affinity with qualities distinctive of the eighteenth century tradition
to indicate the trend along which his form eventually developed.
"Mademoiselle Romaine Lancaux" (2), painted in 1864, and
"Woman with Bird" (3) of c. 1866, are obviously inspired by
Corot,¶ but their form is lighter and more delicate. Nothing in
Corot is as daintily rendered as are, for instance, the flowers in the
background of *"Mademoiselle Romaine Lancaux"*; their unasser-
tive tones of coral, blue and gray subtly coalesce into dainty floating
volumes of almost ineffable lightness. Similarly in *"Lise"* (5) of
1867 and *"Mr. and Mrs. Sisley"* (10) of c. 1868 Renoir adds a
new flavor of distinctive grace and delicacy to the Hals-Velásquez-
Courbet tradition. This tendency to lighten and make more
delicate and graceful what he takes from other painters appears
also in some of Renoir's early landscapes.** *"La Grenouillère"*
(31), obviously founded upon Corot, Manet and Monet, acquires
through the subtle tonal relationships of its soft and gentle color,
a generalized delicacy, a precious quality, and a smooth semi-
glossy surface reminiscent of eighteenth century French painting.††

As Renoir progresses to his more individual form of the mid-
seventies the eighteenth century qualities become increasingly
apparent, even though still as a pervasive feeling rather than as
specific traits. His rendering of subject-matter pertaining to his
own milieu has the delicacy and charm of the Watteau-Lancret-
Boucher-Fragonard tradition, whether he deals with the blithe-
some carefree atmosphere of a Paris crowd eager for holiday
pleasures,‡‡ the *intime* and sedate placidity of interior scenes,§§ the

---

* E.g., Renoir's *"Boy with Cat"* (7) and *"Dancer"* (32).
† E.g., Renoir's *"Mademoiselle Romaine Lancaux"* (2), *"Woman with
Bird"* (3) and *"La Grenouillère"* (31).
‡ E.g., Renoir's *"Odalisque"* (17), *"Harem"* (25) and *"Young Woman
with Rose"* (28).
§ E.g., Renoir's *"Lise"* (5), *"Mr. and Mrs. Sisley"* (10), *"Bather with
Griffon"* (16) and *"Riders in the Bois de Boulogne"* (30).
‖ E.g., Renoir's *"Rowboat"* (6).
¶ Cf., e.g., Corot's *"Woman in Gray"* (569) or *"Woman with the Pearl"*
(570).
** Cf., e.g., Renoir's *"Rowboat"* (6) with Manet's *"Tarring the Boat"*
(609), Renoir's *"La Grenouillère"* (12) with Monet's *"La Grenouillère"*
(628), Renoir's *"Pont-Neuf"* (26) with Pissarro's *"Crystal Palace"* (593),
and Renoir's *"La Grenouillère"* (31) with Manet's *"Croquet Party"* (599).
†† Cf., e.g., the landscape-setting in Lancret's *"Music Lesson"* (490).
‡‡ E.g., *"Moulin de la Galette"* (61 and 62).
§§ E.g., *"Breakfast"* (27), *"In the Studio"* (74) and *"Café Scene"* (81).

dainty naturalness of lovely children and women,* the grace and tranquillity of women at their homely occupations,† or the natural joyful living of people in landscape.‡

"Breakfast" (27) of c. 1872 shows Renoir's debt to Chardin not only in the type and general treatment of the subject-matter but also in the compositional organization and in certain phases of the drawing and execution. Both the expressive drawing and the subtle space-composition are patterned upon the seventeenth century Dutch interior scenes as recast by Chardin into an essentially French form.§ Renoir retains Chardin's characteristic rhythms of objects which tend to project into space and meet at sharp angles, but the objects and the space merge more organically with each other, *i.e.,* the intervals are less pronounced as such, less marked off as units than in Chardin, and the essential framework of the composition is more consistently color.

The accentuated highlights in the porcelain, glass and metallic objects in *"Breakfast"* is another motif taken from Chardin's version of the Dutch form.‖ Chardin eliminated the Dutch surface crudity of paint and the mechanistic character of the accentuated highlights; his method of execution is based upon the Venetian,¶ but it has more delicacy of feeling and of touch than either Titian's or Tintoretto's.** Renoir's adaptation in *"Breakfast"* embodies the color-solidity and subtlety of relationships characteristic of Chardin, but retains somewhat more the accentuated pattern of the Dutch. Renoir's color is brighter and more luminous than in any

* E.g., *"Woman at Spring"* (37), *"Torso"* (52), *"Girl with Jumping Rope"* (57), *"Mademoiselle Jeanne Durand-Ruel"* (59), *"Début"* (66), *"Ingénue"* (68), *"Madame Henriot"* (69).

† E.g., *"Reader"* (40), *"Young Girl Sewing"* (41), *"Girl Sewing Hat"* (67) and *"Woman Crocheting"* (76).

‡ E.g., *"Two Women in Park"* (44) and *"Swing"* (63).

§ Cf., e.g., Chardin's *"Grace before Meal"* (498), *"House of Cards"* (500), *"Industrious Mother"* (501), *"Lesson"* (502) or *"Various Utensils"* (505) with Terborch's *"Guitar Lesson"* (460), Pieter de Hooch's *"Interior of a Dutch House"* (463) and with Vermeer's *"Cook"* (464).

‖ Cf., e.g., Chardin's *"Bottle of Olives"* (497), *"Still Life"* (503), *"Study of Still-Life"* (504) or *"Various Utensils"* (505) with Juriaan van Streek's *"Still-Life"* (468).

¶ The Venetians, the Dutch and Chardin, all owe to van Eyck this use of accentuated highlights in space-compositions of still-lifes. Cf., e.g., Venetian and the Chardin examples here mentioned, with van Eyck's *"Madonna of Lucca"* (321). The later artists replaced van Eyck's miniaturelike precision with broad simplified drawing.

** Cf., e.g., Chardin's *"Various Utensils"* (505) with the still-life in Titian's *"Disciples at Emmaüs"* (350) and in Tintoretto's *"Two Prophets"* (394).

of the prototypes and is an intimate part of a more fluid drawing; as a result the highlights are more vividly colorful, the brushwork in the drawing eliminates more of the representative detail, and the adjustment of light, color and technique imparts those qualities of delicacy and lightness to the texture and weight of the objects which are more definitely French than are the ponderosity and ceramic feeling in Chardin.

The only specific eighteenth century trait apparent in Renoir's work in the seventies is the mother-of-pearl * or delicate porcelain surface † characteristic of Lancret and Boucher, and to a lesser extent of Watteau and Fragonard.‡ Renoir's opalescent surface is still far from the degree of richness, fluidity and iridescence it attains later, and it is not yet as deeply and all-pervasively embedded in the total form,§ but it is much more luminous and colorful than that in the prototypes. The coral wall in *"Pourville"* (80) of 1878, for example, is a glorification of Boucher's mother-of-pearl surface, achieved by a Renoir adaptation of impressionistic technique; its color is richer, more luminous and deeply structural than in any unit in the best work of Watteau, Lancret, Boucher or Fragonard and its drawing is more fluid. ‖

In *"Mademoiselle Jeanne Durand-Ruel"* (59) and *"Madame Henriot"* (69) of the mid-seventies, a pearly tonality imparts a feeling of fragility to the general form, a fragility which adds ethereal charm to the expression of character. The corresponding fragility in eighteenth century French portraiture savors of brittleness and unsubstantiality.¶ In each of these two portraits, Renoir carries the French form to its apotheosis of delicacy, gentleness, daintiness and charm. *"Mademoiselle Jeanne Durand-Ruel"* is allied to the Boucher phase of the tradition by the clean-cut delicate drawing, the one-piece modeling of the face with few and slight shadows, and the smooth surface and porcelainlike texture

* E.g., *"Henriot Family"* (23).
† E.g., *"Two Women in Park"* (44), *"House in Woods"* (48), *"Mademoiselle Jeanne Durand-Ruel"* (59).
‡ E.g., Watteau's *"Autumn"* (472), Lancret's *"Innocence"* (488) and *"Open Cage"* (491), Boucher's *"Diana at the Bath"* (508) and *"Pastoral"* (516), and Fragonard's *"Bathers"* (531) and *"Music Lesson"* (535).
§ Cf., e.g., *"Two Women in Park"* (44) of 1875 with *"Bathers in Forest"* (216) of c. 1897.
‖ Cf., e.g., Watteau's *"Pastoral"* (481), the church spire in Lancret's *"Summer"* (493), Boucher's *"Mill"* (513), the house in front of the castle in Boucher's *"Pastoral"* (516), and Fragonard's *"Bathers"* (531).
¶ Cf., e.g., Boucher's *"Head of Lady"* (509) or *"Marquise de Pompadour"* (512).

of the flesh.* The drawing of the figure as a whole recalls the graceful rigidity characteristic of Lancret,† and seen occasionally in Fragonard and Perronneau.‡ *"Madame Henriot"* represents a sublimation of the Perronneau type of portraiture but without the latter's specious academic tricks and artificial pose.§ Its exquisite delicacy not only exceeds in appeal anything in the whole eighteenth century tradition, not excepting Lancret's *"Music Lesson"* (490), but it is an organic factor in a plastic expression of human character more comprehensive and convincing than can be found in any earlier French portrait. Thus, practically from the start, Renoir made the primarily decorative and illustrative qualities of the antecedent French tradition integral parts of a more fully expressive form.

By the end of the seventies, Renoir's admiration for eighteenth century painting had become an infatuation which led him into grievous pitfalls: ‖ delicacy of color and drawing weakened into softness, and the character of the total form leans toward the inanity, sweetness and chromolike superficial prettiness of Greuze.¶ Renoir, in other words, had not yet assimilated the eighteenth century French traits, since lack of ability to effect integration is always a sign that the coördination between the individual and his environment which constitutes expression, has not taken place.

During the 1880-1887 period Renoir adopted from the earlier French tradition a greater number of specific traits than at any other period, and the form as a whole is much closer to the originals than at any other time in his career. It displays, in varying combinations, the identifying marks of its source: emphasis upon linear contour, smooth mother-of-pearl surface, relatively dry pigment, decorative linear rhythms, pervasively light tonality, exotic porcelain-texture of flesh, patterned composition, occasional tapestry-effects, and a general lyric presentation of subject-matter which tends, at times, toward unreality.

The plastic similarity to the earlier French form is favored by

* Cf., e.g., Boucher's *"Diana at the Bath"* (508) or *"Venus and Vulcan"* (522).

† E.g., Lancret's *"Actress: La Belle Grecque"* (486), the middle figure in *"Music Lesson"* (490), and *"Open Cage"* (491).

‡ E.g., Fragonard's *"Music Lesson"* (535) and Perronneau's *"Girl with Cat"* (526).

§ Cf., e.g., Perronneau's *"Girl with Cat"* (526) or *"Mademoiselle Huquier"* (527), and also Boze's *"Comtesse de Provence"* (540) or *"Lady's Portrait"* (541).

‖ See p. 74.

¶ E.g., Renoir's *"Bohemian"* (90) and *"Fête of Pan"* (96).

the tendency toward overdecoration brought about by the Oriental light and coloring so prevalent in Renoir's work of the early eighties. Indeed, it is this disbalance between decoration and expression which gives to a number of his 1880-1887 pictures much of the superficial decorative and illustrative qualities of eighteenth century French painting. *"Girl with Falcon"* (101), for instance, fails in plastic conviction because of the glare and tinsel-like effect of the Oriental color and light, and the superficiality of its decorative features. On the whole, however, Renoir's form of the period is more substantial plastically than the majority of the French prototypes.

As Renoir progressed through the 1880-1890 decade, he gradually became engrossed in the problem of giving plastic life and blood to the inanities of Watteau, Boucher and Fragonard. In *"Dance in the City"* (135) and *"Dance in the Country"* (136) of 1883, and in *"Children at Wargemont"* (144) of 1884, the decorative features are embedded in more solidly constructed volumes than in the earlier eighties and they participate organically in more comprehensively expressive designs. The decorative rhythms involve volumes and deep space, and become the medium of expressing the naturalness and grace of men, women and children whose movements and attitudes show that they are really alive, not posed as in the work of his French predecessors.* In Renoir's *"Garden Scene"* (161) of c. 1886, the dry, almost brittle, pearly surface of Boucher acquires richer decorative and expressive content by association with impressionistic technique and a miniature type of linear drawing; † in *"Washerwoman and Baby"* (163) of c. 1886 the compositional theme is a movement of volumes in space; the paradox of solidity combined with fragility and generalized lightness and delicacy is achieved by the mutual reënforcement of a classic linear style of drawing, a smooth enamel-like surface and dry color, Oriental in quality and reminiscent also of fresco.

In the eighties Boucher's influence is especially marked in Renoir's nudes and bathing groups ‡—subject-matter much favored by the earlier master.§ Constant use is made of three

* Cf., e.g., *"Children at Wargemont"* (144) with Boucher's *"Luncheon"* (510).
† Cf., e.g., Boucher's *"Pastoral"* (516).
‡ E.g., *"Blond Bather"* (131), *"Bather in Rocky Landscape"* (142), *"Bather Arranging Hair"* (152), *"Bathers"* (164).
§ E.g., Boucher's *"Autumn"* (506), *"Diana at the Bath"* (508), *"Pan and Syrinx"* (515), *"Venus Adorning Herself"* (521), *"Venus Disarming Cupid"* (523).

outstanding Boucher traits: the smooth, hard, enamel-like surface, the pearly-toned flesh and the light and delicate interrelation of volumes, qualities which in Boucher are often found in conjunction with a delicate rendering of extremely dainty poised movement. In Boucher's *"Diana at the Bath"* (508), for example, the relation between Diana's left foot and the area of ground beneath it is so subtle that the toes seem to barely touch the ground; the hands too are drawn with extreme delicacy, but the figures as entities are rendered in the posed idyllic style common in the French tradition of the period. Renoir's drawing, in contrast, is more consistently expressive of reality throughout the picture: his figures are alive and their attitudes and movements seem more free and natural.*

Space-composition in Boucher usually involves only those areas in which clean-cut drawing occurs; thus the precisely drawn foreground stands out against the rest of the picture, which looks like a stage setting or a decorated curtain.† Renoir's organization consists of a rhythmic sequence of volumes throughout the entire picture. Moreover, the feeling of volumes moving in space is conveyed by interrelations of line, light and color, and not as in Boucher ‡ through the primary agency of linear perspective, which emphasizes the contrasts in direction of projecting arms, legs, trees or portions of flying draperies.§ Movement in Renoir is thus more subtle and real than in Boucher; it is also more dynamic because the masses and intervals involved are drawn with color of greater structural quality.

Chiefly through the function of this color, Renoir's figures reacquire the sculpturesque solidity of classic Greek statuary which had been lost in Boucher's primarily decorative rendering of the classic theme. Boucher's form stems less directly from the Greek source than from the versions of it evolved successively by Floren-

* Cf., e.g., Renoir's *"Bathers"* (164).
† This division of the picture into a distinct foreground-scene and a stage-like decorative setting occasionally suggested in Rubens—e.g., *"Bathsheba at the Spring"* (417), *"Garden of Love"* (423)—was adopted by the eighteenth century French painters in general.
‡ And also Rubens—e.g., *"Diana and Her Nymphs Surprised by Satyrs"* (421)—and the Venetians, especially Paolo Veronese—e.g., *"Jupiter Destroying the Vices"* (406).
§ Cf., e.g., Renoir's *"Bathers"* (164) with Boucher's *"Diana at the Bath"* (508), *"Setting of the Sun"* (517) or *"Venus Disarming Cupid"* (523).

tine painters,* Rubens,† Poussin ‡ and French sculptors of the sixteenth and seventeenth centuries,§ in most of whose work the full solidity of classic sculpture had dwindled to the point of fragility, and the fluid grace had been decoratively accentuated. Renoir's color reinstates much of the original sculpturesque quality at the same time that it acquires the delicacy and surface charm characteristic of Boucher.

Renoir's development of the eighteenth century form at this stage of his work reaches its apotheosis in *"Bathers"* (164) of 1887. In this large canvas the pervasive tapestry-effect, the light pearly tonality, the fluid linear patterns, the rhythmic grace and delicate poise of the figures, the porcelain- or bisque-like flesh, are all, not only enhanced in decorative appeal in comparison with Boucher, but are organic parts of an infinitely more expressive form. The painting is a plastic glorification of Boucher's *"Diana at the Bath"* (508).

During the 1890's the eighteenth century French traits in Renoir's work still often determine the character of the form as a whole, even though they have become sublimated by a more positively individualistic treatment than in the eighties. *"Girl in Profile"* (202) is very reminiscent of Watteau in its lavender-coral flesh ‖ and of Boucher in its cameo quality; ¶ *"Head of Girl with Hat"* (210) has the fluidity and general looseness of Fragonard; ** *"Girl with Basket of Flowers"* (188), *"Girls at Piano"* (203) and *"Piano Lesson"* (205) raise the grace and youthful charm of Greuze's figures from the status of superficial illustration to that

* E.g., Botticelli's *"Allegory of Spring"* (337) and *"Birth of Venus"* (338), Raphael's *"Holy Family, of Francis I"* (373), *"Madonna: Belle Jardinière"* (374) and *"Virgin with Blue Diadem"* (376).

† E.g., Rubens' *"Apotheosis of William the Silent"* (415).

‡ E.g., Poussin's *"Holy Family"* (439). Very frequently Boucher draws heavily upon Poussin, particularly in the drawing of men's figures and also in the drawing, modeling and textural quality of stuffs—cf., e.g., Boucher's *"Vulcan Presenting Venus Arms for Aeneas"* (525) with Poussin's *"Arcadian Shepherds"* (437) or *"Blind Men of Jericho"* (438). Renoir makes practically no use of these features of Boucher.

§ E.g., Goujon's *"Fountain of the Innocents"* (399) and especially Girardon's bas-relief *"Bath of the Nymphs"* (461).

‖ E.g., Watteau's *"Autumn"* (472) in which the flesh is heavier than in most of the eighteenth century painters and its surface presents a variety of subtle and rather rich intermingling color-chords.

¶ E.g., Diana's profile in Boucher's *"Diana at the Bath"* (508) and the head of Venus in Boucher's *"Venus and Vulcan"* (522).

** E.g., Fragonard's *"Music Lesson"* (535) or *"Young Woman and Child"* (539).

of robust plastic expression; * *"Nude Seated on Rock"* (192), *"Bathers in Forest"* (216) and *"Reclining Nude"* (217) are each an enriched version of the rhythmic patterns and decorative surface characteristic of the eighteenth century painters as a group.†

Not any of these eighteenth century qualities, however, stands out as relating particularly to the surface as they did in Renoir's earlier period; they are part of the form itself, and result directly from the organic use of color in drawing, modeling and composition. Pigment is now juicier, color flows more freely from area to area and produces more varied and abundant color-chords,‡ surfaces are more iridescent and compositional fluidity, which in the 1880-1887 period was established mainly by linear effects, is now due to more thorough fusion of line, light and color. As a result of the closer coöperation between the plastic means, textures are more solid and real, figures more naturally alive than either in the French prototypes or in Renoir's 1880-1887 version of the French form, and the decorative organization is much stronger.

The main factor in this increased fulness of expression is Renoir's assimilation of the values and meanings of great Venetian painting, a fact particularly apparent in his work of the mid-nineties. In *"Nude in Brook"* (213) of 1895, the pearly surface of Lancret and Boucher is more deeply ingrained in the structure of the flesh than it was in the eighties; the Boucher-like green-coral-lavender color-scheme is greatly enriched by a wider gamut of color and a greater degree of solidity; and the more fluid use of color creates a suffusion which blends the variegated areas in a Titian type of space-volume composition.

"Bathers in Forest" (216) of c. 1897, like *"Bathers"* (164) of 1887, is pervaded with eighteenth century feeling, but the derivations from Girardon, Watteau, Boucher and Fragonard, which in

---

* Cf., e.g., Greuze's *"Broken Pitcher"* (528).

† Cf., e.g., Renoir's *"Nude Seated on Rock"* (192) with Boucher's *"Diana at the Bath"* (508); Renoir's *"Bathers in Forest"* (216) with Boucher's *"Venus Adorning Herself"* (521) and Fragonard's *"Bathers"* (531); and Renoir's *"Reclining Nude"* (217) with Boucher's *"Venus Adorning Herself"* (521) and Fragonard's *"Woman Undressing"* (538).

‡ Color-chords comparable to Renoir's, even in his mid-eighties' period, are of rare occurrence in eighteenth century French painters. The variegated surface in a few Watteaus, Lancrets and Paters are exceptions that prove the rule—e.g., Watteau's *"Autumn"* (472) and *"Game of Love"* (478), Lancret's *"Actors of Italian Comedy"* (485), Pater's *"Comedians in a Park"* (494). Generally the color-areas are delicately modulated by tonal variations of their particular color, and only slightly tinged by the color of the adjoining areas.

the earlier version were primarily decorative, are incorporated in a highly expressive and dynamic Venetian type of composition. Neither in richness and novelty of decorative effects, nor in fulness of expression and creative ingenuity, can the 1887 *"Bathers"* compare with *"Bathers in Forest."* Renoir's modified impressionistic technique, which competes with the Venetian and the eighteenth century characteristics in conferring individuality to the form, contributes much to both the expressive and the decorative aspects of the picture.

"Reclining Nude" (217), also of c. 1897, merits especial attention because it bears very close resemblance to an eighteenth century picture. Boucher is overtly selected as a model, but sufficient modifications prevail to establish a new form of a much higher esthetic grade. The figure has the characteristic mother-of-pearl surface of Boucher and also the lightness and fragility of volume; the head, however, is drawn and modeled by color of a richness and structural solidity comparable to Renoir's best work of the period. The background, in its surface-quality, light and delicate execution, and stage-setting effect, likewise recalls Boucher; but instead of serving as a decorative curtainlike area against which the figure is set, the background functions equally with the figure in a continuous and all-pervasive rhythm of volumes and space-intervals organized through the medium of color. Renoir's composition is thus more dynamic than Boucher's; his color, moreover, is richer and of greater internal luminosity, and the more fluid and subtle drawing yields a delicate variegated color-suffusion.*

After 1900, Renoir's weighty color places the eighteenth century characteristics upon a still more solid foundation. Specific traits of the French tradition appear less frequently, but the general qualities of delicacy, lightness, dainty grace and charm, persistently temper the robustness of the Venetian derivations, the flamboyance of the Rubens elements, and the classic quality adopted from Greek sculpture.† In his latest work contours are more fluid than ever before and the eighteenth century delicacy and decorative charm

---

* Cf., e.g., Boucher's *"Venus"* (520) or *"Venus Adorning Herself"* (521).
† E.g., Renoir's *"Claude in Arab Shirt"* (232), *"Writing Lesson"* (234), *"Judgment of Paris"* (240), *"Caryatids"* (248 and 249), *"Girl with Yellow Hat"* (272), *"Madame Jean Renoir"* (276), *"Bathing Group"* (285), *"At the Bath"* (286), *"Woman with Hat, Reading"* (300). In *"Woman and Children in Landscape"* (228) Renoir plays upon the Fragonard theme consisting of deep-colored, loosely defined foreground masses set off against an illuminated atmospheric background; cf., e.g., Fragonard's *"Souvenir: A Lady Carving her Name"* (536).

are carried over from area to area by the continuous flow of color and the all-embracing atmospheric suffusion.*

FLESH-PAINTING

Renoir's painting of flesh embodies, in general, a blend of elements derived from the forms of the Venetians, Rubens and the eighteenth century French painters, modified by drafts upon Manet and the impressionists. The closest resemblance to the French is to Boucher who most typically represents the eighteenth century type in this respect. Boucher's flesh-painting is based upon characteristics of the flesh of babies and women in Paolo Veronese and Rubens.† From Paolo Veronese, Boucher took the light whitish-pink foundation, the grayish-lavender shadows with pinkish accents, and the tendency to an exotic texture and a smooth one-piece modeling. These features having reached Boucher chiefly by way of Rubens are practically inseparable in Boucher's form from what Rubens himself contributed toward the eighteenth century tradition, namely: the accentuated rose tonality of the flesh, the independent narrow contour-line of color—often red or pink—the active curves of volumes, the bands of reflected light along outlines, and the relative emphasis upon surface-effects at the expense of structural realization of texture. Boucher's own modification of the Paolo Veronese-Rubens characteristics resulted in a type of flesh which is more delicate and fragile, less solid and weighty than in the prototypes, lighter in tone and more exotic in texture; color is less deeply embedded in the form, shadows are slighter and the surface often partakes of a feeling of mother-of-pearl, alabaster, dull porcelain or papier-mâché.‡

Renoir preserves the distinctive delicacy of Boucher's flesh-painting, and its general light tonality, mother-of-pearl surface and

---

* E.g., Renoir's *"Two Figures in Landscape"* (296) and *"Woman in Muslin Dress"* (298).

† Cf., e.g., Boucher's *"Diana at the Bath"* (508), *"Pan and Syrinx"* (515), *"Sleeping Shepherdess"* (518), *"Venus"* (520), *"Venus Adorning Herself"* (521), with Paolo Veronese's *"Happy Union"* (403), *"Mars and Venus United by Love"* (407), *"Venetian Woman"* (409), and with Rubens' *"Apotheosis of William the Silent"* (415), *"Holy Family"* (426), *"Holy Family in Landscape"* (427), *"Romulus and Remus"* (433), *"St. Cecilia"* (434), *"Susanne Fourment"* (435).

‡ Exception must be made in the case of Boucher's *"Venus and Vulcan"* (522) in which the flesh-painting in the woman and cupid retains in appreciable degree the color-solidity of Paolo Veronese's and Titian's.

porcelainlike texture, but the decorative qualities are engrafted upon a substantial foundation of expressive values and thus transform Boucher's pasty surface and artificial effects into a more real and convincing structure.* The rosy glow of the complexion in Boucher's flesh, due to delicate reds in focalized areas and linear contours, conveys the feeling of a cosmetic or a surface-bloom; in Renoir the intensification of the pinks and reds brings out the warmth and glow of real flesh. Renoir's transformations of the Boucher characteristics are accomplished without recourse to the latter's specious technical means. Delicacy of texture and subtle modeling of rounded volumes owe much in Boucher to the linear pink contour and its adjoining band of reflected light, but this device which lends transparency to the flesh results also in fragile, often glasslike, volumes. Renoir dispenses with contour-lines and reflected lights and relies chiefly upon color-relations and the intrinsic structural quality of color; his accentuated highlights in his late work are used, as in Rubens, on the crest of the volume, but they merge more homogeneously with the adjacent color; † when, on rare occasions, Renoir uses a narrow pink contour-line, it also is a more integral part of the flesh and a less obvious decorative element than in Boucher.‡

The Boucher qualities of flesh-painting appear early in Renoir's work. In *"Mademoiselle Romaine Lancaux"* (2) of 1864, they change the Corot form upon which the picture is based, and thus constitute a determining factor in the new expression. During the seventies they are used more creatively: in *"Henriot Family"* (23) the fluid color-drawing adds a floating quality to the delicacy and fragility of Boucher at the same time that the structural color increases the weight and solidity; the mother-of-pearl surface is greatly enriched and all feeling of unreality is eliminated. The dainty, delicate, porcelainlike flesh in *"Mademoiselle Jeanne Durand-Ruel"* (59) has greater individuality and charm than any French prototype and is achieved with fewer and more delicate shadows and with more subtle color-relations.§

---

* Cf., e.g., Renoir's *"Caryatids"* (248 and 249) or *"Reclining Nude"* (217) with Boucher's *"Three Graces"* (519).

† Cf., e.g., Renoir's *"Bathing Group"* (285) with Rubens' *"David Playing on the Harp"* (419).

‡ Cf., e.g., Renoir's *"Mother and Child"* (118), *"Grape Gatherers Resting"* (147) or *"Washerwoman and Baby"* (163) with Boucher's *"Three Graces"* (519) or *"Venus"* (520).

§ Cf., e.g., the middle figure in Lancret's *"Music Lesson"* (490).

During the 1880's, when Renoir was most imbued with the eighteenth century French spirit, his flesh-painting is closer to Boucher's than at any other period; nevertheless, with all the points of similarity, the French form was but a stimulus for experiments tending toward Renoir's own decorative expression. The flesh in *"Nude"* (110) compares with Boucher's at its best * in delicacy of surface, in fragility and lightness of volume and in general appeal. In *"Blond Bather"* (131) an extensive intermingling of white with the Boucher-like pink shadows and attenuated highlights reproduces the familiar alabaster-quality of the earlier French form, but the nacreous surface does not deprive the flesh of its natural feeling and texture, the pink is intensified and related to a greater number of interpenetrating colors, and small areas of blue shadows merge into and lightly tint the general whitish-pink complexion.† Later in the 1880's the pink itself is tinged with coral,‡ and also with lavender,§ and in *"Bathers"* (164) of 1887 the modeling is achieved by positive lavender shadows and brownish-coral middle tones. Thus the pink, which is practically unvaried in Boucher's flesh, became a field of considerable experimentation for Renoir, and a stimulus to his imaginative use of color.

Perhaps the nearest approach in eighteenth century flesh-painting to Renoir's is found in the pearly blue-green-pink-ivory figures in Boucher's *"Autumn"* (506), *"Venus"* (520) and *"Visit of Venus to Vulcan"* (524), which may be compared with the flesh in Renoir's *"Reclining Nude"* (217) of c. 1897. Boucher's flesh has a feeling of paint, its texture is unconvincing, and the color, dull and dry, is of only surface depth; in the Renoir the texture is as delicately rendered as Boucher's, but its color is more expressive of the quality of flesh and the color-modulations are richer, more decorative and better integrated in the texture.‖

In Renoir's late work the porcelain-quality, so prevalent in the Lancret-Boucher-Fragonard tradition, also becomes part of the

* E.g., Boucher's *"Diana at the Bath"* (508).
† The light bluish- or greenish-lavender when used by Boucher—e.g., *"Cupid, a Captive"* (507), *"Head of Lady"* (509) and *"Venus"* (520)—remains a decorative delicate surface-shading with no material effect upon the structure of the flesh itself.
‡ E.g., *"Woman with Fan"* (160).
§ E.g., *"Washerwoman and Baby"* (163).
‖ For similar resemblances and differences, cf. also Renoir's *"Reclining Nude"* (217) with the uppermost figure in Fragonard's *"Bathers"* (531).

flesh itself.* Renoir's progressive increase in degree of illumination, richness, depth and jewel-like character of the color, and the greater fluidity of his drawing, endow the porcelainlike surface with a color voluptuousness and a fleshlike texture and solidity unequalled either in eighteenth century French painting or in Renoir's own earlier work.

PAINTING OF TEXTILES

Textiles in the eighteenth century tradition are closer in appearance to Rubens than to the Venetians, because, as already noted, the French painters adapted the general Venetian form by way of Rubens' modifications of it. The French painting of stuffs carried further Rubens' emphasis upon decoration at the expense of expression.†

Excluding Chardin's textiles which are essentially Venetian, the French fabrics in general are much lighter and more delicate in texture and weight than Titian's, Tintoretto's or Rubens'; they are often thin, papery and unreal, and are usually executed by a mechanistic technique of brush strokes and highlights, superposed on the folds and isolated from the color and texture of the fabric proper; ‡ their drawing partakes of a miniature quality, and the light-patterns, diminished in degree of intensity in comparison with the broad sweeps and streaks of Titian and Tintoretto, yield a shimmering surface-sheen more as in Paolo Veronese and Rubens.§ Decoration, in other words, is obtained speciously by obvious patterns, and expression is often sacrificed to the point that the fabric lacks the feeling of continuity either as a color-unit or as a solid material.||

Renoir, in his varied interpretations of the decorative features of French textile-painting, restored much of the expressive values

* E.g., Renoir's *"Bathers in Forest"* (216) and *"Bathing Group"* (285).
† Cf., e.g., Rubens' *"Annunciation"* (414) with Watteau's *"Figures in Landscape"* (477).
‡ E.g., Watteau's *"False Step"* (475) and *"Fête in a Park"* (476), Fragonard's *"Inspiration"* (533), *"Music"* (534) and *"Study"* (537).
§ Cf., e.g., Watteau's *"Figures in Landscape"* (477) with Rubens' *"Garden of Love"* (423) or *"Annunciation"* (414), and with Paolo Veronese's *"Mars and Venus United by Love"* (407).
|| The exception to this is the best work of Lancret and Pater which tends toward solid Venetian painting, e.g., Lancret's *"Actress: La Belle Grecque"* (486), *"Cage"* (487), *"Mademoiselle Camargo Dancing"* (489) and *"Music Lesson"* (490), and Pater's *"Comedians in a Park"* (494).

of Venetian fabrics, and heightened the plastic significance of each of the original types. In *"Writing Lesson"* (234), for instance, the accentuated patterns of light, color and brushwork are inseparably connected with the fabric of the woman's blouse, and the shimmering sheen is a more iridescent, opalescent and decorative element than, with very few exceptions,* can be found in corresponding units in the earlier French work.† The composite form of this textile represents an ingenious synthesis of characteristic features of Titian,‡ Tintoretto,§ Paolo Veronese,‖ Rubens,¶ Chardin,** and seventeenth century Dutch painting.††

The nearest in French textiles to the color-solidity of Renoir's stuffs is perhaps the pink bow on the left slipper of Watteau's *"Gilles"* (479) ‡‡ and this, in structural quality of color and in lighting-effect, is practically a duplication of the rose ribbon in Velásquez' *"Infanta Marguerite"* (446), although the light- and color-elements in the Velásquez are better merged and the light-pattern is less obvious. The pink hair ribbon in Renoir's *"Girl in Profile"* (202), offering the same problem as in these two pictures, is rendered by color more richly modulated and of greater internal luminosity than in either of the others, and the pattern of light is better merged with the color and texture of the fabric than it is in *"Gilles."*

Patterns of folds in French fabrics are executed by practically the same kind of brush strokes throughout various areas of a picture, the strokes varying only slightly in number and degree of accentuation.§§ Renoir's patterns are entirely free from such mech-

* E.g., Lancret's *"Actors of Italian Comedy"* (485) and Pater's *"Comedians in a Park"* (494).
† Cf., e.g., Watteau's *"Embarkation for Cythera"* (474), Lancret's *"Spring"* (492).
‡ E.g., the red brocade garment at the right in Titian's *"Entombment"* (352).
§ E.g., the dress of Judith in Tintoretto's *"Judith and Holofernes"* (387).
‖ E.g., Paolo Veronese's *"Burning of Sodom"* (401).
¶ E.g., Rubens' *"Annunciation"* (414), *"Garden of Love"* (423) and *"Thomyris"* (436).
** E.g., Chardin's *"Back from Market"* (496).
†† E.g., Terborch's *"Guitar Lesson"* (460).
‡‡ This picture, attributed to Watteau, has numerous plastic qualities which point to Lancret as the more likely painter.
§§ The general differentiation between Watteau's, Lancret's and Pater's respective technique in the painting of sheen and folds of silky materials, seems to be that in Watteau the emphasis is more generally upon the highlights and often to the degree of dramatic overemphasis indicating a direct source in Tintoretto; in the best of Lancret's work there is usually an equality in the activity of the lights and shadows more as in Titian or Bellini; in

anistic repetition; various adjustments of the technique to color
and light produce, even in a single picture, a number of different
effects, which generally bring out a variety of traditional characteristics. For example, in *"Bathing Group"* (285) the dramatic
patterns of light and color which draw and model the skirt of the
sitting figure embody the essence of Watteau's modification of
Tintoretto's form: * the patterns break up the volumes of the
folds, but in distinction to Watteau's use of the motif, the oneness
of texture is retained. Moreover, color is more structural, shadows
are more luminous and colorful than either Watteau's or Tintoretto's; hence the contrast is less abrupt between the highlighted
crest and the depth of the folds, and the pattern of highlighted
streaks is an integral part of the texture as well as of the surface-
decoration of the material. Drama, in other words, is obtained plastically by color-relationships instead of speciously, as in Tintoretto
and Watteau, by overaccentuated contrasts of light and dark.†

The garments of the standing figure at the right in the same
"Bathing Group" illustrate another creative use of the Tintoretto-
Watteau accentuated light-patterns, and the richer effects are obtained chiefly through the introduction of Oriental color-elements.
In the drapery and hat at the lower left, the eighteenth century
pastel tones and pattern of light and color are integral factors of
a unit in which Renoir successfully merges Manet's technique with
Rubens' swirl. Finally, in the drapery on the reclining figure in
the foreground, the eighteenth century type of pattern is much
diminished, but the French lightness, fluidity and delicacy enter
into the rendering of the textile and qualify the Paolo Veronese-
like silvery tonality.

A review of the foregoing study of Renoir's form in relation to
eighteenth century French painting throws into relief the following
outstanding facts: Renoir's color, being more structural than the
earlier French painters', yields a greater degree of convincing reality; his more varied palette and the more imaginative and wider

the characteristic Pater method there is more often a greater reliance for
effect upon a quivering pattern of irregular accentuated shadows in the
depth of the folds.
  * E.g., Watteau's *"Embarkation for Cythera"* (474) and *"Game of Love"*
(478).
  † The pattern of color-and-light streaks in the man's garments in Watteau's *"Music Lesson"* (480) is suggestive of the pattern in this Renoir
unit, but the execution is mechanical, and the color lacks the structural
solidity, the glow and effulgence of Renoir's.

scope in his use of color result in richer decorative effects; decoration itself is more complex at the same time that it is better organized, and it reënforces expression to a greater extent than in the eighteenth century tradition because these two aspects of the form merge more organically with each other. Renoir eliminated the trivial, superficial and mechanistic characteristics of the tradition, and not only retained the delicacy, lightness and dainty charm of the originals but materially heightened the significance of these qualities by his imaginative interpretation of other traditions, in particular the Venetian.

CHAPTER III

RENOIR AND CEZANNE

A JUST appreciation of Renoir involves an estimate of his standing in relation to the greatest of his contemporaries, Cézanne. Such an estimate is doubly necessary for a reason which has nothing directly to do with their actual work, but everything to do with present prevailing opinion in the world of art. So great is Cézanne's renown that most contemporary critics and painters regard him as the greatest, if not the only great, artist of modern times. A Cézanne-cult has grown up, and its existence is responsible for a widespread blindness to the excellence of every other painter, and inevitably also to the most distinctive and important qualities in Cézanne himself. The misconceptions are often buttressed by references to Cézanne's own reported sayings, but these are usually twisted from their context and interpreted without esthetic insight or the least regard for good sense and sound psychological principles. The result is to be seen not only in gross blunders of critical judgment, but in the contemporary forms of academicism in painting itself.

Cézanne's influence has been deservedly very great, and when exercised upon artists capable of grasping and assimilating it, it has borne fruit in such forms as may be seen in the work of Pascin, Picasso, Matisse and Prendergast. Upon innumerable lesser men, victims of this particular idolatry, it has been a blight. It has misdirected their energies, stunted their powers, and filled the exhibitions of recent years with collections of clichés—patterns of planes, blocklike volumes and meaningless distortions—as barrenly imitative of Cézanne as the former fashionable academic rehashes were of Manet, Whistler or Monet. To separate the grain from the chaff in Cézanne's influence is to be true to the ideals of Cézanne himself, whose own painting was intensely individual, and who denounced with all possible vehemence in his own day the stupid and insensitive critics and the academic painters who were the spiritual forbears of his present worshipers. The baleful effects of making a fetish of Cézanne, and the damage done to his own influence and to intelligent appreciation of him, must await discussion in another volume. However, the results of an objective investigation of the largest and most important collection of Cézannes in existence, an investigation directed by the same methods as those followed in the present study of Renoir, throw into such clear relief the salient traits of both of these artists that they may advantageously be summarized here.

Cézanne and Renoir were alike artists of the first rank, in that they enriched the great traditions of art and made them more fully expressive of profound and significant human values. Their specific contributions are widely different, yet each is so deeply grounded in human nature that to avow an unqualified preference for either is to confess to an essential shortcoming in one's own personality. Indeed, the contrast between them is so striking that its perception gratifies immediately our sense of the dramatic. The difference is that between a massive, firmly founded and solidly built cathedral, and a bouquet of bright, glowing flowers, arranged by a person of exquisitely sensitive taste. No normal person wishes to live exclusively either in cathedrals or in flower-gardens; Cézanne and Renoir, discriminately grasped, do not compete with each other, but complement each other, and to laud one at the expense of the other is a disservice to both. It is possible, however, to recognize their equal uniqueness as artistic personalities, and at the same time to point out that in other respects their artistic endeavors were attended with very different degrees of success.

The difference, in brief, was this: Cézanne's interests were very much narrower in range than Renoir's, they never displayed any such capacity for growth, and they never had at their service a comparable command of the medium of paint. By the mid-seventies, Renoir was able to make paint express anything he had to say, and as he grew older he learned, from life and from the traditions, to say constantly more and more. Cézanne struggled his whole life long to get what he had in mind upon canvas, and the marks of the struggle appear in nearly every picture; the efforts were, as he himself felt and said, rarely altogether successful, and the percentage of pictures left unfinished or abandoned by him as failures is immensely larger in his work than in Renoir's.* So much of his energy went into the work of execution that he seems to have

* Many of these abandoned pictures were completed by inferior painters and, ironically enough, are lauded by critics as important and representative Cézannes.

had little or none left to expend in broadening his interests. His paintings testify as unambiguously as do the known facts of his life that the intensity of his mind was equalled by its narrowness, its indifference or aversion to what was irrelevant to his own particular problem. Hence, from the time he outgrew his apprenticeship to Delacroix, Daumier and Pissarro and discovered his own vein, his pictures show little development except in craftsmanship: what he had to say in 1906 was essentially what he had had to say in 1877. Consequently, his work shows no such continuous expansion of range as does Renoir's, no comparable assimilation of constantly wider and deeper values both plastic and human.

From the very beginning Cézanne's interest was in power, the manifestation in Nature of intense force or energy, and in his work he revealed this power in a degree surpassing that of Nature itself. He saw it in terms of geometrical forms, and consequently he rendered every kind of subject-matter, fruit, trees, houses, mountains, human beings, with accentuated blocklike character, in highly patterned designs. The dynamic quality of his form, intense as it is, remains static, it is never, as with Tintoretto or El Greco, the dynamism of active movement. In the very early stages of his career, he attempted the representation of actual motion, but with such rare success that he soon abandoned the attempt altogether. In the creation of his form he made heavy drafts upon the traditions of sculpture and architecture as well as those of painting, and consequently his form is at all times architectonic. Cézanne's integrity and force of personality was so great, he drew his inspiration so directly from Nature, that his patterned planes and cubic masses never, after the first shock of unfamiliarity is past, seem unreal. Indeed, their reality is often overwhelming, but it is an intensely narrow reality, one which omits almost entirely a great many aspects of the natural world. Hence, there is a great lack of variety in his designs, and a still-life, a human figure, or a landscape are all variations on the same architectonic theme. In a literal as well as a figurative sense, his work is monumental: it is weighty, massive, ordered and composed, and seems as though it were built for eternity, but it is also inflexibly rigid. Cézanne shows little capacity for the adjustment of design and compositional organization, as well as of detailed handling, to distinctive types of subject-matter, which makes Renoir's painting an inexhaustible store of fresh and varied insights.

The same absence of essential variety characterizes Cézanne's use of particular plastic means and technical devices. All his pictures consist essentially of a dynamic organization of solid color-masses constructed of planes and set in three-dimensional colorful space; that is, the invariable means by which he secured his incomparable effect of power. Only about four types of such compositional ordering are distinguishable in his work, they vary only slightly, and each is employed indifferently for the painting of still-life, figures and landscapes. His color-schemes and methods of drawing are equally limited, as is his technique, which consists of about half a dozen variations of the impressionistic brush strokes. His modeling involves a characteristic new and important device in color-hatchings by brush strokes, but beneath this a trained eye can readily detect the traditional method of obtaining three-dimensionality of volumes by means of intersecting sets of lines or bands of color. Throughout his career his greatest difficulty was in rendering space, in which he was almost always obliged to resort speciously either to sharp contrasts of color or to heavy contour of actual line in lieu of subtle and specific color-relationships. In his *"Bathers"* (617) of c. 1877, for example, this difficulty led to an excessive piling up of pigment, which is sometimes a quarter of an inch deep; in *"Gardanne"* (619), of about 1885, the heavy line by which a volume is given spatial position stands out to the point of overaccentuation; in *"Nudes in Landscape"* (622), on which he worked from about 1890 to 1906, both heavy pigment and line are strained and forced in order to differentiate volumes from surrounding space. His inability to make pigment a ready instrument of his intention was scarcely ever surmounted; even in his most successful pictures, such as *"Woman with Green Hat"* (623), in which he is really able to say what he means to, the power of the color does not dissolve away wholly the feeling of the paint itself.

In spite of his technical shortcomings, Cézanne was a supreme artist in his ability to make color the fundamental means of all his plastic effects, to use it to build up mass, to fill and organize space, to draw the essential quality of things, and to compose the form as a whole. What he felt as the essential quality of everything, as we have seen, was its power, and his rendering of this is itself often so powerful as to stun and overwhelm the spectator. So profoundly impressive is the effect that the emotional power is not affected by the narrowness of range: however familiar the plastic content of Cézanne's pictures becomes—and to an experienced observer it becomes very familiar—its impact upon the senses and emotions remains. What does wear thin is the intellectual interest. After the observer's feelings have felt the force of the impact, he inevitably wishes, if he is an intelligent being, to analyze it, to understand its objective content, for, as Paul Valéry pointedly says, the authentic critic is interested not only in what the artist does but in *how* he does it.

Cézanne's means have not the variety, the versatility, the precise adjustment to specific purposes, differing often from one place to another in the same picture, that Renoir's have, so that he presents no comparable intellectual stimulus and reward. It is doubtlessly to the fact that after a certain point Cézanne offers so little food for the complete personality that Leo Stein, the most distinguished critic of our day, referred when he wrote that for him Cézanne is "more completely the squeezed lemon than any other artist of anything like equal importance." * Such a judgment, severe as it is, and neglectful of many aspects of Cézanne's work, cannot be too enthusiastically welcomed as a corrective to the prevalent Cézanne-fetishism.

The explanation of the fetishism readily becomes apparent in the light of the facts just pointed out. The stunning impact of Cézanne's power has left the critics and the painters who follow him blindly in a permanent stupor; lacking the capacity to reflect and to see plastically for themselves, they seize upon the obvious technical means by which his designs are carried out and overlook the real grounds of his greatness.

In his *"Nudes in Landscape"* (622), at the end of his career, Cézanne renders in a new form the basic values of both architecture and sculpture, as they are felt in the frieze of the Parthenon; indeed, in all his best work, he gives a penetrating and profound reorganization of Nature, and raises the functional quality of color to the supreme degree. Any one who has learned to see nature and art in their concrete fulness will recognize in this a development of the Venetian tradition of very great and lasting significance; he will also be able to recognize the same tradition in its other present-day developments, and to see through the academic repetition of Cézanne's pattern and technique which is the entire stock in trade of his host of imitators.

Renoir's work offers no such obvious irrelevancies for academic

* Leo Stein, "The A-B-C of Aesthetics," p. 267, Boni & Liveright, New York, 1927.

reproduction and for that reason he has had few imitators. Few too have been the younger painters equipped with the perspicacity to grasp his subtleties and the ability to use them creatively. Those who have possessed these requirements have usually drawn upon Cézanne also, and have made the derivations from each source the means for the development of their own esthetic insight and the expression of their own individuality.

ILLUSTRATIONS

Mademoiselle Romaine Lancaux (2) 1864

Analysis, page 374.

Lise (5)   1867
Analysis, page 374.

Boy with Cat (7)   1868
Analysis, page 376.

Lise (9) c. 1868

In Summer (11)   c. 1868–1869
                    Analysis, page 380.

c. 1868–1869

La Grenouillère (12)   Analysis, page 381.

Canoeists at Chatou (24)

1872

Analysis, page 382.

Mr. and Mrs. Sisley (10)   c. 1868

Analysis, page 378.

Bather with Griffon (16)   1870

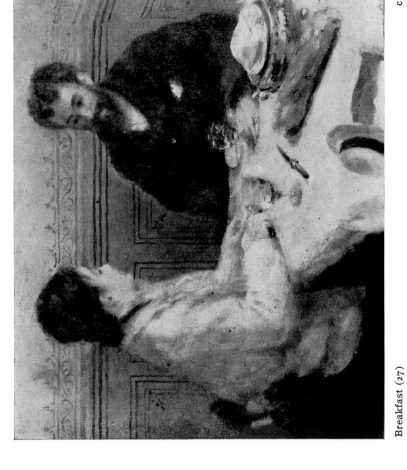

c. 1872

Breakfast (27)

La Grenouillère (31)

Young Woman with Rose (28)   c. 1872
Analysis, page 384.

Opera Box (34)   1874
Analysis, page 385.

Dancer (32)   1874

Woman at Spring (37)   **c. 1874–1875**

Analysis, page 389.

Lacemaker—Vermeer (466)   Reader (40)   c. 1874–1876

Analysis, page 390.

The Vermeer at the left exemplifies the theme of light interpreted in the Renoir at the right.

1875

Two Women in Park (44)

Analysis, page 390.

Young Girl Sewing (41)   c. 1874–1876

Torso (52)   c. 1875

Girl with Jumping Rope (57)   1876

Mademoiselle Jeanne Durand-Ruel (59)   1876
Analysis, page 393.

c. 1871

Analysis, page 382.

Henriot Family (23)

Moulin de la Galette (62)

1876

Analysis, page 394.

247

248

Swing (63)   1876

Analysis, page 395.

At the Milliner's (64) c. 1876

Analysis, page 396.

Madame Henriot (69)　　　　　　　　　　　　　c. 1876

Analysis, page 396.

Jeanne Samary (72)   1877

After the Concert (73)   c. 1877

Café Scene (81)   c. 1878

Woman Crocheting (76)   c. 1877

Woman with Veil (77)   c. 1877

Analysis, page 398.

1878

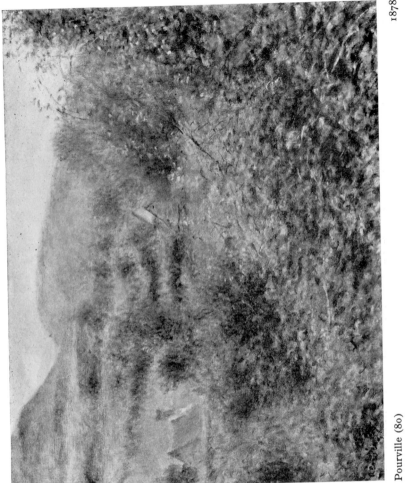

Pourville (80)

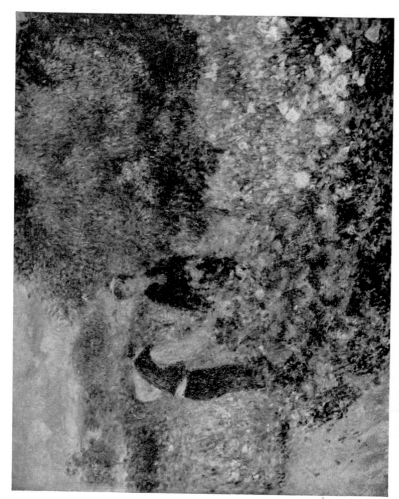

c. 1878

Picking Flowers (85)

After Luncheon (88)　　　　　　　　　　　　　　　　　1879

Analysis, page 399.

Bohemian (90)   1879

Mussel Fishers at Berneval (93)   1879

At the Piano (97)   Late 1870's

Analysis, page 401.

Two Little Circus Girls (99)

Late 1870's

Girl with Falcon (101)   1880
Analysis, page 401.

Mademoiselle Irène Cahen d'Anvers (104) 1880
Analysis, page 402.

Bather, Back Turned (107)   c. 1880

Analysis, page 402.

Capodimonte—Sorrento (112)

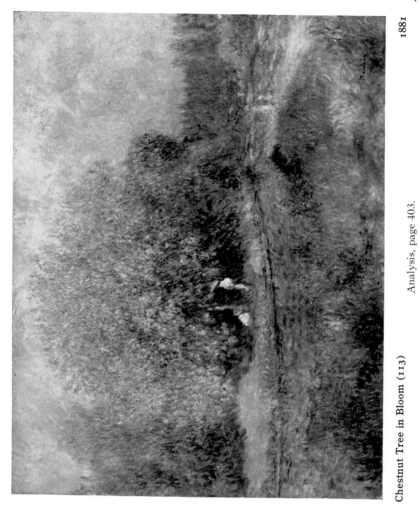

1881

Chestnut Tree in Bloom (113)   Analysis, page 403.

Mesdemoiselles Cahen d'Anvers (117)   1881

Analysis, page 405.

Mother and Child (118)   1881

On the Terrace (119)   1881

Analysis, page 405.

Courtesy of the Art Institute of Chicago

Child in White (134)   1883

c. 1881

Boating at Bougival (124)

c. 1882

Beach Scene, Guernsey (130)

By the Seashore (133)   1883

Analysis, page 407.

Blond Bather (131)   c. 1882
Analysis, page 406.

Dance in the City (135)   1883
Analysis, page 408.

Dance in the Country (136)   1883

Analysis, page 408.

Girl with Parasol (137)   1883

Sailor Boy (141)   1883

Bather in Rocky Landscape (142)   c. 1883–1885
Analysis, page 408.

Summer (150)   c. 1884

1884

Children at Wargemont (144)

Analysis, page 409.

c. 1884

Grape Gatherers Resting (147)

Anemones (156)   c. 1885

Woman with Fan (160)   1886

Garden Scene (161)   c. 1886

Fishing Scene—French Fresco (320)   c. 1344

This early French fresco represents the type of decorative treatment
embodied in the Renoir above.

Mother and Baby (162) c. 1886

Analysis, page 413.

Washerwoman and Baby (163)   c. 1886

Girl Plaiting Hair (165)   c. 1887

Bathers (164)

Diana at the Bath—Boucher (508)

The general form of this Boucher is enormously enriched in decorative and expressive values in the Renoir above. (For details see pages 96 and 205.)

1888

Analysis, page 415.

Bougival (166)

1888

Landscape with Harvester (169)

1888

Red Boat, Argenteuil (170)

Analysis, page 415.

1889

Mt. Ste. Victoire (175)

Girl with Basket   c. 1889
of Fish (177)

Girl with Basket   c. 1889
of Oranges (178)

Girl with Basket of Flowers (188)   Early 1890's

Girl Reading (186)
Analysis, page 416.

Early 1890's

Bather (181)

Late 1880's

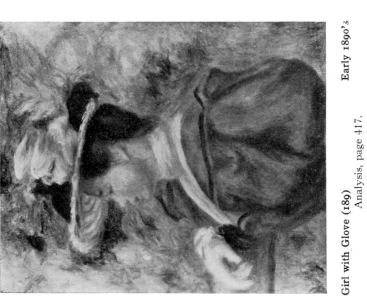

c. 1890

Girl with Straw Hat (196)
Analysis, page 417.

Early 1890's

Girl with Glove (189)
Analysis, page 417.

Analysis, page 417.

Pasture along the Seine (197)

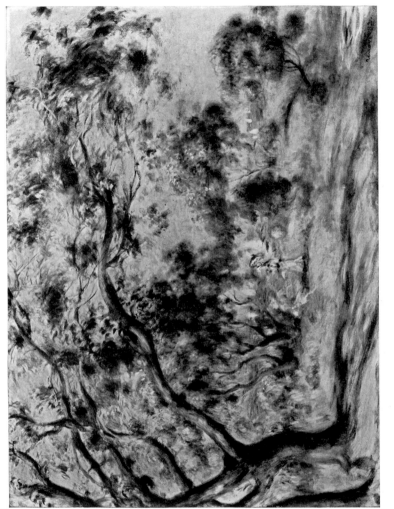

1892

Analysis, page 418.

Noirmoutier (201)

Apple Vender (198)   c. 1890–1891

Analysis, page 418

Girls at Piano (203)   **c. 1892**

Analysis, page 418.

c. 1892

Analysis, page 420.

Near Pont-Aven (204)

c. 1892

Pont-Aven (206)

306

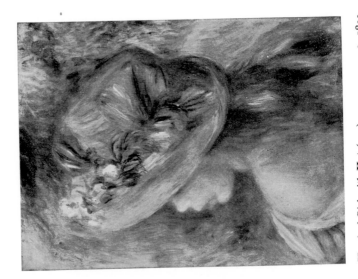

Head of Girl with Hat (210)   c. 1893

Analysis, page 421.

Girl in Profile (202)   c. 1892

c. 1897

Reclining Nude (217)

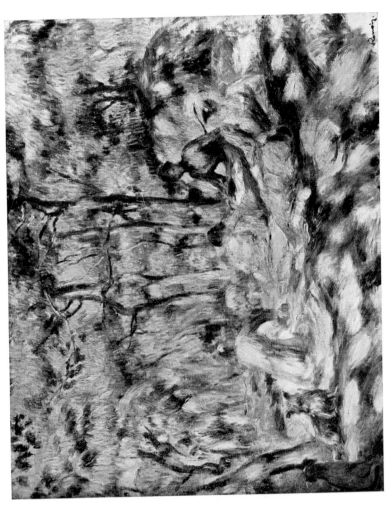

Analysis, page 422.

c. 1893

c. 1894

Analysis, page 422.

Village of Essoyes (212)

Nude in Brook (213)   1895
Analysis, page 422.

Artist's Family (214)   1896

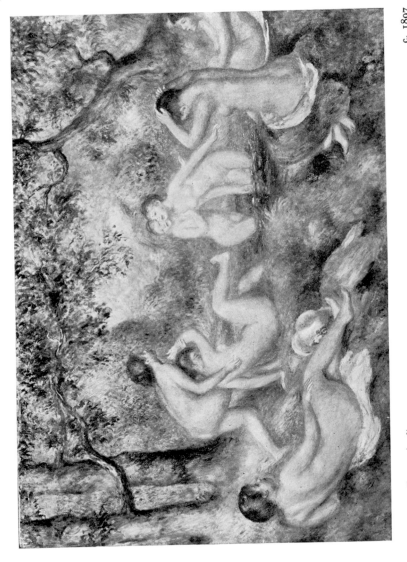

c. 1897

Bathers in Forest (216)

Bath of the Nymphs—Girardon (461)

The subject-matter and graceful movement in this seventeenth century French bas-relief were utilized in attaining the Venetian space-volume type of composition in the Renoir above.

Bather and Maid (218)   Late 1890's

Analysis, page 423.

Nude, Green Background (226)   c. 1902
Analysis, page 424.

Cagnes (219)

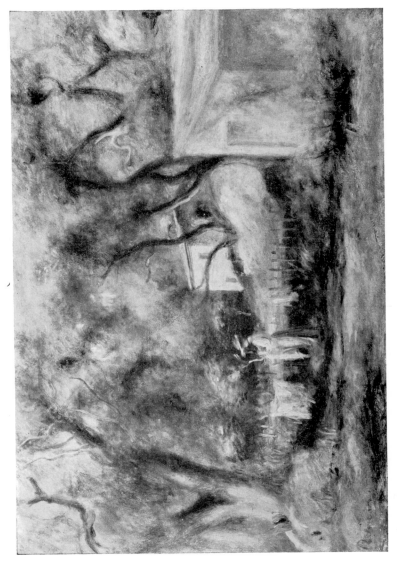

c. 1902

Le Cannet (225)

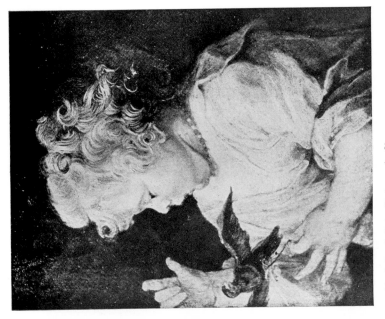

Child of the Artist—Rubens (418)

This Rubens and the four succeeding Renoirs herewith reproduced show the kinship between the two artists in the painting of children.

Jacques Fray, as a Child (230)   1904

Analysis, page 425.

Coco (229)　　　　c. 1903

Claude in Arab Shirt (232)　　c. 1904
Analysis, page 426.

Baby's Breakfast (231)   **c. 1904**

Analysis, page 425.

Embroiderers (233)   c. 1904

c. 1905

Writing Lesson (234)

Apologic page 127

1908

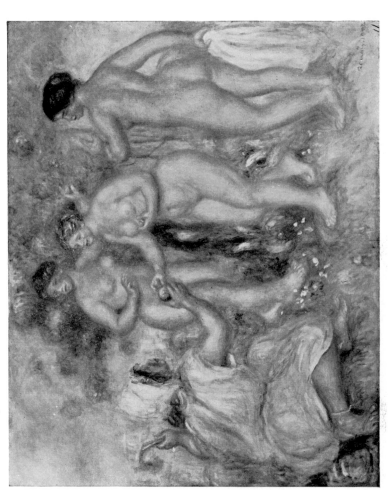

Judgment of Paris (240)

Missia (235)

Analysis, page 427.

c. 1906

Bather Drying Herself (243)　　　　　　　　　　　　　　**c. 1909**
Analysis, page 428.

Promenade (236)   c. 1906

Gabrielle Arising (245)   c. 1909

After the Bath (247)   1910

Original Sin (fragment)
—Michelangelo (341)

Madonna: Belle Jardinière (fragment)—Raphael (374)

Bathsheba at the Spring
—Rubens (417)

Susannah at the Bath (fragment)
—Tintoretto (392)

The various early traditional forms represented in these four pictures were drawn upon by Renoir in the painting reproduced on the opposite page.

Caryatids (248)   c. 1910   Caryatids (249)   c. 1910

Analysis, page 428.

Adam and Eve—Masaccio (325)

The fluid, graceful rhythms of this early
Florentine fresco are embodied, in more
colorful ensembles, in the Renoirs on the
opposite page.

Heads of Two Girls (251)   c. 1910

Woman Sewing (256)   c. 1910

334

Reclining Nude (252)   c. 1910

Sleeping Venus—Giorgione (344)

The Renoir above is a modern version of the Venetian subject-matter, type of composition and general feeling embodied in this Giorgione.

336

Bust of Nude (244)

Woman and Child under Tree (255)

Tea Time (257)   1911

Nude, Back View (259)   c. 1911

Apples (262)

Pomegranate and Figs (277)

Psyche (260)

Cup of Chocolate (263)

Analysis, page 429.

c. 1912

Woman with Black Hair (261)   c. 1911

At the Café (266)   c. 1914

c. 1914

Girl at Gate (267)

c. 1915–1917

Fruit and Bonbonnière (270)

348

Antibes (269)

c. 1915–1917

Woman in Landscape (297)

Landscape with Woman and Dog (275)   c. 1915–1917

Reapers (278)   c. 1915–1917

Seated Nude (279) c. 1915–1917

Analysis, page 431.

Seated Odalisque (280)   c. 1915–1917
                    Analysis, page 431.

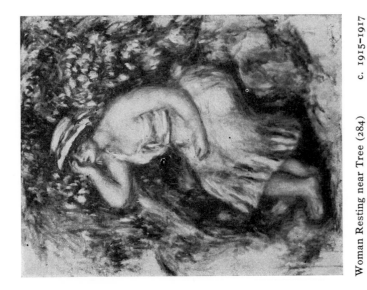

Woman Resting near Tree (284)   c. 1915–1917

Girl with Yellow Hat (272)   c. 1915–1917

1916

Analysis, page 431.

Bathing Group (285)

Nude with Castanets (287)   c. 1916

Standing Figure—Greek Sculpture (311)   c. 300 B.C.

The classic feeling of this early Greek figure is adapted to the theme of an intricate interplay of color in the Renoir on the opposite page.

c. 1917–1919

Reclining Odalisque (293)

c. 1917–1919

Two Figures in Landscape (296)

Standing Odalisque (295)   c. 1917–1919

Woman in Muslin Dress (298)   c. 1917-1919

Figure in Garden (289)

c. 1918

Analysis, page 434.

Group of Bathers (302)

Woman on Hillside (299)   c. 1917–1919

Maternity (303)   c. 1918
Analysis, page 434.

Bathers (301)

c. 1918

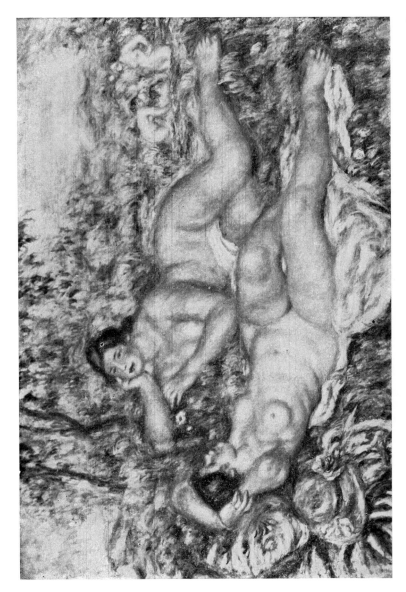

Analysis, page 435.

Nymphs (304)

Chrysanthemums in Vase (306)   c. 1919
Analysis, page 436.

APPENDIX

APPENDIX
BIOGRAPHICAL SKETCH

RENOIR's life was comparatively uneventful, and a brief account of it reads like little more than a bare record of dates. He was born at Limoges on February 23, 1841, and when he was about four years old his family moved to Paris. In 1854 he went to work in a porcelain factory as a painter of ornamental designs, and subsequently made his living by painting fans and window shades. Upon these he frequently reproduced pictures by the old masters, especially by the French painters of the eighteenth century, for whom he thus acquired a great admiration. The clear and transparent tones of all his mature work were also probably a survival of his porcelain-painting. When he was seventeen he entered the studio of Gleyre, where he made the acquaintance of Monet, Bazille and Sisley. His first exhibition at the *Salon* was in 1863, and about the same time he met Pissarro and Cézanne. The year following he was rejected at the *Salon,* but exhibited instead at the *Salon des Refusés*. Between 1865 and 1868 he frequently visited the Forest of Fontainebleau, where he met Diaz, and in 1865 and 1867 his work was again shown at the *Salon*.

Early in the war with Prussia he enlisted in the cavalry, but saw no active service and returned to Paris in 1871. Two years later he met Durand-Ruel, the first dealer to sponsor his work, and in 1874 and 1877 he participated in the general exhibitions of the impressionists. In the seventies and early eighties his previous acquaintance with Cézanne, whom he had always admired, became more intimate. Between 1879 and 1881 he traveled frequently, going to Algiers for six weeks in 1879 and again in 1881, to Guernsey in 1880 and repeatedly thereafter, and to Italy in 1880-1881. He was married in 1880 and his first son, Pierre, was born in 1885.

During the eighties he continued to sketch in the country and after 1885 went regularly each summer to the village of Essoyes in Champagne. He painted with Cézanne at La Roche Guyon in 1886, at Les Martigues and L'Estaque in 1887, and at Aix-en-Provence on frequent occasions between 1886 and 1893. From 1890 to 1893 he spent his summers in Pont-Aven, and in 1895 he made a trip to Spain. His second son, Jean, was born in 1893. In 1899 he had his first attack of rheumatoid arthritis, a malady which eventually crippled him. Claude Renoir, his third son, was born in 1901. Shortly after 1900 he began to go regularly to the Midi, spending one year at Le Cannet and three at Magagnosc, and in 1907 he settled down finally at Cagnes. In 1911 he lost the use of his limbs almost entirely. He died on December 3, 1919.

The dearth of incident in Renoir's actual existence is in striking contrast to the wealth, variety and audacity of his inner life. Except at the time, just before and after 1880, when the resources that had previously sufficed him seemed to be petering out, he had no need to wander afield for material; it is typical of him that when told of Gauguin's departure for Tahiti, his comment was "one can paint so well at Batignolles." His surroundings were those of a *petit bourgeois;* when he finally went to live in the south of France it was for his health's sake; but in the most commonplace scene he could find an inexhaustible source of interest and delight. Even when his success enabled him to live in greater comfort, he was satisfied with the barest of rooms and the simplest of furnishings; the color and light, the grouping of objects, which he cared for above everything, could be found everywhere. When he went to a reception, it is said, he was so absorbed in the burst of color in a flower, the light playing across a face, that he forgot to listen to what was said to him.

He was equally interested in putting upon canvas whatever moved him, and he did it without effort and so far as possible, without interruption. Except under compulsion, he never missed a day's painting in his whole life; in the hospital, awaiting an operation, he propped up a canvas on the bed before him and painted the flowers which had been sent him; and the day his son, who had been wounded, returned to the front, he could find consolation only in painting. He even said *"c'est avec mon pinceau que...j'aime."* He had the utmost admiration for the great painters of the past, who knew their craft so thoroughly, and he expressed his esteem by saying that "the instruction of the museum is the only thing valuable to a painter." He called himself a painter, not an artist, and despised the need for unusual conditions or emotional "inspiration" which condemned other painters to long periods of inactivity. Though he enjoyed music and literature, he gave them up when they threatened to compete with his own work, and though he took pleasure in the companionship of other painters, he had not the slightest interest in theories about art: indeed, he professed to be dismayed when some one suggested entitling one of his pictures *"La Pensée."* His nature was extraordinarily spontaneous, averse to what he considered formal or pretentious, whether in persons or works of art, as well as to everything somber or painful; but he was transported by intense color or brilliant light, and wished his pictures to be full of charm and delight. This *joie de vivre* never left him; it survived through the infirmity of his later years, and the canvases painted with a brush he could not hold unaided were as filled with it as those of his early youth. His life and his art were completely one; there was nothing in himself which he could not put on canvas, and nothing on his canvases which was not completely himself.

ANALYSES

THE following analyses of paintings by Renoir are arranged in chronological order. The space limitations of the volume necessitated an illustrative instead of an exhaustive type of analysis; consequently, in each analysis attention is directed to those objective features of the picture that serve primarily to confirm one or more of the principles treated in the book proper. An attempt has been made to arrange the specified objective features in such a way that they also sum up the salient characteristics of the form of the particular picture.

MADEMOISELLE ROMAINE LANCAUX * (2), dated 1864, is obviously inspired by the traditional French portrait-painting represented by Corot's *"Woman with the Pearl"* (570) and Ingres' *"Madame Marcotte de Sainte-Marie"* (558). A pervasive theme of delicate whitish-grays and grayish-whites, ranging from slate to silver, produces a general silver tonality reminiscent of Corot's. The execution of the figure is also very close to Corot but the total form is not so weighty, it has more of the lightness of the Ingres mentioned above, and a delicacy which was part of Renoir's capital from the start and which indicates an innate affinity with the spirit of the eighteenth century painting. With no distinctive characteristics recognizable as Renoir's own, this early portrait is nevertheless interesting as objective evidence of Renoir's extraordinary skill in painting at the very beginning of his career, and his grasp of the essentials of the great traditions. Here, as usual in his early work, he seems to have had great difficulty in making white pigment render the specific quality of textiles and avoid the feeling of paint.

LISE † (5) painted in 1867, is a good example of Renoir's work in its formative stage, when his main sources were the Barbizon school, Courbet, and the latter's forbears, Hals, Velásquez and Goya. The landscape-setting with its dark greens and tans and its floating ill-defined islands of filtering silver-gray light, comes directly from the *sous-bois* scenes of the Barbizon painters; the flesh, especially in the face, has the smooth surface with dull waxy glow characteristic of

* Illustration, p. 225.
† Illustration, p. 226.

374

Courbet; the brushing throughout is of the Courbet-Velásquez-Hals type; the realization of lacy and transparent materials recalls Goya; the striking black-and-white effect of broad dramatic contrast in the compositional color-and-light organization—one of the outstanding features of the design—is a note taken from Velásquez, as are also the compositional relationships and the picturesquely realistic presentation of the subject-matter. In short, the picture is a fine example of the traditional type of portraiture as Courbet developed it from Hals, Velásquez and Goya. Renoir adds something to the traditional form by better quality of color and a finer sense of plastic relationships; for example, in the unit made up of the flesh and the transparent blouse covering the neck, upper part of the chest and right arm, both the flesh and the fabric are finer in color-quality and are better related to each other than are corresponding units in Goya's rendering of transparent stuffs.* Again, Renoir's painting of the lace parasol in this picture has a finer quality of color and a more convincing reality than Goya's rendering of the black lace-edging around the fichu of *"Doña Tadea Arias de Enríquez"* (544) because Renoir's color makes the unit more positive and real. His enrichment of what he derived from Courbet is perceptible in the flesh and modeling of the woman's head which has a solidity like Courbet's, but in which delicacy supplants the heaviness of the original. The influence of Velásquez appears in the white dress: in its general simplified drawing, the relation of the hand and handkerchief to the skirt,† the black and white contrasts,‡ and the chalky-plaster-wooden quality of surface.§ The dress by its color, lighting and texture is a more strikingly effective compositional factor than one finds in Velásquez or Courbet: its very bright white is enriched by numerous shades of gray, and its texture is enlivened in color-quality by the concentration upon it of a flood of direct open-air sunlight. This illumination and the vivid contrast between the lighted area and the black sash and streamers are adaptations of traits which Manet developed from the Hals-Velásquez-Courbet tradition ‖ and which paved the way for the impressionists' further development of the effects of light playing upon color. Renoir reorganized Manet's broad brush strokes so that they are less perceptible and their form more generalized; in the black sash, for example, they form a pattern of superposed islands of gray light alternating with blackish-gray areas of shadow which lends a lively moiré effect to the surface. This method

---

* Cf., e.g., Goya's *"Infanta María Luisa"* (549) or *"Woman with Fan"* (554).
† Cf., e.g., Velásquez' *"Infanta Doña Margarita de Austria"* (445).
‡ Cf., e.g., Velásquez' *"Infanta Marguerite"* (446).
§ Cf., e.g., Velásquez' *"Court Attendants"* (441) or *"Infanta Doña Margarita de Austria"* (445).
‖ E.g., Manet's *"Dead Christ with Angels"* (600) and *"Eva Gonzalès"* (603).

of execution is a composite of elements and characteristics derived from Manet, Goya, Velásquez and Hals. Other adaptations from the same and from other sources occur in the composition as a whole and are welded into a new and single pictorial entity, chiefly through the medium of color-and-light relations. The derivations from Hals, Velásquez, Goya, Courbet and Manet contained in the figure, for instance, are vividly set off as a unit by a dark background extensively infused with the technique, color-scheme, light- and space-effects of the Barbizon school. This background is linked compositionally with the figure by a sequence of gray, tan and greenish tones, graduated in degree of light-content to form a definite pattern of colored light organized around and back of the vivid white area occupied by the figure itself. Space is rendered by the rhythmic, well-proportioned distribution of these units of gray and greenish light, and by their relations to the brown, tan, gray and green shaded portions of the landscape. As the space at the right recedes to infinity, the dark units are vaguely punctuated by indications of foliage that appear as a rhythmic flow of vague and delicately lighted floating masses which form a subsidiary pattern within the general pattern of colored-light units. The components of this total pattern function differently throughout the setting: they depict the receding plane of the light green ground at the right, contribute to the modeling and surface-texture of the tree trunk at the left, and impart to the entire landscape-setting a well-defined Courbetesque feeling of objects realistically placed in space. The picture, in spite of its extreme reliance upon the traditions, its crude execution, its feeling of paint and its limited palette is, nevertheless, a successful achievement for a young painter. It shows his ability to grasp the meaning of his predecessors' work and to make use of it in the creation of an adequately personal and picturesque form. Two points are worth noting—one as showing Renoir's early ability to handle space-composition, the other as indicating his still incomplete control of color-relations: (1) the exquisiteness of the unit made by the woman's left hand with the space and objects around it, and (2) the lack of finesse in the relations between the gray shadow on the woman's left shoulder and the veil extending down to it from the hat: the veil, of about the same color and tone as the shaded shoulder, seems as color to be out of place in that position.

BOY WITH CAT * (7), of the year 1868, is a remarkable fine, well-organized and skilfully painted picture. It belongs to the Velásquez-Courbet type of portraiture, but is achieved by a different technique, and its color-ensemble embodies the feelings of both power and strength to a greater degree than either Velásquez or Courbet. The general effect is that of Manet's predominatingly black-and-white

* Illustration, p. 227.

color-schemes,* but in execution the only resemblance to Manet occurs in the few places in which perceptible individual brush strokes make a pronounced pattern, such, for example, as in the flowered drapery. The color-organization is infinitely more powerful than any of Manet's because of greater richness, depth and variety in individual colors, qualities which leaven the general theme of light-and-dark contrasts. Particularly eloquent is the color-contrast between the green pillow, the drapery of white, blue and gray, and the mottled marblelike surface of the floor; and no less moving is the very rich and striking pattern of color-areas into which enter the black-and-gray head of the boy, the tortoiseshell patches of the cat, the boy's gray arm, and the deep green pillow with black border and tassel.

The general similarity of the whole picture to Courbet's work is due primarily to certain qualities of color and surface which Renoir adapted from him; for example, Courbet's dull muted tones and slightly waxy surface of paint are particularly noticeable in the green pillow. The color is more solidly structural than Courbet's, the pattern of brushwork takes a more active part in the drawing and modeling of the flesh, and the total design is much more decorative. The boy's flesh has a bizarre textural quality, a decided feeling of cold marble which gives a distinctive character to the whole picture. The quality seems to be born of the light areas of cool slate-gray and the grayish slate-blue shadows which merge into a generalized pattern resembling the surface of marble. In spite of this exotic appearance the quality of color conveys also the feeling of natural flesh.

The form of the picture as a whole differs from Renoir's subsequent work in general qualities of color, tone of shadows in flesh, character of line, and in the action of pattern in drawing and modeling.† The shadows are of slaty gray-blue tone, while in the work of the mid-seventies they are bluish green and are more definitely patterned. The linear effects differ in that there is not the interpenetration of color between areas which is so characteristic of Renoir's mature form of the seventies. The relatively loose contour of the boy's figure tends to suggest an intermingling of the flesh-color with that of the contiguous portions of the setting, but in reality this effect is obtained by the Venetian device of deepening the tone of the flesh to approximate that of the adjoining color-area. The linear definition of the figure has an appearance of broken continuity, but in fact the contour merely varies in content or thickness of pigment, so that its edge is irregular instead of precise or incisive.

The linear pattern made up of the boy's torso, head, arms and crossed legs intertwines compositionally with the rhythmic linear swerves and

* E.g., Manet's *"Dead Christ with Angels"* (600), *"Eva Gonzalès"* (603).
† Cf., e.g., *"Torso"* (52), *"Girl with Jumping Rope"* (57) or *"Mademoiselle Jeanne Durand-Ruel"* (59).

sweeps formed by the cat, the pillow and the folds and swirling edge of the drapery. This composite linear movement is supported by an internal pattern of the brushwork used in drawing and modeling various units of the subject-matter. Variations in the style of brushwork and in color produce diversified decorative patterns in the floor, pillow and drapery, and a pervasive series of slightly swirling rhythms in the flesh. Each of these patterns enlivens the surface and also contributes to the feeling of movement and vitality characteristic of the entire design.

All the objects—cat, pillow, drapery, the boy's torso, legs, hands and head—are nicely placed to form an unaccentuated but well realized space-composition. The decentered figure is counterbalanced at the right and in the upper part of the canvas by the very adequate free space which is made to recede to infinity by the tonal relationship between the dark background and the colors of the figure and other objects. Especially picturesque and subtle in relationships is the unit formed around the cat by the boy's head and arms; another unit of space-pattern is created at the lower right by the relationships between the drapery, the boy's legs, the floor and the receding deep space of the background.

The picture is very striking, powerful and distinctive, and the color is rich and deep. The convincing realism of Velásquez and Courbet is raised to a higher plastic status by Renoir's more effective line, space-pattern, color-contrast and, particularly, color-relations. The whole form breathes life and reality, and is perhaps the most powerful of Renoir's early achievements. It is more important, for instance, as a contribution to the traditions than *"Lise"* (5), *"Mr. and Mrs. Sisley"* (10), or, indeed, than any other picture of approximately the same stage of development. It is a stronger picture than most of Velásquez' or Courbet's. Although the form is not original, nothing in it is lifted bodily from any other painter: the brushwork itself and the use made of it, the drawing, the rendering of the flesh, the composition, the color-relations and the extensive slaty gray-blue shadows are different from anything in Manet, Courbet or Velásquez.

MR. AND MRS. SISLEY * (10), of about 1868.

The color-scheme of this picture, with its vivid notes and reënforcing contrasts, supplies a novel and distinctive foil for elements taken from other artists: from Corot in the rendering of the landscape, from Courbet in the painting of the woman's flesh, and from Manet in the drawing of the man. Interest centers in the sequence of color-areas, all of which, either by their own brightness (as in the woman's red, yellow and white dress) or by their contrast with adjacent areas (as in the black and gray garments of the man), contribute to a bizarre

* Illustration, p. 232.

color-pattern. The most striking part of this pattern, and the one which imparts to the design its essential piquancy and power, is the colorful dress of the woman which is a riot of vivid contrasts of colors and patterns. The bell-shaped skirt is a sequence of alternating bright red and yellow stripes; two panniers of a bright red, akin to that used by Tintoretto, edged with orange-red fringe and partly covered by transparent gray flounces, come in sharp contact with the vivid red bolero and the gray-white transparent guimpe. The red and yellow contrasts, of somewhat Spanish character, are to be found in other color-contexts in other painters, in Courbet and Manet for example,* but the particularly picturesque part they play here in conjunction with the other components of the color-scheme is entirely novel. The colors of the woman's dress and flesh are effectively set off by the various greens and grays of the landscape, and by the black, gray and white components of the man's figure. Conversely, the latter's blackish-gray tones are reënforced as color-factors by the more positive and more varied colors of their setting—silver-green foliage, orange-red flower-bed, bright green lawn, ivory-gray path and gray ground.

The landscape shows essential features of Courbet's in the peculiar raw green, and of Corot's in the lightness of foliage, silvery illumination and diffuse atmosphere; the foliage is not so delicate and floating as in Corot at his best, but is more lightly rendered than in Courbet and the green is not so crude.† At the upper left corner these borrowed features are given a novel cast by the accentuated pattern of diffuse light green patches, which supply the compositional need, at this point, for a focal concentration of color and light. Because of this accentuated pattern of light, the upper left area becomes part of a diagonal sequence of contrasting color-areas which sweeps upward from the lower right corner and is counterbalanced in direction by another sequence of color-areas comprising the figure of the man, the large striped fold at the front of the woman's dress, the general plane of the path and lawn, and the slightly indicated grayish-brown tree trunks and slate-gray house at the upper right of the landscape. Included in this compositional pattern is an area of shadow surrounding the figures which is worthy of special note because, functioning primarily as space, it forecasts Renoir's much later use of similar shadow-effects to convey the feeling of volumes set in a pocket of space.‡

The drawing and the modeling of the figures are done in the styles of Courbet and Manet. The grayish tone of the woman's flesh is midway between Courbet's dull gray in *"Head of Baby"* (583) and the

* E.g., Courbet's *"After the Hunt"* (582) and Manet's *"Boy with Fife"* (596).
† Cf., e.g., Corot's *"Dancing Nymphs"* (563), Courbet's *"Pond in the Valley"* (587).
‡ Cf., e.g., *"Promenade"* (236) of c. 1906.

warmer ivory complexion in his *"Woman with Pigeons"* (589). The similarity to Courbet is increased by the light-and-shadow modeling, the smooth roundness of the volume, which has no marked accentuation of either highlights or deep shadows, and by the dull glow of the waxy surface. Manet's influence is perceptible in the man's head, with its relatively flattened profile, its black-and-white effect, and its simplified modeling, and in the broadly painted, relatively flat areas of black and gray fabrics, with their slight pattern of a few broad brush strokes which render folds and suggest the feeling of adequately solid volumes enclosed within the garments. No Manet portrait, however, has the firmly constructed illustrative appeal of *"Mr. and Mrs. Sisley"*; no color of Courbet's has an equal degree of luminosity, and no Corot color-ensemble has the variety, quaintness and picturesqueness of this Renoir. The drawing is not tight for a picture of this period; indeed its relative looseness and naïvely awkward grace yield a very charming, dainty framework for the picturesque color-relations.

The picture as a whole reveals Renoir's undeveloped personality and his imperfect control of paint. The surface is dry, heavy and devoid of pleasing sensuous quality, with the actual paint felt as a material object rather than as an esthetic medium. Neither flesh nor garments have sufficient substantial or textural realism; the lighted area at the upper left, and also a Goya-like linear contour of light around the man's shoulder and arm are conventionally relied upon to help set off the figure in space. Finally, realism is carried almost to the point of photographic literalism in the strands of the fringe on the woman's dress, the veins of the man's hand, the seams in the gloves, and in minor details of the collar and necktie.

IN SUMMER * (11), of c. 1868-1869, represents the student phase of Renoir's work of the pre-1870 period. The realistic rendering of the sitter, the smooth surface and grayish tone of the flesh, the rather conventionalized drawing of the various objects, and the crude quality in the green of the background—all these are the familiar Courbet features which Renoir at this period used so frequently. Nevertheless, the color and, indeed, the entire composition are better illuminated than in Courbet; the colors are brighter and lighter both in tone and weight, they carry better, and their ensemble is far richer than that in any corresponding Courbet.† Much of the vividness, brightness and picturesqueness of the design is due to the spotted pattern of sunlight in the foliage. This adaptation of a device familiar in Bazille ‡ and the early Monet, § is used here with broad individual brush strokes which constitute practi-

---

* Illustration, p. 229.
† Cf., e.g., Courbet's *"Midday Dream"* (584) or *"Nude"* (585).
‡ E.g., Bazille's *"Family Party"* (634).
§ E.g., Monet's *"In the Garden"* (627) and *"La Grenouillère"* (628).

cally the sole point of kinship with Manet. The light of the patches is colored by strokes of whitish green disseminated among the varied darker tones of green, so that the pattern is one of color as well as of light and of shapes. Some of the patches are vaguely outlined as by a faint halo of light and thus acquire the floating quality of islands of color and light. The concentration of light in relatively large focal areas immediately to the right and left of the girl's head is very effective in setting off the figure à *contre jour* and in creating spatial relations between it and the background. The method is specious, however, and never recurs in Renoir's matured form.

As a portrait, this picture is very successful, but in it Renoir has not yet found his personal form or method of expression. Its distinction is that it is a conversion of traits not original with Courbet into a form more individual than Courbet's own.

LA GRENOUILLERE * (12), painted c. 1868-1869, is a definitely impressionistic picture, quite like an early Monet † or Manet,‡ but with a deeper color and a more firmly knit organization. The color-scheme, though dark, is neither dull nor somber, and is more reminiscent of Courbet than of Manet or Monet. A pervasive deep green, which gives the keynote and general tonality to the color-ensemble, is punctuated with a few small notes of blue, red, silver and brown, but its general dark tone is relieved by a large area of light extending at the right from the sky to the water in the foreground. Drawing is simplified in the extreme; figures are flat, more generalized even than in Manet, and they are silhouetted by a broad linear contour. The technique in general is very close to that of Manet or of Monet's early work, but the brush strokes are more varied in shape, direction, and size, and in their use in drawing and compositional organization. This better command of technique, together with the rich, well-illuminated color, makes of the picture a personal rendering of the impressionists' form in a stronger and higher type of plastic organization. Surfaces, however, still preserve the feeling of pigment, especially in the rendering of the trees and boats.

In FREDERIC BAZILLE (15), painted before 1870, Renoir experiments with a color-scheme of grays and a type of composition borrowed from Corot,§ but the ensemble is less juicy in color than a good Corot and less subtle in organization of space. The picture is noteworthy in that it shows scarcely a trace of Courbet's influence, which

---

* Illustration, p. 230.
† Cf., e.g., Monet's *"La Grenouillère"* (628) or *"Landing-stage at Argenteuil"* (629).
‡ Cf., e.g., Manet's *"Departure of Folkestone Boat"* (601 and 602) or *"Tarring the Boat"* (609).
§ Cf., e.g., Corot's *"Studio"* (568).

at this stage of Renoir's work was usually more in evidence than any other.

HENRIOT FAMILY* (23), of c. 1871, shows that at an early stage of his career Renoir was a colorist of the first rank and that he was already saturated with the spirit of the eighteenth century French tradition. The color-ensemble, which at first sight appears as a gray monochrome, is soon revealed as an extremely subtle interplay of greens, blues, browns and pinks, all so delicately modulated that their respective nuances, melting into each other, confer upon the pervasive gray tonality the subtle color-richness and the subdued glow of a pearl. A few positive notes of lustrous black, the relatively large areas of coral, and the numerous islands of multinuanced grayish light, not only form vivid patterns of their own but punctuate the general color-ensemble with dramatic contrasts which contribute much to both the strength and the formal organization of the composition. The extremely fluid drawing of figures and objects is in great part responsible for the pervasively subtle color-harmony. The simplifications of Manet's are carried to a further degree of generalization and the loosely defined contours, helped by large areas of unpainted gray canvas, become the vehicle by which each plastic unit blends with and appears to melt into the surrounding space. Subtle adjustments of tone and color retain adequate clean-cutness in the definition of space-intervals and deep distance, and the conjoined action of drawing and color creates an all-pervasive suffusion which envelops the landscape with a pearly-silvery atmosphere more colorful and luminous than Corot's. The suffusion and the ubiquitous fluidity of color and drawing impart a floating quality to the total composition. The technique of broad irregular brush strokes adds a quivering pattern which enlivens the ensemble without disturbing the extreme placidity of the scene. In the treatment of the woman's gown in the foreground, the pattern of the brushwork and the shadows in the folds represent a version of Pater's method of rendering similar materials.†

CANOEISTS AT CHATOU ‡ (24), of 1872, in its color-scheme, color-quality, light-content, drawing and technique, is a characteristic picture of the early seventies. Renoir, emerging from Courbet's influence, was experimenting with the broken color, sunlight and technique of his closer contemporaries, Monet, Manet and Sisley.

The color-scheme does not yet fall within the blue-green-ivory category of the mid-seventies, inasmuch as it is dominated by the extensive area of the bright red boat which extends diagonally across

* Illustration, p. 246.
† Cf., e.g., Pater's "Gallant Conversation" (495).
‡ Illustration, p. 231.

practically the entire width of the foreground. Scattered notes of somewhat lower tones of red occur in nearly all sections of the canvas. Sunlight, in an accentuated pattern of alternating areas and spots of light and shadow, brightens only the surface of the color, a defect which makes the dark areas dull and deprives the lighted colors of luster and internal luminosity; in other words, light and color do not yet blend as organically as in the mid-seventies. The contrasts between spots of concentrated light and areas of dark unilluminated color are practically replicas of similar decorative features in typical early landscapes of the impressionists.* The contrasts are forerunners of Renoir's later experiments with decorative effects of light upon color in the exotic landscapes of the early eighties.†

Technique is one of the means by which the picture is organized, and in the different areas it varies in type and degree of accentuation of its pattern, in perceptibility and direction of individual brush strokes, and in compositional function. This accentuated pattern of brush strokes running in contrasting directions is not adequately supported by either depth or solidity of color, and hence the color-movement is factitious.

The picture is interesting chiefly as an example of Renoir's enrichment of the impressionistic form, mainly by varied color-chords and more fluid Manet-like drawing of the figures. The ensemble is more colorful and juicy than an average picture by Monet, Manet or Sisley, and it represents a better plastic embodiment of decorative and illustrative values.

PONT-NEUF (26), painted in 1872, testifies by its composition, color-scheme and drawing to the influence of Pissarro as represented in *"Crystal Palace"* (593), painted in 1871. In both pictures the generalized, loosely defined figures are drawn and modeled with small, flat, Manet-like touches, and much use is made of linear perspective and of blue shadows cast upon the ground to help set the objects and figures in space. The modifications introduced by Renoir institute a significant departure from Pissarro's form. The figures are more alive and are better located in space, the blue shadows upon the ivory ground are organized in a more lively pattern of patches, and each shadow occupying a vaguely semicircular area functions as a plane and seems to support each of the figures, much as a pedestal supports a statue. The effective repetition of the color of these shadows makes the picture predominantly blue, in marked distinction to Pissarro's usually more variegated color-scheme. The blue is of a brighter shade than that in the blue-ivory ensembles of the mid-seventies, but because of its relation to the large expanse of ivory foreground, and to the

* E.g., Monet's *"La Grenouillère"* (628), Sisley's *"Flood"* (615).
† E.g., *"Gondola on the Grand Canal"* (125).

few, small and scattered punctuations of red, the color-organization in *"Pont-Neuf"* may be perhaps considered as the birth of the later blue-ivory color-scheme.

In YOUNG WOMAN WITH ROSE * (28) of c. 1872, the color-scheme of deep rose-red and warm flesh tone, the surface-quality of the color, the muted internal glow and the flashy pattern of light are derived directly from Delacroix,† but the technique is closer to Manet's and Courbet's. Courbet's influence is transformed in the interest of a better textural rendering of flesh, and also of a more sensuously pleasing organization of the surface-color. Color is not yet adequately structural and conveys only the superficial effect of textiles and flesh; the pigment itself still retains the feeling of crude paint, especially in the whites. The picture has the unreal papery quality of a stage-setting, and its chief claim to attention is that it shows the muted tone and color and the dramatic light-effect which Renoir adopted from Delacroix and two years later raised to the high estate represented by *"Opera Box"* (34). The vast difference between the two pictures indicates that in the interval Renoir had grasped much more fully the meaning of Delacroix and had acquired the ability to convert it, largely by the structural use of color, into a more fully expressive Venetian form.

RIDERS IN THE BOIS DE BOULOGNE (30) is dated 1873, but its enormous size, its free use of Courbet traits, its labored execution, banal color, and academic character, all indicate that Renoir was engaged in painting it during a period of several years prior to 1873. The Courbet influence is especially evident in the waxy surface, the tight realistic drawing, and the painting of flesh. Renoir contributes notes of his own in a more luminous and lighter-toned color-scheme of silvery gray, slightly relieved by blues, greens and pinks, and in an enrichment of the flesh by the addition of considerable pink to the complexion, a few greenish gray-blue shadows and a general color of greater internal luminosity. Without forming a definite pattern the slight shadows contribute to the three-dimensional solidity of the woman's head, and this makes a contrast to the one-piece type of modeling in the relatively flat profile of the boy. The color is dry and uninteresting and in most of the areas the pigment is heavy, especially in the painting of the flesh and in the horses, although bare canvas appears in a considerable number of scattered spots. The picture is skilfully painted throughout, but is still the work of a student: the figures are posed, the horses are stilted in their move-

* Illustration, p. 236.
† Cf., e.g., Delacroix's *"Death of Sardanapalus"* (572) or *"Study of Reclining Woman"* (574).

ment and look as if they were made of wood, and the whole design has a strong savor of academicism.

MADAME X (33), dated 1874, has none of the richness and decorative quality which make *"Opera Box"* (34) of the same year, a masterpiece. The paint is dry, the color lacks luster, the drawing is flaccid and the total effect is monochromatic. The ensemble recalls both Courbet * and Carrière.†

OPERA BOX ‡ (34), dated 1874. The most significant plastic feature of this picture is its unconventional, compact and extremely effective composition attained mainly by an extraordinarily skilful realization of space. The main constituents of the design fill the canvas to its borders but, in spite of their compact grouping, the picture is not overcrowded nor do the objects seem jammed or huddled together. This required extreme subtlety and finesse in the handling of space and resulted in a picturesque placing of the volumes.§ The ubiquitous fluidity of the composition is due to the combined effects of spatial adjustment of volumes, delicate tonal modulations, subtle color-relations between juxtaposed areas, and the Manet-like brush strokes which overlap contours and cause adjacent units to interpenetrate.

The unconventionality of the pictorial organization results from restoring compositional equilibrium to the decentered main figure by means of interdependent and reënforcing rhythms and contrasts. In the process each of the constituent volumes—arms, hands, heads, bodies, curtain, ledge of the box—by virtue of its color, size, direction and relation to its context, enters into a well-defined, all-inclusive compositional pattern of rhythms and contrasts which assembles within its irregular diamond-shaped framework the pyramidal figure of the woman extending through the width of the foreground, and the slanting oblong area occupied by the man at the upper left. The framework of this compositional pattern is a set of broad bands—actual bands in the woman's dress, and band-shaped volumes and planes elsewhere. The method of organizing this theme consists, in the main, of paralleling some of the bands in several large units, and contrasting them to other sets of similarly paralleled bands.

The striking character and movement of the composition is due in large part to the ingenious interplay of broad areas of light and dark

* E.g., Courbet's *"Wounded Man"* (590).
† E.g., Carrière's *"Little Girl Counting"* (635).
‡ Illustration, p. 237.
§ One of the fine subsidiary designs of masses in space occupies the area of the woman's head and the space immediately back of it into which her hair delicately floats off; another is constituted by her left sleeve and its lace cuff, each of which rests convincingly in its own space.

color which alternate throughout the design. These areas form a pattern which is focalized in the large unit of the woman's face and chest, an area illuminated with a soft, warm, muted glow. From this broad spotlight, the pattern of light radiates along the sinuous, bluish silver-white bands of the woman's dress and sleeves, and finally ramifies throughout the entire expanse of the picture. In this, as in the similarly organizing light-pattern of the mid-seventies, the constituents of the pattern are objects some of which are of light color, others dark. This means that Renoir is still far from his later more imaginative replacement of the natural color and degree of illumination of objects by richer, more active and more original color-and-light effects.* The distribution of the units of the light-pattern in *"Opera Box"* through the pattern of dark colors form a complex organization of color- and light-areas which binds background and foreground into a single all-inclusive pattern; in other words, the subsidiary areas of space and mass in both foreground and background all unite with the constituents of the principal figure in a total compositional pattern of color-areas. The component areas of this pattern are not as a rule sharply delineated; consequently, the color-transition between them is comparatively fluid, notably between the white and the black, or between the red and the ivory-gold. This fluidity is increased by a ubiquitous slightly wavy contour produced by variety in brushwork and in thickness of pigment.

Renoir's progress over his earlier work is evidenced particularly in the rendering of textiles and flesh. The painting of the textiles is broad, simplified, delicate, and fluid; their color has a more lively sensuous quality than in Renoir's earlier work, it is better organized as pattern and conveys a more real feeling of texture. Another long stride forward appears in the extraordinarily rich, lustrous and solid quality of the blacks. Previously, Renoir's blacks have been dull, relatively painty, more as in Velásquez than as in Manet; in this picture the black materials surpass in depth, lusciousness, glow and feeling of life any corresponding textile in Titian or Velásquez, in Courbet or Manet, or in Renoir's own previous treatment of similar stuffs.† A corresponding advance appears in his painting of transparent materials, such as the light portions of the woman's dress and her delicate lace cuff. In the latter, the flesh is felt to be actually present beneath the filmy fabric, without the accentuation of either flesh or textile noticeable in the painting of the transparent sleeve and dress-yoke in the 1867 *"Lise"* (5). Renoir's better union of color and light

* Cf., e.g., *"Woman in Muslin Dress"* (298) of c. 1917-1919.
† Cf., e.g., Titian's *"Young Man in Black"* (371), Velásquez' *"Infanta Marguerite"* (446) or *"Lady with Fan"* (448), Courbet's *"Woman with Pigeons"* (589), Manet's *"Boy with Sword"* (597), and also Renoir's *"Lise"* (5) or *"Mr. and Mrs. Sisley"* (10).

in *"Opera Box"* differentiates the filmy material from the flesh, and at the same time merges them more organically into a single unit embodying the feeling of both the flesh and the fabric.

The flesh-painting is transitional between that of his earlier work and of his mid-seventies' form. The flesh is much lighter in tone than in the previous work, more delicate and transparent in texture, and more subtly modeled with much less shadow. The flesh of the woman's face and chest, for instance, represents a form midway between that of the Titian-Delacroix type in *"Young Woman with Rose"* (28) and the more delicate, luminous, glowing, colorful and convincing flesh in *"Torso"* (52), *"Girl with Jumping Rope"* (57) or *"Mademoiselle Jeanne Durand-Ruel"* (59). His earlier brown and gray shadows in the modeling have given place here to very slight delicate tones of greenish blue, which occur in only small areas, along the contour of the face and nose, at the corners of the mouth and under the lower lip. The resulting lack of contrast between lighted and dark areas gives to the modeling a smooth one-piece effect and makes the face relatively flat. This reduction of shadows in the flesh, the use of greens and blues in the shadows, and the flattening of the volume of the head, are all very likely due to Manet's influence.* From the same source come the generalized brushwork, the epigrammatic drawing of the flowers, the black-and-white effect of the color-organization, and the lustrous quality of the blacks. All of these derivations, however, have been significantly altered and blended with qualities more directly associated with earlier traditions. The woman's face, for instance, bears more resemblance to the old-fashioned traditional type of painting than to Manet's. The loose drawing of the face approaches that in Renoir's best work of the mid-seventies, but in comparison with the definitely fluid color in, for example, *"Torso"* (52) or *"Girl with Jumping Rope"* (57), the fluidity of contour in *"Opera Box"* is obtained speciously by obvious breaks in continuity of pigment and by a linear contour of shadow. Renoir's progress toward the form represented by *"Two Women in Park"* (44) or *"Girl with Jumping Rope"* is revealed by comparing the use of colored shadows in the modeling of flesh in *"Opera Box"* and in the two pictures named; in each, the shadow of the chin is continued over upon the neck, and very slight modulations of tone within the passage of shadow convey an adequate suggestion of space. In *"Opera Box"* the means employed, and the effort required, are readily perceptible, while in the two later pictures one observes the well-defined effect without being conscious of the means involved.

The drawing of the man's head is looser than that of the woman's and its surface is mottled by ill-defined brushing. In its looseness, delicacy and floating lightness, and in the subtle and effective render-

* Cf., e.g., Manet's *"Olympia"* (607).

ing of a figure in shadow, the figure of the man is extremely close to the typical Renoiresque figures in the earlier *"Henriot Family"* (23), and to a lesser extent to those in *"Moulin de la Galette"* (62) of 1876.

In sum, *"Opera Box"* represents a definite break from the heavy form of Courbet, from the latter's blocklike modeling, gray tonality, lack of sensuous appeal and general heaviness. It is already impregnated with Renoir's distinctive feeling for subtle, rich and delicate color-relations, and for lightness and sensuous quality of stuffs and surfaces. Nevertheless, deficient internal illumination of color brings the picture essentially into the old-master category of painting, represented by Titian or Velásquez.*

PROMENADE IN WOODS (35), dated 1874, exemplifies in its color-scheme and general treatment, steps in Renoir's transition from the period of the predominance of Courbet's influence to Renoir's attainment of his characteristic form of the mid-seventies. The black-and-white effect of the color-organization and the crude Barbizon-like greens are reminiscent of Renoir's *"Lise"* (5) of 1867. The textiles have less of the feeling of paint than in *"Lise,"* the surface is not so drab or dull as in *"Mr. and Mrs. Sisley"* (10) of c. 1868, and the technique differs from that in either, in that practically the entire surface of the painting is of rugged impasto, patterned in irregular curlicue and criss-cross brush strokes not unlike Monet's. The individual brush strokes contrast usually in degree of tone rather than in actual color; they cross each other and overlap, but their color-components do not interpenetrate, the pigment is not fluid and there are no real color-chords. A resemblance to Constable's technique appears in the treatment of the foreground, especially in the rugged surface of the path on the right, a resemblance due as much to solid and weighty color as to the pattern of brushwork and the technique itself.† The brush strokes differ somewhat from Constable's and their color is more luminous.‡

The drawing of the figures is freer, more spontaneous and less tight than in Renoir's earlier form. The grace and charm in the movement and expression of the two figures are marks of Renoir's progress toward the form of the mid-seventies.

* See also chapter "Development of Renoir's Form," pp. 55-56.
† Cf., e.g., Constable's *"Hay-Wain"* (557).
‡ Cf. Renoir's *"Glade"* (246) of c. 1909 in which the spirit of Constable's form is realized in delicate tones of pink, blue and silver, without a trace of Constable's technique. Cf. also Renoir's *"Trees"* (281) of c. 1915-1917, in which the vigor, strength and color-quality of Constable are attained by richer and more varied color and looser drawing than in the prototype and by a modified impressionistic technique.

In WOMAN AT SPRING* (37) of c. 1874-1875, Renoir treats a classic theme which goes back through Ingres and the eighteenth century French tradition to the Italian Renaissance.† The influence of Corot appears in the delicate greens, grays and silvery tones, and that of the impressionists in the brushwork and lighting. The broadly treated landscape is rendered mainly by brush strokes which are more colorful than Manet's and more active compositionally. The color-scheme is very simple: two large areas—the ivory-toned figure and the green setting—punctuated by notes of orange in the hair and red in the lips, and relieved of monotony by the vividly illuminated flesh and spots of light in the landscape. The strength of the color-organization and the lightness and daintiness of the total form are achieved by fineness of relationships between color and light in the drawing of individual parts and between figure and setting. The compositional problem, that of unifying figure and background, is solved in part by rhythmic repetition of units of the general light-pattern, in part by relations in degree of voluminousness between masses in various parts of the picture, and by repetition of areas in which brush strokes unite with color and light to make quite definite patterns. The figure is more voluminous than the objects in the background and is more sharply patterned although the brush strokes are less perceptible than in the setting; it is illuminated more brightly, and forms a vivid focus in a pattern of light which includes the clumps of grass and the bushes and waterfall in the setting. The background as a whole, with its elevation of distance to the top of the canvas, forms a screen, but the effect of actually receding space is secured by loose drawing, modulations of tone, and a pattern of light and dark areas in which the light areas become delicate volumes floating in a silvery atmosphere. Variety in the background is achieved by the greater depth of space at the left. In both the figure and the setting, a profusion of areas of silver and light blue, highly patterned with brush strokes and points of light, aid materially in unifying the composition. The pattern of light anticipates in its dramatic effect the 1880 type of nude-in-landscape in which light is focalized upon the figure and vividly set off by the deeply colored landscape.

GREENHOUSE (39), of 1874-1876, is a play upon the impressionistic theme of color, light and technique, and in this respect it has numerous points in common with *"Two Women in Park"* (44) of 1875. The blue-green-ivory color-scheme of the period is extensively punctuated by the red and white flowers set amongst the green foliage; smooth areas of uniform color and thin pigment alternate with more

* Illustration, p. 239.
† Cf., e.g., Ingres' *"Spring"* (561), Watteau's *"Autumn"* (472), Botticelli's *"Birth of Venus"* (338).

variegated units rendered in rugged impasto with accentuated high-lights; and the emphasis upon light-and-dark contrasts creates a rather obvious color-drama. The light-content of color is less than that in *"Two Women in Park"* and greater than that in *"Dancer"* (32) of 1874.

READER * (40), of 1874-1876, offers a novel version of the color-scheme of the mid-seventies attained by the activity of a large slanting ray of colored sunlight which falls directly upon the girl's hair, face and fichu, and also vividly illuminates the background-drapery above her head, and parts of the book in her hands. This diagonal shaft of light is painted with thick rugged pigment in irregular spots, strokes and dabs of juicy paint, which produce a texture like that of heavy porcelain or ceramic. The ray of light is permeated through and through with extremely rich color-chords of iridescent bright reds, yellows and blues, which produce a vivid plastic drama with the various tones of blue in other parts of the color-pattern. As the multi-colored light descends across the canvas it produces the effect of a spotlight cast upon a tray of solid, rich, sparkling, brightly colored jewels. The solidity of the color, its freedom from superficial glitter or tinsel-quality, and its firm integration in the drawing and light give substantiality to the extremely decorative pattern and a rugged expressiveness to the total form. Color is as organically integrated in the texture of the objects as it is in Renoir's best work of the mid-seventies, so that illustration is rendered plastically through the medium of color. The picture may be considered as an enriched version of the theme of dramatic contrast between light and color, familiar in Vermeer.†

In TWO WOMEN IN PARK ‡ (44), of 1875, the impressionistic theme of out-of-door light-effects upon colorful objects takes the form of lighted areas alternating with areas in shadow—a premonition of the pattern of islands of light in pictures of 1876. The color of each of the main units of subject-matter functions either as a dark or as a light element in the total compositional rhythm of light-and-dark con-trasts; and each area in turn is flecked with an irregular internal pattern: the dark units with a pattern of colored light, the lighted areas with a pattern of colored shadows. Thus, the theme of light-and-dark contrast is carried uninterruptedly throughout the picture, and is greatly varied in the degree of accentuation and in the size and relations of its components. Contributing to the liveliness and variety of the pattern is the ingeniously adapted impressionistic brush-

* Illustration, p. 240.
† Cf., e.g., Vermeer's *"Cook"* (464), *"Girl Reading Letter"* (465), *"Lace-maker"* (466) or *"Woman with Pearl Necklace"* (467).
‡ Illustration, p. 241.

work. Broad brush strokes in the foreground run in practically all directions and increase the decorative value of the general pattern by accentuating the mottling of dark colors within the lighted areas and of light colors within the dark. Likewise, small irregular strokes and dabs in the background are adapted to the general character of the design; besides helping in the drawing and modeling of the bushes and creating a sunlit atmosphere around them, the pattern of the brushwork, in conjunction with the color and light, dots the dark green bushes with a surface-pattern of small spots of light yellow and yellowish green, and the lighted bushes with touches of darker green. In a few areas on the lawn itself and in the figure in blue, the pattern of the technique is diminished to the point that the surface appears comparatively uniform and the color unbroken. However, even these comparatively broad areas of color are also internally mottled by a subtle change in the degree of illumination of their color. These relatively uniform areas serve as a foil to the others, and the contrast further emphasizes the characteristic motif of the total pattern. The impressionistic theme gains crispness, life and individuality by Renoir's juicy and luminous color, his judicious distribution of vivid high-lights and accents of deep lustrous darks, and his picturesque composi-tional organization of the subject-matter.* Much of the vividness of the lighted areas is due to their contiguity with emphatic dark units and also to their rugged surface of irregularly thick spots and dabs of pigment. One of these focal units of light—the flowers in the woman's hand—recalls Monet in its pattern of color, light and tech-nique; another—the lighted bush at the extreme upper left—is remi-niscent of effects obtained in the *sous-bois* scenes of Diaz and Daubigny; † in the face of the woman in the foreground, the pattern of light and color together with the rugged surface of the paint draws and models the volume and imparts to the head adequate three-dimensionality and to the flesh the novel textural quality of a luminous crinkly ceramic.

The alternating rhythm of the lights and darks throughout the canvas, and the echoes in the upper background of the accentuated light and dark units in the foreground, help to make the components of the pyramidal mass of the two figures participate in two diagonal sequences of vertical planelike volumes. Figures and bushes thus enter into a compositional receding rhythm of colorful light and dark upright units, and the oblique-horizontal plane of the ground serves as a setting.

ENGLISH PEAR TREE (47) generally ascribed to about 1875, is a combination of the undeveloped Renoir features of the

* Cf., e.g., Monet's *"Girl in Garden"* (625).
† E.g., Diaz' *"In the Forest"* (576), Daubigny's *"On the Seine"* (580).

late sixties or early seventies. Light throughout fails to illuminate or enrich the color: in the foliage it produces a soft cottony effect not unlike that in the Essen *"Lise"* (5) of 1867, and in *"Mr. and Mrs. Sisley"* (10) of c. 1868; lack of color in the light of the sky breaks all plastic continuity between that area and the rest of the picture. The influences in color and general treatment of the subject-matter are, as in Renoir's early landscapes, those of the Barbizon school, modified in some areas by small accentuated brush strokes, and in others by diffuse drawing and loosely interpenetrating tones which lead toward the richly colored surfaces of Renoir's later work.

SELF-PORTRAIT (51), of c. 1875, seems to be an experiment in which Renoir wandered into paths different from those of his daily use. The result is a striking realization of human character done with extreme simplicity, directness and vigor. The luminous light-colored face is vividly contrasted against the deep dark-green back-ground, interspersed with vague streaks of gray and permeated with an internal luster. The complexion is of a more uniform pink than is usual in the mid-seventies; that is, instead of the usual accentuations of pink on the cheeks and lips, that tone is carried over the whole texture of the flesh by an active pattern of brush strokes. The greenish blue, less well defined as shadows than in typical pictures of the period, occurs only as dispersed notes in the generalized color-pattern of the face. The technique on the whole is a slightly modified form of Monet's rugged impasto and pattern of ribbonlike brush strokes. The individual strokes are less emphasized than in Monet and the impressionistic method of execution is combined with, and reënforced by, solid color, Manet-like simplifications in the drawing, and a very forceful directness of statement.

MADAME HENRIOT AS A PAGE (55) of c. 1875-1876, is of the conventional type of portrait-painting current in France at the end of the nineteenth century, more manufactured than inspired. The color-scheme is a radical departure from the blue-green-ivory palette of the mid-seventies, the color is thin without internal luminosity and the entire surface is drab and dull. Except for the pink-toned ivory complexion and its blue-green shadows, and for the mottling of the large uniform areas of the background, there is scarcely a distinctive Renoir trait of the period, nor any redeeming plastic feature to save the painting from total lack of interest. The composition reverts to late Venetian academic portraiture.*

* Cf., e.g., Moretto's *"Italian Nobleman"* (380), Moroni's *"Ludovico Madruzzo"* (384).

MADEMOISELLE JEANNE DURAND-RUEL * (59), dated 1876, one of the most successful pictures of Renoir's entire career, embodies the form and spirit of the eighteenth century French tradition, but enormously enriched as an expression of the charm, daintiness and naïve grace of childhood. How far Renoir had progressed in three years in the use of color is seen by comparing the picture with *"Riders in the Bois de Boulogne"* (30). Both pictures have a generally gray monochrome color-scheme but the grays which pervade the flesh, garments and background in the later picture are of a much richer sensuous quality, and they are modulated with nuances of delicate blue, green, ivory and pink that combine to form an all-inclusive pearly, silvery-blue tonality. This tonality imparts a lightness and delicacy to the total design, it adds to the decorative appeal, and it harmonizes with the dainty drawing of the figure and the translucent porcelainlike texture of the flesh. The figure has the delicacy, almost the fragility, of a Dresden statuette. The few accents of darker colors which punctuate the light-colored design are judiciously located in widely separated areas: in the black shoes at the lower part of the picture; in the brownish hair at the top; in the broad blue portion of the surbase; and in the small irregular dabs of reddish pink which enliven the surface of the wall with an unobtrusive floral motif. These punctuations, like everything else in the picture, contribute to the essential delicacy and charm of the figure and its simple surroundings.

The realization of space is commensurate with the dainty rendering of textiles and flesh. The figure is very subtly differentiated from the background, particularly around the head and shoulders and along the right side of her body, where the light-value of the color in figure and background is approximately equal. The effect of space on the right side of the picture is also convincingly real but is achieved partly by the conventional method of a slight shadow cast by the figure upon the wall.

A noteworthy feature of the ensemble is the departure from the usual technique of the period in the painting of the dress, in which long narrow brush strokes are used to realize the textural quality and construct the decorative pattern. The narrowness of the strokes and the definiteness of their individuality suggest that they may be a forerunner of the characteristic brush strokes of 1877-1878.

A curious and undoubtedly intentional distortion in the drawing and modeling of the head, which makes it seem more like a mask than a full three-dimensional volume, adds a piquant charm to the design. Modeling is achieved by color-relations between the few, very slight, and delicately toned shadows, and the pearly light flesh. The painting of the face is derived directly from the eighteenth century masters, but the exotic texture is so perfectly blended with the naturalness

* Illustration, p. 245.

of the drawing and general expression that no artificiality intervenes to impair this genuine plastic embodiment of very real human values.

MOULIN DE LA GALETTE* (62), dated 1876, is, in spirit and general composition, similar to certain early pictures of Manet, Monet, and Bazille,† in which literal illustration is more in evidence than expressive plastic form. Even as an illustration the painting rises to no very high rank, because the movement of the dancers and the activities of the other figures seem exaggerated. The figures, broadly drawn and flatly painted, are not well organized with the other masses in a compositional unity, and there is an additional plastic defect in the use of color and light. Small areas of lighted color, which emerge as illuminated islands from among the darker colors of their setting, are organized as a lively pattern of color-light units encompassing the entire picture. Though these islands are tinged with color and are somewhat iridescent, their pattern is primarily one of light, relatively isolated from the rest of the color-organization. Renoir's later use of a similar light-color pattern results in compositions of greater decorative value and finer color-quality, in which the pattern plays an important part in establishing both the unity and expressive value of the design.‡

The chief points of interest in the picture are certain superb passages of painting—as, for example, the dancing figure in pink at the left—and the good command of space in separate units of space-composition. The latter, however, fail to enter into organic connections with each other or with the composition as a whole; consequently the picture is largely a series of fragments or relatively isolated episodes.

The color also falls short of Renoir's standard in sensuous quality and in giving plastic substance to the form. Its consistent dullness, due to lack of internal luminosity, limits the function of both color and light to surface decoration. An obvious lack of structural quality in the color still further undermines the reality and conviction of the design. Even though the units are skilfully drawn and modeled, color does not fulfill its plastic functions as adequately as it does in the more successful pictures of the period. Color-chords in the flesh, for example, are only surface deep, and in most of the garments their decorative appeal is detracted from by the disproportionate impact of the isolated islands of light. Only in the pinkish white-coral dress of the dancer at the left are the color-chords really a part of the

* Illustration, p. 247.
† E.g., Manet's *"Concert at the Tuileries"* (598), Monet's *"In the Garden"* (627) and *"Luncheon"* (630), and Bazille's *"Family Party"* (634).
‡ Cf., e.g., *"Picnic"* (211) of c. 1893 or *"Bathers in Forest"* (216) of c. 1897.

fabric. An imperfect integration of color and light is responsible also for the fact that the color-contrasts are obtained speciously. The contrasts are numerous and vivid but the accentuated pattern of light predominates and thus renders impossible a fine adjustment of color-relationships. The lack of placidity in the picture and the complexity the beholder feels in the design, result inevitably from the unsatisfactory coördination of the means of execution.

MOULIN DE LA GALETTE (61), of 1876, is apparently a sketch for the Louvre picture (62), to which it is superior in color, general plastic strength, spontaneity of expression and directness of execution. The color is more luminous, the color-chords richer and more varied, the space-volume units are better related to each other and are more tightly bound together in compositional unity.

SWING * (63), dated 1876, presents one of the familiar out-of-door Parisian scenes which Renoir painted so frequently in the mid-seventies. Like the other pictures of this type and period, it is permeated with eighteenth century French feeling, and the main motif of the organization is the colored light which filters through the foliage of the trees and patterns the shaded landscape and figures with illuminated spots or islands. It shares with *"Moulin de la Galette"* (62), painted in the same year, the technique of modified Manet-like brush strokes, the crude, sensuously jarring Barbizon-school green in part of the foliage, and the variation of the green-blue-ivory color-scheme by an extensive use of coral tone in the islands of light and in the white fabrics. The painting of the flesh is also similar in both pictures; the faces are patterned with shadows cast from the trees, and the complexion, instead of having the usual pervasively ivory tonality of the period, is chiefly a combination of rose-pink tones and vague greenish-blue shadows.

The technique, the color and the pattern of light are more successfully handled in *"Swing"* than in *"Moulin de la Galette"*; the islands of light, for instance, are better integrated with the color and substance of the objects which they decorate, and the coral tones pervade the other colors and form richer and more subtle color-relations. The all-inclusive spotted pattern of light and shade is more ingeniously varied in size, color, degree of accentuation, and in the range of its compositional activity; moreover, the activity of the constituents of the pattern shifts in emphasis from the lighted islands in the middle distance and background to spots of dark which pattern the light-colored path in the foreground.† The Manet-type of drawing

* Illustration, p. 248.
† Cf. with later versions of this in *"Apple Vender"* (198) of c. 1890-180¹ and *"Woman Gardening"* (215) of c. 1896.

in the figures is varied by the introduction of a Goya-Lancret quality, particularly in the small figures at the upper right. The appeal of the latter suffers, however, from their relatively heavy drawing and a painty texture of pigment, and from an inadequate realization of space between this group and the arm of the woman in the foreground. The unpleasant green is less obtrusive in "Swing" than in "Moulin de la Galette," the color-ensemble is more sensuously pleasing, and the accentuated decorative pattern of light and dark is not nearly so much isolated from color. In short, the decorative and the expressive aspects of the design blend more organically in the form.

AT THE MILLINER'S * (64), of c. 1876, exemplifies Renoir's experimentation in the mid-seventies with simplified expressive drawing in the style of Manet and Degas. Renoir's use of this drawing imparts a feeling of freshness, charm and spontaneity to the entire composition and furnishes an epigram of the situation with the enhanced vitality of new and fresh insight. While only a sketch in point of execution the picture is charged with the values of a successful and complete painting. The episode is rendered in a few touches, each so significant that not only are the individual figures alive and real, but the entire composition vibrates with vitality and convincing reality. In the small expanse of the canvas, the three figures are so distributed in relation to each other and to the space around and between them, that their compact arrangement gives a pictorial completeness to the fragmentary episode depicted, while avoiding all effect of compression or compositional overcrowding.† The color-scheme shares in this economical and fruitful use of means: it is mostly black and white, reënforced and dramatized by a few small punctuations of red and by numerous areas of bare canvas.

MADAME HENRIOT ‡ (69), of c. 1876, is one of the most successful of Renoir's mid-seventies' experiments with relatively monotone colors. It is rendered with such an extreme degree of finesse, delicacy and lightness, that the whole picture seems to have been merely breathed upon the canvas. The color-scheme, a variation upon the familiar blue-green-ivory, has an almost imponderable pearly translucence enriched by subtle modulations of the most delicate pastel shades. It is a light bluish-silver harmony, with only a slight admixture

* Illustration, p. 249.
† Other pictures which illustrate Renoir's ability to *fill* his canvas, with no feeling of its being overcrowded, are "Opera Box" (34), "After the Concert" (73), "Flower in Hat" (185), "Girl Reading" (186), "Two Girls with Hats" (193), "Two Girls Reading" (207), "Writing Lesson" (234), "Woman Reading" (238), "Heads of Two Girls" (251).
‡ Illustration, p. 250.

of pale green in the background, but the very eloquent punctuations by the vivifying darks in the woman's hair and eyes, dispel all sense of monotony. The pigment is thin and transparent and the fine-grained surface of the canvas, in the relatively uncovered parts, adds to the subtle surface-variations within the general monochrome. The very light, delicate, almost robin's-egg blue of the imponderable background seems to float forward and envelop the figure within its ethereal substance; the figure, in turn, swims into its surrounding color-filled space and merges with the setting in an indissoluble unit, each component of which retains its identity of shape, texture and form, and its position in subtly defined space. All these relationships are effected by delicate fluid colors that cause each volume and its surrounding space to melt into a single unit and to harmonize with all other similar and subtly contrasting units in a continuous smooth compositional flow. Between the hand, wrist and arm this continuous color-flow is mediated by a series of unobtrusive, extremely delicate bluish-lavender tones, hardly to be considered as shadows; in fact, in their subtle relation to the pink of the flesh they constitute a large fluid color-chord rather than an organized pattern of shapes. The absence of shadows as such is even more noticeable in the one-piece modeling of the face.

The whole picture suggests a delicate Goya of the very finest type, but Goya never approached the subtlety and delicacy, nor the floating, almost vaporous, quality infused in this painting. It is a sublimated version of outstanding characteristics of the eighteenth and late seventeenth century traditions represented by Perroneau, Boze, Largillière and Boucher, with none of their specious effects or mechanistic devices. A delicacy and transparency of the textiles, far exceeding anything in antecedent French painting, is realized by subtly related tones internally saturated with light. Light plays no part in the picture either in the form of patterns, accentuated contrasts, or focalized area, but the total composition is immersed in a bright mellow light totally free from glare. Subtle modifications of tone or intensification of light-content within the colors modulate the all-pervasive illumination to produce variations and contrasts of the color itself. The continuous area of light, for example, flowing through the color from the woman's left shoulder diagonally across the whole bodice down to her hands, is a vague and generalized spotlight, faintly echoed in other parts of the picture, which contributes to the color-ensemble much of the quality of the orient of a pearl.

An appealing fragility, entirely free from brittleness, is part of the expression. The flesh is extraordinarily fleshlike, and the textiles are real and dainty. It is the eighteenth century form carried to its apotheosis, the pinnacle of Renoir's exquisite lightness and delicacy.

WOMAN WITH VEIL * (77), of c. 1877, is unusual in color-scheme and general appearance and the total effect is much like that of Seurat's black-and-white drawings.† The blues and greens of the mid-seventies have been subdued to a level of tone that blends with the dark colors of the woman's shawl. The flesh is not so smooth nor so patterned with shadows as in the earlier form and its surface is vaguely marked with a brushing of very narrow strokes characteristic of the 1877-1878 technique.‡ Small strokes are used all over the canvas in the pointillist manner of Pissarro's short commalike touches with which Renoir experimented in a number of pictures in the late seventies.§

The unusual color-ensemble, the delicate tonal modeling and the vibrating surface of the whole canvas are reënforced in their expressive and decorative appeal by the extraordinarily subtle drawing of the dainty *profil perdu* and the poised pink-blue-green hands, by the transparent rendering of the veil, and by the textural reality of the soft, woolly plaid shawl. It is a superb picture, giving the composite effect of a Seurat, a Goya and, in its flatness, a Manet.

MADAME CHARPENTIER AND HER CHILDREN (79), dated 1878, has but few traces of Renoir's usual spontaneity, freedom and naturalness of expression. The general effect is conventional, banal, unexciting, and the color-ensemble is dull. The blacks, which are luminous in so somber a picture as *"Opera Box"* (34) of 1874, are here mere areas of dull paint, unappealing as color and unsuccessful in rendering textural quality in either the woman's gown or the dog's fur. The color of the flesh is practically like that of the mid-seventies, with slight bluish-green shadows, vague color-chords, and relatively smooth surface broken up by brushwork; but the thick, somewhat pasty impasto of the flesh and the absence of internal luminosity of its color, make the texture relatively unreal and the volumes deficient in solidity. With the exception of occasional sharply defined areas, the drawing is in general also that of the preceding period, with the same degree of loose contour; the child on the couch is so loosely outlined that its drawing tends toward the flabby character in Renoir's bad pictures of 1879. The application of paint, with its obvious reliance upon thick impasto and pattern of brush strokes to produce a factitious solidity of fabrics, is far below Renoir's standard of excellence. Equally factitious and literal are the decorative screen in the background with its illustratively rendered peacocks, and the pat-

---

* Illustration, p. 255.
† Cf., e.g., Seurat's *"Artist's Mother"* (636).
‡ E.g., *"Jeanne Samary"* (72) and *"Head of Margot"* (86).
§ E.g., *"Spring Landscape"* (75), *"Garden of the Artist"* (82), *"Picking Flowers"* (85), *"Head of Margot"* (86), *"Madame Murer"* (87).

terned tapestry of the sofa. This tapestry is a mere succession, almost a jumble, of juxtaposed multicolored units conveying little or no feeling of the substance of the material or the solidity of the volume. A similar lack of inspiration appears in the banal compositional distribution of the subject-matter; that is, a sequence of volumes in space extends across the canvas from the lower left foreground to the upper right background, and this unit is counterbalanced mechanically by the triangular formation of the two children and the large area occupied by the woman's figure and expanded black skirt.

The sole source of real esthetic pleasure in the picture is the painting of the still-life at the upper right of the canvas, particularly in the distribution and relation in space of its various units— the objects on the table, the chair, the legs of the chair and table, the plane of the floor, the curtain at the back, and the well-realized space receding underneath the table back into the distance behind the curtain. Nevertheless, even the fine quality of this still-life painting suffers in comparison with some of Renoir's other achievements in that line, for example, in *"After Luncheon"* (88). The still-life in the latter has color of finer sensuous quality and greater luminosity, the drawing is looser, more fluid and more generalized, and the modeling is obtained more by color-relations and not, as in the picture under discussion, mainly by the obvious use of thick impasto working in conjunction with light-and-dark contrasts to realize three-dimensional quality in the various objects. This sort of painting represents the bad influence of Delacroix in color and of Monet in technique: the degree of reality obtained is partly destroyed by a basic undercurrent of unconvincing substantiality which lessens the appeal of the total unit. The technique throughout the picture is also eclectic; it is a combination of Dutch seventeenth century methods, Fantin-Latour's and Hans Thoma's modifications of that style, Monticelli's manner of applying paint in lumps and, to a small extent, the impressionistic individual brush strokes.

The ensemble is a typical conventional group-portrait, plastically weak, and only mildly pleasing as a decorative illustration.

JEANNE SAMARY (83), of c. 1878, illustrates one of Renoir's unsuccessful efforts to merge figure and background in compositional unity. The plum-colored background encroaches upon the shadows of plum-lavender tone at the contour of the face, thereby preventing harmonious relationship between figure and background.

AFTER LUNCHEON * (88), dated 1879. The one-piece type of flesh-modeling, the pervasively light complexions and the smooth

* Illustration, p. 258.

enamel-like surface indicate the trend of Renoir's development from the form of the mid-seventies toward that of the early eighties and that of 1885-1887. The patterns of green shadows in the flesh which aid in the modeling in the mid-seventies are practically absent; instead, the complexion in the women's faces is mottled very subtly by the inter-penetration of transparent glazes of pale bluish-green tones and deli-cate nuances of pink. The results are two outstanding traits of the form of the early eighties—the one-piece type of modeling, and the smooth surface of the flesh in which there is no trace of brushwork. The pronounced three-dimensionality of the man's head, achieved here primarily by modeling with nuances of pinks and greens, is an antici-pation of the fully rounded volumes so characteristic of Renoir's form of the mid-eighties.

The color-ensemble is of the general blue-green-ivory type of the mid-seventies with hardly a trace of the enriched palette of the typical pictures of 1879. The technique of generalized brushwork of the same earlier period also prevails, but the later, narrow, ribbon-like brush strokes are used in rendering the blouse of the seated woman. The color-scheme is less luminous than that of either the mid-seventies or the best pictures of 1878, and the individual colors are not so bright as those of the early eighties. Parts of the surface, however, are enriched by color-chords and subtle modulations of tone. A great part of the still-life, for instance, is really an aggregation of iridescent units, and the highlights in raised impasto are themselves color-chords of several tones. The ubiquitous smooth, light and delicate porcelainlike surface is a sublimated version of this characteristic feature in the eighteenth century painters.

The picture has some beautiful passages of painting and some plastic units of great strength and charm; instances of these are the color-form of the man's head, the poised movement in the lighting of the cigarette, and the exquisitely realized unit of space-composition in the still-life. The form of the picture as a whole partakes of the weakness common to many of Renoir's pictures of 1879; for example, the loose drawing in the woman at the left tends to diffuseness, and the mottling of the color and the modulations of light in her garments lead to flabby and unsubstantial solidity and texture.

AT LA GRENOUILLERE (89), dated 1879, offers another ex-ample of Renoir's weak form of this period, with its flabby draw-ing, unintegrated suffusion, and lack of significant definition and organization of plastic and representative components. Renoir's problem here seems to have been to enhance the effects of Corot's silvery filmy atmosphere by means of a lavender-blue suffusion. But the suffusion stands out like an isolated floating mist or a rising steam and fails to unify the volumes and their spatial intervals in a continuous color-flow. The woman's shoulder, for instance, appears to be part of the water back of it, thus breaking the rhythm of the space-composition and sacrificing too much of reality of expression to effects primarily decorative.

AT THE PIANO * (97), said to have been painted in the late seventies, has not, in clean-cut form, any of the characteristics of the typical pictures of the ascribed period. Instead of the increased palette and brightness of the 1878-1879 period, the color-scheme is low-keyed, a subtly modulated black-and-white effect of dark blues, browns and bluish ivory. The sparsely used reds, blues, greens and yellows in some of the mottled areas of background and floor are so low in tonality, and their light-content so small, that they do not alter the essentially black-and-white effect of the total composition. The concentration of direct light upon the bluish-white area occupied by the figure, in conjunction with the dark mahogany-brown of the piano, brings out skilfully the dramatic emphasis of the color-organization. Graceful fluidity of drawing prevails throughout the picture, and subtle color-chords abound in the ivory flesh with its pink accents and green shadows. The only traits which might link the picture with the typical work of the 1878-1879 period are a tendency toward diffuseness in definition of volumes and spatial intervals, and the technique of thin and small haphazard brush strokes used in the floor and background at the left, which recall similarly treated areas in *"Pourville"* (80) of 1878, and *"After Luncheon"* (88) of 1879.

"At the Piano" obviously represents a distinctive version of Courbet's form, in which the latter's somber and heavy black-and-white effects have been raised to a high degree of subtlety and fluidity.†

In GIRL WITH FALCON ‡ (101) of 1880, plastic expression is sacrificed to decoration and illustration. Drawing and modeling are soft, drama is obvious and specious, the bright and sensuously appealing color is superficial and tinsel-like, and decorative illustration is carried almost to the point of theatricality. The full decorative possibilities of the Oriental color-scheme are still unrealized and the picture suffers from the unsubstantial effects and surface prettiness of Renoir's work of 1879.

The two portraits, MADEMOISELLE GRIMPEL WITH BLUE RIBBON (102) and MADEMOISELLE GRIMPEL WITH RED RIBBON (103), of 1880, are typical examples of superb painting and feeble plastic expression. The contour in *"Mademoiselle Grimpel with Red Ribbon"* is flaccid, and in *"Mademoiselle Grimpel with Blue*

* Illustration, p. 261.
† Cf., e.g., Courbet's *"Woman with Pigeons"* (589).
‡ Illustration, p. 263.

Ribbon" the relations between head and shoulder are inharmonious. In both portraits, the overaccentuation of bright colors and of vivid effects of concentrated light results in flashy superficial effects totally absent in Renoir's best portrait work of the 1870's. This flashiness, together with the meticulous rendering of textiles, particularly of the lace trimming in *"Mademoiselle Grimpel with Red Ribbon,"* is the analogue in painting of the facile use of words which is derogatorily termed "fine writing." Even as low grade as these pictures are for Renoir, they would compare very favorably with Manet's treatment of a similar type of portraiture and design. Manet's *"Mademoiselle de Bellio"* (605), for instance, is essentially a display of flashy virtuosity, with no genuine characterization of the sitter; the surface and textures are all extremely painty and there is a total lack of fine relationships between color, light, line, space and mass.

MADEMOISELLE IRENE CAHEN D'ANVERS * (104), dated 1880, is one of the numerous commissioned portraits of this year which sink to the level of decorative illustration. As in the others, the outstanding characteristics are a flood of light upon flesh and textiles, bright colors vividly contrasted, and the meticulous painting of the details of fabrics. The treatment of the background as a patterned area of foliage takes away from the baldness of the overemphasized illustrative factors in the other portraits of this group, and a better control of the compositional relations of background to foreground results in a fine concordance between the dark green setting and the brightly lighted pale-blue figure sharply profiled against it.

BATHER, BACK TURNED † (107), of c. 1880, is typical of that group of single nudes in landscape painted in the early eighties and characterized by a contrast between a spotlighted figure and a setting of deep tones of blue, green and purple-mahogany. The flesh, delicately shaded in lavender gray-green, is thickly painted except at its contact with the landscape, its surface is smoothly rugged, and its texture is like that of a rough heavy porcelain. At the contact of the body with the landscape, the color of the background in many places slightly overlaps that of the body. The traits carried over from the mid-seventies appear in the relatively loose definition of contour and, more specifically, in the treatment and color-scheme of the drapery, with, however, these significant differences: the drapery is heavier in execution, the surface is more rugged, impasto is accentuated in the highlights, the brush strokes are smaller, their pattern is less defined and less expressive of the folds and texture of the fabric.‡

* Illustration, p. 264.
† Illustration, p. 265.
‡ Cf., e.g., *"Torso"* (52) of c. 1875.

As is typical of some of Renoir's work in the early eighties, thick pigment in highlighted spots adds to the decorative character of the ensemble.

NAIAD (108), of c. 1880, departs from the other nude-in-landscape compositions of the period in that practically the entire background is patterned by brush strokes which contribute to the liveliness of the landscape and to the contrast with the flesh of the figure. The organization of these strokes in a pattern of patches forecasts the technique characteristic of pictures of 1883 and 1884, but the patches are as yet not definitely marked off as individual units of a pattern.* The flesh is very richly modulated with subtle color-chords of interpenetrating blues, lavenders, pinks and greens; and the loose contour of its positive and firmly drawn volumes results from overflow of color into adjacent units. The area of light-toned pink around the cheeks seems to anticipate the linear contour of light characteristic of the modeling of heads in the early nineties.

NUDE (110), supposedly painted c. 1880, has practically no trait in common with pictures of that date. It anticipates the form of the mid-eighties in the pastel color-ensemble, the relatively tight drawing, the long parallel brush strokes, and the smooth Boucher-like mother-of-pearl surface of the flesh. The form of the mid-eighties, however, appears only in an embryonic stage: the sharp, hard, incisive contour of the left arm, for example, is obtained with the help of an actual line, which neither merges entirely with the form of the arm as a whole nor becomes part of the space around the volume; the precision characteristic of the 1885-1887 drawing is still lacking, and there is not that coöperation between contour, color, shadow and light which in the middle of the decade yields fully rounded sculpturesque volumes. The figure has a sort of loose floating quality, and its location in space is not clearly defined.

CHESTNUT TREE IN BLOOM † (113), dated 1881, is one of the comparatively rare, typically impressionistic pictures painted by Renoir. Multicolored sunlight spreads throughout the composition; it heightens the sparkle of the extremely glowing and juicy greens, yellows, pinks and blues, and creates a wide range of nuances of each of these colors, particularly the blues. The technique in general is impressionistic, and color and pattern of brushwork are the principal active elements in the drawing; hardly more than one or two spots of color define the extremely simplified figures and indicate precisely

---

* Cf., e.g., *"Girl with Parasol"* (137), *"Sailor Boy"* (141), *"Bather in Rocky Landscape"* (142), *"Girl in Field"* (145), *"Madame Renoir"* (148).
† Illustration, p. 267.

their position in the landscape. The strokes of thick impasto which draw and model the flowers and foliage of the chestnut tree are interspersed with spots of bare canvas and small areas only slightly covered with a transparent layer of green, pink, yellow or blue. The uneven crinkly pigment of the juxtaposed contrasting colors through-out the picture adds an appealing texture to the entire surface.

The composition is based upon a curvilinear theme and is extraor-dinarily effective. The large expanse of multicolored and patterned space to the right moves backward from the immediate foreground in an encircling sweep around the solid compact island to the left upon which stand the large tree and the two figures. This compositional relationship imparts a pervasive feeling of life and movement to the entire organization. The total effect of the landscape, with its variegated bunches, clumps and clusters of flowers and foliage, and its well-defined clouds, is that of a rich multicolored bouquet floating upward in a clear cerulean atmosphere. Renoir, in short, has carried Monet's technique, color and light to infinitely greater heights of decoration and expression than were ever reached by any of the impressionists.

LUNCHEON OF THE BOATMEN (116), of 1881, is interesting chiefly as a transitional step from the forms of the middle and late seventies to the typical work of the early eighties. The enriched palette of the end of the seventies with its abundant color-chords * has been engrafted upon the general form of the mid-seventies,† and the drawing is midway between the looseness in the late seventies and the precise clean-cut delineation of contour in the eighties. The very loose drawing of the still-life recalls in a less well-realized form the corresponding unit in *"After Luncheon"* (88) of 1879. Elsewhere contours are slightly encroached upon by the color of the adjacent areas but, on the whole, outlines are sharper than in Renoir's work of the late sev-enties. The organization of the color-areas recalls the work of the mid-seventies but it has none of the isolated islands of light used so frequently at that period in pictures of similar out-of-door scenes.‡ The areas of light blend with the adjacent colors more as in *"After the Concert"* (73) of c. 1877.

The flesh is richer in color than in the mid-seventies: a warm rose tone pervades the complexion and deepens to a red slightly tinged with brown in the shaded parts, with scarcely a trace of the greenish-blue shadows of the earlier period. The flesh is more thickly painted than in pictures of the seventies but less so than in the typical work

* E.g., *"Café Scene"* (81), *"Dreamer"* (91) and *"Mussel Fishers at Berne-val"* (93).
† E.g., *"Moulin de la Galette"* (62) and *"After the Concert"* (73).
‡ Cf., e.g., *"Moulin de la Galette"* (61 and 62) or *"Swing"* (63).

of 1881.* In common with the latter, the surface of the picture is decoratively enhanced in certain small areas by spots of raised impasto. As in *"On the Terrace"* (119), painted in the same year, the technique combines features of the seventies with tendencies toward characteristics of the early eighties: the plants, water and boats in the setting are treated in the impressionistic manner typical of paintings of 1877-1878; † the garments and other accessories in the foreground are executed in broad brush strokes reminiscent of those of the mid-seventies; ‡ and the uniform surface of the flesh, which is practically free from perceptible pattern of brushwork, forecasts the 1883 type of painting.§ The picture belongs to the category of decorative illustration, and is inferior in plastic strength to Renoir's best work in that field.‖ The figures on the whole seem somewhat posed, too intent in their action or expression, a frequent occurrence in Renoir's outdoor groups of people; the tablecloth conveys the feeling of crude paint rather than of color or textile; the arm of the man to the right is monotonous in color and academic in general effect; and the space around the glasses, fruit dish and bottles is nôt sufficiently well rendered to avoid the jumbled appearance of the still-life. In painting this picture Renoir was obviously interested more in reworking his forms of the seventies than in creating a design in line with his major experiments of the early eighties.

MESDEMOISELLES CAHEN D'ANVERS ¶ (117), dated 1881, is interesting chiefly as an example of extraordinary technical skill. The children's dresses, for example, represent Renoir's finesse in handling paint; the fabrics proper are real and solidly colorful, the lacy materials are filmy and diaphanous, and the color-chords in the pink and blue sashes are extremely rich. The figures also are skilfully drawn, modeled and painted and they express adequately the character of the children. Color, in general, lacks internal luminosity and the picture as a whole is a badly organized series of such disparate units as the light pastel tones and delicate drawing of the figures and the dark heavily painted Delacroixesque color of the setting.

ON THE TERRACE ** (119), dated 1881. Highly decorative colors, bright illumination, and charm of subject-matter are responsible for the popular appeal of the picture. Decoration, however, is accentuated

* Cf., e.g., *"Mother and Child"* (118).
† Cf., e.g., *"Madame Murer"* (87).
‡ Cf., e.g., *"Two Women in Park"* (44).
§ Cf., e.g., *"Girl with Parasol"* (137) or *"Sailor Boy"* (141).
‖ E.g., *"Two Women in Park"* (44), *"After the Concert"* (73), *"Café Scene"* (81), *"Dance in the Country"* (136), *"Children at Wargemont"* (144).
¶ Illustration, p. 268.
** Illustration, p. 270.

at the expense of expressiveness, hence the design is esthetically weak. The vivid colors in the foreground impress the senses strongly, but they lack depth and fail to convey a feeling of adequate solidity in the objects, and their well-balanced decorative organization is attained by comparatively obvious means. The direction, size, shape and pattern of the brush strokes, as well as the contour of objects, serve chiefly to give literal information about the subject-matter.

The treatment of space offers the main source of interest. A sharp contrast between foreground and background in color, drawing and manner of execution, sets off the clean-cut, vividly colored figures from the ill-defined greenish landscape as from a screen, yet space appears to recede subtly through the hazy atmosphere. A pattern of variously accentuated areas of subdued light around and immediately back of the figures helps carry the eye backward to the distant houses and sky through a rhythmic series of subtly varied space-intervals. This receding movement of space is perceived as through a network of lines, which extend in all directions and, together with the diffuse type of drawing, confer upon the background the decorative character of a Chinese pattern. The comparatively few volumes in the background and their simplified drawing and color-scheme throw into sharp relief the compact grouping of figures and objects in the foreground. The placing of a focus of vivid red—the girl's hat—above the center of the canvas relieves the relatively encumbered lower part of the design. Compositionally and pictorially, the picture is a decorative illustration of low grade for a man of Renoir's general status.

BLOND BATHER * (131), painted c. 1882, marks, by its abundance of eighteenth century French characteristics, particularly Boucher's, a well-defined advance toward the pictures of 1883 and 1885-1887. The signs of this transition appear in the general light-toned ensemble, the pervasive grace of the figure, the clean-cut definition of volumes, the mother-of-pearl surface and alabaster texture of the flesh, the delicately modulated coral-white complexion, the attenuated highlights and the subdued lightly-toned pink, blue and lavender shadows.

While the general clean-cut effect is well on the way toward its final form in the mid-eighties,† it varies throughout the picture in degree of sharpness and in the means employed. On the whole, the sharp definition of contour results from immediate contact of adjoining areas, with no assistance from any intermediary line.‡ The linear effect in the face is quite sharp and, in conjunction with the delicate

---

* Illustration, p. 275.
† Cf., e.g., *"Bathers"* (164) of 1887.
‡ Cf., e.g., *"Nude"* (110) of c. 1880, in which a thin line is used to emphasize the contour of volumes and to set them in space.

shadows and highlights, it imparts to the head a well-defined solidity, even though the face itself is as usual relatively flat. Contour is also sharp around the figure's abdomen, but between the setting and her back the contact is not quite so incisive as in the face. The outline of the right arm shows a curious combination of looseness and sharpness, particularly noticeable from a distance; close inspection reveals that the color-areas, which from afar appear diffuse at their contact, do not actually interpenetrate but are very delicately adjusted to one another in terms of their respective content of color, tone and light. The fluid grace of the general drawing is intensified in the delicate fluffy hair which seems to flow away from the woman's body like a stream of delicate coral-toned mist.

BY THE SEASHORE * (133), dated 1883, is one of the few pictures of the early eighties in which bright sunlight is not emphasized as a pervasively decorative, expressive and compositional factor. In all other respects it bears the identifying marks of the period: in general color-scheme and tonality, in type of drawing and modeling, in surface and texture of flesh, and in technique. The impasto is thinner than in other typical pictures of 1883; † the color is less vivid and luminous; and the light-content is diminished commensurately throughout the picture to accord with the relatively subdued color-ensemble. This all-inclusive color-effect contributes to the unity of the design and imparts a feeling of subtlety and delicacy. The surface of the flesh has less of the one-piece effect than is usual at this period because the thick impasto on the front of the face, patterned by well-defined bristle marks, forms a contrast with the smoothly painted cheeks.

The unconventional compositional relationship between figure and background adds much interest and piquancy to the picture. The figure is slightly decentered toward the left, and the landscape, while functioning as a decorative screenlike setting, also creates a dynamic space-composition of cliffs and rocks at the left, and a continuous expanse of free space at the right. The compositional arrangement thus becomes in itself a contrast between an ordered sequence of volumes and space-intervals and a vista of open landscape; it represents a version of the old masters' wall-and-window type of compositional setting,‡ which was used frequently and diversely by Renoir at all periods of his career.§ As an entity, the picture is a striking example both of Renoir's extensive debt to Boucher and of how, by

---

* Illustration, p. 274.
† Cf., e.g., "Girl with Parasol" (137), "Sailor Boy" (141).
‡ E.g., Tintoretto's "Venetian Senator" (395).
§ E.g., "Naiad" (108), "Nude Seated on Rock" (192), "Girl on Balcony at Cagnes" (258), "Girl in Landscape" (268).

means of color, Boucher's decorative qualities have been converted into integral parts of an expressive form.*

DANCE IN THE CITY † (135) and its pendant DANCE IN THE COUNTRY ‡ (136), of 1883, are outstanding achievements in Renoir's work of the early eighties. Their extraordinary pictorial quality is due principally to their vivid color-drama, fine plastic adjustment of constituents, and fitting coördination of space-composition to identity of design—complex in *"Dance in the Country,"* extremely simple in the other canvas.

Movement is freer and more active in *"Dance in the Country,"* more stately and restrained in *"Dance in the City."* In each, the movement results as much from the compositional relationships between the figures and the setting as from the drawing of the dancers themselves. Space in *"Dance in the Country"* revolves around and together with the figures; from the lower right corner it swings to the left and right, and upward and backward from the free expanse in front of the couple to the distance realized with extreme subtlety in the charming blue background at the top. Movement and drama are communicated to this space-setting by the variety in color, shape, size, direction, degree of solidity, and manner of grouping of the objects and plastic units.

The different type of movement in *"Dance in the City"* results also, in great part, from the compositional treatment of space, but of another sort. The principal movement of the composition consists of a large, majestic, graceful upward sweep from the lower right corner to the upper left, and it is balanced by relatively static planes at the upper right and the lower left—the wall and the floor. The space-composition is correspondingly simple: space surrounds the dancing couple, and the background in its two upright sections repeats the general verticality of the two figures, and duplicates rhythmically their contrasts in technical execution, surface pattern and degree of activity in their space-volume constituents.

BATHER IN ROCKY LANDSCAPE § (142), of c. 1883-1885, according to general belief was painted in 1885, but no distinctive characteristics of the form of the mid-eighties could be abstracted and identified. The flesh, in color and texture, leans toward the heavy porcelain type of the 1885 pictures, but its rugged surface and substance, and its modeling with few highlights and shadows give an effect very different from the flesh of the period. Moreover, the figure is decidedly flat, very unlike the sculpturesque volumes of 1885.

* Cf., e.g., Boucher's *"Venus"* (520).
† Illustration, p. 276.
‡ Illustration, p. 277.
§ Illustration, p. 280.

The picture has much in common with *"Sailor Boy"* (141) of 1883. The flesh, especially in the legs, is practically identical in both pictures, in general color, in the use of lavender and coral shadows at contour, in the manner of execution and in the textural feeling, with perhaps a little more blue in *"Bather in Rocky Landscape"* and with less sharpness of contour. The resemblance between the two pictures is even more evident in their backgrounds: in each, the setting is a highly patterned organization of multicolored units in which Oriental color and sunlight appear in a subdued form, and in which brush strokes play an important compositional part by their varied length, width and direction, and by their being grouped in patches or islands of contrasting color and degree of light. Likewise in both pictures, figure and background are relatively on a par in decorative value and in general compositional activity of the components. It seems, in short, that the plastic characteristics of *"Bather in Rocky Landscape"* are more closely affiliated with Renoir's work of the early eighties than with that of 1885. If the ascribed date, 1885, is correct, the picture represents another instance of Renoir's experimentation with earlier forms * by means perfected in the intervening years.

CHILDREN AT WARGEMONT † (144), dated 1884. This large canvas stands out as one of the most novel and important achievements of Renoir's entire career. It is unique in color-scheme, in complexity of the plastic problems involving space-composition and color-organization, and in the scope of the technical means employed. Additional novelty is brought about by an extraordinarily ingenious adaptation of his own form of the moment to a distinctive version of the eighteenth century French tradition.

The uniqueness of the color-ensemble consists principally in its greatly varied nuances of delicate bright colors—orange, red, blue, green, tan and ivory—all of approximately equal degree of illumination, and with no sharp contrast of dark and light tones. The color-contrasts are nevertheless vivid and the colors, arranged compartmentally, form a lively pattern. This pattern is accentuated because of the relatively sharp contact of the contrasting areas, and it is complex because of the great variety of color in the internal constituents in the individual units as well as in their total pattern. The relatively even distribution of the light throughout the canvas assembles all the contrasting effects within an all-inclusive pastel tonality which blends with the Oriental character of some of the color-compartments.

The quality of the pigment coöperates with that of the colors themselves to produce the paradoxical effect of juicy dryness, the juiciness of the paint recalling Renoir's *"Mother and Child"* (118) of 1881,

* E.g., *"Naiad"* (108) of c. 1880.
† Illustration, p. 282.

and the dryness of the pastel tones forecasting the cool light-toned pictures of the 1885-1887 period.* Color-chords abound throughout the picture, but their component nuances do not always intermingle freely; they interpenetrate with varying degree of fluidity and richness and produce a series of diversified color-effects: subdued modulations in the floor, the wall and the framework of the couch; more pronounced color-variations in the red of the girl at the right; rich multicolored pattern in the portion of the curtain seen below the table; an extraordinarily colorful area in the basket.

The use of light, particularly in its contributions to the exotic quality of the color-ensemble and to the clean-cut definition of space, is a direct outcome of Renoir's experiments with color and light in the early eighties, after his observation of sunlight effects in Algiers. Sunlight permeates every part of the composition as if the scene were located out-of-doors or as if the room were illuminated from all sides. Yet with all the pervasive brightness there is no glitter, for light and color work conjointly to achieve reality as well as variety in both the decorative and the expressive aspects of the design. The light varies in color-content as it moves through the composition; it partakes of a subtle silver blue-green tone in the left section of the picture and acquires a pinkish-tan tonality as it touches and penetrates the objects and spatial intervals at the right. The light varies also in degree of accentuation and in plastic quality and function. In the few areas where light is relatively pronounced as pattern, it contributes as much to the plastic reality of the object as to its decorative appeal. In the curtain above the table, for instance, the light not only adds vividness and glow to the surface of the Oriental tones but merges with the solid colors and penetrates into the substance of the material. Likewise, the unaccentuated highlights on the hair of the girl reading are subsidiary as pattern to the part they play in the delicate and fluffy texture of the hair. In the flesh the subdued highlights blend with the color in a practically undisturbed one-piece effect, and the general coral-orange complexion—a harmony of delicate pinkish-and greenish-yellows, orange, rose, and silvery and lavendery white— is evenly saturated with light and only slightly patterned with unobtrusive lavender shadows. The texture of the flesh has a mother-of-pearl and a ceramic or porcelain quality which accords well with the exotic character of the color-organization; it retains however more of the general feeling of flesh than does, for instance, the more naturalistic painting of flesh in Renoir's *"Sailor Boy"* (141) of 1883. It is also more solid, less fragile than in the latter picture, and more nearly approaches in surface and texture the flesh in Renoir's *"Head of Girl"* (173) painted in the late eighties.

*E.g., *"Garden Scene"* (161), *"Washerwoman and Baby"* (163) and *"Bathers"* (164).

A very striking compositional effect is obtained by the division of the picture into two large sections, each partitioned off, as it were, by the unit composed of the curtain, the left edge of the table and the table leg, and each section contrasting with the other in color-scheme and in character of space-composition. While the right half of the picture is composed of numerous and multicolored units arranged in subtle volume-space relationships, the chromatic organization in the left section is essentially a gamut of blues, and the space-composition involves only a few objects and relatively free space. The two sections are unified organically by rhythmic echoes in each of the predominating color- and space-character of the other, and the picture as a whole offers one of the most varied and complex space-compositions to be found in Renoir's entire work.

With all its individuality in color, technique, flesh-painting and compositional organization, *"Children at Wargemont"* is nevertheless a synthesis of traits characteristic of Renoir's work of the three years immediately preceding. The blue of the vase and of the standing girl's dress, and also its manner of application by broad brushing, are not unlike the painting of the garments in *"Sailor Boy."* The bouquet on the table, in color, brushwork and iridescence, is like the bunch of flowers in the hand of *"Girl with Parasol"* (137); the up-holstery of the sofa, the basket with its rich color-chords, the curtain, the flowers, leaves and vase, and the area of the tablecloth to the right of the chair, are painted in a technique very close in effect to that of the basin, jug and floor in *"Mother and Child"* of 1881. These areas have, in common with the latter picture, a thick impasto, broad brushwork, and superposed units of decoration; the essential difference is that brush strokes in the earlier picture are much more pronounced and their active pattern is one of the main determinants of the specific character of the design, while the surface in *"Children at Wargemont"* has an evenly uniform ruggedness produced by relatively regular mark-ings of the brush bristles in the thickness of the pigment. This general grained appearance of the surface is occasionally interrupted at the junction of two differently colored areas by a slight break in the texture of the impasto which produces the effect of an indented line set in between the raised edges of the contiguous areas.

The technique, much more generalized than in Renoir's typical work of the same period,* tends to achieve the smooth one-piece effect of the 1885-1887 pictures; there is, however, no feeling of fresco such as appears in the later work, nor of sculpturesque masses; and while outlines of objects and shapes are clean-cut and well defined, the linear drawing is not tight, and the contours are neither so continuous nor so precise as in the 1885-1887 period. The picture thus exemplifies Renoir's

* E.g., *"Girl in Field"* (145), *"Grape Gatherers Resting"* (147), *"Summer"* (150).

transition from his form of the early eighties to that of the mid-eighties. In itself it embodies a highly personal conception of several traditions of the past—the Venetian, Chardin's, Boucher's and Fragonard's—* as well as of the subject-matter of the moment. Compared with Renoir's presentation of a similar type of subject-matter in *"Madame Charpentier and her Children"* (79) of 1878, *"Children at Wargemont"* is infinitely superior as portraiture, as pictorial presentation, and in plastic construction.

MADAME RENOIR (148), of c. 1884, presents in an inferior form, a combination of traits characteristic of the years 1881, 1883 and 1884. The color of the face recalls that in *"Mother and Child"* (118) of 1881 but without its rich color-chords; the generalized pattern in the flesh resembles that in the legs of *"Sailor Boy"* (141) of 1883, but the texture in *"Madame Renoir"* is less solid and the surface, smoother and less rich in color, has a heavy porcelain-quality which forecasts the painting of flesh in the 1885-1887 period. The general heavy impasto throughout the picture bearing vague marks of the brush bristles, and the pervasive pastel tonality of the ensemble, are characteristic of Renoir's work in 1884. Influences of Cézanne are suggested by the blue linear contour around part of the body, and by the tendency of long parallel strokes to be grouped in a pattern of patches and to function as planes. The figure, however, has none of Cézanne's plastic solidity, its apparent weight being due more to the actual heaviness of the paint than to the plastic relationships of its component color-planes. Its volumes have relatively little three-dimensional quality, the massiveness of the torso being attained speciously by layers of heavy impasto on the projecting parts.

Drawing and modeling are much below Renoir's standards; in the torso, for example, despite the specious resort to actual line of contour, the modeling fails to convey a feeling of adequate continuity in the volumes either as color or as structure. Defective adjustment in the constituents of drawing and modeling are responsible for the faulty relationships between the woman's body and her right arm and between the figure and the background. Space back of the woman's right shoulder and arm, for instance, is so inadequately realized that the background appears to project forward thereby destroying compositional balance. The picture is inferior also in the handling and control of the paint. Its quality varies much throughout the composition: the thickly painted hat with its coarsely applied pigment and lack of sensuous appeal in its color creates a jarring note in the ensemble.

* Cf., e.g., Tintoretto's *"Susannah at the Bath"* (393), Chardin's *"Industrious Mother"* (501), Boucher's *"Diana at the Bath"* (508), Fragonard's *"Music Lesson"* (535).

MADEMOISELLE BERARD (149), of c. 1884, is interesting as an adaptation of Renoir's form of the moment to an interpretation of the type of convincing realistic portraiture represented by Holbein. The facial features and contour, sharply defined by incisive linear drawing, are almost photographic in representative detail. The color-scheme, dominated by brown, dull mahogany-red and light blue, is toned down in degree of luminosity to approximate that of the proto-type. The subtle modeling of the head with its inconspicuous areas of light and shadow, and the smooth mother-of-pearl or enamel-like surface of the flesh, give a new, distinctive and more delicate character to the Holbein form.

BATHER ARRANGING HAIR (152), dated 1885, has the tight drawing, sculpturesque modeling and mother-of-pearl tonality of the period, but the form is atypical in several respects. The figure, with its flesh of uneven thick impasto irregularly pitted, and its rich, juicy and softly glowing color recalls *"Mother and Child"* (118) of 1881. The pastel quality of the color in general, the compact parallel planes and the pattern of patches formed by long and broad brush strokes in the setting, differ only slightly from these characteristics in the work of 1884. With all the thickness of the pigment and vigorous brushwork, the form is light and delicate. The deep mahogany hair is a dark but luminous focal area very effective in the bright color-organization which otherwise is free from any sharp contrast of large color-units.

MOTHER AND BABY * (162), of 1886, is one of those few pic-tures of the mid-eighties painted on plaster-covered canvas. The pig-ment is thin, dry and very evenly applied, the surface of the flesh is enamel-like in its smoothness, and the color-scheme of pale tones of delicate blue, light green, pink-coral and dull orange has a general effect suggestive of water color and fresco combined. The general plastic theme is of contrasts in color, drawing and technique. The major contrasts are between the relatively precise drawing of the figure and the vaguely indicated landscape with its generalized effect of tapestry; between the smoothly painted flesh and the pattern of brush strokes in the setting; and between the pinkish-white flesh, the delicate green, relieved by pink-coral and blue, of the background, and the light blue, bluish white and dull orange of the garments. Against the loosely drawn background the figures of woman and infant are as sharply outlined in their component parts as in a clean-cut pen-and-ink drawing. The lines indicating folds of flesh in the baby's legs con-tribute to their three-dimensional quality and also form an accentuated linear pattern which is continued by the light-and-shadow pattern made

* Illustration, p. 287.

by the folds of the woman's skirt. The green and blue modulations in these shadows are applied in transparent washes and organized in geometrical areas; they produce an effect not unlike that of a Cézanne water color. The flesh is very similar to that in Renoir's *"Bathers"* (164) of 1887; it has the same general complexion, smooth texture, uninterrupted continuity of surface, and one-piece modeling with lack of pronounced shadows and highlights; but the figures are much more delicate, lighter in weight than in the later picture and are not sculpturesque. The volumes are nevertheless solid, well rounded and clearly located in space, but they have a lightness and delicacy of texture exceeding that of the finest porcelain. The ensemble embodies, in a form characteristic of the mid-eighties, values intrinsic to motherhood in a setting saturated with the lyricism and charm of landscape.

DAUGHTERS OF CATULLE MENDES (167), dated 1888, is an attempt to recast some of the salient traits of the 1885-1887 pictures in a new form. The bizarre color-scheme is a combination of the terra cotta tones of the 1885-1887 period, with the pastel and Oriental color-effects of the early eighties. The orange-brown or terra cotta is deeper in tone than in *"Girl Plaiting Hair"* (165) of c. 1887, it is mottled by modulations of yellow, purple and red, and its large areas serve as a color-setting for the figures. The latter, painted in a color-scheme combining Oriental with pastel effects, are vividly set off by the surrounding deep tones, and the contrast is emphasized by the intense illumination directly focussed upon the figures. The positiveness of this light and its relative circumscription result in a theatrical spotlight-effect as in Renoir's inferior portraits of the early eighties.* The most significant departures from the 1885-1887 form consist in a less incisive linear drawing, a patterning of the flesh with vague bristle marks or a generalized brushwork, and an enrichment of the complexion by a charming blending of pinks and lavender-blues. The blue shadows, diffuse rather than sharply compartmental, are more like those in the flesh of the mid-seventies than in that of the eighties.

The technique in the floor and garments is of the ribbonlike strokes of the 1884 period. The girls' dresses, painted in alternating streaks of pastel tones of pink, blue and ivory, greatly varied in content of light, offer a rich gamut of color-chords, but the fabrics convey no feeling of textural reality. A hard metallic quality pervades all the objects—the flowers and other accessories of the setting as well as the flesh and textiles—and gives a heaviness and an unreal exotic character to the total form. The picture was obviously an experiment with a particular color-problem, and the fact that Renoir never

* E.g., *"At the Concert"* (100), *"Mademoiselle Grimpel with Blue Ribbon"* (102), *"Mademoiselle Grimpel with Red Ribbon"* (103).

attempted it again indicates that he sensed its limitations and considered it futile.

BOUGIVAL * (166); RED BOAT, ARGENTEUIL † (170); SUNSET ON THE SEINE AT ARGENTEUIL (171); and ARGENTEUIL BRIDGE (172) are typical of Renoir's land-scapes painted in or about 1888. They all have the distinctive rugged surface and the technique of positive brush strokes vigorously applied in small brushfuls of juicy thick paint saturated with deeply glowing color; but particular emphasis in each picture upon a specific aspect of the general form establishes marked differences in their respective design. In *"Red Boat, Argenteuil"* the primary emphasis is upon dramatic exotic color-contrasts and bizarre angular shapes and linear patterns. The sparkling multicolored ensemble and the accentuated linear features are organized around a vivid red focus in patterned flat areas of bright and juicy, but not very structural, color. *"Argenteuil Bridge"* offers an exotic orange-and-blue color-scheme dominated by deep terra cotta tones. The plastic problem in *"Sunset on the Seine at Argenteuil"* centers around effects of light upon color to convey the feeling of sunlighted atmosphere. In *"Bougival,"* color, light and compositional pattern, more daringly used than in the other of these landscapes of 1888, accomplish an outstandingly individual and very forceful design. Deep purple, interspersed with terra cotta tones, dominates the exotic color-scheme; it embraces the entire foreground—the extensive riverbank and the swirling arabesque of foliage—and enframes the intensely illuminated area of water and sky. Light not only floods the central area of distant landscape with concentrated sun-light, but it penetrates into the substance of all the colors, producing an all-pervasive deep glow and contributing a jewel-like quality to the rich, dark, dense, velvety foreground. The daring contrast between the dark enframing area and the brilliantly lighted vista produces an extremely dramatic effect and a novel rendering of landscape.

VARANGEVILLE (174), another landscape of c. 1888 in which many contrasts of vivid colors saturated with light determine the character of the design, retains in well-defined manner such charac-teristic features of the eighties as the Oriental color-and-light effects and the Cézanne type of accentuated brushwork of parallel broad strokes. The Oriental color-scheme with orange-red overtones prevails in the entire foreground, except for a few areas where it is attenuated by light green; the orange red is duplicated in smaller areas in the sky and tempered by blue; between these two horizontal broad bands of foreground and sky dominated by the orange red, is

* Illustration, p. 292.
† Illustration, p. 294.

an almost unrelieved solid area of deep green consisting of the closely packed trees in the middle distance. Foreground and sky are each striated by a lively pattern of parallel brush strokes; these, running in a contrasting direction in each of the two areas, form a dramatic counterbalancing rhythm which comes to rest in the placid area of dense green foliage in the middle, in which the pattern of the brush strokes is reduced to a few small dabs or dots on the highlights. Color and the compositionally active pattern of the technique communicate a particularly lively, dramatic and decorative character to the design, which anticipates the flamelike motif frequently used in Renoir's late landscapes.* The multicolored units in the foreground appear to be actually on fire and to flame upward toward the sky in which a brightly illuminated area, not unlike a rainbow, seems to reverberate the glow and brilliance of the conflagration below.

In GIRL READING † (186), painted in the early nineties, naturalistic expression of human intentness is embodied in a highly decorative bouquetlike color-ensemble. Blues, reds, pinks, greens and yellows, all juicy, intense and fully saturated with light are set in vivid contrast against each other throughout the picture. An exotic quality pervades the color-organization, but its sparkle, glow and vividness lack the accentuated glare or glitter of the earlier use of Oriental color-and-light effects. The color-scheme is organized in a pattern of large areas, each with its own internal pattern and contrasts. Practically all the units are striated by long parallel brush strokes of rugged impasto which, varying greatly in the different areas in degree of accentuation and in direction, impart a feeling of lively movement to the composition and contribute added elements of decoration and of drama to the plastic expression of the subject. This all-over activity of the technique favors the loose definition of contour and the free interpenetration of color throughout all areas. The composite color-effect of the picture is that of a large single color-chord, extremely rich, radiant and glowing and of extraordinarily fresh tonality. The quantity and intensity of the pink in the flesh represents a step toward the form of the early nineties. The pink amounts to a pervasive rose suffusion and in conjunction with greenish-blue shadows, pink highlights and loose contour, it gives to the head a marked three-dimensional quality. This set of relationships between color, light, shadow and contour, is evidence that Renoir has reached the stage of growth that capacitates him to make what was exotic in the eighties, serve ends definitely in line with the expression of his own natural self. The solidity of the color, merging with the sensuous quality, con-

---

* E.g., *"Figure in Garden"* (289) of c. 1917-1919 and *"Group of Bathers"* (302) of c. 1918.
† Illustration, p. 298.

verts the design into a version of the eighteenth century French tradition, weightier and more expressive as well as more decorative than the prototypes.* The picture is another example of Renoir's ability to arrange in a small canvas many objects in compact space with no overcrowding and in a well-balanced composition.

In GIRL WITH GLOVE † (189), of the early nineties, the relationship between the subtle light-shadow modeling in the face and the extremely fluid drawing by washes of color and loose contour yields the effect of a delicate three-dimensional volume floating off into the background. Active brushwork in the setting converts the different tones of green, flecked with subdued light, into a series of very slight, loosely defined volumes, resembling in a generalized form the pattern and color of tapestry. The compositional figure-to-background relationship is thus treated in a manner similar in principle to that in "*Head of Girl with Hat*" (210), of c. 1893, but with greater emphasis upon contrasts of color and pattern: the bright red gown and the intensely lustrous white glove and collar, relatively uniform as color-areas, are dramatically set off by each other and by the cool green background actively patterned with light and brush strokes.

In GIRL WITH STRAW HAT ‡ (196), painted c. 1890, Renoir selected one element, the lavender, from his mid-eighties' form and developed it as a theme in a dynamic space-volume type of composition. Lavender is used in the modeling of the flesh and also in the background where it appears, interspersed with green and yellow, in two diagonal broad bands separated by a band of yellow. These areas of contrasting color in the setting assume the form of vaguely defined volumes, which appear to move in deep space around the girl's head, the focus of the total space-composition. Weight and solidity are concentrated in the component masses of the figure; this fact, and the placing in a foreground plane of the overhanging foliage at the top, increase the dynamic effect of the rhythmic organization of the volumes as they recede from the accentuated foreground masses to the less pronounced volumes and intervals in the background.

PASTURE ALONG THE SEINE § (197), painted c. 1890, represents perhaps Renoir's closest approach to the forcefulness, power and general form of Cézanne. The resemblance is increased by the technique of hatchings and pattern of patches and planes which build up trees and hills into weighty and definite masses. Brushwork and color-scheme are in the main those of the 1884 period, but the pastel

* Cf., e.g., Fragonard's "*Boy as Pierrot*" (532).
† Illustration, p. 299.
‡ Illustration, p. 299.
§ Illustration, p. 300.

colors in the sky, the Oriental yellow overtones in the distant hills, and the broad brush strokes and pattern of patches have more positiveness than in the earlier form, and the deep solid greens establish a forceful contrast with the pastel and Oriental color-areas.

APPLE VENDER * (198), of c. 1890-1891, belongs to that group of 1888-1893 landscapes characterized by rhythmic movement of volumes in space. The volumes, here, are light and delicate and actively patterned by islands of light and patches of dark color. The luminous atmosphere throughout the landscape results from Oriental color blending with impressionistic lighting and technique.

BATHER (199), dated 1892. The known date of this picture conflicts with the plastic characteristics because most of the distinctive traits of the mid-eighties are present and even accentuated: the outline of the figure is sharp, incisive; the pastel-toned flesh, with its lavender shadows and hard texture, has the characteristic porcelain, almost majolica, type of surface. Similar exotic qualities pervade the texture of the entire setting: rocks, water and plants, though of a different color-scheme than the figure, are practically the same in appearance and feeling; not a single unit bears any identifying quality expressive of its respective substance. The picture is interesting as a decorative design in which the figure, much alive and expressively drawn, is on a par in color-quality and textural feeling with the objects of the background.

The use in NOIRMOUTIER † (201), of 1892, of a definite arabesque-theme entails a general linear emphasis which combines the graceful flow in Renoir's pictures of the seventies with the more pronounced pattern of the eighties. To accord with this theme most of the volumes are flattened and rendered in sinuous patterns, while a succession of other and more rounded volumes creates a second curvilinear movement. The interplay of the two motifs—that of the linear effects and that of the three-dimensional volumes—achieves compositional balance as well as a series of dramatic contrasts. Long, narrow and curvilinear brush strokes carry out the accentuated linear effects in practically all the constituents of the landscape. The rich pattern of islands of variegated colored light in the foreground brings out the solidity and textural qualities in the areas thus illuminated. In short, the decorative factors merging with the expressive render the spirit of landscape in a pattern of iridescent colors which conveys the feeling of a sweeping arabesque-movement.

GIRLS AT PIANO ‡ (203), painted c. 1892, represents perhaps the most complete crystallization of the essentials, boiled down to their

* Illustration, p. 302.
† Illustration, p. 301.
‡ Illustration, p. 303.

basic indispensables, of what Renoir had learned up to this time. The most striking novelty of this picture is its color-scheme of pastel shades of green, blue, pink, yellow, coral, each in an infinite number of nuances and all subtly pervaded with generalized Oriental tones. The differences in the pastel-effect from that in *"Children at Warge-mont"* (144), of 1884, concern not only the way the colors are related to produce the novel effect but the manner of application of the paint: it is very smoothly and evenly applied in *"Girls at Piano,"* while in the other painting the impasto is thicker and the surface rough and bristle-marked. The treatment of the flesh differs from that in Renoir's antecedent work although it is based upon his own prior types of drawing and modeling. A subtle suffusion of coral-pink and green pervades the faces, large areas of interspersed pink adorn the cheeks, and diffuse greenish-blue shadows, very subtly related to the lighter colors, form an unobtrusive pattern. In the arms and hands, the colors, with practically no perceptible pattern of light and shadow, blend more closely with each other and give to the modeling a uniform one-piece effect. Delicate but real three-dimensional solidity in the figures is obtained by perfect fusion of varied proportions of light and color. This fine example of modeling with color, one of the highwater marks of Renoir's achievements in this respect up to the early nineties, is accomplished by a synthesis of his own creations in technique, drawing and use of color. The incisive linear drawing of the 1885-1887 period is retained in sufficient degree to give clean-cut definition to contour, but assisted by more successfully merged light and color it lends to the volumes the feeling of greater naturalness prevalent in Renoir's work after 1890.

The painting as a whole bears a closer resemblance to Ingres than does any picture of the mid-eighties, but the intrinsic quality of the color and its integration in the substance of objects, completely convert the elements suggestive of Ingres into organic parts of the form. Compared with *"Madame Rivière"* (559), which represents Ingres at his best, Renoir's color actually builds up the texture of flesh and fabrics; Ingres' is mainly a superficial fill-in between linear contours, it merely imitates surface quality or ornament without being incorporated in the substance of the objects. Ingres' color, moreover, when bright seems like tinsel compared to Renoir's; and when dark it is, as color, dull. A comparison of almost identical tones in the two pictures reveals Renoir's infinitely finer feeling for the immediate sensuous quality of color *per se.**

The precise linear drawing and the well-defined three-dimensional modeling in *"Girls at Piano"* illustrate very forcibly Renoir's capacity

---

* Cf. also from the same point of view Renoir's *"Girl with Basket of Flowers"* (188) with Ingres' *"Mademoiselle Rivière"* (560).

to make of his own earlier forms implements for the creation of new and fuller plastic designs. The elements of the 1885-1887 form have here lost their identity as such, and are applied to purposes more comprehensive plastically, more in line with Renoir's own nature, and of more profound human significance. The porcelainlike surface, the tapestry-effects, and the dry color are generalized and woven into the very body of the new ensemble. The convincing reality of the textiles results from subtle relationships between loose contour and highlights that blend with the color with no accentuated sharp patterns; that is, the decorative value of the color-and-light pattern is an integral part of the expression of the materials as solid real stuffs. The instrumental function of light, and its high degree of activity even when not accentuated, are shown in numerous ways: light mottles and otherwise varies the color; light is subtly fused with color or rendered in pronounced patches; it favors the interpenetration of small color-units and the production of rich juicy color-chords. Similarly, space, either accentuated as distance or as part of space-volume units, is coördinated with color to give individuality to each grouping of units and to the composition as a whole.

Illustration and decoration of the classic type of Ingres' are merged with the distinctive qualities of the eighteenth century French tradition, but the form is infinitely richer in content of color-values than either of the prototypes. Decorative illustration is carried to a high degree of expression because of the integration of color and pattern in convincing plastic units which convey profound human values good in their own right. Conversely, the charm of youth and the individuality of the girls depicted are enhanced by the intrinsic appeal of the bright, delicate, cheerful, pastel-like color-ensemble.

NEAR PONT-AVEN * (204), of c. 1892, relates itself to that well-defined type of 1888-1893 landscapes characterized by daring contrasts between bright exotic colors. The color scheme, with its orange, yellow and a bright magenta, is as exotic as a Gauguin landscape; it acquires richness and vitality by the bright sunlight which floods the picture and produces rich overtones reminiscent of the Oriental effects but free from glitter or glare. As in *"Mt. Ste. Victoire"* (175), of 1889, the individual trees are constructed by hatchings of short parallel strokes of thick pigment. The foreground is rendered by a succession of broad ill-defined areas of contrasting colors in a pattern not unlike Cézanne's familiar patches.† Also as in Cézanne, the brush strokes within the individual patches tend to run in a parallel direction but Renoir's strokes are less perceptible and more varied in their length. Hence the strokes in one patch of color, not being so

* Illustration, p. 304.
† Cf., e.g., the foreground plane in Cézanne's *"Gardener"* (620).

evenly aligned at their contact with those of the adjacent patches, tend to merge with the constituents of the adjoining areas, and to diminish the sharpness of their contrast in color, shape and direction. Renoir's handling of the pigment itself achieves a greater variety of color-effects than does Cézanne's: Renoir's brush strokes in the center of the individual patches are loaded with pigment intensely saturated with color, and as the color extends toward and reaches the edges of the patch, its substance diminishes to the thinness of a wash or glaze; thus the color, naturally lowered in degree of intensity at the boundaries of the areas, flows more freely into the varied colors of the adjoined patches. In the central part of the sky, just above the uppermost distant small tree, Renoir almost duplicates the effect of a Cézanne patch-motif, with its alignment of the parallel brush strokes and the intensification of the color along one edge of the patch. Renoir's modification of Cézanne's devices are genuinely creative, quite in line with his own general technique and form of the period.

In HEAD OF GIRL WITH HAT * (210), of c. 1893, may be recognized the loose drawing and patterns of light of the middle seventies, the increased palette and impressionistic illumination of the early eighties, the lavender shadows and tapestry-quality of the 1885-1887 period—all with significant modifications by which their plastic values and compositional activity are greatly increased. The sharp and precise drawing of *"Girl in Profile"* (202), of c. 1892, is replaced here by such looseness of contour and fluidity in all areas of the picture that the figure seems to flow into the background. The subtle interweaving of the component parts of foreground and background converts the whole composition into an uninterrupted sequence of light delicate volumes floating in subtly realized space. This intimate commingling of all areas in the picture imparts delicacy and fluidity to the all-over pattern of multicolored islands of light. The technique by which the quasi-volumes in the background are executed produces an effect both vaguely reminiscent of the tapestry-quality of the 1887 *"Bathers"* (164) and forecasting the compositional fluid blending of foreground and background typical of Renoir's latest period.† The general effect of the picture embodies the charm and delicacy of the eighteenth century French painters, made both more decorative and more substantial by the greater sensuous appeal and structural quality of color, the finer feeling for relationships and especially by the deeper integration of color in a fully expressive plastic design.‡

* Illustration, p. 306.
† Cf., e.g., *"Two Figures in Landscape"* (296).
‡ Cf., e.g., Fragonard's *"Boy as Pierrot"* (532).

422   APPENDIX

PICNIC * (211), of c. 1893, is of a much higher plastic status than
the majority of landscapes of this period because the color is richer
and more iridescent, and functions more assertively in the design. The
islands of light which figure so actively in Renoir's pictures of the
mid-seventies † are here merged with the patches of brush strokes
characteristic of his work of 1883 and 1884, and form a highly patterned
all-embracing organization of solid color-light units in compact space.
Compared to similar patterns of color and light in Renoir's earlier
work ‡ the component units in "Picnic" are more solid, they are drawn
with color that penetrates more deeply into the structure of the objects,
yields a richer textural quality, saturates more thoroughly the areas
of light, and establishes relations between the individual patches which
transform the accentuated pattern into a fluid uninterrupted sequence
of solid color-light masses. The patches literally melt into each other
at the same time that each retains its identity as a positive unit of the
assertive color-pattern. Variations from area to area in color, degree
of effulgence and definiteness of shape, determine the specific character of the drawing, modeling and decorative quality of each detail of
the subject-matter. The brightness of the color, the varying sharpness
of its contrasts, and the unabated flow of the bright, iridescent, sparkling color-areas all over the canvas, create a more positive and
richer color-suffusion than that in any prior work of Renoir's. The
general advance is due to the fact that color, more effulgent and jewel-
like, serves richer and fuller expressive and compositional purposes
and also yields a more powerful decorative effect.

VILLAGE OF ESSOYES § (212), probably painted c. 1894, is
interesting for its pervasive toned-down sunlight, its fluid drawing,
its patterned design of angular roofs and houses, and its eighteenth
century lavender-coral suffusion.

NUDE IN BROOK ‖ (213), of 1895, shows how Renoir selects
component colors of an organization to serve diverse plastic purposes.
The lavender of the shadows of the figure, for example, becomes a
slate-blue above the left shoulder and defines a pocket of space into
which the shoulder fits; in another section of the canvas the blue is
toned down to represent water, and in still another part of the landscape it carries space backward and upward. The orange of the right
leg is changed in tone in the background and is modeled by brush

* Illustration, p. 308.
† E.g., "Moulin de la Galette" (62) or "Swing" (63).
‡ E.g., "Sailor Boy" (141) of 1883 or "Grape Gatherers Resting" (147) of
c. 1884.
§ Illustration, p. 309.
‖ Illustration, p. 310.

strokes and light into a slight volume of foliage. Other tones of the flesh are deepened in the background to represent, variously, diffuse areas of space, slightly voluminous trees, and clumps of foliage. The mottled surface of the flesh is repeated in the background by means of units of light interspersed in areas of more positive color and more patterned than in the flesh. These areas melt into each other and form a vaguely indicated landscape pervaded by the generalized feeling of a tapestry-setting.

In conformity with this principle of organization by means of color, the girl's towel and garments are slight three-dimensional volumes made up of various intensified flesh-tones and patterned by linear streaks and mottled areas, which rhythmically repeat, in color, linear effect, light-and-shadow, spatial arrangement, solidity and surface-texture, the various parts of the figure. In short, the colors which, by their intrinsic quality and tonal interrelationships participate in the rendering of the figure, contribute also to other plastic effects in the other areas of the picture.

BATHER AND MAID * (218), of the late nineties, offers a combination of traits characteristic both of the nineties and of the first years after 1900. The latter appear rather as anticipations than as fully developed identifying marks; the treatment of the background, for example, resembles that in *"Promenade"* (236) of c. 1906, in the subtlety of relations between tree trunk and distant bushes, and in the way the fluffy, vaguely defined bushes themselves melt into each other; but nowhere in the picture is there the free overflow of color at contours so characteristic of the later work. Again, the pervasive subtlety of the entire design and also the delicate painting of the nude are reminiscent of *"Nude, Green Background"* (226), of c. 1902; but the painting of the flesh in *"Bather and Maid"* is not so solid, its drawing not so fluid, and the delicacy and subtlety of the ensemble is subsidiary to the Courbetesque solidity of the standing woman's head, and to the bold contrast effected by the large focus of red in her blouse. The traits which link the picture to the late nineties are more positive than those suggesting the later period; the individual colors, the contrasts and patterns in the standing figure are quite similar to those in *"Artist's Family"* (214) of 1896, and the painting of the water is very close in effect and execution to that in *"Nude in Brook"* (213) of 1895. The most interesting parts of the picture are the pastel-colored garments at the left, and the painting of the nude. Both units are elaborations of the exquisite daintiness of Boucher's drawing and of the light tones, especially the pinks, of his color-scheme. The flesh is extraordinarily dainty, and its texture recalls both the fragility and the hardness of glass.

* Illustration, p 314.

With all its exquisite passages of painting, its skilful placing of volumes in space, and its very effective pictorial organization, the painting is banal and academic; it lacks the spark of life and seems as if Renoir had painted a parody of his form by producing what the official *Salon* would pronounce excellence in art.

SEATED BATHER, READING (224), supposedly painted c. 1900, has the loose drawing of the late nineties, but a distinctive character of surface and texture: the substance of all the objects, including the chair, mantelpiece, draperies, and the woman's hair and flesh, has the quality of a heavy tile or a piece of majolica or enamel; and the surface, divided into a series of small areas, has a pattern and sparkle reminiscent of mosaics. Figure and setting—as in *"Bather"* (199) of 1892 *—are on a same compositional footing as regards surface and texture. Decoration is accentuated throughout the picture, but expression is nevertheless adequately convincing: the figure appears intent in her reading, and all the constituents of the setting are felt to be real objects despite their exotic, jewel- or mosaic-like sparkle and enamel-majolica texture.

In NUDE, GREEN BACKGROUND † (226) of c. 1902, Renoir carries out a novel experiment in the use of red to obtain new effects both in flesh-painting and in total color-organization. The flesh has the ivory tone and mother-of-pearl surface of the nineties but is punctuated in various areas by notes of brownish-red which form units of local color-contrast and also become parts of a general pattern of red areas that embraces foreground and background. Each of these units serves different plastic purposes: just above the left shoulder of the figure one small patch of brownish red models a solid sprig of foliage, another gives the effect of receding space; in the center of the background on the left an area of orange represents a vaguely defined portion of foliage and also contributes to the tapestry-quality. In the face the red gives the effect of highlight, as well as making a localized color-pattern; in the wrists and hands it dominates both light and shadow, and along the arms a lighter shade of it defines the contour and aids in building up the volume and organizing space. It thus not only makes up its own decorative pattern, but conveys the transferred value of reflected fire-light and plays an important part in all the basic plastic functions.

The two main elements in the picture, the figure and the background, are each characterized by a quiet subtle movement of rhythms. The subordinate volumes which make up the figure and form a general arabesque-sequence merge into each other by gentle transitions, with-

* See analytical data, Appendix, p. 418.
† Illustration, p. 315.

out jutting abruptly out into space at any point, so that though the figure is adequately real and solid it never has the effect of sculpture. Similarly, the contrast between the figure and the background is never sharp or dramatic: in both units there is a soft, gentle flow of delicate color, gradual transition from light to shadow, and unemphatic movement of volumes in space. The arabesque-character of the figure is repeated in the background, but very vaguely, because of the prevailingly blurred contours. The texture of both parts is very natural, with a slight decorative distortion in the tapestry-quality in the background and the mother-of-pearl quality in the flesh. The unifying pattern of reds is also subtle: individual notes do not stand out as points of accentuation, but merge gradually into adjacent colors, in conformity with the general design of quiet, slowly moving rhythmic flow.

JACQUES FRAY, AS A CHILD * (230), dated 1904, is a remarkably fine plastic realization of the charm of childhood. It is a typical red-rose picture of the period, with marvelously loose fluid drawing which establishes a general continuous color-flow throughout the canvas and yields subtle spatial relations between the head and the dark green background. It is a strong full-bodied version of Renoir's form of portraiture in the early nineties: † color is more solid and more deeply ingrained in the texture of the flesh. The background is not unlike that in Jacques-Louis David's "*Madame Chalgrin*" (555) and "*Madame Récamier*" (556) in its mottled surface obtained by irregular brush strokes unevenly loaded with pigment. Similar effect and technique frequently occur with varying degree of accentuation and diverse plastic activity in Renoir's work after 1890.‡

BABY'S BREAKFAST § (231), of c. 1904, from the standpoint of technical problems and human values, invites comparison with two pictures by Rubens, "*Child of the Artist*" (418) and "*Hélène Fourment and her Children*" (424). The Renoir presents a wider range of problems, they are solved in better plastic terms, and the expression is fuller and more convincingly rendered. The framework of the organization is a compartmental pattern of broad contrasting color-areas, of which the extensive deep red of the woman's blouse is the focal unit. Subsidiary patterns of bands and stripes affect most of the areas and vary in kind and degree of perceptibility. Each compositional unit assumes a distinct plastic character: the table and back-

---

* Illustration, p. 318.
† Cf., e.g., "*Child Reading*" (184), "*Girl with Yellow Cape*" (191), "*Girl in Profile*" (202), "*Two Girls Reading*" (207), "*Head of Girl with Hat*" (210).
‡ E.g., "*Girl with Yellow Cape*" (191), "*Madame Renoir in Dressing Gown*" (200), "*Coco*" (229), "*Baby's Breakfast*" (231).
§ Illustration, p. 320.

ground are solid planes, the objects on the table are delicate volumes, and the figures are weighty planelike masses. The relationships between the color, direction and position of these planes and masses, create a rhythmic organization of space-volume units in an original version of the traditional pyramidal type of composition.

The distribution of the masses brings about a series of enframing activities throughout the design. The plate, mug and hands at the lower left form a circular group of small volumes, very subtly related to each other and to the plane of the spoon suspended in free space in their center. The figure of the baby is a pyramidal volume set at right angles to the pyramidal planelike mass of the woman's body, and is enframed by the latter in two different manners: on a two-dimensional plane, the area occupied by the woman's blouse forms an enframing red setting extending above and to the sides of the baby's head and shoulders; in three-dimensional space, the woman's head, arms and hands encircle the baby's body in an embracing movement around the unit of space in which the baby is set. In turn, the body of the woman is set at an angle to the background plane and is enframed by its tan and blue color-areas. Finally, the upright plane in the background, in relation to the slanting horizontal plane of the table in the foreground, creates an open V-shaped angle of deep space which encloses the other constituents of the total space-composition—the group of figures and objects. The degree of three-dimensional quality in the volumes grows as their rhythm moves from the flat planes of the background and table to the delicate masses of the still-life, the flattened volume of the woman's body, and the fully rounded volumes in the child. These contrasts in degree of voluminous quality, as well as those in the position of the masses and planes, are emphasized by the contrasts in color and the comparatively sharp contour of the areas.

CLAUDE IN ARAB SHIRT * (232), of c. 1904, embodies the essence of eighteenth century French delicacy, lightness and charm, integrated by solid and weighty color and extremely fluid drawing. One of the outstanding features of the design is its simplicity and directness. The figure, dominated by bright mellow rose, is placed against an equally bright green background. In spite of the small number of colors, few other Renoirs equal this one in singing quality of color, and the vividness of the drama and the exotic charm of the color-design are not excelled by the most daring and complex ventures of Matisse's. This color-design illustrates what color-relations *per se,* when rightly adjusted, can do to make a picture carry out to full extent a wealth of human values. This painting shows also how much an unobtrusive pattern, organically merged with the form, can contribute to the fulness of plastic expression.

* Illustration, p. 319.

ANALYSES 427

WRITING LESSON * (234), of c. 1905, exemplifies Renoir's use of red to achieve a novel interpretation of various traditional compositional forms. The extensive red area of background sets off by contrast the pyramidal organization of the principal masses, it participates in the enframing arrangement of volumes around other volumes, and it also contributes to the enclosure of a mass between others in compressed space. The interweaving of these various compositional types of organization produces a pulsating rhythm of volumes in space, generally Venetian in character but altered by modified traits of other traditions. The woman's blouse, for example, has the reality of texture of the best of Tintoretto's fabrics † and the surface sheen of Paolo Veronese's,‡ and the decorative and expressive phases of each of these Venetian traits are enhanced by patterns of highlights reminiscent of Rubens' § and Watteau's, ‖ by subtle spatial relations of volumes recalling Chardin's,¶ and by a surface gleam resembling Terborch's.** Moreover, the color of this green-blue blouse is iridescent to a degree not attained in any of the prototypes; numerous stripes and bands add a lively pattern to the surface and also divide the area into subsidiary masses which participate in the general compositional movement of volumes in space. The novel and unusually decorative color-ensemble is well integrated in a design which conveys convincingly the values of childhood, motherly care, and the reality of human activity in home surroundings.

MISSIA †† (235), of c. 1906, retains the familiar tapestry-effect of Renoir's earlier work, but in a generalized form, with looser drawing, and richer, more structural and better illuminated color. The tapestry unit is no longer primarily a setting but a factor commensurate in color and compositional activities with the figure.‡‡ The total form, while reminiscent in general feeling of the highly decorative work of some of the seventeenth and eighteenth century French portraitists, is richer in plastic and human content than the prototypes in the tradition.§§ The picture is to the Largillière-Nattier-Boucher type of portraiture what

---

* Illustration, p. 322.
† E.g., Tintoretto's *"Paradise"* (389).
‡ E.g., Paolo Veronese's *"Burning of Sodom"* (401).
§ E.g., Rubens' *"Annunciation"* (414).
‖ E.g., Watteau's *"Game of Love"* (478).
¶ E.g., Chardin's *"Back from Market"* (496).
** E.g., Terborch's *"Guitar Lesson"* (460).
†† Illustration, p. 324.
‡‡ Cf., e.g., Renoir's *"Woman in Blue, with Bonnet"* (158) or *"Bathers"* (164).
§§ Cf., e.g., Largillière's *"Artist's Family"* (470) or *"Charlotte Amelia Ragotsky"* (471), Nattier's *"Madame Henriette"* (482), *"Madame Louise"* (483) or *"Princesse de Condé as Diana"* (484), Boucher's *"Madame de Pompadour"* (511), Fragonard's *"Study"* (537).

"Girl with Basket of Flowers" (188) of the early nineties or *"Head of Girl with Hat"* (210) of c. 1893 is to the Greuze type; that is, a realization in plastic terms of the human values of the subject-matter which these other painters rendered chiefly by illustrative and decorative means of only surface depth.

BATHER DRYING HERSELF * (243), of c. 1909, is compositionally an organization of very dynamic volume-space relationships raised to the peak of decorative and expressive heights. The figure as a whole is not only definitely placed in space but its component parts—head, arms, breasts and legs—are each accentuated as volumes, each occupying its own area of well-defined space. The pronounced solidity and three-dimensionality of the figure are obtained by structural color and an assertive pattern of light and shadow, a combination which yields sculptural quality and great decorative richness. Compositional unity between figure and background is achieved by a succession of rhythms of volumes and intervals, each richly and variously colored, lighted and patterned. The volume of projecting foliage about the nude's head and shoulders seems to extend forward like the fingers of a hand and draw the head into a pocket of space, thus making of that portion of the figure and of the background parts of the general theme of space-volume relationships. This unit of foliage, rendered in dark green marked with stripes of lighter green, adds striking decorative values to the unit composed of the head, foliage and pocket of space.

Another important agent of compositional unification is the interplay of two large three-dimensional patterns, one formed by the head, arms and white towel, the other by the nude's right leg, the trunk of the tree, and the horizontal strip of dark grass on the left. The right leg, as belonging to the pattern which includes objects in the landscape, is less solid than the other leg, but more so than the tree trunk, and thus in a sense serves as a bridge in the continuity of rhythms between figure and background. Similarly, the patch of light which, by its conjunction to surrounding darker color, models the tree trunk, is related by its shape to patches of light in the figure, but the latter are productive of a more massive solidity. An interplay between volumes, spatial units, shapes, areas of light and dark color, takes place throughout the canvas, so that each constituent serves as a contributing factor to the decorative and expressive values of the form as a whole.

CARYATIDS † (248 and 249), of c. 1910, illustrate Renoir's plastic amplification, through his growth in the use of color, of the motifs

* Illustration, p. 325.
† Illustrations, p. 330.

ANALYSES 429

in ancient sculpture and eighteenth century French painting which preoccupied him in the 1885-1887 period. In these two pictures he embodies perhaps to a greater extent than anywhere else in his work, the graceful fluidity of classic sculpture and also the mother-of-pearl surface of the earlier French tradition in its richest version.*

The glowing rose-colored figures, as exquisitely rendered as anything in his previous work, are more solidly constructed, and their color partakes at one and the same time of the qualities of fresco and of human flesh. The flesh is modeled by a dappling pattern of dovetailing areas of light and dark, and the fluidity of this pattern, together with the subtlety of its color- and tone-relationships, contributes much to the fluid grace of the figures themselves. Variations in the use of the dappling pattern occur in each composition and in each figure. On the right side of the figure to the left, in No. (248), the areas of lighter color are accentuated as highlights and are so loosely outlined that they form a continuous sinuous band which extends from head to foot and conveys a feeling of exquisitely graceful movement. This band is paralleled on the left by three similar curvilinear bands alternately of shadow and light each so little interrupted in the continuity of their component areas that their respective sinuous movement is perceived as that of a continuous linear area. A great technical achievement is that the light and dark areas produce the linear effects themselves and also their rhythmic punctuations. Corresponding shifts of emphasis in the constituents of the pattern in the other figures increase the composite feeling of movement by the variety of effects obtained.

The grace of the figures and the strength of their plastic structure, together with the fresco-quality suggested in the surface, produce a general effect reminiscent of Masaccio's *"Adam and Eve"* (325) and Signorelli's *"Hell—Paradise"* (336), without the latter's overemphasis upon linear anatomical definition.

CUP OF CHOCOLATE † (263), of c. 1912, ranks with Renoir's highest achievements in imaginative use of color and in fulness of decorative and expressive content. The color-theme consists essentially in a dramatic interplay of three main colors—red, blue and ivory—occupying large distinct areas, but each modulated by nuances of the others. Thus the flesh, brownish red in general, is vaguely tinged with lilac or lavender; the whitish-ivory tablecloth is permeated in its shadows with rose, lavender, coral and light blue, which blend into color-chords; the cerulean-blue drapery is streaked with bluish white

* Cf., e.g., the Greek bronze *"Standing Figure"* (311), Boucher's *"Three Graces"* (519).
† Illustration, p. 343.

and tinged with rose; the skirt, bluish purple in general, has stripes of vague brown and whitish blue; the bunch of violets is a complex of blue, brown, purple, deep coral, white, fringed with a contour of green modulated by blue; the cup and pot are likewise made up of one of the predominating colors varied and enriched by nuances of the other two.

To speak paradoxically, yet with accuracy, it is a red picture dominated by blue; for, though a deep brownish-red determines the characteristic appearance of the flesh and enters into the composite color-identity of the other areas, the blue, concentrated in the large area of background-drapery and in the woman's skirt in the foreground, competes for supremacy with the red chiefly because of its brightness and luminosity. As a result of the emphasis upon one color in each of the objects or areas of the canvas, the color-design is an accentuated pattern of contrasting color-patches which balance each other in direction, shape, position and plastic content. The structural quality of the color, the firmness of the drawing and modeling, and the definiteness in the placing of the objects create a series of rhythmic throbs of solid color-units dynamically related to each other in deep space, which is filled with a suffusion formed by the overtones of the three principal colors.

The movement of the volumes involves a compositional arrangement of four main planes, each a positive contrast to the others—the vertical background, the horizontal table-top, the forward slanting torso, the vertical-oblique front of the table and side of the figure. The thrust and counterthrust of these planes, establishing numerous effects of perspective, aid materially in giving picturesqueness as well as three-dimensional spaciousness to the composition. No less active as compositional agent is the pattern of highlights occurring as two distinct types of iridescent islands—relatively small spots in the face, cup and bunch of violets, and stripes or bands in the skirt, tablecloth and background-drapery. Wherever they occur, the highlights enter into the drawing and modeling of the volumes and the rendering of space, and participate also, by their punctuating rhythm, in the throb of masses in space. Variation in their shape, size and proportionate amount of light and color confers variety upon the character of the masses, the quality of the light and the degree of contrast in color-relations.

The composition is particularly successful as a placing of many objects in relatively limited space, with complex relationships brought into order and balance by all-embracing rhythms. The feelings of weight and solidity in the volumes, of reality in the textures, of repose in the figure, and of intime charm in the scene of everyday life, are not only conveyed with depth and conviction but are embodied in a plastic form which enriches these feelings with a wealth of decorative qualities unusual even for Renoir.

SEATED NUDE* (279) and SEATED ODALISQUE † (280), two typical examples of Renoir's form of c. 1915-1917, differ plastically from each other in the relations established in each between figure and setting.‡ The background in *"Seated Nude"* consists of two draperies of contrasting color, treated as juxtaposed broad planes, which long streaks of light and color transform into a series of elongated slight volumes representing folds of textiles and units of space. These color-volumes echo the shape, direction and general pattern of the component parts of the figure, but differ from them in color and degree of solidity. The shape and three-dimensional quality of the other objects in the setting, as well as their location in relation to each other, are also adapted to the specific character of the pulsating rhythm of compact volumes which move within the shallow space between foreground and background.

In *"Seated Odalisque"* the two large areas that make up the setting contrast with each other in their content of volumes and space: a large expanse of free space at the left extends diagonally from the lower right to the extreme upper left, and is counterbalanced by a compact set of flattened volumes in the area at the right which moves forward from the upper left background toward the right foreground. These two contrasting parts of the setting, by their relationships to each other and to the figure, produce a sweeping circular movement, within which the rhythmic duplication of units becomes more frequent and more positive as the movement progresses from the lower right, forward, upward and backward toward the left and then from the upper left downward toward the right. The climax of this compositional rhythm is reached in the figure, in which the volumes are more numerous, solid and colorful and also more compactly grouped than anywhere else in the picture.

BATHING GROUP § (285), dated 1916.‖ The powerful and all-pervasive color-drama of the picture results not only from striking contrasts of bright colors, but also from the interaction of all the elements in the design. Drama is indeed woven into the very fabric of the form as a quality inherent in each of the fundamental plastic factors; the abstract value of drama, in other words, is conveyed by the integrated ensemble, of which the basic element is color. A great variety of effects in color-drama is obtained throughout the picture by a changing interplay of the plastic constituents. For example, in

* Illustration, p. 352.
† Illustration, p. 353.
‡ To be read in connection with the general discussion of the type in chapter "Development of Renoir's Form," pp. 142-143.
§ Illustration, p. 355.
‖ To be read in connection with the general discussion of this picture in chapter "Development of Renoir's Form," pp. 144-150.

the color-focus of the composition—the two distant small nudes approximately in the center of the canvas—the drama due to the movement of the figures is reënforced by the color-contrast with the immediate setting. At the right of the composition, in the area occupied by the three large figures, the drama results only partly from the vivid color-variety in garments, flesh, tree trunk and foliage, and to a greater extent from the accentuated pattern of these variegated areas and from their contrasting directions. Moreover, the spots and streaks of colored light which pattern some of these units and glow with a jewel-like effulgence are dramatic in their own right, and contribute a distinctive quality to the color-drama of this entire area. At the left of the canvas, the color-drama is reënforced by the contrast between the peaceful, slowly undulating movement of the standing rose-red nude and the throbbing rhythm of the swirling clumps of multicolored foliage back of her. Again, the outstanding dramatic feature in the foreground is the contrast of the solid, fully rounded, red and silver-gray figure with the relatively flat plane of blue-green, yellow and brownish-red grass upon which the figure reclines. Finally, the dramatic note in the sky is occasioned by the irregular streaks of light which interrupt the large expanse of blue, and by the contrasts of the blue with the enframing areas of green, orange and yellow foliage.

All these varied aspects of the color-drama, and the technical means by which they are rendered, are distinguishable from each other only upon analysis; they blend harmoniously within the composite color-organization, to which they lend variety and interest by the rise and fall in the degree of intensity of their respective dramatic qualities. This is abstract drama in its highest estate because achieved by the activity of aspects and compositional functions of color.

No less ingenious than the variegated effects of the color-drama is the complex set of compositional plans of organization, which also establish, by their harmonious relationships, a great array of esthetic effects. The two small nudes which in the middle distance echo the color, the iridescent luminosity and the voluminousness of the large figures in the foreground, may be selected as a focal point toward which converges the movement of the main masses in the picture. These two figures with the landscape about them, form a composition of their own, of the extremely generalized type characteristic of Renoir's latest work.* Large clumps of foliage, revolving around this central compositional focus, form an enframing enclosure which expands forward and on all sides into the still larger frame made by the sky and the figures in the foreground. The composite effect is that of a pulsating rhythm of large color-volumes around two small figures seen as in a vista, in the distance.

An alternative conception of the compositional plan is an organiza-

* Cf., e.g., *"Two Figures in Landscape"* (296).

tion of three main vertical sections: first, the area occupied by the compactly grouped figures and trees at the right; second, the middle portion of the picture which encircles the area at the right in a wide semicircular sweep of accentuated space from the upper right of the picture through the sky and down to the water and the extreme lower right corner; the third section, paralleling the second in its enframing sweep, flows downward from the upper left corner to the lower right in an uninterrupted rhythmic sequence of solid volumes and colorful spatial intervals. The three sections contrast with each other in degree of accentuation of volumes and of space, and are unified by the qualities of light, drawing, technique and especially of color and movement, which they all share.

The picture may also be conceived as a unity of two organizations—the right and left halves of the canvas—each a balanced composition in itself, yet also expanding the other. Contrast between these two sections is established chiefly by the relative degree of accentuation of the units of space and volume. The right half is a series of well-defined volumes and intervals interlocking in a compact and highly patterned space-composition. The left half is itself conceivably divisible into two parts, one of which is mainly a large expanse of receding space, and the other a compact organization of volumes in shallow space. The two contrasting halves of the total picture are unified by an uninterrupted flow of colorful atmosphere which is punctuated by equally colorful volumes and in which all the plastic constituents participate.

In each of the foregoing plans of organization, Renoir's familiar arabesque-formation is a constant factor, but its compositional function here is much more comprehensive than in his previous use of it. In the earlier forms,* the arabesque was more easily resolvable into separate arabesques of light, line and color, whereas in this picture its plastic constituents are more completely interfused, the arabesque is one of robust volumes, and is thus infinitely more expressive as well as more highly decorative. This rich and full-bodied arabesque winds its way through practically every area of the canvas, taking, in turn, the general course of a large circle, an ellipse, a scroll-like spiral or an S-shaped curve. Its movement takes place in deep space as well as on the plane of the canvas, so that over and above the two-dimensional flow of color-volumes, the arabesque carries in its all-pervasive rhythm a continuous in-and-out movement of masses, and is thus an integral part of composition in both two and three dimensions. The picture, in short, carries the Venetian type of composition to newer heights of esthetic expression and to a richer realm of decorative qualities.

---

* E.g., *"Bathers"* (164), *"Noirmoutier"* (201), *"Bathers in Forest"* (216).

GROUP OF BATHERS * (302), painted c. 1918, is a very fine realization of Renoir's latest type of color-design in which a deep rose-red pervades the all-embracing suffusion, permeates the overflow of color in the loose contours, and dominates the color-organization. The movement of the figures is quietly fluid and rhythmic, and the vaguely defined patterns, no less than the volumes and their circumambient space, are active participants in the all-inclusive compositional rhythm of color-masses.

The composition is much simpler and more compact than that in *"Bathing Group"* (285), the rose of the flesh is deeper in tone, the sky more dramatic and multicolored, and the general color-effect is more decidedly red. The pictures are similar in the quiet swirl of their masses, and in both the large volumes of figures and foliage in the foreground enframe the group of small nudes in the middle distance. The emphasis upon a large area of open space in *"Bathing Group"* and upon compact grouping of volumes in *"Group of Bathers"* determines the difference in the respective types of space-composition. The larger areas of green and blue in the former picture and the greater predominance and deeper tone of rose in *"Group of Bathers"* are responsible for pronounced differences in the color-ensemble of these two paintings.

In *"Group of Bathers,"* in the nude at the left, at the contour which should define the figure's back against the immediate setting, the back appears detached from the body, obviously because of a lack of a proper coördination in the use of line, color, light and space in the drawing. The defect detracts nothing from the high plastic status of the picture and is noteworthy only because similar faults are rarely found in Renoir's best work.

MATERNITY † (303), of c. 1918, is one of Renoir's most successful plastic organizations and one of the most appealing of his bright color-ensembles. Deep rose tones dominate the greens, blues and yellows, and give to the picture the characteristic red tonality of his latest work. The composite red is resolvable into numerous tones and nuances: the flesh is a deep rose; the large expanse of the woman's blouse is more positively red; the small brush strokes of red interspersed in the areas of other colors are variously affected by their respective color-context. In the overflow of color from area to area the overtones are carried throughout all parts of the design and yield a rich, weighty and all-enveloping suffusion in which warm tones of red prevail.

The color is weighty and not heavy, solid and neither massive nor painty, and it is everywhere vivified by dramatic contrasts and by islands of iridescent light. Drawing is primarily a matter of color; everything is fluid and floating and, with no suggestion of sharp or

* Illustration, p. 363.
† Illustration, p. 365.

tight contour anywhere, the features and parts of the body in each of the figures are well defined as entities and as integral parts of the composition. The trees and house in the background are more loosely outlined and less definite in representative detail; they are structural color-volumes, much enriched by glowing islands of light, and they offer in their ensemble a most effective contrast to the main part of the design.

The extraordinary sensuous richness of the ensemble, and the fundamental parts which color plays in the drawing and in the organization of the composition show an enormous advance over Renoir's earlier versions of the same subject-matter.* As in his best work of the late period, the Oriental color-scheme in this picture has been sublimated to the highest degree: there is no suggestion of glitter, glare, overaccentuated overtones, or any trace of unintegrated color. The Oriental colors have been so much enriched, made so much more solid and juicy, and are so much more essentially active in the drawing, that they have become an all-inclusive and deeply ingrained part of glowing color-chords. Chiefly because of this growth in the use of color, the human values intrinsic to the subject-matter are conveyed with much greater charm, poignancy and reality than in any of Renoir's previous versions.

NYMPHS † (304), of c. 1918, is perhaps the largest picture painted by Renoir at the end of his career. Almost the entire canvas is occupied by two life-size nudes reclining in the foreground of a bright and colorful landscape, in the upper right distance of which is a group of equally well-defined, but smaller bathers. The components of the subject-matter—figures, garments and landscape—form a rich pattern of iridescent areas, dominated variously by bright and luminous reds, blues, greens and yellows in many nuances of each. Red, of the familiar rose tone of Renoir's latest work, pervades the ensemble, and its shades extend from a deep red that recalls raw flesh to the most delicate pinks of the tea-rose.

The intense illumination of the color is responsible for a degree of effulgent iridescence not excelled in any other of Renoir's work. The succession of the iridescent multicolored units throughout the canvas produces a highly decorative, extraordinarily rhythmic color-pattern, a continuous flow of effulgent islands of colorful light: progressing from side to side, for instance, the foreground at the left—pillow, hat and draperies—is a shimmering ensemble of red tones ranging from vermilion and deep rose-madder to pale pinkish-rose, and interspersed with lemon-yellow, light blue and streaks of light; adjoining this area is an island of light, with green as the most conspicuous color; then

* Cf., e.g., *"Mother Nursing Baby"* (155) of 1885, *"Mother, Child and Cat"* (159) of 1886, and *"Mother and Baby"* (162) of c. 1886.
† Illustration, p. 367.

follows the drapery under the figure, in which the predominating color is white toned with bluish-slate shadows; succeeding this is a reddish-rose area which suggests the color and movement of flames rather than of the depicted foliage or grass. A literally innumerable quantity of similar flamelike units are scattered throughout the landscape and echo the fluid sinuous grace of the figures; they are greatly varied in content of color and light and in degree of accentuation of their movement, and they contrast with and balance each other in adjoining and in widely separated sections of the canvas. A flood of sunlight pervades the almost crystal-clear atmosphere, unifies the effulgence of the variegated color-units and adds vividness to the color-ensemble and to the reality of the open-air scene.

This picture, hanging in the Louvre in the same gallery with *"Moulin de la Galette"* (62) of 1876, offers an opportunity to confirm Renoir's growth in the handling of the familiar islands of light. Both pictures are primarily decorative illustrations in which a general dissemination of iridescent units of light constitutes the main decorative motif. In the later picture the color- and light-elements of the patches are merged into single units which are integral parts of the total color-organization; moreover, the patches, over and above their increased decorative value, portray the essential feeling of the structure, texture and surface of the represented materials. The corresponding units in the earlier picture not only are less rich in color-content, but appear isolated from the color-context and total color-organization, and often seem to be merely superposed upon the surface which they decorate. The advance in *"Nymphs,"* in other words, consists in a successful blending of the color-light patches with the substance of the objects and the total form of the picture.

An equally important advance is perceptible in the compositional function of these patches or islands of color and light; the greater variety of color within the patches in the later picture establishes more numerous and more effective compositional contrasts and relationships with all the other colorful elements of the design. In short, what was formerly scarcely more than a surface-pattern has acquired the qualities of a glorified bouquet of luminous variegated flowers interspersed with clusters of sparkling multicolored jewels. The picture is a fine example of color conveying the abstract feeling of voluptuousness which always accompanies esthetic pleasure at its supreme height.*

CHRYSANTHEMUMS IN VASE † (306), said to be the last picture painted by Renoir, is a superb example of the plastic realization of the feeling of voluptuousness intrinsic to richly colorful flowers.

---

* For further details on *"Nymphs"* (304) see chapter "Development of Renoir's Form," p. 143.
† Illustration, p. 368.

The colors, by their relations to each other as well as by their individual sensuous quality, convey, independently of the fulness of feeling in the flowers themselves, the abstract qualities of glow, iridescence, lusciousness and voluptuous charm. A flow of glowing color seems to well up from the vase, to spread in all directions and permeate all parts of the design, like a thick foaming liquid condensing into volumes of color as it rises. The composition is of the characteristic late type, in which a positive unit in the foreground is inseparably fused with the setting by the interflow of their respective colors. The identity of the individual flowers diminishes in degree of positiveness as the constituents of the bouquet recede toward the background and, with no break in continuity, the non-representative swirls of color in the setting carry back into infinite space the feelings intrinsic to the flowers themselves. The compactly organized color-movement of the form as a whole reflects the same voluptuous abandon as that in Renoir's latest paintings of nudes. Comparisons with Renoir's flowerpieces of earlier periods * show a progressive development of the expressive power of his color, corresponding to that illustrated by his treatment of figures and landscape.

* E.g., the dark and heavy *"Easter Flowers"* (1) of 1864, the impressionistic *"Moss Roses"* (50) of c. 1875, the Manet-like *"Roses in Blue Vase"* (98) of the late seventies, the glary *"Flowerpiece"* (114) of 1881, the clean-cut *"Anemones"* (156) of the mid-eighties, the warm-colored *"Pitcher of Flowers"* (180) of c. 1889, and the loosely drawn and color-suffused *"Flowers in Green Vase"* (239) of c. 1907.

CATALOGUE DATA

CATALOGUE DATA *

THE two following lists contain the titles of the pictures and other works of art, together with their corresponding numbers, as they appear in the text. The paintings by Renoir are arranged in chronological order, and the works belonging to each year are listed alphabetically. Unless otherwise specified, Renoir's pictures listed are painted in oil on canvas. To assist in identification, such descriptive details are given as the size of the paintings and the collections in which they are to be found. The first enumerated dimension is the height of the picture. The Renoir exhibitions referred to are as follows: "The Classical Period of Renoir—1875-1886," held at M. Knoedler & Company, New York, in 1929; "Renoir," held at Musée de l'Orangerie, Paris, in 1933, the references to which relate to the second edition of the catalogue.

Following the enumeration of Renoir's work, another list, "Miscellaneous Works of Art," commencing with No. 307, includes data on such paintings, sculpture, frescoes, tapestries, etc., referred to in the text as having a bearing on Renoir's work. Works in this list are classified alphabetically under the tradition or individual artist to which they belong, and the order of the traditions and artists is roughly chronological.

For the purpose of convenience, the titles in both lists are given in English and also in the language of the country in which the pictures are to be seen. When proper names and titles of persons occur in the designation of pictures, they are given in the language of their country.

(A) PAINTINGS BY RENOIR

NO.   1864

1. **Easter Flowers.** 51¼" x 38½". Dated. Collection Oskar Reinhardt, Winterthur, Switzerland. "Stilleben." Pages 48n, 437n.

* The inclusion of page references converts this section into a supplementary index. The letter n after a number indicates that the reference is contained in a footnote on the page so numbered.

NO.

2. **Mademoiselle Romaine Lancaux.** 32" x 25½". Dated. Collection Madame Barret-Decap, Paris. Renoir Exhibition, Musée de l'Orangerie, Paris, 1933, No. 1, "Portrait de petite fille." Pages 49-50, 200, 200n, 210, 374. Illustration, page 225.

Circa 1866

3. **Woman with Bird.** 32¼" x 26". Collection Baron Herzog, Budapest. "Ászany egy maddáral." Pages 200, 200n.

Circa 1866-1867

4. **Diana, the Huntress.** 77½" x 52". Private Collection, New York. Reproduced in "Burlington Magazine," London, Nov., 1929. Page 48n.

1867

5. **Lise.** 71" x 44½". Dated. Folkwang-Museum, Essen, i. W., Germany, No. 257. Pages 48n, 49n, 56n, 60n, 113n, 154, 193, 200, 200n, 374-376, 386, 386n, 388, 392. Illustration, page 226.

Circa 1867

6. **Rowboat.** 9¾" x 13¼". Collection Ed. Esmond, Paris. Renoir Exhibition, Musée de l'Orangerie, Paris, 1933, No. 2, "La barque." Pages 50, 57, 200n.

1868

7. **Boy with Cat.** 48¾" x 26¼". Dated. Collection Frau Eduard Arnhold, Berlin. "Knabe mit Katze." Pages 48n, 50, 200n, 376-378. Illustration, page 227.

Circa 1868

8. **Alfred Sisley.** 32" x 26". Private Collection, Paris. Renoir Exhibition, Musée de l'Orangerie, Paris. 1933. No. 5. "Portrait de Sisley." Page 48n.

9. **Lise.** 18½" x 15½". Barnes Foundation No. 874. Pages 48n, 49, 49n, 59, 59n, 60n, 113n, 153. Illustration, p. 228.

10. **Mr. and Mrs. Sisley.** 41¼" x 29½". Wallraf-Richartz-Museum, Cologne, No. 1199. "Das Ehepaar Sisley." Pages 48n, 49n, 50, 56n, 113n, 177n, 200, 200n, 378-380, 386n, 388, 392. Illustration, page 232.

Circa 1868-1869

11. **In Summer.** 33½" x 23¼". National-Galerie, Berlin, No. 1073. "Im Sommer." Pages 48n, 113n, 380-381. Illustration, page 229.
12. **La Grenouillère.** 24½" x 35½". Collection Oskar Reinhardt, Winterthur, Switzerland. Pages 200n, 381. Illustration, page 230.

1869

13. **Artist's Father.** 24" x 18". Dated. City Art Museum, St. Louis, Mo., Accession No. 37.33. Page 60n.

Circa 1869

14. **Barges on the Seine.** 18" x 25¼". Louvre. "Chalands sur la Seine." Page 48n.

Before 1870

15. **Frédéric Bazille.** 41¾" x 29". Louvre. Page 381.

1870

16. **Bather with Griffon.** 72½" x 45¼". Dated. Estate of Alfred Cassirer, Berlin. "Badende mit Hund." "Renoir Exhibition, Musée de l'Orangerie, Paris, 1933, No. 7, "La baigneuse au griffon." Pages 48n, 50n, 56n, 82n, 177n, 200n. Illustration, page 233.
17. **Odalisque.** 27¼" x 48½". Dated. Private Collection, New York. Pages 50n, 51n, 80n, 200n.
18. **Woman's Portrait.** 32" x 25½". Dated. Collection Oscar Schmitz, Zurich. "Damenbildnis." Page 48n.

1871

19. **Capitaine Darras.** 32" x 25½". Dated. Staatliche Gemälde-Galerie, Dresden, No. 2608. "Offiziersbildnis." Pages 50n, 51n, 80n.
20. **Madame Maître.** 51¼" x 32¾". Dated. Collection René Lecomte, Paris. Pages 50n, 51.

NO.
21. **Still-Life with Bouquet.** 29½" x 23¼". Dated. Collection Gaston Bernheim de Villers, Paris. Exhibition of Vollard Collection, Knoedler Galleries, New York, 1933, No. 23, "Nature morte au bouquet." Pages 50n, 51n.

Circa 1871

22. **Head of Madame Maître.** 14½" x 12½". Smith College, Museum of Art, Northampton, Mass., No. 24:16-1. Page 48n.
23. **Henriot Family.** 45" x 64¼". Collection Etienne Bignou, Paris. Renoir Exhibition, Musée de l'Orangerie, Paris, 1933, No. 9, "La famille Henriot." Pages 50n, 51, 60n, 61n, 73n, 110n, 125n, 202n, 382, 388. Illustration, page 246.

1872

24. **Canoeists at Chatou.** 32" x 39½". Dated. Collection Adolph Lewisohn, New York. Renoir Exhibition, Musée de l'O-rangerie, Paris, 1933, No. 10, "Les canotiers à Chatou." Pages 50n, 52, 53, 54-55, 64n, 382-383. Illustration, page 231.
25. **Harem.** 61" x 51¼". Dated. Collection Matsukata, Paris. "Parisiennes habillées en Algériennes." Pages 50n, 51n, 80n, 200n.
26. **Pont-Neuf.** 30" x 37¾". Dated. Collection Ralph M. Coe, Cleveland. Pages 50n, 51-52, 200n, 383.

Circa 1872

27. **Breakfast.** 19¼" x 23½". Barnes Foundation No. 45. Pages 50n, 53, 59n, 61n, 89n, 127, 200n, 201. Illustration, page 234.
28. **Young Woman with Rose.** 11" x 9¾". Louvre—gift of Mr. Ernest May. "Femme demi-nue couchée." Pages 50n, 51n, 80n, 177, 200n, 384, 387. Illustration, page 236.

1873

29. **Landscape.** 18½" x 24¼". Dated. Collection Albert Poul-lot, Paris. Renoir Exhibition, Musée de l'Orangerie, Paris, 1933, not catalogued, "Paysage." Pages 50n, 54-55.
30. **Riders in the Bois de Boulogne.** 102¾" x 89". Dated. Kunsthalle, Hamburg, No. 1567. "Reiterin im Bois de Boulogne." Pages 200n, 384, 393.

Circa 1873

31. **La Grenouillère.** 17¾" x 21½". Collection Carlo Z. Thomsen, Hamburg. Pages 50n, 53-54, 97n, 121n, 200, 200n. Illustration, page 235.

1874

32. **Dancer.** 56" x 36½". Dated. Collection Joseph E. Widener, Elkins Park, Pa. Renoir Exhibition, Musée de l'Orangerie, Paris, 1933, No. 17a, "Danseuse." Pages 50n, 55, 56-58, 58n, 59, 60n, 64, 116n, 153, 177, 193n, 200n. Illustration, page 238.

33. **Madame X** (Madame Hartmann). 72½" x 48¾". Dated. Louvre No. 499. Page 385.

34. **Opera Box.** 31¾" x 25½". Dated. Collection Samuel Courtauld, London. Renoir Exhibition, Musée de l'Orangerie, Paris, 1933. No. 17, "La loge." Pages 50n, 55-56, 58, 153, 177, 192, 193n, 384, 385-388, 396n, 398. Illustration, page 237.

35. **Promenade in Woods.** 31¾" x 25½". Dated. Collection Paul Rosenberg, Paris. Renoir Exhibition, Musée de l'Orangerie, Paris, 1933. No. 18, "La promenade." Page 388.

Circa 1874-1875

36. **Path in the Field.** 23¼" x 29". Louvre—gift of Mr. Charles Comiot. "Chemin montant dans les hautes herbes." Pages 50n, 55.

37. **Woman at Spring.** 54¼" x 33¼". Barnes Foundation No. 908. Pages 61n, 63n, 64, 64n, 115n, 201n, 389. Illustration, page 239.

Circa 1874-1876

38. **Girl with Cat.** 21½" x 18". Collection Benjamin E. Lévy, Paris. Renoir Exhibition, Musée de l'Orangerie, Paris, 1933, No. 32, "La jeune fille au chat." Pages 51n, 68n.

39. **Greenhouse.** 23¼" x 28¾". Collection D. W. T. Cargill, Stanmore, Lanark, Scotland. Renoir Exhibition, Musée de l'Orangerie, Paris, 1933, No. 20a, "La serre." Page 389.

40. **Reader.** 17¾" x 14½". Louvre. "La liseuse." Pages 58n, 61n, 63n, 64, 65, 68n, 84n, 201n, 390. Illustration, page 240.

NO.
41. Young Girl Sewing. 25½" x 21¼". Collection Etienne Bignou, Paris, "La couseuse." Pages 61n, 63n, 65, 84n, 20in. Illustration, page 242.

1875

42. Madame Choquet. 29" x 23½". Dated. Collection Madame Halvorsen, Oslo, Norway. Renoir Exhibition, Musée de l'Orangerie, Paris, 1933, No. 22. Pages 51n, 64.
43. Mademoiselle Legrand. 32" x 23½". Dated. Collection J. and G. Bernheim-Jeune, Paris. Renoir Exhibition, Musée de l'Orangerie, Paris, 1933. No. 21, "La fillette attentive." Pages 58n, 63n, 64.
44. Two Women in Park. 23½" x 28¾". Dated. Barnes Foundation No. 289. Pages 52n, 55n, 58n, 61n, 62n, 63n, 64n, 67, 69, 70, 70n, 71, 82n, 84n, 89n, 201n, 202n, 387, 389, 390-391, 405n. Illustration, page 241.

Circa 1875

45. Beautiful Season: Conversation. 23¼" x 15½". Collection Ambroise Vollard, Paris. Exhibition of Vollard Collection, Knoedler Galleries, New York, 1933, No. 25, "La belle saison: la conversation." Pages 68n, 89n, 90n.
46. Beautiful Season: Promenade. 23¼" x 13". Collection Ambroise Vollard, Paris. Exhibition of Vollard Collection, Knoedler Galleries, New York, 1933, No. 24, "La belle saison: la promenade." Pages 68n, 89n, 90n.
47. English Pear Tree. 25½" x 32". Collection Fauchier Delavigne, Paris. Renoir Exhibition, Musée de l'Orangerie, Paris, 1933, No. 6a, "Le poirier d'Angleterre." Page 391.
48. House in Woods. 15¼" x 18½". Barnes Foundation No. 860. Pages 58n, 67, 70, 71, 202n.
49. Meditation. 18" x 15". Collection Madame Georges Menier, Paris. Renoir Exhibition, Musée de l'Orangerie, Paris, 1933. No. 23, "La songeuse." Page 125n.
50. Moss Roses. 13¾" x 10½". Collection Paul Jamot, Paris. Renoir Exhibition, Musée de l'Orangerie, Paris, 1933, No. 25, "Roses mousseuses." Pages 68n, 437n.

NO.

51. Self-Portrait. 15" x 12¼". Collection Henry Bernstein, Paris. Renoir Exhibition, Musée de l'Orangerie, Paris, 1933, No. 24, "Portrait de l'artiste par lui-même." Page 392.

52. Torso. 32" x 26". Barnes Foundation No. 9. Pages 56n, 58-60, 58n, 60n, 61n, 62n, 63n, 64, 64n, 65, 72n, 82n, 113, 116n, 123n, 130n, 153, 178-179, 180, 193, 193n, 201n, 377n, 387, 402n. Illustration, page 243.

53. Woman in Blue. 7¾" x 5¾". Barnes Foundation No. 31. Page 60n.

Circa 1875-1876

54. Girl in Striped Dress. 24" x 19¾". Collection Paul Rosenberg, Paris. Renoir Exhibition, Musée de l'Orangerie, Paris, 1933, No. 36, "Femme à la robe rayée." Pages 58n, 61n, 66.

55. Madame Henriot as a Page. 63½" x 41". Collection Stephen C. Clark, New York. Renoir Exhibition, Musée de l'Orangerie, Paris, 1933, No. 27, "Madame Henriot en travesti." Page 392.

1876

56. Child with Watering Can. 39½" x 28¾". Dated. Private Collection, New York. Reproduced in "The Classical Period of Renoir," Knoedler & Company, New York, 1929, Plate II, "L'enfant à l'arrosoir." Pages 58n, 64, 68n.

57. Girl with Jumping Rope. 42½" x 28". Dated. Barnes Foundation No. 137. Pages 58n, 60n, 61n, 63n, 64n, 65, 72n, 87n, 115n, 181n, 182n, 193, 193n, 194n, 201n, 377n, 387. Illustration, page 244.

58. Mademoiselle Charpentier, Seated. 38½" x 28¾". Dated. Collection E. Tournon, Paris. Renoir Exhibition, Musée de l'Orangerie, Paris, 1933, No. 31, "Portrait de Mademoiselle Charpentier, assise." Pages 51n, 68n.

59. Mademoiselle Jeanne Durand-Ruel. 44" x 29½". Dated. Collection Madame André F. Aude, Paris. Renoir Exhibition, Musée de l'Orangerie, Paris, 1933, No. 28. Pages 56n, 58, 58n, 60n, 63n, 64, 64n, 66, 68n, 72n, 130n, 202, 202n, 210, 377n, 387, 393. Illustration, page 245.

NO.
60. **Mademoiselle Muller.** 21½" x 18½". Dated. Collection J. and G. Bernheim-Jeune, Paris. Renoir Exhibition, Musée de l'Orangerie, Paris, 1933. No. 30, "La chevelure." Pages 68n, 69.
61. **Moulin de la Galette.** 31" x 45¼". Dated. Collection John Hay Whitney, New York. Pages 58n, 63n, 66, 200n, 395, 404n.
62. **Moulin de la Galette.** 30¾" x 45". Dated. Louvre No. 495. Pages 52n, 58n, 61n, 63n, 66, 68n, 200n, 388, 394, 395, 404n, 422n, 436. Illustration, page 247.
63. **Swing.** 35¾" x 28". Dated. Louvre No. 494. "La balançoire." Pages 58n, 61n, 63n, 66, 68n, 201n, 395-396, 404n, 422n. Illustration, page 248.

Circa 1876

64. **At the Milliner's.** 13" x 9¾". Fogg Art Museum, Harvard University, Cambridge, Accession No. 1934.31. Pages 68n, 89n, 396. Illustration, page 249.
65. **Bouquet before Mirror.** 36½" x 28¼". Collection Baron Robert de Rothschild, Paris. Renoir Exhibition, Musée de l'Orangerie, Paris, 1933, No. 34, "Le bouquet devant la glace." Page 51n.
66. **Début.** 25½" x 19¾". National Gallery, Millbank, London, No. 3859. Page 201n.
67. **Girl Sewing Hat.** 25½" x 21¼". Collection Paul Rosenberg, Paris. "Jeune fille cousant un chapeau." Page 201n.
68. **Ingénue.** 22" x 18¼". Collection Jakob Goldschmidt, Berlin. Reproduced in "The Classical Period of Renoir," Knoedler & Company, New York, 1929, Plate IV. Page 201n.
69. **Madame Henriot.** 27¼" x 21¼". Collection Paul Rosenberg, Paris. Pages 58n, 60n, 63n, 64, 64n, 66-67, 68n, 201n, 202, 203, 396-397. Illustration, page 250.
70. **Madame Henriot in the Field.** 28¾" x 17". Collection Paul Rosenberg, Paris. "Madame Henriot dans les champs." Page 60n.

1877

NO.

71. **Head of Woman and Flowers.** 52″ x 23½″. (Painted on cement.) Dated. Collection Durand-Ruel, Paris and New York. "Tête de femme et fleurs." (Peinture sur ciment.) Page 68n.

72. **Jeanne Samary.** 18″ x 17¼″. Dated. Collection Comédie Française, Paris. Renoir Exhibition, Musée de l'Orangerie, Paris, 1933, No. 37. Pages 65n, 69, 89n, 90n, 398n. Illustration, page 251.

Circa 1877

73. **After the Concert.** 73½″ x 46¼″. Barnes Foundation No. 862. Pages 58n, 60n, 61n, 63n, 66, 87n, 182, 396n, 404, 404n, 405n. Illustration, page 252.

74. **In the Studio.** 18″ x 15″. Collection Madame Kröller, Amsterdam. "In het atelier." Pages 68n, 200n.

75. **Spring Landscape.** 15″ x 20¾″. Collection Durand-Ruel, Paris and New York. Renoir Exhibition, Musée de l'Orangerie, Paris, 1933, No. 38, "Paysage de printemps." Pages 68n, 100n, 398n.

76. **Woman Crocheting.** 16″ x 12¾″. Barnes Foundation No. 108. Pages 58n, 60n, 61n, 62n, 63n, 65, 68n, 87n, 113, 173, 180-181, 201n. Illustration, page 254.

77. **Woman with Veil.** 24″ x 20″. Louvre—Koechlin bequest. "Femme à la voilette, en profil perdu." Pages 68n, 398. Illustration, page 255.

Circa 1877-1878

78. **Madame Georges Charpentier.** 19″ x 15¾″. Louvre No. 500. Page 51n.

1878

79. **Madame Charpentier and her Children.** 60½″ x 74¾″. Dated. Metropolitan Museum of Art, New York, No. R 291-1. Pages 398-399, 412.

80. **Pourville.** 18″ x 21¾″. Dated. Barnes Foundation No. 6. Pages 65n, 69, 70-71, 75, 81, 82n, 124, 130n, 140n, 202, 401. Illustration, page 256.

Circa 1878

NO.
81. **Café Scene.** 15" x 13½". Collection O. Gerstenberg, Berlin. "Im Café." Pages 71-72, 74n, 186n, 200n, 404n, 405n. Illustration, page 253.
82. **Garden of the Artist.** 61" x 39¼". Collection Durand-Ruel, Paris and New York. Renoir Exhibition, Musée de l'Orangerie, Paris, 1933, No. 83, "Le jardin de l'artiste." Page 398n.
83. **Jeanne Samary.** 16" x 12½". Collection Comte Frédéric Pillet-Will, Paris. Exhibition "Le décor de la vie sous la III° République de 1870 à 1900," Pavillon de Marsan, Paris, 1933, No. 284. Page 399.
84. **Margot.** 39¼" x 32". Collection Durand-Ruel, Paris and New York. Renoir Exhibition, Musée de l'Orangerie, Paris, 1933, No. 39a, "La tasse de chocolat." Page 68n.
85. **Picking Flowers.** 20½" x 25¼". Art Institute, Chicago. (Coburn Collection.) Pages 68n, 100n, 398n. Illustration, page 257.

Circa 1878-1879

86. **Head of Margot.** 11¼" x 9½". Barnes Foundation No. 920. Pages 86n, 398n.
87. **Madame Murer.** 24" x 20". Barnes Foundation No. 712. Pages 65n, 68n, 398n, 405n.

1879

88. **After Luncheon.** 39½" x 32¼". Dated. Staedelsches Kunstinstitut, Frankfurt a.M., No. S.G. 176 "Frühstücksszene im Freien." Pages 74n, 75, 89n, 399-400, 401, 404. Illustration, page 258.
89. **At La Grenouillère.** 28" x 34½". Dated. Collection D. David-Weill, Paris. Renoir Exhibition, Musée de l'Orangerie, Paris, 1933, No. 44, "A La Grenouillère." Pages 74, 74n, 75n, 400.
90. **Bohemian.** 28¾" x 21¼". Dated. Collection Paul Rosenberg, Paris. Renoir Exhibition, Musée de l'Orangerie, Paris, 1933, No. 42, "La bûcheronne (La bohémienne)." Pages 74, 74n, 76, 203n. Illustration, page 259.

NO.

91. **Dreamer.** 19½" x 24". Dated. Collection M. Knoedler & Co., Inc., New York. Reproduced in "The Classical Period of Renoir," Knoedler & Company, New York, 1929, Plate VII, "La songeuse." Pages 74n, 186n, 404n.

92. **Marine: the Wave.** 25½" x 39". Dated. Art Institute, Chicago, No. 845. (Palmer Collection). Pages 74n, 75n.

93. **Mussel Fishers at Berneval.** 69" x 51¼". Dated. Collection Durand-Ruel, Paris and New York. Renoir Exhibition, Musée de l'Orangerie, Paris, 1933, No. 46, "Pêcheuses de moules à Berneval." Pages 74, 74n, 116n, 404n. Illustration, page 260.

94. **Rose Tree at Wargemont.** 25¼" x 31½". Dated. Collection Baron Robert de Rothschild, Paris. Renoir Exhibition, Musée de l'Orangerie, Paris, 1933, No. 43, "Les rosiers à Wargemont." Pages 74, 74n, 75n.

95. **Wargemont.** 32" x 39¼". Dated. Collection Madame Halvorsen, Oslo, Norway. Renoir Exhibition. Musée de l'Orangerie, Paris, 1933, No. 48, "Paysage à Wargemont." Pages 74n, 75n.

Circa 1879

96. **Fête of Pan.** 23½" x 28¼". Collection Madame Alfred Bérard, Paris. Renoir Exhibition, Musée de l'Orangerie, Paris, 1933, No. 51, "La fête de Pan." Pages 74n, 75n, 203n.

Late 1870's

97. **At the Piano.** 36½" x 29". Collection Mrs. Martin A. Ryerson, Chicago. Page 401. Illustration, page 261.

98. **Roses in Blue Vase.** 21¾" x 18¼". Barnes Foundation No. 538. Page 437n.

99. **Two Little Circus Girls.** 51" x 38½". Art Institute, Chicago, No. 847. (Palmer Collection.) Pages 71, 72-74, 89n, 188n. Illustration, page 262.

1880

100. **At the Concert.** 39½" x 31½". Dated. Private Collection. Paris. Renoir Exhibition, Musée de l'Orangerie, Paris, 1933, No. 53, "Au concert (Dans la loge)." Pages 77n, 78n, 79n, 414n.

NO.

101. Girl with Falcon. 49½″ x 30¾″. Dated. Collection Durand-Ruel, Paris and New York. Renoir Exhibition, Musée de l'Orangerie, Paris, 1933, No. 52, "La fillette au faucon." Pages 77n, 78n, 79n, 80n, 104n, 132n, 204, 401. Illustration, page 263.

102. Mademoiselle Grimpel with Blue Ribbon. 17¾″ x 13¾″. Dated. Collection H.-J. Laroche, Paris. Renoir Exhibition, Musée de l'Orangerie, Paris, 1933, No. 55, "Portrait de Mademoiselle Grimpel au ruban bleu." Pages 77n, 78n, 79n, 104n, 401-402, 414n.

103. Mademoiselle Grimpel with Red Ribbon. 17¾″ x 13¾″. Dated. Collection H.-J. Laroche, Paris. Renoir Exhibition, Musée de l'Orangerie, Paris, 1933, No. 54, "Portrait de Mademoiselle Grimpel au ruban rouge." Pages 77n, 78n, 79n, 104n, 401-402, 414n.

104. Mademoiselle Irène Cahen d'Anvers. 25¼″ x 21¼″. Dated. Collection Léon Reinach, Paris. Renoir Exhibition, Musée de l'Orangerie, Paris, 1933, No. 57. Pages 77n, 78n, 402. Illustration, page 264.

105. Paul Cézanne. 21¼″ x 17″. (Pastel). Dated. Art Institute, Chicago, Accession No. 27.1601. Pages 88n, 89n.

106. Sleeping Girl with Cat. 47¼″ x 35½″. Dated. Private Collection, Paris. Reproduced in "Ausstellung Auguste Renoir, 41 Werke aus den Jahren 1873-1910," Thannhauser Moderne Galerie, Munich, No. 7, "La femme au chat." Page 76n.

Circa 1880

107. Bather, Back Turned. 19″ x 15″. Collection M. Knoedler & Co., Inc., New York. Pages 77n, 79n, 80n, 402. Illustration, page 265.

108. Naiad. 10½″ x 8½″. Collection Durand-Ruel, Paris and New York. Exhibition "Quelques œuvres importantes de Corot à van Gogh," Galeries Durand-Ruel, Paris, 1934, No. 37, "Naïade." Pages 77n, 79n, 80n, 403, 407n, 409n.

109. Nude. 17¾″ x 13¾″. Collection H.-J. Laroche, Paris. Renoir Exhibition, Musée de l'Orangerie, Paris, 1933, No. 60, "Nu." Pages 77n, 79n.

110. Nude. 31½″ x 25½″. Musée Rodin, Paris. "Femme nue." Pages 77n, 82n, 90, 211, 403, 406n.

Circa 1880-1881

NO.

111. Experimental Garden at Algiers. 21¼″ x 25½″. Private Collection, Paris. Reproduced in catalogue of sale of Jules Strauss Collection, Galeries Georges Petit, Paris, December 15, 1932, No. 77, "Le jardin d'essai à Alger." Pages 77n, 82n.

1881

112. Capodimonte-Sorrento 21¼″ x 25½″. Dated. Collection Durand-Ruel, Paris and New York. Renoir Exhibition, Musée de l'Orangerie, Paris, 1933, No. 64. Pages 77n, 78n, 81, 81n, 82n, 100n, 130n. Illustration, page 266.

113. Chestnut Tree in Bloom. 28″ x 35″. Dated. National-Galerie, Berlin, No. 1007. "Blühender Kastanienbaum." Pages 77n, 81, 81n, 82, 82n, 100n, 403-404. Illustration, page 267.

114. Flowerpiece. 21¾″ x 18¼″. Dated. Kunsthalle, Hamburg, No. 2355. "Blumenstück." Pages 77n, 79n, 80n, 437n.

115. Fruit of the Midi. 20″ x 27″. Dated. Art Institute, Chicago, No. 2155. (Ryerson Collection.) Pages 77n, 79n, 88, 132n

116. Luncheon of the Boatmen. 50½″ x 68″. Dated. Phillips Memorial Collection, Washington, D. C. Pages 76n, 404-405.

117. Mesdemoiselles Cahen d'Anvers. 46¾″ x 29″. Dated. Collection J. and G. Bernheim-Jeune, Paris. Exhibition "Le décor de la vie sous la 111ᵉ République de 1870 à 1900," Pavillon de Marsan, Paris, 1933, No. 285. Pages 51n, 77n, 79n, 405. Illustration, page 268.

118. Mother and Child. 47½″ x 33½″. Dated. Barnes Foundation No. 15. Pages 74n, 77n, 78n, 79n, 80n, 82n, 86n, 89, 181n, 188n, 197n, 210n, 405n, 409, 411. Illustration, page 269.

119. On the Terrace. 39½″ x 31½″. Dated. Art Institute, Chicago. (Coburn Collection.) Pages 77n, 78n, 79n, 83, 84n, 86n, 405-406. Illustration, page 270.

120. Railroad Bridge at Chatou. 21¼″ x 25½″. Dated. Louvre. "Le pont du chemin de fer à Chatou." Pages 77n, 81n, 82n, 100n.

NO.
121. **Venice.** 21¼" x 25½". Dated. Collection Durand-Ruel, Paris and New York. "Venise." Pages 77n, 81, 81n, 100n.
122. **Vesuvius.** 22¾" x 31½". Dated. Collection Durand-Ruel, Paris and New York. "Le Vésuve." Pages 77n, 79n, 80n, 81n.

Circa 1881

123. **Algerian Woman.** 21½" x 18". Collection Durand-Ruel, Paris and New York. Renoir Exhibition, Musée de l'Orangerie, Paris, 1933, No. 66, "L'Algérienne." Pages 51n, 77n, 79n, 80n.
124. **Boating at Bougival.** 21¼" x 25¾". Barnes Foundation No. 210. Pages 77n, 81, 81n, 82, 82n, 101n. Illustration, page 272.
125. **Gondola on the Grand Canal.** 20¾" x 25¼". Private Collection, Amsterdam. "Gondel op het Groote Kanaal." Renoir Exhibition, Musée de l'Orangerie, Paris, 1933, No. 65, "Venise. Gondole sur le Grand Canal." Pages 77n, 79n, 81, 81n, 157, 383n.
126. **St. Mark's Church.** 24¾" x 32¼". Staatsgalerie, Munich. "Die Markuskirche." Pages 77n, 79n.

1882

127. **Ali.** 20½" x 11". Dated. Collection Durand-Ruel, Paris and New York. "Jeune garçon arabe." Pages 77n, 79n, 80n.
128. **Madame Lériaux.** 21¼" x 18". Dated. Kunsthalle, Hamburg, No. 2354. Pages 77n, 79n, 80n.
129. **Young Girl with Bonnet.** 16½" x 12¼". (Pastel). Collection A. L. Tietz, Cologne. "Mädchen mit Käpchen." Reproduced in "Exposition d'art français: peinture du XIXme & XXme siècle," E. J. van Wisselingh & Co., Amsterdam, 1933, No. 33, "La jeune fille au bonnet." Page 89n.

Circa 1882

130. **Beach Scene, Guernsey.** 21¼" x 25½". Barnes Foundation No. 10. Pages 77n, 78n, 79n, 81n, 82n, 83, 84n, 86n, 101n, 141-142, 158. Illustration, page 273.

NO.
131. **Blond Bather.** 31½" x 24¾". Collection Alfred Gold, Paris. Renoir Exhibition, Musée de l'Orangerie, Paris, 1933, No. 67, "La baigneuse blonde." Pages 72n, 77n, 83, 204n, 211, 406-407. Illustration, page 275.

1883

132. **Apples in Dish.** 21¼" x 25¾". Dated. Fogg Art Museum, Harvard University, Cambridge, Accession No. 1934.29. (Coburn bequest.) Page 88.

133. **By the Seashore.** 36¼" x 28½". Dated. Metropolitan Museum of Art, New York, No. R 291-2. (H. O. Havemeyer Collection.) Pages 77n, 78n, 97n, 407. Illustration, page 274.

134. **Child in White.** 23½" x 19". Dated. Art Institute, Chicago, No. 2153. (Ryerson Collection.) Pages 77n, 78n. Illustration, page 271.

135. **Dance in the City.** 71" x 35½". Dated. Collection Durand-Ruel, Paris and New York. Renoir Exhibition, Musée de l'Orangerie, Paris, 1933, No. 69, "La danse à la ville." Pages 72n, 77n, 78n, 83n, 84-86, 87, 87n, 89n, 92, 204, 408. Illustration, page 276.

136. **Dance in the Country.** 71" x 35½". Dated. Collection Durand-Ruel, Paris and New York. Renoir Exhibition, Musée de l'Orangerie, Paris, 1933, No. 68, "La danse à la campagne." Pages 72n, 77n, 78n, 84-86, 87, 87n, 89n, 90n, 92, 204, 405n, 408. Illustration, page 277.

137. **Girl with Parasol.** 51¼" x 31½". Dated. Barnes Foundation No. 189. Pages 77n, 84-86, 87, 89n, 90, 94n, 112n, 125n, 403n, 405n, 407n. Illustration, page 278.

138. **Madame Caillebotte with Dog.** 36¼" x 28¾". Dated. Collection Wildenstein & Co., Paris and New York. "Madame Caillebotte avec chien." Pages 77n, 79n.

139. **Madame Clapisson** (Woman with Fan). 31¾" x 25½". Dated. Art Institute, Chicago, No. 2157. (Ryerson Collection. Pages 77n, 78n.

140. **Near Mentone.** 27¼" x 33½". Dated. Collection John T. Spaulding, Boston. Page 82n.

141. **Sailor Boy.** 51¼" x 31½. Dated. Barnes Foundation No. 325. Pages 72n, 77n, 83n, 84-86, 87, 89n, 90, 110, 403n, 405n, 407n, 410, 412, 422n. Illustration, page 279.

Circa 1883-1885

NO.
142. Bather in Rocky Landscape. $46\frac{3}{4}'' \times 36\frac{1}{2}''$. Collection Jacques Balsan, Paris. Renoir Exhibition, Musée de l'Orangerie, Paris, 1933, No. 78, "Baigneuse." Pages 204n, 403n, 408-409. Illustration, page 280.

1884

143. Bust of Girl. $25\frac{1}{4}'' \times 20\frac{1}{2}''$. Dated. Collection Henry Bernstein, Paris. Renoir Exhibition, Musée de l'Orangerie, Paris, 1933, No. 74, "Buste de jeune fille." Page 78n.
144. Children at Wargemont. $50'' \times 68''$. Dated. National Galerie, Berlin, No. 1008. "Der Nachmittag der Kinder in Vargemont." Pages 88n, 91-92, 97n, 104, 204, 204n, 405n, 409-412, 419. Illustration, page 282.
145. Girl in Field. $31\frac{1}{2}'' \times 25\frac{1}{4}''$. Dated. Collection Josse Hessel, Paris. Renoir Exhibition, Musée de l'Orangerie, Paris, 1933, No. 73, "L'été." Pages 88n, 89n, 90, 403n, 411n.
146. Madame Renoir at the Gate. $32'' \times 26''$. Dated. Collection Mrs. Ralph Booth, Detroit. Page 88n.

Circa 1884

147. Grape Gatherers Resting. $21\frac{1}{4}'' \times 25\frac{1}{2}''$. Barnes Foundation No. 937. Pages 88n, 89n, 90-91, 123n, 188n, 198n, 210n, 411n, 422n. Illustration, page 283.
148. Madame Renoir. $25\frac{1}{2}'' \times 20\frac{1}{4}''$. Pennsylvania Museum of Art, Philadelphia. Pages 88n, 403n, 412.
149. Mademoiselle Bérard. $13\frac{3}{4}'' \times 10\frac{1}{2}''$. Collection Paul Rosenberg, Paris. Renoir Exhibition, Musée de l'Orangerie, Paris, 1933, No. 76. Page 413.
150. Summer. $26\frac{1}{4}'' \times 22\frac{1}{4}''$. Barnes Foundation No. 933. Pages 88n, 89n, 90n, 91, 123n, 411n. Illustration, page 281.
151. Three Pears. $9'' \times 12\frac{1}{4}''$. Barnes Foundation No. 49. Pages 88n, 91.

1885

152. Bather Arranging Hair. $36\frac{1}{4}'' \times 28\frac{3}{4}''$. Dated. Collection Durand-Ruel, Paris and New York. "Baigneuse." Pages 93n, 204n, 413.

NO.

153. **In the Garden.** $67\frac{1}{4}'' \times 44\frac{1}{2}''$. Dated. Collection O. Gerstenberg, Berlin. "Das Paar im Garten." Page 94n.

154. **Mademoiselle Chapuis with Hoop.** $49\frac{1}{4}'' \times 29\frac{1}{2}''$. Dated. Private Collection, New York. Reproduced in catalogue of sale of "Collections de Messieurs S..... et S.....," Galeries Georges Petit, Paris, 1932, No. 29, "La fillette au cerceau." Page 94n.

155. **Mother Nursing Baby.** $31\frac{3}{4}'' \times 25\frac{1}{2}''$. Dated. Collection Philippe Gangnat, Paris. "Jeune femme allaitant son bébé." Pages 93n, 94, 95, 435n.

Circa 1885

156. **Anemones.** $16'' \times 13''$. Barnes Foundation No. 532. Page 437n. Illustration, page 284.

157. **Redheaded Girl in Yellow Hat.** $21\frac{1}{2}'' \times 18''$. Collection Mr. and Mrs. Edwin Chester Vogel, New York. Pages 93n, 98n.

158. **Woman in Blue, with Bonnet.** $11\frac{1}{4}'' \times 9\frac{1}{4}''$. Barnes Foundation No. 1060. Page 427n.

1886

159. **Mother, Child and Cat.** $28\frac{3}{4}'' \times 21\frac{1}{4}''$. Dated. Private Collection, New Orleans, La. Pages 93n, 435n.

160. **Woman with Fan.** $22'' \times 18''$. Dated. Barnes Foundation No. 938. Pages 83n, 93n, 94-95, 95n, 96, 97, 98n, 124n, 183n, 211n. Illustration, page 285.

Circa 1886

161. **Garden Scene.** $21\frac{1}{4}'' \times 25\frac{3}{4}''$. Barnes Foundation No. 161. Pages 93n, 94-95, 95n, 98n, 204, 410n. Illustration, page 286.

162. **Mother and Baby.** $32'' \times 25\frac{1}{2}''$. Collection Chester Beatty, London. Renoir Exhibition, Musée de l'Orangerie, Paris, 1933, No. 80, "La mère et l'enfant." Pages 93n, 94-95, 95n, 413, 435n. Illustration, page 287

163. **Washerwoman and Baby.** $32'' \times 25\frac{3}{4}''$. Barnes Foundation No. 219. Pages 84n, 93n, 94-95, 95n, 98n, 124n, 188n, 204, 210n, 211n, 410n. Illustration, page 288.

1887

NO.
164. Bathers. 45¼" x 67". Dated. Collection Carroll S. Tyson, Jr., Chestnut Hill, Philadelphia. Pages 84n, 85n, 93, 93n, 94, 95, 96-98, 111, 124n, 130n, 158, 204n, 205n, 206, 207, 211, 406n, 410n, 414, 421, 427n, 433n. Illustration, page 290.

Circa 1887

165. Girl Plaiting Hair. 22" x 18½". Collection Sydney W. Brown, Baden, Switzerland. Renoir Exhibition, Musée de l'Orangerie, Paris, 1933, No. 84, "La natte." Pages 72n, 93, 93n, 94, 96, 97, 98, 414. Illustration, page 289.

1888

166. Bougival. 21¼" x 26". Dated. Collection Durand-Ruel, Paris and New York. Renoir Exhibition, Musée de l'Orangerie, Paris, 1933, No. 87. Pages 53n, 99n, 100n, 103, 111n, 415. Illustration, page 292.

167. Daughters of Catulle Mendès. 64¼" x 51¼". Dated. Collection Wildenstein & Co., Paris and New York. Renoir Exhibition, Musée de l'Orangerie, Paris, 1933, No. 85, "Les filles de Catulle Mendès au piano." Pages 103, 414.

168. Girl with Sheaf of Grain. 25½" x 21¼". Dated. Collection Dr. Max Meirowsky, Berlin. "Das Mädchen mit den Garben." Page 99n.

169. Landscape with Harvester. 25½" x 31¾". Dated. Barnes Foundation No. 240. Pages 101, 101n, 103. Illustration, page 293.

170. Red Boat, Argenteuil. 21¼" x 25½". Dated. Barnes Foundation No. 126. Pages 99n, 100n, 103, 111n, 129, 415. Illustration, page 294.

171. Sunset on the Seine at Argenteuil. 21¼" x 25½". Dated. Collection Durand-Ruel, Paris and New York. Renoir Exhibition, Musée de l'Orangerie, Paris, 1933, No. 86, "La Seine à Argenteuil." Pages 99n, 415.

Circa 1888

172. Argenteuil Bridge. 21¼" x 25½". Marie Harriman Gallery, New York. Pages 99n, 415.

NO.

173. Head of Girl. 16¼" x 12½". Barnes Foundation No. 1000. Pages 72n, 104-105, 107, 410.

174. Varangeville. 21¼" x 25½". Collection Alex. Reid & Lefèvre Ltd., London. Exhibition of Vollard Collection, Knoedler Galleries, New York, 1933, No. 28. Pages 102n, 415-416.

1889

175. Mt. Ste. Victoire. 21½" x 25¾". Dated. Barnes Foundation No. 288. Pages 80n, 101, 101n, 102, 103, 109, 111n, 158, 420. Illustration, page 295.

Circa 1889

176. Girl in Gray-Blue. 26" x 20½". Barnes Foundation No. 222. Pages 105, 106n, 115n.

177. Girl with Basket of Fish. 51¼" x 16". Barnes Foundation No. 53. Page 107n. Illustration, page 296.

178. Girl with Basket of Oranges. 51¼" x 16". Barnes Foundation No. 65. Pages 107n, 198n. Illustration, page 296.

179. Girl with Marguerites. 25½" x 21¼". Collection J. and G. Bernheim-Jeune, Paris. Renoir Exhibition, Musée de l'Orangerie, Paris, 1933, No. 88, "La jeune fille aux marguerites." Pages 85n, 107n.

180. Pitcher of Flowers. 16" x 13". Barnes Foundation No. 156. Page 437n.

Late 1880's

181. Bather. 23½" x 21¼". Nasjonalgalleriet, Oslo, No. 1166. Baderinde." Pages 72n, 85n, 104. Illustration, page 298.

182. Nude Wading. 16¼" x 13¼". Barnes Foundation No. 228. Page 107n.

Early 1890's

183. Brunette. 16¼" x 12½". Collection N. and M. Mullen, Philadelphia. Pages 105n, 106n.

184. Child Reading. 12¾" x 16¼". Barnes Foundation No. 51. Pages 105n, 106n, 107, 425n.

185. Flower in Hat. 25½" x 21¼". Art Institute, Chicago, No. 2156. (Ryerson Collection.) Page 396n.

NO.

186. Girl Reading. 21¾" x 18¼". Staedelsches Kunstinstitut, Frankfurt a.M., No. S. G. 177 "Lesendes Mädchen." Pages 105n, 107, 396n, 416-417. Illustration, page 298.

187. Girls' Heads. 16" x 12½". Barnes Foundation No. 474. Page 106n.

188. Girl with Basket of Flowers. 32" x 25½". Barnes Foundation No. 944. Pages 195n, 198n, 206, 419n, 428. Illustration, page 297.

189. Girl with Glove. 21¾" x 18¼". Barnes Foundation No. 167. Pages 105n, 106n, 107, 108, 129, 417. Illustration, page 299.

190. Girl with Pink Bonnet. 16¼" x 13". Barnes Foundation No. 118. Pages 105n, 106n.

191. Girl with Yellow Cape. 21¾" x 18½". Barnes Foundation No. 120. Page 425n.

192. Nude Seated on Rock. 25½" x 21¼". Barnes Foundation No. 274. Pages 207, 207n, 407n.

193. Two Girls with Hats. 16" x 12¾". Barnes Foundation No. 130. Page 396n.

1890

194. Green Trees. 10¾" x 14½". Dated. Barnes Foundation No. 542. Page 97n.

Circa 1890

195. Girl Reading. 24½" x 21¼". Collection Dr. Georges Viau, Paris. Renoir Exhibition, Musée de l'Orangerie, Paris, 1933, No. 93a, "Jeune fille lisant." Page 85n.

196. Girl with Straw Hat. 18" x 15". Collection Wildenstein & Co., Paris and New York. Renoir Exhibition, Musée de l'Orangerie, Paris, 1933, No. 89, "Fillette au chapeau de paille." Pages 104-105, 417. Illustration, page 299.

197. Pasture along the Seine. 21" x 25½". Collection Alex. Reid & Lefèvre Ltd., London. Exhibition of Vollard Collection, Knoedler Galleries, New York, 1933, No. 29, "Pâturage au bord de la Seine." Pages 89n, 102n, 417-418. Illustration, page 300.

Circa 1890-1891

198. Apple Vender. 25½" x 21¼". Barnes Foundation No. 8. Pages 101n, 103, 395n, 418. Illustration, page 302.

1892

NO.

199. **Bather.** 32" x 25½". Dated. Collection Durand-Ruel, Paris and New York. Renoir Exhibition, Musée de l'Orangerie, Paris, 1933, No. 94, "Baigneuse." Pages 418, 424.

200. **Madame Renoir in Dressing Gown.** 9" x 7". Dated. Collection N. and M. Mullen, Philadelphia. Page 425n.

201. **Noirmoutier.** 25¾" x 32". Dated. Barnes Foundation No. 163. Pages 28, 101n, 103, 112n, 113, 122, 140n, 418, 433n. Illustration, page 301.

Circa 1892

202. **Girl in Profile.** 16½" x 12¾". Barnes Foundation No. 302. Pages 105n, 106, 106n, 108, 116, 206, 213, 421, 425n. Illustration, page 306.

203. **Girls at Piano.** 45¾" x 35". Louvre No. 492. "Jeunes filles au piano." Pages 80n, 105n, 106n, 107, 108, 116n, 206, 418-420. Illustration, page 303.

204. **Near Pont-Aven.** 21¼" x 25½". Collection Alex. Reid & Lefèvre Ltd., London. Exhibition of Vollard Collection, Knoedler Galleries, New York, 1933, No. 31, "Environs de Pont-Aven." Pages 102n, 420-421. Illustration, page 304.

205. **Piano Lesson.** 44" x 31". Estate of Paul Guillaume, Paris. Renoir Exhibition, Musée de l'Orangerie, Paris, 1933, No. 96, "Jeunes filles au piano." Pages 105n, 206.

206. **Pont-Aven.** 18" x 21¾". Barnes Foundation No. 242. Pages 53n, 102n, 103. Illustration, page 305.

207. **Two Girls Reading.** 18¼" x 22". Barnes Foundation No. 107. Pages 105n, 106n, 107, 108, 396n, 425n.

208. **View from Montmartre.** 13" x 16¼". Barnes Foundation No. 144. Pages 102n, 123n.

Circa 1893

209. **Cagnes Landscape with Three Figures.** 25½" x 32". Collection Alphonse Bellier, Paris. Renoir Exhibition, Musée de l'Orangerie, Paris, 1933, No. 100, "Paysage de Cagnes aves trois personnages." Page 102n.

210. **Head of Girl with Hat.** 16¼" x 12¾". Barnes Foundation No. 299. Pages 105n, 106n, 107, 116, 116n, 183n, 186, 206, 417, 421, 425n, 428. Illustration, page 306.

NO.
211. **Picnic.** 21¼" x 25¾". Barnes Foundation No. 567. Pages 53n, 89n, 102n, 103, 394n, 422. Illustration, page 308.

Circa 1894

212. **Village of Essoyes.** 21" x 26". Collection Alex. Reid & Lefèvre Ltd., London. Exhibition of Vollard Collection, Knoedler Galleries, New York, 1933, No. 33, "Le village d'Essoyes." Page 422. Illustration, page 309.

1895

213. **Nude in Brook.** 32" x 25½". Dated. Barnes Foundation No. 301. Pages 108-109, 110n, 116n, 123n, 124, 158, 183n, 184, 207, 422-423. Illustration, page 310.

1896

214. **Artist's Family.** 68" x 54". Dated. Barnes Foundation No. 819. Pages 86n, 108, 109-110, 140n, 158, 190n, 423. Illustration, page 311.

Circa 1896

215. **Woman Gardening.** 17¼" x 21". Barnes Foundation No. 884. Page 395n.

Circa 1897

216. **Bathers in Forest.** 29" x 39¼". Barnes Foundation No. 901. Pages 80n, 86n, 89n, 105, 106, 107, 108, 110-111, 115, 158, 160, 172, 172n, 183n, 202n, 207, 207n, 208, 212n, 394n, 433n. Illustration, page 312.
217. **Reclining Nude.** 25¾" x 61¼". Barnes Foundation No. 903. Pages 183n, 207, 207n, 208, 210n, 211, 211n. Illustration, page 307.

Late 1890's

218. **Bather and Maid.** 57" x 37½". Collection J. and G. Bernheim-Jeune, Paris. Renoir Exhibition, Musée de l'Orangerie, Paris, 1933, No. 104. "La toilette de la baigneuse." Pages 423-424. Illustration, page 314.

CATALOGUE DATA 463

Early 1900's

NO.

219. Cagnes. 10¾″ x 17½″. Barnes Foundation No. 19. Page 122n. Illustration, page 316.

220. Houses at Cagnes. 10½″ x 11½″. Barnes Foundation No. 146. Pages 122n, 123n.

221. Strawberries and Almonds. 7″ x 12¾″. Barnes Foundation No. 99. Page 127n.

222. View of Cagnes. 12½″ x 18″. Barnes Foundation No. 859. Pages 89n, 122n, 123n.

223. Woman and Child in Field. 18″ x 21¾″. Barnes Foundation No. 111. Page 116n.

Circa 1900

224. Seated Bather Reading. 8½″ x 12¼″. Collection Dr. Georges Viau, Paris. Renoir Exhibition, Musée de l'Orangerie, Paris, 1933, No. 103, "Baigneuse assise lisant." Page 424.

Circa 1902

225. Le Cannet. 15¼″ x 21″. Barnes Foundation No. 245. Pages 54n, 121. Illustration, page 317.

226. Nude, Green Background. 36¼″ x 28¾″. Barnes Foundation No. 28. Pages 423, 424-425. Illustration, page 315.

Circa 1902-1903

227. Bather with Legs Crossed. 45¾″ x 34½″. Collection Josse Hessel, Paris. Renoir Exhibition, Musée de l'Orangerie, Paris, 1933, No. 108, "La grande baigneuse aux jambes croisées." Pages 183n, 184.

228. Woman and Children in Landscape. 10½″ x 14½″. Barnes Foundation No. 543. Page 208n.

Circa 1903

229. Coco. 9¾″ x 7½″. Barnes Foundation No. 70. Pages 117n, 118n, 119, 120n, 425n. Illustration, page 319.

1904

NO.
230. **Jacques Fray, as a Child.** $16\frac{1}{2}'' \times 13''$. Dated. Collection Madame Val, Paris. Renoir Exhibition, Musée de l'Orangerie, Paris, 1933, No. 110, "Enfant écrivant." Page 425. Illustration, page 318.

Circa 1904

231. **Baby's Breakfast.** $25\frac{3}{4}'' \times 21\frac{1}{4}''$. Barnes Foundation No. 132. Pages 425-426, 425n. Illustration, page 320.
232. **Claude in Arab Shirt.** $21\frac{1}{2}'' \times 18\frac{1}{4}''$. Barnes Foundation No. 935. Pages 175, 426. Illustration, page 319.
233. **Embroiderers.** $39\frac{1}{2}'' \times 32''$. Barnes Foundation No. 239. Pages 118n, 119, 119n, 120, 120n, 197. Illustration, page 321.

Circa 1905

234. **Writing Lesson.** $21\frac{1}{2}'' \times 25\frac{3}{4}''$. Barnes Foundation No. 150. Pages 80n, 118n, 119, 120n, 195n, 196n, 208n, 213, 396n, 427. Illustration, page 322.

Circa 1906

235. **Missia.** $36\frac{1}{4}'' \times 29''$. Barnes Foundation No. 565. Pages 117n, 118n, 119, 119n, 120, 120n, 123, 174n, 183n, 184, 187n, 427-428. Illustration, page 324.
236. **Promenade.** $64\frac{3}{4}'' \times 50\frac{3}{4}''$. Barnes Foundation No. 571. Pages 58n, 115, 116, 117n, 142, 190n, 193n, 379n, 423. Illustration, page 326.
237. **Two Figures in Lane.** $10\frac{1}{4}'' \times 9''$. Barnes Foundation No. 62. Page 54n.
238. **Woman Reading.** $21\frac{1}{2}'' \times 18''$. Barnes Foundation No. 169. Pages 117n, 174n, 183n, 396n.

Circa 1907

239. **Flowers in Green Vase.** $13\frac{1}{2}'' \times 12''$. Barnes Foundation No. 531. Page 437n.

1908

NO.

240. Judgment of Paris. 32″ x 39¾″. Dated. Collection Madame Halvorsen, Oslo, Norway, "Döm af Pâris." Renoir Exhibition, Musée de l'Orangerie, Paris, 1933, No. 114, "Jugement de Pâris." Pages 123n, 125n, 126, 189n, 190, 208n. Illustration, page 323.

Circa 1908

241. Fruit on White Cloth. 6½″ x 16¼″. Collection N. and M. Mullen, Philadelphia. Page 127n.

Circa 1909

242. Apple and Pear. 6¾″ x 10″. Barnes Foundation No. 243. Page 127n.

243. Bather Drying Herself. 36¼″ x 29″. Barnes Foundation No. 68. Pages 123n, 125n, 127, 183n, 184, 187n, 428. Illustration, page 325.

244. Bust of Nude. 19″ x 22″. Barnes Foundation No. 157. Pages 123n, 124n, 125n, 126, 183n, 184, 185n. Illustration, page 336.

245. Gabrielle Arising. 24¾″ x 20¾″. Barnes Foundation No. 232. Page 124n. Illustration, page 327.

246. Glade. 8″ x 13″. Barnes Foundation No. 26. Page 388n.

1910

247. After the Bath. 37½″ x 29¾″. Dated. Barnes Foundation No. 142. Pages 123n, 124n, 125n, 126, 168n, 195n, 198n. Illustration, page 328.

Circa 1910

248. Caryatids. 51¼″ x 17¾″. Barnes Foundation No. 918. Pages 124n, 183n, 184, 208n, 210n, 428-429. Illustration, page 330.

249. Caryatids. 51¼″ x 17¾″. Barnes Foundation No. 919. Pages 124n, 183n, 184, 208n, 210n, 428-429. Illustration, page 330.

250. Fruit. 9″ x 15¾″. Barnes Foundation No. 27. Pages 127n, 128.

251. Heads of Two Girls. 21½″ x 18½″ Barnes Foundation No. 233. Page 396n. Illustration, page 332.

NO.
252. **Reclining Nude.** 26½" x 61". Barnes Foundation No. 97.
Pages 123n, 125n, 127, 145n, 168n, 183n. Illustration,
page 334.

253. **Self-Portrait.** 16½" x 13". Collection Durand-Ruel, Paris
and New York. Renoir Exhibition, Musée de l'Orangerie,
Paris, 1933, No. 120, "Portrait de l'artiste, au chapeau
blanc." Illustration, frontispiece.

254. **Two Pomegranates.** 8" x 14¾". Barnes Foundation No.
29. Page 127n.

255. **Woman and Child under Tree.** 21¼" x 25½". Barnes
Foundation No. 257. Page 122. Illustration, page 337.

256. **Woman Sewing.** 25½" x 21¼". Barnes Foundation No.
900. Pages 118n, 119, 193n. Illustration, page 333.

1911

257. **Tea Time.** 36¼" x 29". Dated. Barnes Foundation No.
478. Pages 127n, 129, 195n, 197. Illustration, page 338.

Circa 1911

258. **Girl on Balcony at Cagnes.** 17" x 20½". Barnes Foundation No. 98. Pages 195n, 407n.

259. **Nude, Back View.** 32" x 25¾". Barnes Foundation No.
284. Pages 123n, 124, 125n, 126. Illustration, page 339.

260. **Psyche.** 25¾" x 32". Barnes Foundation No. 217. Pages
123n, 125n, 126. Illustration, page 342.

261. **Woman with Black Hair.** 19¼" x 16¾". Barnes Foundation No. 1. Page 132. Illustration, page 344.

Circa 1911-1912

262. **Apples.** 8" x 16¼". Barnes Foundation No. 17. Pages
127n, 128. Illustration, page 340.

Circa 1912

263. **Cup of Chocolate.** 21½" x 25½". Barnes Foundation No.
14. Pages 129, 145n, 190n, 195n, 429-430. Illustration,
page 343.

Circa 1913

264. **Bananas and Oranges.** 8" x 11". Barnes Foundation No.
2. Page 127n.

NO.
265. **Fruit and Cup.** 9″ x 14″. Barnes Foundation No. 61. Pages 127n, 128.

Circa 1914

266. **At the Café.** 22¾″ x 19¼″. Barnes Foundation No. 40. Page 127n. Illustration, page 345.
267. **Girl at Gate.** 20″ x 25¼″. Barnes Foundation No. 255. Page 122. Illustration, page 346.
268. **Girl in Landscape.** 13½″ x 10½″. Barnes Foundation No. 11. Pages 132, 407n.

Circa 1915-1917

269. **Antibes.** 10¾″ x 16″. Barnes Foundation No. 4. Pages 117n, 131-132. Illustration, page 348.
270. **Fruit and Bonbonnière.** 9½″ x 12½″. Barnes Foundation No. 39. Pages 132, 175n. Illustration, page 347.
271. **Garden of the Post-Office at Cagnes.** 9¼″ x 15½″. Barnes Foundation No. 106. Pages 122n, 123n.
272. **Girl with Yellow Hat.** 16″ x 14¼″. Collection N. and M. Mullen, Philadelphia. Page 208n. Illustration, page 354.
273. **In the Orchard.** 18½″ x 21″. Collection N. and M. Mullen, Philadelphia. Page 137n.
274. **Landscape with Two Women.** 14″ x 11″. Barnes Foundation No. 535. Page 136n.
275. **Landscape with Woman and Dog.** 18″ x 20″. Barnes Foundation No. 541. Pages 135n, 136n, 137n, 138-139. Illustration, page 350.
276. **Madame Jean Renoir.** 13″ x 16¼″. Barnes Foundation No. 159. Page 208n.
277. **Pomegranate and Figs.** 9″ x 15¾″. Barnes Foundation No. 24. Page 175n. Illustration, page 341.
278. **Reapers.** 13¾″ x 12½″. Barnes Foundation No. 896. Page 141. Illustration, page 351.
279. **Seated Nude.** 16″ x 13″. Barnes Foundation No. 16. Pages 142n, 143, 188n, 198n, 431. Illustration, page 352.
280. **Seated Odalisque.** 20½″ x 18½″. Barnes Foundation No. 237. Pages 142n, 431. Illustration, page 353.
281. **Trees.** 16″ x 12″. Barnes Foundation No. 215. Page 388n.
282. **Two Girls among Bushes.** 17½″ x 21¼″. Barnes Foundation No. 818. Page 136n.

NO.

283. **Woman at Rest in Landscape.** 12″ x 8¾″. Barnes Foundation No. 220. Page 136n.

284. **Woman Resting near Tree.** 25½″ x 21¼″. Barnes Foundation No. 139. Pages 132, 136n. Illustration, page 354.

1916

285. **Bathing Group.** 28¾″ x 36½″. Dated. Barnes Foundation No. 709. Pages 8on, 86n, 118n, 130n, 144-150, 168n, 169n, 171n, 172n, 175n, 183n, 186n, 187n, 189n, 190n, 195n, 196, 197n, 208n, 210n, 212n, 214, 431-433, 434. Illustration, page 355.

Circa 1916

286. **At the Bath.** 16″ x 11¾″. Collection Georges Keller, Paris. "Au bain." Page 208n.

287. **Nude with Castanets.** 21″ x 16″. Barnes Foundation No. 147. Pages 58n, 188n, 189n. Illustration, page 356.

Circa 1917-1919

288. **Farm House.** 12½″ x 18¼″. Barnes Foundation No. 47. Page 122.

289. **Figure in Garden.** 15½″ x 19½″. Barnes Foundation No. 877. Pages 135n, 136n, 137n, 139-140, 416n. Illustration, page 362.

290. **Girls in Garden.** 19¾″ x 23½″. Barnes Foundation No. 931. Pages 117n, 169n, 174n.

291. **Landscape with Figure in Yellow.** 10¼″ x 9″. Barnes Foundation No. 588. Page 136n.

292. **Nude on Couch.** 8¼″ x 16½″. Barnes Foundation No. 1142. Page 142n.

293. **Reclining Odalisque.** 9″ x 12″. Barnes Foundation No. 921. Pages 142-143, 142n, 195n. Illustration, page 358.

294. **Riviera Landscape.** 12¼″ x 11″. Barnes Foundation No. 596. Pages 135n, 136n, 137n, 139.

295. **Standing Odalisque.** 16¼″ x 12½″. Barnes Foundation No. 1136. Pages 8on, 143-144. Illustration, page 360.

296. **Two Figures in Landscape.** 9½″ x 12″. Barnes Foundation No. 587. Pages 117n, 135n, 136n, 137-138, 137n, 145n, 172, 172n, 209n, 421n, 432n. Illustration, page 359.

NO.

297. **Woman in Landscape.** 9″ x 13¾″. Barnes Foundation No. 922. Pages 135n, 136n, 137, 137n. Illustration, page 349.

298. **Woman in Muslin Dress.** 25½″ x 23½″. Barnes Foundation No. 145. Pages 132-135, 136n, 142, 195n, 198n, 209n, 386n. Illustration, page 361.

299. **Woman on Hillside.** 13¾″ x 12″. Barnes Foundation No. 585. Pages 140-141, 140n. Illustration, page 364.

300. **Woman with Hat, Reading.** 16″ x 19¾″. Barnes Foundation No. 932. Page 208n.

Circa 1918

301. **Bathers.** 26½″ x 32″. Barnes Foundation No. 902. Pages 188n, 189n, 198n. Illustration, page 366.

302. **Group of Bathers.** 19¼″ x 23½″. Barnes Foundation No. 945. Pages 416n, 434. Illustration, page 363.

303. **Maternity.** 20″ x 15¾″. Collection Georges Keller, Paris. "Maternité." Pages 175, 434. Illustration, page 365.

304. **Nymphs.** 43¼″ x 63″. Louvre. "Baigneuses — Les nymphes." Pages 116n, 118n, 143, 144, 183n, 435-436, 436n. Illustration, page 367.

305. **Seated Figure in Landscape.** 10½″x 12½″. Barnes Foundation No. 38. Page 198n.

Circa 1919

306. **Chrysanthemums in Vase.** 15¾″ x 13¾″. Barnes Foundation No. 838. Pages 436-437. Illustration, page 368.

(B) MISCELLANEOUS WORKS OF ART

Egyptian Mural Paintings (various centuries B.C.)

307. Examples in British Museum. Page 98.

Greek Carving (circa 400 B.C.)

308. **Reclining Figure.** Small bone carving. Barnes Foundation No. A 98. Page 188n.

Greek Sculpture (circa 400 B.C.)

French Fresco (circa 1344)

320. **Fishing Scene.** Chambre de la Garde-Robe, Palais des Papes, Avignon. "Le vivier." (Fresque.) Page 95n. Illustration, page 286.

Eyck, Jan van (1385-90—1441)

321. **Madonna of Lucca.** Staedelsches Kunstinstitut, Frankfort a.M., No. 944. "Madonna von Lucca." Page 201n.

Pisanello or Pisano, Antonio, formerly called Vittore (1397-99—1455)

322. **Princess of the Este Family.** Louvre No. 1422a. "Portrait d'une princesse de la famille d'Este." Pages 96n, 134n.

French Miniature (End XIVth or beginning XVth century)

323. **Hares.** Book of Hunting of Gaston Phébus. Bibliothèque Nationale, Paris, MSS. Fr. "Les lièvres." Livre de la Chasse, de Gaston Phébus. Reproduced in "The French Primitives and Their Forms," Barnes and de Mazia, p. 63, Barnes Foundation Press, Merion, Pa., 1931. Page 95n.

Gothic Tapestry (XVth century)

324. **Woman with Falcon.** Collection Octave Homberg. Page 95n.

Masaccio (1401-1428)

325. **Adam and Eve.** Fresco. Cappella Brancacci, Chiesa di Santa Maria del Carmine, Florence. "Adamo ed Eva." (Affresco.) Page 429. Illustration, page 331.

Francesca, Piero della (1416?-1492)

326. **Reception of Queen of Sheba by Solomon.** Fresco. Chiesa di San Francesco, Arezzo. "Incontro della Regina Saba con Salomone." (Affresco.) Pages 95n, 126n.

Gozzoli, Benozzo (1420-1498)

327. **Journey of the Magi.** Frescoes. Palazzo Riccardi, Florence. "Il viaggio dei Magi." (Affreschi.) Pages 95n, 126n.

Bellini, Gentile (1426-9—1507), School of

Carpaccio, Vittore (1450-1522)

NO.
340. St. Stephen Preaching at Jerusalem. Louvre No. 1211. "Prédication de Saint Etienne à Jérusalem." Page 192n.

Michelangelo (1475-1564)

341. Original Sin. (Fragment.) Fresco. Palazzo Vaticano, Cappella Sistina, Rome. "Il peccato originale." (Dettaglio.) (Affresco.) Page 126n. Illustration, page 329.

342. Original Sin and Expulsion from Eden. Fresco. Palazzo Vaticano, Cappella Sistina, Rome. "Il peccato originale e l'espulsione dal Paradiso terrestre." (Affresco.) Page 148n.

Giorgione (1477-78—1510)

343. Concert in the Open Air. Louvre No. 1136. "Le concert champêtre." Pages 126n, 145n, 148n, 150n, 168n, 169n.

344. Sleeping Venus. Staatliche Gemälde-Galerie, Dresden, No. 185. "Schlummernde Venus." Pages 63n, 127n, 145n, 148n, 150n, 168n, 178-179, 190, 192n. Illustration, page 335.

345. Tempest. Accademia, Venice. "La tempesta." Page 169n.

Titian (1477?-1576)

346. Alfonso da Ferrara and Laura di Dianti. Louvre No. 1590. Pages 56n, 185.

347. Bacchus and Ariadne. National Gallery, London, No. 35. Pages 138n, 168n, 169n, 171-172, 172n, 175, 183n, 186n, 194n.

348. Christ and the Magdalene. National Gallery, London, No. 270. Pages 148n, 169n, 172, 172n, 174, 180, 192n.

349. Danaë Receiving Rain of Gold. Prado No. 425. "Dánae recibiendo la lluvia de oro." Pages 186n, 190n, 192, 194n.

350. Disciples at Emmaüs. Louvre No. 1581. "Pèlerins d'Emmaüs." Pages 53n, 172n, 175n, 186n, 201n.

351. Emperatriz Doña Isabel de Portugal. Prado No. 415. Page 192.

352. Entombment. Louvre No. 1584. "La mise au tombeau." Pages 111n, 113n, 172n, 196, 213n.

Raphael (1483-1520)

NO.

372. **Descent from the Cross.** Galleria Borghese, Rome, No. 369. "La deposizione dalla Croce." Page 148n.

373. **Holy Family, of Francis I.** Louvre No. 1498. "La Sainte Famille, dite de François Ier." Page 206n.

374. **Madonna: Belle Jardinière.** Louvre No. 1496. "La belle jardinière." Pages 126n, 206n. Illustration (fragment), page 329.

375. **Transfiguration.** Pinacoteca Vaticana, Rome, No. N. 333. "La Trasfigurazione." Page 148n.

376. **Virgin with Blue Diadem.** Louvre No. 1497. "La Vierge au diadème bleu." Page 206n.

French Tapestry (circa 1490)

377. **Scene of Courtly Life.** Pennsylvania Museum of Art, Philadelphia. Page 95n.

Correggio, Antonio Allegri da (1494-1534)

378. **Marriage of St. Catherine.** Louvre No. 1117. "Mariage de Sainte Catherine." Page 53n.

379. **Venus, Mercury and Cupid.** National Gallery, London, No. 10. Page 53n.

Moretto (da Brescia) (1498-1555)

380. **Italian Nobleman.** National Gallery, London, No. 1025. Page 392n.

French Tapestry (circa 1500)

381. **Concert in the Open Air.** Louvre—legacy Bareiller. "Le concert champêtre." Page 95n.

Clouet, François (1510?-1572)

382. **Woman's Head.** Barnes Foundation No. 809. Page 85n.

Clouet, François (attributed to)

383. **Elisabeth d'Autriche.** Louvre No. 130. Page 85n.

Moroni, Giovanni Battista, or Giambattista
(1510-25—1578)

NO.
384. **Ludovico Madruzzo.** Art Institute, Chicago, No. 29.912—
Collection Mr. and Mrs. C. H. Worcester. Page 392n.

Tintoretto, Jacopo Robusti, called (1518-1594)

385. **Esther and Ahasuerus.** Prado No. 388. "Esther ante
Asuero." Page 198n.
386. **Head of a Man.** Louvre No. 1467. "Portrait d'homme."
Pages 66n, 182.
387. **Judith and Holofernes.** Prado No. 389. "Judith y Holofernes." Pages 198n, 213n.
388. **Origin of the Milky Way.** National Gallery, London, No.
1313. Pages 111n, 183n, 184n, 187n.
389. **Paradise.** Louvre No. 1465. "Le Paradis." Pages 135n,
196, 427n.
390. **Queen of Sheba and Solomon.** Prado No. 394. "Visita de
la Reina de Saba a Salomón." Page 198n.
391. **St. George and the Dragon.** National Gallery, London,
No. 16. Pages 149n, 169n, 172, 172n, 183n, 187n, 194n.
392. **Susannah at the Bath.** Kunsthistorisches Museum, Vienna, No. 239. "Susanna im Bade." Pages 126n, 127n.
Illustration (fragment), page 329.
393. **Susannah at the Bath.** Louvre No. 1464. "Suzanne au
bain." Pages 168n, 185n, 187n, 412n.
394. **Two Prophets.** Barnes Foundation No. 807. Pages 53n,
175n, 185, 187n, 201n.
395. **Venetian Senator.** Barnes Foundation No. 836. Pages
135n, 407n.
396. **Vincenzo Morosini.** National Gallery, London, No. 4004.
Pages 66n, 182, 187n.
397. **Woman of Samaria.** Barnes Foundation No. 823. Pages
66n, 190n.
398. **Young Venetian Girl.** Prado No. 382. "La dama que
descubre el seno." Page 184n.

Goujon, Jean (circa 1520-circa 1566)

399. **Fountain of the Innocents.** Bas-reliefs. Square des Innocents, Paris. "Fontaine des innocents." Page 206n.

Veronese, Paolo Caliari, or Cagliari, called (1528-1588)

NO.

400. Baptism of Christ. Barnes Foundation No. 800. Pages 135n, 188n, 195n.

401. Burning of Sodom. Louvre No. 1187. "L'incendie de Sodome." Pages 86n, 135n, 195n, 197, 197n, 213n, 427n.

402. Feast at the House of Simon the Pharisee. Louvre No. 1193. "Le repas chez Simon le Pharisien." Pages 185n, 195n, 197n.

403. Happy Union. National Gallery, London, No. 1326. Pages 183n, 185n, 187n, 189n, 209n.

404. Holy Family. Louvre No. 1191. "Sainte Famille." Page 198n.

405. Jesus Healing Peter's Mother-in-Law. Louvre No. 1191 bis. "Jésus guérit la belle-mère de Pierre." Page 198n.

406. Jupiter Destroying the Vices. Louvre No. 1198. "Jupiter foudroyant les Vices." Page 205n.

407. Mars and Venus United by Love. Metropolitan Museum of Art, New York, No. V 6-1. Pages 183n, 195n, 209n, 212n.

408. Unfaithfulness. National Gallery, London, No. 1318. Pages 112, 183n, 185n, 187n.

409. Venetian Woman. Barnes Foundation No. 837. Pages 183n, 187n, 209n.

410. Vision of St. Helena. National Gallery, London, No. 1041. Page 195n.

411. Wedding at Cana. Louvre No. 1192. "Les noces de Cana." Pages 181n, 185n, 187n.

Hindu-Persian Miniature (circa 1550)

412. Head Servant. Detail from "Princes of the House of Tīmūr," by Mīr Sayyid Alī or Abdus Samad (the portraits of Akbar, Jahānjīr and Shāh Jahān—in the pavilion opposite Humāyūn—were added by an Indian artist circa 1622). British Museum. Page 134n.

Rubens, Sir Peter Paul (1577-1640)

413. Adoration of the Kings. Prado No. 1638. "La adoración de los reyes." Pages 187n, 191n.

414. Annunciation. Barnes Foundation No. 813. Pages 188n, 195n, 212n, 213n, 427n.

NO.
415. **Apotheosis of William the Silent.** National Gallery, London, No. 187. Pages 187n, 206n, 209n.
416. **Baron Henri de Vicq.** Louvre No. 2111. Page 119.
417. **Bathsheba at the Spring.** Staatliche Gemälde-Galerie, Dresden, No. 965. "Bathseba am Springbrunnen." Page 205n. Illustration, page 329.
418. **Child of the Artist.** Kaiser-Friedrich-Museum, Berlin, No. 763. "Bildnis eines Kindes des Meisters." Page 425. Illustration, page 318.
419. **David Playing on the Harp.** Barnes Foundation No. 812. Pages 188n, 190n, 210n.
420. **Diana and Callisto.** Prado No. 1671. "Diana y Calisto." Page 187n.
421. **Diana and her Nymphs Surprised by Satyrs.** Prado No. 1665. "Diana y sus ninfas sorprendidas por faunos." Pages 186n, 188n, 189n, 205n.
422. **Diana Returning from the Hunt.** Staatliche Gemälde-Galerie, Dresden, No. 962a. "Dianas Heimkehr von der Jagd." Page 188n.
423. **Garden of Love.** Prado No. 1690. "El jardín del amor." Pages 195n, 205n, 212n, 213n.
424. **Hélène Fourment and her Children.** Louvre No. 2113. "Hélène Fourment et ses enfants." Page 425.
425. **Holy Family.** Metropolitan Museum of Art, New York, No. R 82-2. Page 189n.
426. **Holy Family.** Prado No. 1639. "La Sagrada Familia con Santa Ana." Pages 187n, 188n, 209n.
427. **Holy Family in Landscape.** Barnes Foundation No. 849. Pages 187n, 190n, 209n.
428. **Horrors of War.** National Gallery, London, No. 279. Page 188n.
429. **Ixion Deceived by Juno.** Louvre—Collection Schlichting. "Ixion trompé par Junon." Pages 126n, 127n.
430. **Judgment of Paris.** National Gallery, London, No. 194. Pages 126, 145n, 190.
431. **Peace and War.** National Gallery, London, No. 46. Page 127n.
432. **Rape of Leucippus' Daughter.** Alte Pinakothek, Munich, No. 321. "Der Raub der Töchter des Leukippos." Pages 126n, 127n, 149n.

NO.

433. **Romulus and Remus.** Pennsylvania Museum of Art, Philadelphia—Johnson Collection. Pages 187n, 209n.
434. **St. Cecilia.** Metropolitan Museum of Art, New York, No. R 82-9. Pages 183n, 187n, 209n.
435. **Susanne Fourment.** National Gallery, London, No. 852. (Known as "Chapeau de Paille.") Pages 187n, 209n.
436. **Thomyris.** Louvre No. 2084. "Thomyris, reine des Scythes, faisant plonger la tête de Cyrus dans un vase rempli de sang." Page 213n.

Poussin, Nicolas (1594-1665)

437. **Arcadian Shepherds.** Louvre No. 734. "Les bergers d'Arcadie." Page 206n.
438. **Blind Men of Jericho.** Louvre No. 715. "Aveugles de Jéricho." Page 206n.
439. **Holy Family.** Louvre No. 714. "Sainte Famille." Page 206n.
440. **Summer, Ruth and Boaz.** Louvre No. 737. "L'été, Ruth et Booz." Pages 138n, 150n.

Velásquez, Don Diego de Silva y (1599-1660)

441. **Court Attendants.** Prado No. 1174. "Las meninas." Pages 193n, 375n.
442. **Don Juan de Austria.** Prado No. 1200. "El bufón llamado 'Don Juan de Austria'." Page 55n.
443. **Felipe IV.** National Gallery, London, No. 745. "Philip IV." Page 181.
444. **Felipe IV, in his Youth.** Prado No. 1182. Page 181n.
445. **Infanta Doña Margarita de Austria.** Prado No. 1192. Pages 57n, 181n, 193, 375n.
446. **Infanta Marguerite.** Louvre No. 1731. Pages 55n, 56n, 65n, 119n, 177n, 178n, 181, 181n, 182n, 192, 193n, 213, 375n, 386n.
447. **Infanta María Teresa, when Three Years Old.** Kunsthistorisches Museum, Vienna, No. 615. "Die Infantin Margareta Theresia im Alter von drei Jahren." Pages 56n, 57n, 182n.
448. **Lady with Fan.** Wallace Collection, London, No. 88. Pages 65n, 177n, 386n.

Vermeer, Jan (1632-1675)

464. **Cook.** Rijksmuseum, Amsterdam, No. 2528a. "Het keukenmeisje." Pages 65n, 201n, 390n.
465. **Girl Reading Letter.** Staatliche Gemälde-Galerie, Dresden, No. 1336. "Brieflesendes Mädchen am offenen Fenster." Pages 65n, 390n.
466. **Lacemaker.** Louvre No. 2456. "La dentellière." Pages 65n, 390n. Illustration, page 240.
467. **Woman with Pearl Necklace.** Kaiser-Friederich-Museum, Berlin, No. 912b. "Die junge Dame mit dem Perlenhalsband." Pages 65n, 390n.

Streek, Juriaan van (circa 1632—circa 1678)

468. **Still-Life.** Louvre No. 2437. "Nature morte." Pages 53n, 128n, 201n.

Hobbema, Meindert (1638-1709)

469. **Watermill.** Louvre No. 2404. "Moulin à eau." Page 67n.

Largillière, Nicolas de (1656-1746)

470. **Artist's Family.** Louvre No. 491. "Portrait de Largillière, de sa femme et de sa fille." Page 427n.
471. **Charlotte Amelia Ragotsky.** National Gallery, London. No. 3883. "Princess Ragotsky." Page 427n.

Watteau, Antoine (1684-1721)

472. **Autumn.** Louvre No. 990 "L'automne." Pages 202n, 206n, 207n, 389n.
473. **Buck.** Louvre No. 984. "L'indifférent." Pages 135n, 195n.
474. **Embarkation for Cythera.** Louvre No. 982. "Embarquement pour Cythère." Pages 195n, 213n, 214n.
475. **False Step.** Louvre No. 989. "Le faux pas." Page 212n.
476. **Fête in a Park.** Wallace Collection, London, No. 391. Page 212n.
477. **Figures in Landscape.** Barnes Foundation No. 801. Pages 195n, 212n.
478. **Game of Love.** National Gallery, London, No. 2897. "La gamme d'amour." Pages 207n, 214n, 427n.

NO.
479. **Gilles.** Louvre No. 983. Page 213.
479A. **Jupiter and Antiope.** Louvre No. 991. "Jupiter et Antiope." Page 79n.
480. **Music Lesson.** Wallace Collection, London, No. 377. Page 214n.
481. **Pastoral.** Louvre No. 992. "Pastorale." Pages 71n, 202n.

Nattier, Jean Marc (1685-1766)

482. **Madame Henriette.** Louvre No. 661. "Madame Henriette, fille de Louis XV." Page 427n.
483. **Madame Louise.** Musée de Versailles, No. 2183. "Madame Louise, fille de Louis XV." Page 427n.
484. **Princesse de Condé as Diana.** Metropolitan Museum of Art, New York, No. N 21-1. Page 427n.

Lancret, Nicolas (1690-1743)

485. **Actors of Italian Comedy.** Louvre No. 470. "Les acteurs de la comédie italienne." Pages 135n, 145n, 207n, 213n.
486. **Actress: La Belle Grecque.** Wallace Collection, London, No. 450. Pages 203n, 212n.
487. **Cage.** Louvre No. 472. "La cage." Page 212n.
488. **Innocence.** Louvre No. 469. "L'innocence." Page 202n.
489. **Mademoiselle Camargo Dancing.** Wallace Collection, London, No. 393. Pages 66n, 212n.
490. **Music Lesson.** Louvre No. 468. "La leçon de musique." Pages 135n, 200n, 203n, 210n, 212n.
491. **Open Cage.** Barnes Foundation No. 814. Pages 183n, 202n, 203n.
492. **Spring.** Louvre No. 462. "Le printemps." Pages 54n, 213n.
493. **Summer.** Louvre No 463. "L'été." Pages 71n, 202n.

Pater, Jean-Baptiste-Joseph (1696-1736)

494. **Comedians in a Park.** Louvre No. 690. "Comédiens dans un parc." Pages 135n, 197n, 207n, 212n, 213n.
495. **Gallant Conversation.** Wallace Collection, London, No. 458. "Conversation Galante." Page 382n.

Chardin, Jean-Baptiste Siméon (1699-1779)

NO.
496. **Back from Market.** Louvre No. 99. "La pourvoyeuse." Pages 213n, 427n.
497. **Bottle of Olives.** Louvre No. 107. "Le bocal d'olives." Pages 53n, 127n, 201n.
498. **Grace before Meal.** Louvre No. 92. "Le bénédicité." Page 201n.
499. **Grace before Meal.** Louvre No. 93—Collection La Caze. "Le bénédicté." Page 66n.
500. **House of Cards.** National Gallery, London, No. 4078. Page 201n.
501. **Industrious Mother.** Louvre No. 91. "La mère laborieuse." Pages 201n, 412n.
502. **Lesson.** National Gallery, London, No. 4077. Page 201n,
503. **Still-Life.** Barnes Foundation No. 530. Pages 53n, 127n, 201n.
504. **Study of Still-Life.** National Gallery, London, No. 1258. Pages 53n, 127n, 201n.
505. **Various Utensils.** Louvre No. 101. "Ustensiles variés." Pages 53n, 66n, 201n.

Boucher, François (1703-1770)

506. **Autumn** (or "Shepherdess with Sporting Loves"). Wallace Collection, London, No. 447. Pages 204n, 211.
507. **Cupid, a Captive.** Wallace Collection, London, No. 432. Page 211n.
508. **Diana at the Bath.** Louvre No. 30. "Diane sortant du bain." Pages 85n, 96, 97n, 116, 145n, 187n, 202n, 203n, 204n, 205, 205n, 206, 206n, 207n, 209n, 211n, 412n. Illustration, page 291.
509. **Head of Lady.** Metropolitan Museum of Art, New York, No. B 66-1. Pages 202n, 211n.
510. **Luncheon.** Louvre No. 50a. "Le déjeuner." Page 204n.
511. **Madame de Pompadour.** National Gallery of Scotland, Edinburgh, No. 429. Pages 95n, 135n, 427n.
512. **Marquise de Pompadour.** Wallace Collection, London, No. 418. Pages 66n, 202n.
513. **Mill.** Louvre No. 3018. "Le moulin." Pages 71n, 202n.
514. **Nest.** Louvre No. 34. "Le nid." Page 97n.

NO.

515. **Pan and Syrinx.** National Gallery, London, No. 1090. Pages 187n, 204n, 209n.

516. **Pastoral.** Louvre No. 35. "Pastorale." Pages 71n, 202n, 204n.

517. **Setting of the Sun.** Wallace Collection, London, No. 486. Page 205n.

518. **Sleeping Shepherdess.** Louvre No. 32. "La bergère endormie." Pages 51n, 66n, 97n, 187n.

519. **Three Graces.** Louvre No. 47. "Les trois Grâces." Pages 183n, 188n, 189n, 210n, 429n.

520. **Venus.** Metropolitan Museum of Art, New York, No. B 66-2. Pages 187n, 188n, 208n, 209n, 210n, 211, 211n, 408n.

521. **Venus Adorning Herself.** Louvre No. 43. "La toilette de Vénus." Pages 187n, 204n, 207n, 208n, 209n.

522. **Venus and Vulcan.** Louvre No. 46—Collection La Caze. "Vénus chez Vulcain." Pages 85n, 116, 203n, 206n, 209n.

523. **Venus Disarming Cupid.** Louvre No. 44. "Vénus désarme l'Amour." Pages 204n, 205n.

524. **Visit of Venus to Vulcan.** Wallace Collection, London, No. 429. Page 211.

525. **Vulcan Presenting Venus Arms for Æneas.** Louvre No. 36. "Vulcain présentant à Vénus des armes pour Enée." Page 206n.

Perronneau, Jean-Baptiste (1715-1783)

526. **Girl with Cat.** National Gallery, London, No. 3588. Pastel. Pages 66n, 203n.

527. **Mademoiselle Huquier.** Louvre No. 1890. Pastel. (No. 74 in "Catalogue des Pastels," 1930). "Portrait de jeune fille tenant un petit chat." Pages 66n, 203n.

Greuze, Jean Baptiste (1725-1805)

528. **Broken Pitcher.** Louvre No. 372. "La cruche cassée." Pages 75n, 207n.

529. **Dairy Maid.** Louvre No. 372a. "La laitière." Page 75n.

Fragonard, Jean Honoré (1732-1806)

530. **Bacchante Asleep.** Louvre No. 294. "Bacchante endormie." Page 76n.

NO.

531. Bathers. Louvre No. 293. "Baigneuses." Pages 71n, 183n, 188n, 202n, 207n, 211n.

532. Boy as Pierrot. Wallace Collection, London, No. 412. Pages 66n, 75n, 417n, 421n.

533. Inspiration. Louvre No. 298. "L'inspiration." Page 212n.

534. Music. Louvre No. 296. "La musique." Page 212n.

535. Music Lesson. Louvre No. 291. "La leçon de musique." Pages 75n, 202n, 203n, 206n, 412n.

536. Souvenir: A Lady Carving her Name. Wallace Collection, London, No. 382. Page 208n.

537. Study. Louvre No. 297. "L'étude." Pages 212n, 427n.

538. Woman Undressing. Louvre No. 295. "La chemise enlevée." Pages 66n, 188n, 207n.

539. Young Woman and Child. Louvre No. 300. "Jeune femme." Pages 95n, 183n, 188n, 206n.

Boze, Joseph (1744-46?—1826)

540. Comtesse de Provence. Louvre No. 673. Pastel. (No. 8 in "Catalogue des Pastels," 1930.) Pages 66n, 203n.

541. Lady's Portrait. Louvre—Legacy of Mademoiselle Cécile Garnier. Pastel. (No. 5 in "Catalogue des Pastels," 1930.) "Portrait de femme." Pages 66n, 203n.

Goya y Lucientes, Francisco José de (1746-1828)

542. Doctor Galos. Barnes Foundation No. 5. Pages 65n, 66n, 193, 193n.

543. Doña Isabel Cobos de Porcel. National Gallery, London, No. 1473. Page 65n.

544. Doña Tadea Arias de Enríquez. Prado No. 740. Pages 57n, 193n, 375.

545. Don José Alvarez de Toledo y Gonzaga, el Duque de Alba. Prado No. 2449. Page 53n.

546. Don Luis María de Cistue, as a Child. Collection Mr. and Mrs. John D. Rockefeller, Jr., New York. Reproduced in "Goya", Loan Exhibition, Knoedler Galleries, New York, 1934, No. 10 Page 65n.

547. Duques de Osuna and their Children. Prado No. 739. "Los Duques de Osuna y sus hijos." Page 53n.

548. Family of Carlos IV. Prado No. 726. "La familia de Carlos IV." Page 53n.

NO.
549. **Infanta María Luisa.** Metropolitan Museum of Art, New York, No. 30.95.243—Bequest of Theodore M. Davis. Page 375n.
550. **Juanita Mazarredo.** Collection Mr. and Mrs. J. Watson Webb, New York. Reproduced in "Goya", Loan Exhibition, Knoedler Galleries, New York, 1934, No. 11. Page 66n.
551. **Maja Dressed.** Prado No. 741. "La maja vestida." Page 193n.
552. **Maja Nude.** Prado No. 742. "La maja desnuda." Pages 65n, 193.
553. **Majas on the Balcony.** Metropolitan Museum of Art, New York, No. G 74-8. Pages 193n, 194n.
554. **Woman with Fan.** Louvre No. 1704a. "Femme à l'éventail." Pages 194, 375n.

David, Jacques-Louis (1748-1825)

555. **Madame Chalgrin.** Louvre No. 199a. Page 425.
556. **Madame Récamier.** Louvre No. 199. Page 425.

Constable, John (1776-1837)

557. **Hay-Wain.** National Gallery, London, No. 1207. Page 388n.

Ingres, Jean Auguste Dominique (1780-1867)

558. **Madame Marcotte de Sainte-Marie.** Louvre. Page 374.
559. **Madame Rivière.** Louvre No. 427. Page 419.
560. **Mademoiselle Rivière.** Louvre No. 428. Page 419n.
561. **Spring.** Louvre No. 422. "La source" Page 389n.
562. **Turkish Bath.** Louvre. "Bain turc." Page 93n.

Corot, Jean-Baptiste Camille (1796-1875)

563. **Dancing Nymphs.** Louvre No. 138. "Nymphes dansantes." Pages 112n, 379n.
564. **Landscape.** Barnes Foundation No. 586. Page 54n.
565. **Marcoussis: Road across Fields.** Collection Paul Rosenberg, Paris. Reproduced in "Corot", Loan Exhibition of Figure and Landscape Paintings, Knoedler Galleries, New York, 1934, No. 21, "Marcoussis: Route à travers champs." Page 54n.

NO.
566. **Road to Méry, near La Ferté-sous-Jouarre.** Collection Paul Rosenberg, Paris. Reproduced in "Corot", Loan Exhibition of Figure and Landscape Paintings, Knoedler Galleries, New York, 1934, No. 17, "Chemin de Méry, près La Ferté-sous-Jouarre." Page 61n.

567. **Spinner.** Collection Paul Rosenberg, Paris. "Corot", Loan Exhibition of Figure and Landscape Paintings, Knoedler Galleries, New York, 1934, No. 6, "La fileuse." Page 61n.

568. **Studio.** Louvre No. 157. "L'atelier." Page 381n.

569. **Woman in Gray.** Barnes Foundation No. 533. Page 200n.

570. **Woman with the Pearl.** Louvre. "La femme à la perle." Pages 50n, 200n, 374.

Delacroix, Ferdinand Victor Eugène (1798-1863)

571. **Algerian Women.** Louvre No. 210. "Femmes d'Alger." Pages 51n, 132n, 149n.

572. **Death of Sardanapalus.** Louvre. "La mort de Sardanapale." Pages 177n, 384n.

573. **Odalisque.** Louvre—Collection Moreau-Nélaton, I. Page 51n.

574. **Study of Reclining Woman.** Louvre—Collection Moreau-Nélaton, I. "Etude de femme couchée." Pages 51n, 177n, 384n.

575. **Triumph of St. Michael.** Barnes Foundation No. 32. Page 149n.

Diaz de la Peña, Narcisse Virgilio (1808-1876)

576. **In the Forest.** Louvre No. 2861. "Sous-bois." Page 391n.

577. **Road.** Louvre No. 43. "La route." Page 67n.

Daumier, Honoré (1808-1879)

578. **Ribalds.** Barnes Foundation No. 22. Page 66n.

Rousseau, Pierre Etienne Théodore (1812-1867)

579. **Edge of Forest of Fontainebleau.** Louvre No. 827. "Sortie de la forêt de Fontainebleau du coté de Brôle." Page 113n.

Daubigny, Charles-François (1817-1878)

NO.
580. **On the Seine.** Pennsylvania Academy of the Fine Arts, Philadelphia—Edward H. Coates Memorial Collection. Pages 54n, 391n.
581. **Sunset on the Oise.** Louvre No. 31. "Soleil couchant sur l'Oise." Page 67n.

Courbet, Gustave (1819-1877)

582. **After the Hunt.** Metropolitan Museum of Art, New York, No. C 83-22. Page 379n.
583. **Head of Baby.** Barnes Foundation No. 124. Page 379.
584. **Midday Dream.** Institute of Arts, Detroit, No. 42, Accession No. 27.202. Page 380n.
585. **Nude.** Barnes Foundation No. 810. Pages 65n, 177n, 380n.
586. **Painter's Studio.** Louvre. "L'atelier." Page 177n.
587. **Pond in the Valley.** Metropolitan Museum of Art, New York, No. C 83-5. Page 379n.
588. **Spring.** Louvre. "La source." Pages 48n, 177n.
589. **Woman with Pigeons.** Barnes Foundation, No. 824. Pages 380, 386n, 401n.
590. **Wounded Man.** Louvre No. 144. "L'homme blessé." Pages 177n, 385n.
591. **Young Bather.** Metropolitan Museum of Art, New York, No. C 83-18. Pages 48n, 177n.

Jongkind, Barthold (1819-1891)

592. **Marine.** Dated 1863. Pennsylvania Museum of Art, Philadelphia—Collection W. L. Elkins. Page 54n.

Pissarro, Camille (1831-1903)

593. **Crystal Palace.** Dated 1871. Collection Durand-Ruel, Paris and New York. Pages 52n, 200n, 383.
594. **Garden.** Dated 1876. Barnes Foundation No. 324. Page 67n.
595. **Woman at the Well.** Dated 1882. Art Institute, Chicago, No. 840—Palmer Collection. Page 100n.

Manet, Edouard (1832-1883)

596. **Boy with Fife.** Circa 1866. Louvre No. 173. "Le fifre." Page 379n.

NO.

597. **Boy with Sword.** Dated 1861. Metropolitan Museum of Art, New York, No. M. 311-1. Page 386n.

598. **Concert at the Tuileries.** Painted in 1862. National Gallery, Millbank, London, No. 3260. Page 394n.

599. **Croquet Party.** Painted in 1873. Staedelsches Kunstinstitut, Frankfurt a.M., No. 1476. "Die Croquetpartie." Page 200n.

600. **Dead Christ with Angels.** Painted in 1864. Metropolitan Museum of Art, New York, No. M 311-4. Pages 375n, 377n.

601. **Departure of the Folkestone Boat.** Circa 1869. Collection Oskar Reinhardt, Winterthur, Switzerland. "Abfahrt des Folkestoner Dampfer." Page 381n.

602. **Departure of the Folkestone Boat.** Circa 1869. Collection Carroll S. Tyson, Jr., Chestnut Hill, Philadelphia. Page 381n.

603. **Eva Gonzalès.** Painted in 1869. National Gallery, Millbank, London, No. 3259. Pages 57n, 375n, 377n.

604. **In a Boat.** Painted in 1879. Metropolitan Museum of Art, New York, No. M 311-8. Pages 89n, 149n.

605. **Mademoiselle de Bellio.** Dated 1878. Collection Wildenstein & Co., Paris and New York. Page 402.

606. **Mademoiselle Voisin.** Circa 1880. Barnes Foundation No. 162. Page 62n.

607. **Olympia.** Dated 1865. Louvre No. 613a. Page 387n.

608. **Picnic.** Dated 1863. Louvre No. M 71. "Le déjeuner sur l'herbe." Page 65n.

609. **Tarring the Boat.** Circa 1870. Barnes Foundation No. 166. Pages 52n, 62n, 67n, 200n, 381n.

Degas, Edgar (1834-1917)

610. **After the Bath.** Barnes Foundation No. 290. Page 177n.

611. **At the Milliner's.** Dated 1882. Metropolitan Museum of Art, New York, No. D 363-13. Page 89n.

612. **Dancers Practicing at the Bar.** Metropolitan Museum of Art, New York, No. D 363-19. Page 57n.

613. **Four Dancers on Stage.** Barnes Foundation No. 307. Page 57n.

Sisley, Alfred (1839-1899)

614. **Edge of the Forest in Spring.** Louvre No. 547. "Lisière de forêt au printemps." Page 81n.

615. **Flood.** Dated 1872. Collection Durand-Ruel, Paris and New York. "L'inondation." Page 383n.

616. **River Scene with Ducks.** Dated 1881. Barnes Foundation No. 224. Pages 67n, 81n.

Cézanne, Paul (1839-1906)

617. **Bathers.** Circa 1877. Barnes Foundation No. 906. Pages 49n, 219.

618. **Bathers, Five Nudes.** Circa 1880. Barnes Foundation No. 93. Page 91n.

619. **Gardanne.** Circa 1885. Barnes Foundation No. 917. Pages 123n, 219.

620. **Gardener.** Late 1880's. Barnes Foundation No. 534. Page 420n.

621. **Landscape.** Water color. Barnes Foundation No. 651. Page 95n.

622. **Nudes in Landscape.** Circa 1906. Barnes Foundation No. 934. Pages 219, 220.

622A. **Still-Life.** Circa 1885. Barnes Foundation No. 910. Page 91n.

623. **Woman with Green Hat.** Circa 1888. Barnes Foundation No. 141. Page 219.

Monet, Claude (1840-1926)

624. **Etretat.** Dated 1886. Metropolitan Museum of Art, New York, No. 31.67.11—Bequest of Lillie P. Bliss, 1931. Page 100n.

625. **Girl in Garden.** Dated 1873. Barnes Foundation No. 857. Pages 62n, 391n.

626. **House Boat.** Barnes Foundation No. 730. Page 67n.

627. **In the Garden.** Painted in 1867. Louvre No. 418. "Au jardin." Pages 380n, 394n.

628. **La Grenouillère.** Painted in 1869. Metropolitan Museum of Art, New York, No. M 74-3. Pages 52n, 200n, 380n, 381n, 383n.

629. **Landing-Stage at Argenteuil.** Dated 1868. Collection M. Knoedler & Co., Inc., New York. Page 381n.

NO.
630. Luncheon. Louvre No. 412. "Le déjeuner." Pages 61n, 394n.

631. Madame Monet Embroidering. Dated 1875. Barnes Foundation No. 197. Page 51n.

632. Monsieur Cogneret. Dated 1880. Barnes Foundation No. 725. Page 62n.

633. Spring Trees by the Lake. Dated 1888. Pennsylvania Museum of Art, Philadelphia—Collection W. L. Elkins. Page 100n.

Bazille, Frédéric (1841-1870)

634. Family Party. Louvre No. 15. "Réunion de famille." Pages 380n, 394n.

Carrière, Eugène (1849-1906)

635. Little Girl Counting. Pennsylvania Museum of Art, Philadelphia—Collection W. L. Elkins. Page 385n.

Seurat, Georges (1859-1891)

636. Artist's Mother. Conté pencil. Museum of Modern Art, New York, No. 62—Collection Lillie P. Bliss. Page 398n.

Matisse, Henri-(1869-   )

637. Reclining Odalisque. Barnes Foundation No. 923. Page 144n.

INDEX*

Academism, 7-8, 13, 38, 216, 220, 384, 385, 392, 405, 424
Animism, 3
Arabesque, 97, 100, 101, 110, 111, 112-113, 139, 140, 150, 415, 418, 424, 425, 433
Art
and life, 26, 30, 155, 373
and perception, 27
and philosophy, 42-43
and religion, 163, 164, 165, 166
and science, 4, 7, 8, 37n, 38
function of, 165-166
manufactured, 28-29, 392
subconscious in, 40
work of, 19, 163
Art and Education, Dewey, Barnes, de Mazia, etc., 42n
Art as Experience, John Dewey, 18n, 29n, 37n, 166n
Atmosphere, 81, 100, 101, 111, 112, 120, 131, 132, 133, 134, 138, 139, 140, 141, 144, 336, 379, 382, 389, 391, 400, 406, 415, 418, 433
see also Suffusion
compared to Venetian, 171
Background, 57, 64, 108, 110, 179n, 180, 389, 402, 406, 412
and foreground compared to French, 205, 208, 208n
compositional relation to foreground, 96, 97, 100, 105, 107, 108, 109, 113, 125-126, 133, 135, 140, 142, 143, 144, 375, 376, 381, 386, 389, 391, 392, 393, 397, 399, 405, 406, 407, 408, 409, 413, 417, 421, 424, 425, 428, 431, 435, 437
Barbizon school, 47, 48, 54, 55, 61n, 67, 113, 130, 374, 376, 388, 392, 395
Barnard, George, 29n

Barnes, Albert C., *The Art of Henri-Matisse*, 26n, 30n
Barnes Foundation, vii, x
Bazille, Frédéric, 371, 380, 394
Family Party (634), see p. 491
Beethoven, 27-28, 29, 42, 131n
Behavior, vii, 34-35, 36
Bellini, Gentile (school of), 192n
Reception of a Venetian Ambassador at Cairo, in 1512 (328), see p. 472
Bellini, Giovanni, 191-192, 213n
Madonna and Child (329), see p. 472
Madonna of the Little Trees (330), see p. 472
Benton, Thomas, 29n
Biographical Sketch, 371-373
Black-and-White, 398, 401
compared to Courbet, 48
-ensemble, *see* Color-scheme
Manet-like, 380, 387
Black, quality of, 55, 56n, 382, 386, 387, 398
Botticelli, Alessandro, 206n, 389
Allegory of Spring (337), see p. 472
Birth of Venus (338), see p. 472
Pietà (339), see p. 472
Boucher, 51, 66, 71, 83, 96, 97, 116, 126, 151, 183, 187, 188, 189n, 199, 200, 202, 203n, 204-206, 207, 208, 209-212, 397, 403, 406, 407, 412, 423, 427, 429n
Autumn (506), see p. 483
Cupid, a Captive (507), see p. 483
Diana at the Bath (508), see p. 483
Head of Lady (509), see p. 483
Luncheon (510), see p. 483
Madame de Pompadour (511), see p. 483

---

* The arrangement of the preceding section—Catalogue Data—makes it serve as a supplementary index.

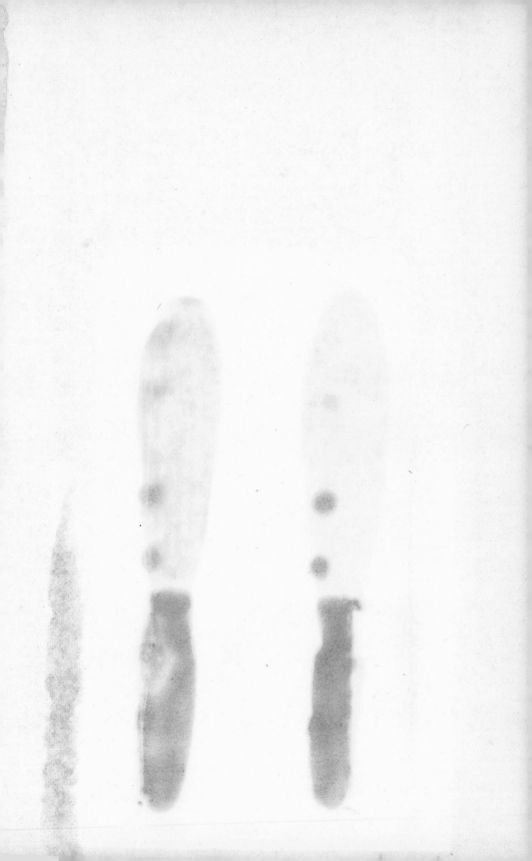